INDISCRIMINATE AND DISPROPORTIONATE ATTACKS IN INTERNATIONAL LAW

This book unveils gaps, inconsistencies, and barriers to accountability emerging from the intersections between IHL and ICL in the definition and treatment of indiscriminate and disproportionate attacks as *jus in bello* violations.

The book identifies and explains the unresolved legal problems surrounding the prevention and control of indiscriminate and disproportionate attacks as international war crimes, and critically unpacks the macroscopic implications of these problems for international adjudications. It goes on to address the challenges posed by these attacks as key causes of civilian victimisation in war.

The author demonstrates that the Rome Statute of the ICC must be either re-interpreted or amended in order to prosecute and punish the most recurring forms of indiscriminate and disproportionate attacks. Not doing so would mean impairing the ability of this institution to pursue the most important objectives declared by its founding treaty. The book concludes by offering interpretative solutions and two amendment proposals for the Rome Statute to bridge the gaps and overcome the antinomies identified.

Volume 24 in the series Studies in International and Comparative Criminal Law

Studies in International and Comparative Criminal Law

General Editor: Michael Bohlander

Criminal law had long been regarded as the preserve of national legal systems, and comparative research in criminal law for a long time had something of an academic ivory tower quality. However, in the past 15 years it has been transformed into an increasingly, and moreover practically, relevant subject of study for international and comparative lawyers. This can be attributed to numerous factors, such as the establishment of ad hoc international criminal tribunals and the International Criminal Court, as well as to developments within the EU, the UN and other international organisations. There is a myriad of initiatives related to tackling terrorism, money laundering, organised crime, people trafficking and the drugs trade, and the international 'war' on terror. Criminal law is being used to address global or regional problems, often across the borders of fundamentally different legal systems, only one of which is the traditional divide between common and civil law approaches. It is therefore no longer solely a matter for domestic lawyers. The need exists for a global approach which encompasses comparative and international law.

Responding to this development this new series will include books on a wide range of topics, including studies of international law, EU law, the work of specific international tribunals, and comparative studies of national systems of criminal law. Given that the different systems to a large extent operate based on the idiosyncracies of the peoples and states that have created them, the series will also welcome pertinent historical, criminological and socio-legal research into these issues.

Recent titles in this series:

The Emergence of EU Criminal Law:
Cyber Crime and the Regulation of the Information Society
Sarah Summers, Christian Schwarzenegger, Gian Ege and Finlay Young

Transitional Justice and the Prosecution of Political Leaders in the Arab Region: A Comparative Study of Egypt, Libya, Tunisia and Yemen
Noha Aboueldahab

Caribbean Anti-Trafficking Law and Practice
Jason Haynes

The Construction of Guilt in China: An Empirical Account of Routine Chinese Injustice
Yu Mou

The Amicus Curiae in International Criminal Justice
Sarah Williams, Hannah Woolaver and Emma Palmer

Principles of German Criminal Procedure, Second Edition
Michael Bohlander

Principles of Chinese Criminal Procedure
Liling Yue

Principles of Indonesian Criminal Law
Topo Santoso

Principles of Polish Criminal Procedure
Jaroslaw Zagrodnik and Kazimierz Zgryzek

Contemporary Challenges to Criminal Justice: Liber Amicorum for Ralph Henham
Edited by Paul Behrens

Indiscriminate and Disproportionate Attacks in International Law: Bridging the Accountability Gap
Luigi Daniele

Indiscriminate and Disproportionate Attacks in International Law

Bridging the Accountability Gap

Luigi Daniele

•HART•
OXFORD • LONDON • NEW YORK • NEW DELHI • SYDNEY

HART PUBLISHING

Bloomsbury Publishing Plc

Kemp House, Chawley Park, Cumnor Hill, Oxford, OX2 9PH, UK

1385 Broadway, New York, NY 10018, USA

Bloomsbury Publishing Ireland Limited, 29 Earlsfort Terrace, Dublin 2, D02 AY28, Ireland

HART PUBLISHING, the Hart/Stag logo, BLOOMSBURY and the Diana logo are trademarks of Bloomsbury Publishing Plc

First published in Great Britain 2026

A catalogue record for this book is available from the British Library.

A catalogue record for this book is available from the Library of Congress.

ISBN: HB: 978-1-50997-607-2
ePDF: 978-1-50997-609-6
ePub: 978-1-50997-608-9

Typeset by Compuscript Ltd, Shannon

For product safety related questions contact productsafety@bloomsbury.com

To find out more about our authors and books visit www.hartpublishing.co.uk. Here you will find extracts, author information, details of forthcoming events and the option to sign up for our newsletters.

CONTENTS

Background: Inequality as Continuity between War and Law 1

1. Civilian Victimisation in Armed Conflicts in History and Theory 13
   1.1. Introduction 13
   1.2. International Humanitarian Law as *Koinè*, and its 'Dark Sides' 16
   1.3. Civilians in the Interstate Warfare of the *Jus Publicum Europaeum*......19
   1.4. Civilian Resistance at the Origins of the Civilians/Combatants Legal Dichotomy 22
   1.5. Civilians at War, the Partisan, and the Problem of Guerrilla Warfare..27
   1.6. Civilian Victimisation in Contemporary Wars. Notes for an Aetiological Enquiry: Why do Liberal Democracies Strike Non-Combatants? 31

2. Indiscriminate and Disproportionate Attacks in International Humanitarian Law..38
   2.1. The Fundamental IHL Prescriptions Governing Targeting Decisions, between 'Military Necessity' and 'Humanity'.......................38
      2.1.1. Distinction 46
      2.1.2. Proportionality 56
      2.1.3. Precautions..64
   2.2. The IHL Prohibitions of Indiscriminate and Disproportionate Attacks under Additional Protocol I..71
   2.3. Interplay of the Targeting Principles: In Search of Systematic Coherence...79
   2.4. Reframing the Distinction–Proportionality Nexus 81
      2.4.1. Incidentality of the Civilian Harm as Systematic Cornerstone of the Law of Targeting..82
      2.4.2. Incidentality between Distinction and Proportionality............83
      2.4.3. Incidentality and Precautions...84
      2.4.4. A Serious Misconception: 'Balancing' Incidentality with Military Advantage 85
      2.4.5. Multi-Component Objects, *Pars Pro Toto* Determinations of Military Objectives and the 'Synecdoches' Capsizing Incidentality...88

2.5. Recentralising Incidentality of the Civilian Harm as *Conditio Sine Qua Non* for Proportionality Assessments 93
2.6. The Interpretative Auxilium of *Mens Rea* Categories: Incidentality as a Threefold Dividing Line between Distinction and Proportionality 95

3. Indiscriminate and Disproportionate Attacks at the Origins of International Criminal Law: From Nuremberg to the ICTY 99
3.1. Indiscriminate Warfare at the Origins of International Criminal Law 99
3.1.1. The Axis's Indiscriminate 'Total War': War Crimes in Nuremberg 105
3.1.2. Hiroshima, Nagasaki, and the *Einsatzgruppen* Case: At the Origins of Double Standards 108
3.1.3. Kelsen's *Privilegium Odiosum* and Radbruch's Second *Verleugnungsformel*: 'Equality, the Core of Justice' 115
3.2. The ICTY Jurisprudence on Indiscriminate and Disproportionate Attacks as War Crimes 121
3.2.1. Overcoming the IACs–NIACs Dichotomy: The *Tadić* Lesson 123
3.2.2. Indiscriminate and Disproportionate Attacks as Conduct Indicating the Intent of the Crime of Terror 128
3.2.3. Indiscriminate and Disproportionate Attacks as Conduct Indicating the Intent of Direct Attacks on Civilians 131
3.3. Critical Knots in the ICTY Jurisprudence 140
3.3.1. In Search of Objective Parameters Indicating the Indiscriminate Character of Attacks: The Circular Error Probable 140
3.3.2. The *Gotovina* 'Scandal': The 'End of Indiscriminate Attacks'? 141
3.3.3. Indiscriminate and Disproportionate Attacks as Reckless Attacks on Civilians, and the Fragility of Case-by-Case Inferences: Back to Victor's Justice? 147

4. Indiscriminate and Disproportionate Attacks in Contemporary War Crimes Law: Born to be Blunt? 150
4.1. Indiscriminate and Disproportionate Attacks as Turning Points for the ICC at 30: Two Alternative Futures for the Court (and Warfare) 150
4.2. Indiscriminate and Disproportionate Attacks in the Rome Statute of the ICC: In Search of Lost Enforcement 155
4.2.1. The War Crimes Regime of the Rome Statute: Structure of Article 8 and Common Elements 157

4.2.2. The Elements of the Crimes of Direct Attacks on Civilians and Civilian Objects....163
4.2.3. Indiscriminate Attacks as Direct Attacks on Civilians and Civilian Objects? The ICC Jurisprudence....167
4.2.4. The Contradictory Elements of the Crime of (Clearly) Disproportionate Attacks....171
4.2.5. Old Challenges and New Possibilities: Toward the First ICC Adjudication of Disproportionate Attacks....178
4.3. An 'Unduly Expanded Legal Shield' for the Military?....180
4.3.1. The 2015 Attack against the Kunduz MSF Hospital: The Problem of Recklessness....182
4.3.2. Western Loopholes for Russian War Crimes? Indiscriminate and Disproportionate Attacks in the War against Ukraine....187
4.3.3. Gaza 2023–24: A Genocide by Means of Indiscriminate and Disproportionate Attacks?....192
4.3.3.1. Pre-Justifying Indiscriminate and Disproportionate Attacks: Entire Populations of 'Human Shields'....197
4.3.3.2. Indiscriminate and Disproportionate Attacks Nipped in the Bud: 'Every School, Every Mosque, Every Second House' as a 'Military Objective'....202
4.3.3.3. Rewriting IHL Proportionality to Accommodate the Destruction of Victim Groups as 'Collateral': Of 'Incidental' and 'Proportionate' Genocides....205
4.4. Cassese's Prognosis Confirmed, and the Normalisation of Indiscriminate and Disproportionate Attacks....209

5. Bridging the Accountability Gap: Delivering Justice for Indiscriminate and Disproportionate Attacks....212
5.1. Jurisprudential Avenues for Ensuring Accountability, *Lex Lata*....212
5.1.1. Indiscriminate Attacks as Direct Attacks on Civilians: The Missing Piece of the Puzzle....213
5.1.2. A Long-Overdue Step Forward: Applicability of the *Dolus Directus* in the Second Degree/Indirect Intent *Mens Rea* Standard....219
5.1.3. The War Crime of Disproportionate Attacks: Achieving Harmonisation with IHL Proportionality Through Indirect Intent....224
5.1.3.1. Distinguishing Disproportionate Attacks from Indiscriminate Attacks under War Crimes Law....224
5.1.3.2. Indirect Intent against the 'Monarchy' of the Military Commander....227

5.2. The Limits of Interpretative Solutions: Racialised Hierarchies of Civilian Protection and Racialised Hierarchies of War Crimes Law Enforcement 233
5.3. An Agenda for the Assembly of the State Parties to the Rome Statute: *Lex Ferenda* Avenues for Restoring Accountability 238
5.3.1. Toward a New War Crime Offence of Indiscriminate Attacks 239
5.3.2. Amending the War Crime of Disproportionate Attacks 241
5.3.3. Roxin and the Future Roles of Criminal Sciences 243

Index *247*

Background: Inequality as Continuity between War and Law

Whenever legal scholars have debated the histories and theories behind the foundations of the law of armed conflicts,[1] this legal framework has always been analysed as being locked in a structural anomaly; using the law to regulate such exceptional, extremely violent, and anarchical situations as armed conflicts. This has resulted in the omnipresent reference to the notorious sentence by Cicero, who, in the famous *Oratio Pro Milone*, asserted '*silent enim leges inter arma*' – the laws are silent amidst the clash of weapons.[2]

Less often noted is the context in which Cicero advanced this statement, epitomising an important aspect of the events surrounding it: the belonging of suspect (Milo) and victim (Clodius) to two different, and opposed, social and political groups. Milo, in fact, was a member of the *optimates* faction (the patrician Senatorial majority seeking to limit the powers of the popular assemblies), while Publius Clodius, killed by Milo's guards, although of aristocratic heritage, was a leader of the *populares* (faction favouring the cause of the commoners), and had been a Tribune of the Plebs, passing many laws in favour of the urban poor.

The killing of Clodius, therefore, triggered outrage and disorders, with the subsequent trial surrounded by radical tensions in Rome. Due to these tensions, historians report that crowds of *populares* gathered in the *forum* to witness the trial, demanding justice for Clodius. Accounts of the trial recall that Cicero was so agitated by these tensions that his oration was poor and unconvincing.[3] At the end of the trial Milo was convicted. Only then did Cicero rewrite the oration as he had wanted to declaim it, composing what has then been considered a masterpiece of

[1] Terminologically, hereinafter 'laws of war' and 'law of armed conflicts' are used to indicate both *ius ad bellum* and *ius in bello*; '*ius in bello*' is used to indicate the framework comprising both international humanitarian law (IHL), and international criminal law (ICL) norms applicable in armed conflicts, in particular war crimes.

[2] Cicero, *Pro Milone*, FH Colson (ed) (Bristol Classic Press, 1991) IV, 11.

[3] 'So Pompey, while it was still night, posted his soldiers on the heights so as to command the forum, and Milo, fearing that Cicero might be disturbed at the unusual sight and conduct his case less successfully, persuaded him to be brought in a litter to the forum and to wait there quietly until the jurors assembled and the court-room was filled. Now Cicero, as it would seem, was not only without courage under arms, but also felt fear when he began to speak, and in many trials he hardly ceased quivering and trembling after his eloquence had become high and sustained. … He took no rest at all during the night before, so that his lack of sleep and his great anxiety did him harm, and he was thought inferior to himself in his plea' (Plutarch, *Parallel Lives*, VII, *Demosthenes and Cicero, Alexander and Caesar*, B Perrins (trs) (Harvard University Press, 1967) XXXV, 171).

the *ars oratoria*. This anecdotal background behind the famous quote well represents a crucial and recurring problem in the analysis of the relationships between armed conflicts and legal structures, that is the inescapable tension between power relations, inequality, and the regulation of war.

Ancient history gives other examples of how war has always been considered an antithesis to law and equality, as a realm in which what only matters are power, force, victory and subjugation. This aspect emerges clearly from an equally famous dialogue accounted by Thucydides. The exchange takes place between an Athenian and a Melian envoy, at the time when the two cities where at war, in 416 BC. According to the Greek historian, the Melian representative, addressing the Athenians, stated:

> Your military preparations are too far advanced to agree with what you say, as we see you are come to be judges in your own cause, and that all we can reasonably expect from this negotiation is war, if we prove to have right on our side and refuse to submit, and in the contrary case, slavery.

The answer of the Athenian envoy was emblematic:

> For ourselves, we shall not trouble you with specious pretences … of how we … are now attacking you because of wrong that you have done us – and make a long speech which would not be believed … since you know as well as we *do that right, as the world goes, is only in question between equals in power, while the strong do what they can and the weak suffer what they must.*[4]

The core of this conception lasted until the beginning of the modern era. It is well synthetised in the words of Gianbattista Vico, who polemically wrote, in the first half of the 1600s, that international law (back then, *ius gentium*) was still 'a law by which the victors govern the blind fury of the weapons and the unbridled insolence of victories, and the vanquished console the damage of wars and the subjugation of the conquests.'[5] In late modernity military supremacy and entitlement to employ it to subjugate entire populations gained a constitutive function in the relation between war and law, with colonialism structurally excluding entire hemispheres from the community of the 'civilized nations'.[6]

Contemporary international law both antagonised and actualised at the same time this nexus between war, victory and law. The post-World War II International Military Tribunals, for example, adjudicating solely the crimes of the Nazi and Japanese defendants, brought the selectivity of enforcement

[4] Thucydides, *History of the Peloponnesian War*, R Crawley (trs) (Everyman, 1993), cited in M Sassoli, AA Bouvier, and A Quintin, *How does Law Protect in War? Cases, Documents and Teaching Materials on Contemporary Practice in International Humanitarian Law*, Vol I, 3rd edn (ICRC, 2001) 5 (emphases added).

[5] GB Vico, 'Epistola Dedicatoria Premessa alla Sifilide di Girolamo Fracastoro' in *Epistole* 1, i–xxi (Laboratorio dell'Istituto di Storia del Pensiero Filosofico e Scientifico Moderno, 2007, Eng tr of this author).

[6] M Koskenniemi, 'Race, Hierarchy and International Law: Lorimer's Legal Science' (2016) 27 *European Journal of International Law* 415.

of the laws constraining the waging of war to a new supranational dimension. It is worth recalling that the Nuremberg judgment itself acknowledged that the power to establish the Tribunal arose simply from the Allies' victory, and Germany's surrender, affirming that

> The making of the Charter was the exercise of the sovereign legislative power by the countries to which the German Reich unconditionally surrendered; and the undoubted right of these countries to legislate for the occupied territories has been recognised by the civilised world.[7]

Ultimately, this nexus between victory and selective material jurisdiction has long been criticised by leading authors as an emblem of 'victor's justice'.[8] The chance to recap this crucial debate clearly escapes the possibility of this introduction, but the remarks of two eminent jurists, personally appointed in their professional capacities to the two international tribunals, seem particularly illuminating and elucidative. First, Justice Robert Jackson, chief United States Prosecutor at Nuremberg, during the 1945 London International Conference on Military Trials, when discussing the elements of crimes comprised in the material jurisdiction of the Tribunal, stated:

> The second element [of the crime] is 'it must be carried out by Axis powers'. We would think that had no place in any definition because it makes an entirely partisan declaration of law. If certain acts in violation of treaties are crimes, they are crimes whether the United States does them or whether Germany does them, and we are not prepared to lay down a rule of criminal conduct against others which we would not be willing to have invoked against us.[9]

At the origins of modern international criminal justice, therefore, one of the leading jurists involved in its establishment noted that its substantive law was being built upon a highly selective premise, one that continental criminal lawyers would identify as paradigm of the 'type of author'.[10]

Second, Radhabinod Pal, dissenting judge of the International Military Tribunal for the Far East, when discussing the nature of customary international law as construed by the military tribunal, wrote:

> The people should not merely be conscious of their law but they must live their law, – they must act and conduct themselves according to it. This living according to law is required not as a mere form of manifestation but also as a means of cognition of

[7] IMT, *Judgement, Law of the Charter*, The Avalon Project – Yale Law School, at avalon.law.yale.edu/imt/judlawch.asp.

[8] See, inter alia, D Zolo, *Victors' Justice: From Nuremberg to Baghdad* (trs MW Weir) (Verso, 2020); RH Minear, *Victors' Justice. Tokyo War Crimes Trials* (Princeton University Press, 1972); T McCormack, Y Tanaka and G Simpson (eds), *Beyond Victor's Justice? The Tokyo War Crimes Trial Revisited* (Martinus Nijhoff Publishers, 2011). More extensively, see ch 3 of this volume.

[9] R Jackson, *International Conference on Military Trials: London 1945, Minutes of Conference Session of July 23*, The Avalon Project – Yale Law School, at avalon.law.yale.edu/imt/jack44.asp.

[10] See n 28 below.

> customary law. When the conduct of the nations is taken into account the law will perhaps be found to be that only a lost war is a crime.[11]

Victory or defeat, in other words, as ultimate formants of legal authority and determinant of the distinction between lawful and criminal conduct.

The post-World War II international criminal tribunals effectively failed to adjudicate major violations of already codified international humanitarian law (IHL)[12] prescriptions by allied powers, notably the atomic bombings of Hiroshima and Nagasaki, the deadliest indiscriminate attacks in the entirety of the war. Laws to combat impunity for civilian victimisation in war, indeed, have since brought a sort of primigenial brand of unfairness.[13]

The remarks recalled unveil a theoretical and normative problem still affecting international law today, which is the continuity between the struggles to prevail in war, the outcomes of the wars themselves, and the reproduction of power hierarchies between states (decided by their defeat or victory) in the law-making functions shaping international criminal justice. The unequal enforcement of the laws of war arises from this continuity. Issues of inequality and selectivity in the enforcement of the law of armed conflict and of war crimes law have a long, uninterrupted history that continues today. From one historical stage to another, post-war international laws, rather than serving the purpose of restoring the principle of equality, and rather than sanctioning the commission of the most serious violations irrespectively of the nationality of the perpetrators, have in truth been shaped by the hegemonic equilibriums established by the war itself, with the aim of maintaining and reproducing them.[14] It is therefore possible to identify a structural philosophical collision between war and law as domains governed, respectively, by two irreducibly conflicting paradigms: that of prevailing against enemies through military supremacy, on the one hand; and that of equalising the sphere of rights and duties of unevenly powerful actors through unified standards, on the other. From this angle, the relationship between war and law emerges as relationship between opposite polarities, with war demanding an axiology of inequality to prevail over enemies, and law promoting a teleology of equality to coexist as peers. This is ultimately the essence of the framing of law and legal policies, on the one hand, and war and violence, on the

[11] 'International Military Tribunal for the Far East, The Dissenting Opinion of the Member of India (Justice Pal)' in N Boister and R Cryer (eds), *Documents on the Tokyo International Military Tribunal: Charter, Indictment, and Judgments* (Oxford University Press, 2008) 863.

[12] See eg Art 25 Hague Convention (IV) *Respecting the Laws and Customs of War on Land and Its Annex: Regulations Concerning the Laws and Customs of War on Land*, adopted 18 October 1907, entered into force 26 January 1910, stipulating 'The attack or bombardment, by whatever means, of towns, villages, dwellings, or buildings which are undefended is prohibited'.

[13] See ch 3, section 3.1 of this volume.

[14] As it has been noted, 'The dominant theory of the laws of war is of them 'regulating' war; an alternative view is that they merely enable, constitute, and perpetuate it' (F Mégret, 'Theorizing the laws of war' in A Orford, F Hoffman and M Clark (eds), *The Oxford Handbook of the Theory of International Law* (Oxford University Press, 2016) 773).

other, as historical and theoretical contraries in the Enlightenment-liberal legal thinking tradition.[15]

This problematic knot accompanies the whole history of ideas on the laws of war in modernity, as nexus of continuity between victory in war and assumption, in particular, of international criminal law-making (and justice-establishing) functions. This nexus has marked the historical experience of great powers and their contributions to international law. The current world order model, after all, has emerged from a war in which great powers have been responsible for serious violations of the laws of war, and at the same time main legislators of the mechanisms to bring war crimes to justice.

This historical ambivalence has continued to exert influence not only over the selective administration of international justice, but also, and arguably more radically, on how the most recently codified treaties to protect civilians in armed conflicts (notably for this analysis, the Rome Statute of the ICC) were ultimately shaped by power relations.[16]

Thinking about these aspects, one is reminded of the words of Michel Foucault:

> No matter what philosophic-juridical theory may say, political power does not begin when the war ends. The organization and juridical structure of power, of States, monarchies, and societies, does not emerge when the clash of arms ceases. War has not been averted. War obviously presided over the birth of States: right, peace, and laws were born in the blood and mud of battles. This should not be taken to mean the ideal battles and rivalries dreamed up by philosophers or jurists: we are not talking about some theoretical savagery. The law is not born of nature, and it was not born near the fountains that the first shepherds frequented: the law is born of real battles, victories, massacres, and conquests which can be dated, and which have their horrific heroes; the law was born in burning towns and ravaged fields. It was born together with the famous innocents who died at break of day.[17]

This vision led Foucault to the overturn of the famous Clausewitz assumption, according to which 'war is the continuation of politics by other means'.[18] As the French philosopher asserted,

> [I]f power is indeed the implementation and deployment of a relationship of force, rather than analysing it in terms of surrender, contract, and alienation, or rather than analysing it in functional terms as the reproduction of the relations of production, shouldn't we be analysing it first and foremost in terms of conflict, confrontation, and war? … Power is war, the continuation of war by other means. At this point, we can

[15] Since the dawn of Natural Law thinking; see R Tuck, *The Rights of War and Peace. Political Thought and the International Order from Grotius to Kant* (Oxford University Press, 1999).

[16] See chs 4 and 5 of this volume.

[17] M Foucault, *Society Must be Defended, Lectures at the Collège de France 1975–76*, D Macey (trs), M Bertani and A Fontana (eds) (Picador, 2003) 50.

[18] C Von Clausewitz, *Vom Kriege* (first published 1932, Dümmlers Verlag); M Howard and P Paret (trs, eds), *On War* (PUP, 1989) Book One, 87.

> invert Clausewitz's proposition and say that politics is the continuation of war by other means.[19]

According to Foucault's conception, even the law was a continuation of the frame of domination constituted by war. He consequently described his own research as

> interested in defining and discovering, beneath the forms of justice that have been instituted, the order that has been imposed, the forgotten past of real struggles, actual victories, and defeats which may have been disguised but which remain profoundly inscribed.

An intellectual effort, in other words, 'interested in rediscovering the blood that has dried in the codes, and not, therefore, the absolute right that lies beneath the transience of history'.[20] Foucault's conception explicitly aimed to move the lenses of intellectual enquiry away from the law and its assumptions, in favour of the analysis of the material struggles of history, wars, and how they forged the social, political and legal orders arising from them.

Despite the compelling nature of Foucault's insights, a comprehensive embrace of this perspective would inevitably leave a multitude of critical issues unassessed. By exclusively examining power relations through the lens of domination, and focusing only on material battles, victories and defeats, there is a risk of overlooking numerous other important mechanisms. This intellectual perspective would risk, in particular, obscuring the mechanisms of *mediation* between historical struggles and ideas shaping the political and legal dialectics of modernity.[21] Consequently, this could neglect the intricate web of alliances between different social groups producing the affirmation of ruling powers, and their primacy in shaping of the law, both nationally and internationally.

Within this context, the work of Antonio Gramsci – in particular his theory of hegemony – assumes particular relevance. Numerous scholars, seeking to highlight the transformative potential of emancipatory theories of international law, have extensively argued that even in the international arena transnational dominant powers assert their authority *over their social adversaries* by securing *the consensus of their social allies*.[22] Not only wars and material struggles for power, therefore, assume crucial importance, but also theoretical struggles for the highest cultural influence. In other words, not only material force, but also capacity of intellectual direction, and ability to portray the interests of a specific class, social group, state, or even a bloc of states, as universal.

[19] Foucault (n 17) 15.

[20] ibid, 56.

[21] On the role of mediation in the theory of sovereignty, and its impact on the conceptualisation of the relation between law and violence in Spinoza, Hegel, Benjamin, Schmitt and Kelsen, see eg B De Giovanni, *Kelsen e Schmitt. Oltre il Novecento* (ESI, 2018) 19–107; see also C Capograssi, 'Considerazioni sullo Stato' in *Opere* (Giuffrè, 1959) 332–74.

[22] A Gramsci, *Quaderni dal Carcere*, V Gerratana (ed) (Einaudi, 1975) Quaderno 25 (XXIII), § 5.

In this light, legal analyses reacquire centrality, and it makes sense to enquire where do the categories of the laws of war stand within the struggles for the direction of the international community. This Gramscian perspective on the complexities of power relationships forms part of the theoretical background of this book.[23] It establishes the understanding that, on a global scale, law, legal concepts and legal institutions exist within the same realm of political and economic power struggles and are inherently entwined with them. Every legal claim becomes part of this field of tensions, facing on one side the demands of transnational ruling powers and, on the other, those of freedom, dignity, and emancipation of marginalised, impoverished, colonised and subaltern groups. International lawyers, therefore, should look at the international legal field 'as a plural and fragmented terrain of contestation rather than as a monolith'. Adopting this view would acknowledge that international law and its institutions provide important arenas for progressive action, with the consequence of 'expanding the space of transformative politics based on the nexus between freedom, peace, and social justice'.[24] This potential has indeed been one of the integral elements in the process leading to the codification of human rights law. It is worth noting the scholarship underscoring the often-overlooked significance of the decolonisation and its crucial contribution to the rise of contemporary international law. Counterbalancing the attention directed at eurocentrism and colonial mindsets,[25] scholars have illustrated the world-leading functions of political leaders, jurists and diplomats of the Global South in setting the premises of the international human rights agenda since the late 1960s.[26]

Hence, whilst power relations, military force and supremacy have been central in international law-making processes and in the dynamics of its enforcement, it is reasonable to ask if any breakthrough intervened in modernity and how, from this point of view, IHL and international criminal law (ICL) are situated. This breakthrough over inequalities – at least the formal inequalities before the law – has been the pillar of the bourgeois revolutions of the late eighteenth century. Their epochal legal achievement was to reorganise the foundations of sovereignty around the ideals of the juridical Enlightenment, driving peoples from the condition of subjected of absolute monarchies to citizens of early-modern democracies.

[23] See inter alia D Kennedy, 'Antonio Gramsci and the Legal System' (ALSA Forum, 1982) 6, 32–39; D Litowitz, 'Gramsci, Hegemony, and the Law' (2000) *BYU Law Review* 515; S Buckel and A Fischer-Lescano, 'Gramsci Reconsidered: Hegemony in Global Law' (2009) 22 *Leiden Journal of International Law* 437.

[24] B Rajagopal, *International Law from Below. Development, Social Movements and Third World Resistance* (Cambridge University Press, 2003) 23.

[25] See, inter alia, A Anghie, *Imperialism, Sovereignty and the Making of IL* (Cambridge University Press, 2004); M Koskenniemi, 'Histories of IL, Dealing with Eurocentrism' (2011) 10 *Rechts Geschichte* 152.

[26] D Jensen, *The Making of International Human Rights. The 1960s, Decolonization, and the Reconstruction of Global Values* (Cambridge University Press, 2016).

Equality before the law was pivotal in this process, and both philosophically and historically the struggles for the formalisation of this principle became the main constituent of the concept of Rule of Law. This is true, in particular, from the point of view of the history of criminal law, in which the Enlightenment theories[27] progressively shaped secular bulwarks to protect citizens from inequalities and arbitrariness, projecting the standards of the Rule of law into the realm of penal systems. Not only, in fact, is every liberal penal system normatively centred on the principle of equality before the law, but it is a foundational condition of every democratic theory about the function of punishment (whether it is general or special prevention, both in their positive or negative declinations)[28] that the same offences are to be treated in the same way, no matter who commits them. Sanctions, in other words, are attached to actions, rather than to authors. Equality, therefore, is both criterion of normative coherence, axiological parameter to evaluate a system of penal norms, and teleological measure of the effectiveness of its enforcement. On the contrary, 'criminal law of the author' is the formula used by continental penal theorists to synthetise the set of features characterising the penal systems of authoritarian and totalitarian regimes, aimed at the repression of particular categories of subjects and groups, labelled as enemies.[29]

The persisting selectivity of IHL and ICL has elements of this illiberal tendency, actualised when imperial powers identify specific categories of enemies to be brought to justice even at serious geopolitical costs, thus implying an imperative moral duty to do so, while refusing to subject themselves, their allies and their actions to the same judicial scrutiny, under the same legal parameters. In this respect, 20 years after the entry into force of the International Criminal Court (ICC), many authors discuss the limits of international criminal justice and how they intersect the problem of selectivity.[30] The consensus around this institutional

[27] Such as C Beccaria, *Dei Delitti e Delle Pene*, first published 1764, A Burgio (ed) (Feltrinelli, 2005); CLS Montesquieu, 'Lo spirito delle leggi, XII, 2' in M Armandi (ed), *Dizionario delle idee. Le radici liberali della politica e del diritto* (Editori Riuniti, 1998); G Filangieri, *The Science of Legislation, from the Italian Gaetano Filangeri* (Emery and Adams, 1806).

[28] See S Moccia, *Il diritto penale tra essere e valore. Funzione della pena e sistematica teleologica* (ESI, 1992); A Baratta, 'Principi del diritto penale minimo. Per una teoria dei diritti umani come oggetti e limiti della legge penale' (1985) 3 *Dei delitti e delle pene* 445; A Baratta, *Criminologia critica e critica del diritto penale*, 2nd edn (Meltemi, 2019); P Costa, 'Il principio di legalità. Un campo di tensione nella modernità penale' (2007) 36 *Quaderni Fiorentini per la storia del pensiero giuridico moderno* 8; A Ashworth and J Horder, *Principles of Criminal Law*, 7th edn (Oxford University Press, 2013).

[29] L Ferrajoli, *Diritto e ragione. Teoria del garantismo penale* (Laterza, 2011); S Moccia (ed), *Diritti dell'uomo e sistema penale* (ESI, 2002); E De Cristofaro, *Codici della persecuzione. I giuristi e il razzismo nei regimi nazista e fascista* (Giappichelli, 2008); toward degrees of admissibility of criminal law against internal and external 'enemies', see G Jakobs, 'Kriminalisierung im Vorfeld einer Rechtsgutsverletzung' (1985) 97 *Zeitschrift für die gesamte Strafrechtswissenschaft*, 751; *contra*, see D Salas, *La volonté de punir. Essai sur le populisme pénal* (Pluriel, 2005); concerning the purpose of punishment in international criminal justice, see F Jessberger and J Geneuss (eds), *Why Punish Perpetrators of Mass Atrocities?: Purposes of Punishment in International Criminal Law* (Cambridge University Press, 2020).

[30] There are several problems in keeping the norms of the Statute compliant to the safeguards of the legality principle, and its corollaries, for example: lack of stringency and definiteness of the types of offences; clauses of expressed analogy; extreme breadth of hermeneutical operations allowed to judges (see M Shahabuddeen, *Does the Principle of Legality Stand in the Way of Progressive Development of*

framework, more than many others, appears to have been adversely affected by the inequalities and relativities of its enforcement.[31] Looking at the different objectives solemnly declared and remarked in the Prologue to the Rome Statute of the ICC, the lack of enforcement for the crimes committed by agents of hegemonic states has often been indicated as representing a major failure. This led scholars to confirm the tendency to 'double-standards' in ICL enforcement, or, as Damaška puts it, a 'discrimination against those who violate human rights on a citizenship basis'.[32] This discriminatory selectivity has prompted authors to develop a radical critique of international criminal justice, articulated in many positions and studies, and culminating in questioning the desirability itself of institutions such as the ICC. This jurisdiction has often been depicted as an instrument of colonial domination, standing guard over the hegemonic equilibrium of the international legal sphere. There are also those who have accused this institution of embodying a model of 'criminal law of the enemy' *par excellence*,[33] or those who see in it simply a symbolic gesture.[34]

Whilst many of these arguments have several merits in terms of ideology critiques,[35] their inherent risk lies in sidestepping any endeavours to enhance the effectiveness of this legal framework in fulfilling its general-preventive functions, including in anti-hegemonic directions. From a Gramscian standpoint,[36] conceiving modern ICL as a construct shaped by power politics should not constitute a conclusion, useful to dismiss further efforts, but a premise. The real challenge, in this sense, would be not to merely point out power's 'footprint' on the development and functioning of this legal field, but rather to identify how power relations have adversely affected its normativity, equal enforcements, and – consequently – develop paths to overcome its limits.[37]

Law? (2004) 2 *Journal of International Criminal Justice* 1007; on the Rome Statute as system characterised by a 'crisis of guarantees' and safeguards for the accused, see M Caianiello and E Fronza, 'Il principio di Legalità nello Statuto della Corte Penale Internazionale' in G Carlizzi et al (eds), *La Corte penale internazionale. Problemi e prospettive* (Vivarium, 2003) 308; there is no norm in the Statute about the purpose of punishment, which contributes to confidence in retribution (see R Henham, 'The Philosophical Foundations of International Sentencing' (2003) 1 *Journal of International Criminal Justice* 64; the Statute preamble is characterised by a teleological overload of declared goals, some contrasting between one another and many others, requiring a difficult balance (see M Damaška, *What is the Point of International Criminal Justice?* (2008) *Yale Law School Faculty Scholarship Series*, Paper 1572).

[31] See D Zolo, 'The double-track approach to international criminal justice' (2007) 5 *Journal of International Criminal Justice* 799.

[32] Damaška (n 30) 361.

[33] See D Pastor, *El derecho penal del enemigo en el espero del poder punitivo internacional* in M Cancio Melia and DCG Jara Diez (eds), *Derecho penal del enemigo. El dicurso penal de la exclusion* (BdeF, 2006) 475 ff.

[34] DL Rother and CW Mullins, *Symbolic Gestures and the Generation of Global Social Control: the International Criminal Court* (Lexington Books, 2006).

[35] T Krever, 'International Criminal Law: An Ideology Critique' (2013) 26 *Leiden Journal of International Law* 701.

[36] See in particular Buckel and Fischer-Lescano (n 23).

[37] The issue is more extensively discussed in L Daniele, 'The International Criminal Court between Human Rights and Realpolitik' in G Oberleitner (ed), *International Human Rights Institutions, Tribunals, and Courts* (Springer, 2018) 355–76.

The current developments in the pursuit of leadership accountability for the probable war crimes and crimes against humanity committed during the last, full-scale 2022 Russian invasion of Ukraine, and in the Israeli total destruction of Gaza, with the recent arrest warrants issued by the ICC, seem to point in a new direction. This shift assumes particular significance for the challenge of adjudicating probable crimes committed by powerful Western allies. Missed opportunities of the ICC in this respect, in fact, have often been justified on the basis of *realpolitik* considerations. However, an arrest warrant swiftly issued against the head of state of one of the biggest nuclear world powers does not leave much space for future framings of international criminal justice inspired by *realpolitik* pragmatism, demanding public opinions to assume in premise the limits to equal enforcements imposed by power relations between states.[38]

Within this background, IHL and war crimes law assume a crucial relevance. Indiscriminate and disproportionate attacks, in particular, stand out as topical test bench for the equal application of international law. The prohibition of indiscriminate and disproportionate attacks, in fact, appear to condense in both definition and international criminalisation a paradigmatic example of the problems described so far.

When codified in the 1977 Additional Protocol I to the four 1949 Geneva Conventions, these prohibited attacks represented the culmination of the historical efforts to restrain the conduct of hostilities of belligerents, by means of legally balancing considerations military necessity and the principle of humanity. This balance, normatively struck, and the source of numerous prescriptions, finds in the mentioned prohibitions two exemplary systematisations, outlawing 1) attacks of a nature to strike lawful targets and protected persons and objects without distinction, as well as 2) attacks which may be expected to cause excessive incidental civilian harm (a notion including incidental loss of life, injury to civilians, damage to civilian objects, or a combination thereof) in comparison to the concrete and direct military advantage anticipated.

As the following chapters will discuss in detail, the whole normative fabric of contemporary IHL converges in these two prohibitions. Nonetheless, the drafters of the Rome Statute of the International Criminal Court, called upon to codify the war crime offences punishing the commission of indiscriminate and disproportionate attacks, introduced significant modifications to the IHL lineaments of the two prohibitions. This process included, on the one hand, unavoidable reformulations of the prohibitions, inevitable in the process of 'translation' of IHL norms in the realm of individual criminal liability, such as the introduction of the necessary *mens rea* thresholds. On the other hand, through efforts of powerful states' delegations, drafters also opted for debatable choices decisively weakening civilian protection in armed conflicts, such as refraining from criminalising explicitly

[38] See D Bosco, *Rough Justice: The International Criminal Court in a World of Power Politics* (Oxford University Press, 2013); A Pues, *Prosecutorial Discretion at the International Criminal Court* (Hart Publishing, 2020).

indiscriminate attacks, or adding new concepts unknown to IHL in the definition of the offence of disproportionate attacks.[39]

This book presents an account of the repercussions of these choices, and endeavours to propose potential avenues to overcome the accountability gaps they have produced. Relatedly, it highlights how the understanding of these prohibitions has been a crucial field of contestation in the last decades. In particular, the competing paradigms constituting the opposite normative polarities of every IHL prescription – that is, civilian protection, on the one hand, and military necessity, on the other – appear to have been very differently balanced against each other by various interpreters, depending on how attacking forces were geopolitically situated, following the same ally/enemy dichotomies indicated by authors warning against the general dangers of double standards in international legal discourses.[40] The result has been a frequently unequal construction of the normativity of IHL and ICL on the basis of the geopolitical positionalities of Western authors, and of the military actors whose hostilities were under scrutiny, particularly during the war on terror.

While the related dangers have been extensively discussed in relation to the unequal institutional mobilisation to enforce the prohibition against aggression, and to give effect to its international criminal protection, the risks of laws of war scholarship reproducing a 'tale of two IHLs', strictly or permissively construed depending on the collocation of attacking forces around these enemy/ally lines has attracted much less attention. *Ius in bello*, however, is structurally organised around the principle of equality of belligerents,[41] relies on enforcement mechanisms with a lower degree of big powers' protagonism and politicisation (at least in comparison to the *ius contra bellum* in the UN Charter security architecture),[42] and can

[39] See, inter alia, JC Lawrence and KJ Heller, 'The First Ecocentric Environmental War Crime: The Limits of Article 8(2)(b)(iv) of the Rome Statute' (2007) 20 *Georgetown. International Environmental Law Review* 61; see also H Olàsolo, *Unlawful Attacks in Combat Situations: from the ICTY's Case Law to the Rome Statute* (Brill Nijhoff, 2007) 80–91.

[40] See *ex multiis* R Wilde, 'Hamster in a Wheel: International Law, Crisis, Exceptionalism, Whataboutery, Speaking Truth to Power, and Sociopathic, Racist Gaslighting' *Opinio Juris*, 17 March 2022, at opiniojuris.org/2022/03/17/hamster-in-a-wheel-international-law-crisis-exceptionalism-whataboutery-speaking-truth-to-power-and-sociopathic-racist-gaslighting; A Kotova and N Tzouvala, 'In Defense of Comparisons: Russia and the Transmutations of Imperialism in International Law' (2022) 116 *American Journal of International Law* 710. See also K Ambos, 'Ukraine and the Double Standards of the West' (2022) 20 *Journal of International Criminal Justice* 875, and J Dugard, 'The Choice Before Us: International Law or a "Rules-Based International Order?"' (2023) 36 *Leiden Journal of International Law* 223.

[41] See A Roberts, 'The Equal Application of the Laws of War: A Principle Under Pressure' (2008) 90 *International Review of the Red Cross* 931; V Koutroulis, 'And Yet It Exists: In Defence of the "Equality of Belligerents" Principle' (2013) 26 *Leiden Journal of International Law* 449.

[42] See N Krisch, 'International Law in Times of Hegemony: Unequal Power and the Shaping of the International Legal Order' (2005) 16 *European Journal of International Law* 369; M Hakimi, 'The Jus ad Bellum's Regulatory Form' (2018) 112 *American Journal of International Law* 151; OA Hathaway. 'How the Erosion of U.S. War Powers Constraints Has Undermined International Law Constraints on the Use of Force' (2023) 14 *Harvard National Security Journal* 336; G Pecorella, *The United States and the Crime of Aggression* (Routledge, 2021).

count on less contested jurisdictional premises enabling the international pursuit of individual criminal liability for its most serious violations (at least in comparison to the limits of the ICC jurisdictional regime on the crime of aggression).[43] These features, rendering IHL more equally and horizontally enforceable across states and blocs of allied states, appear to raise even higher dangers of appropriation and mimicking, by rival big powers, of Western big powers' and allies' approaches eroding the civilian protective purposes of IHL,[44] and opposing the equal enforcement of war crimes law as universal instrument of prevention of its most serious violations.[45] This propensity to differentiate conduct of hostilities legal standards on the basis of the hostilities, in other words, reveals particularly problematic in relation to IHL and war crimes law, since their equal application represents their best chance to remain a shared, minimum legal and moral ground of compliance even between enemies at war, or amidst escalating blocs' confrontations (and growing readiness to new wars),[46] rendering all the more urgent a critical reflection on its unequal relativisations, and how to overcome them.

[43] KJ Heller, 'Who is Afraid of the Crime of Aggression?' (2021) 19 *Journal of International Criminal Justice* 999; K Ambos, 'The Crime of Aggression after Kampala' (2010) 53 *German Yearbook of International Law* 463; C Kreß and S Barriga (eds), *The Crime of Aggression: A Commentary* (Cambridge University Press, 2017).

[44] See A Cassese, 'Terrorism is also Disrupting Crucial Legal Categories of International Law' (2001) 5 *European Journal of International Law* 993; N Quenivet, 'The "War on Terror" and the Principle of Distinction in International Humanitarian Law' (2010) 3 *Colombian Yearbook of International Law* 155.

[45] See SD Murphy, 'American Servicemembers' Protection Act' (2002) 96 *American Journal of International Law* 975; J Bava and K Ireland, 'The American Service-Members' Protection Act: Pathways to and Constraints on US Cooperation with the International Criminal Court' *Law & Policy Lab*, June 2016, Stanford Law School, at law.stanford.edu/wp-content/uploads/2016/07/Ireland-and-Bava-The-American-Servicemembers-Protection-Act-Pathways-to-and-Constraints-on-U.S.-Cooperation-with-the-ICC.pdf; in the press, more recently, see J Scahill, 'U.S. Hypocrisy on War Crimes Is a Gift to Putin' *The Intercept* (10 February 2023), at theintercept.com/2023/02/10/us-russia-putin-war-crimes.

[46] See *ex multiis* MF Cancian and E Heiginbotham, 'The First Battle of the Next War: Wargaming a Chinese Invasion of Taiwan', Centre for Strategic and International Studies, January 2023, at csis-website-prod.s3.amazonaws.com/s3fs-public/publication/230109_Cancian_FirstBattle_NextWar.pdf.

1

Civilian Victimisation in Armed Conflicts in History and Theory

1.1. Introduction

If observed through the lenses of the long history of international law, the contemporary concept of the civilian is relatively recent. The problem of the involvement of civilians in war, however, is older, from the point of view of both their participation in the hostilities (in contrast to regular armies), and – conversely – from the point of view of the absolute and relative prohibition of their victimisation (absolute in relation to intentional targeting, and relative in relation to incidental civilian harm).

Non-combatants have been a target of organised violence since the earliest historical accounts of wars, and records of mass victimisation of civilians date back to ancient history. A history of civilian victimisation in armed hostilities should with no doubt include, to mention few examples: the killing of the men of Melos and the enslavement of women and children of the island after its conquest by Athens, during the Peloponnesian War;[1] the fall of Carthage in the Third Punic War, when Roman legions razed the city to the ground;[2] the deeds of Attila and the Huns who, in the words of Roman historians, 'ground almost the whole Europe into dust' in the mid-fifth century;[3] the sack of Jerusalem in the 1099 Crusade;[4] the massacres of Genghis Khan and the Tamerlane between the end of the thirteenth and the beginning of the fourteenth centuries;[5] the eight million civilians killed or displaced during the Thirty Years War;[6] the French destruction of German regions on its eastern border at the end of the seventeenth century;[7] the killing of about 150.000 civilians during the royalist uprising in the Vendée in 1794;[8] the hundreds of thousands of civilian victims of the imperial and colonial

[1] Thucydides, *History of the Peloponnesian War*, R Crawley (trs) (Everyman, 1993) book 5, chs 84–116.

[2] AE Astin et al (eds), *The Cambridge Ancient History*, Vol. VIII, *Rome and the Mediterranean to 133 B.C.*, 2nd edn (Cambridge University Press, 1989); and D Scullard, *A History of the Roman World, 753 to 146 B.C.* (Routledge, 2002) 316 ff.

[3] EA Thompson, *The Huns* (Wiley-Blackwell, 1999) 103.

[4] PK Davis, *Besieged: 100 Great Sieges from Jericho to Sarajevo* (Oxford University Press, 2003) 57 ff.

[5] R Grousset, *The Empire of the Steppes: A History of Central Asia* (Rutgers University Press, 1970).

[6] J Childs, *Armies and Warfare in Europe, 1648–1789* (Homs & Meier, 1982) 152 ff.

[7] ibid.

[8] AJ Joes, 'Insurgency and Genocide: La Vandée' in *Small Wars and Insurgencies* (1998) IX, 3, 37 ff.

wars,[9] between Dutch, Russians, French and Italians respectively in Indonesia,[10] Caucasus,[11] Algeria[12] and Ethiopia,[13] in the first half of the twentieth century.

There are countless further examples that a historiography of civilian victimisation in war should account for. In the twentieth century, civilians who lost their lives due to wars and their consequences are estimated by some authors to number more than 50 million.[14]

In such a historiography, colonialism would require a specific study, due to its ability to transform the physical destruction of entire populations – that is, genocides (usually by means of a combination of mass killing and mass displacement) – through war.[15] This was particularly the case when colonial powers faced armed uprising of the colonised or guerrilla warfare backed by civilian populations. As Sartre puts it:

> Against partisans backed by the entire population, colonial armies are helpless. They have only one way of escaping from the harassment which demoralises them and tends towards a Dien Bien Phu. This is to eliminate the civilian population. As it is the unity of a whole people that is containing the conventional army, the only anti-guerrilla strategy which will be effective is the destruction of that people, in other words, the civilians, women and children. Torture and genocide were the colonialists' answers to the uprising of the natives. And that answer, as we know, is useless if it is not definitive and total. A determined population, unified by its fierce and politicised partisan army, will not let itself be intimidated, as it was in the heyday of colonialism, by a massacre 'as a lesson'. On the contrary, this will only increase its hatred. It is no longer a matter of arousing fear but of physically liquidating a people. And as this is not possible without at the same time eliminating the colonial economy and the colonial system; the settlers panic, the colonial powers grow tired of sinking manpower and money into a conflict with no solution, the masses at home end up opposing the continuation of barbaric wars and the colonies become independent states. There do exist, however, cases where the genocidal solution to popular wars is not held back by innate contradictions. Total genocide then reveals itself as the foundation of anti-guerrilla strategy. And, under certain circumstances, it would even present itself as the ultimate objective, either immediately or gradually.[16]

[9] S Howe, 'Colonising and Exterminating? Memories of Imperial Violence in Britain and France' (2010) 2 *Histoire Politique* 11; O Le Court Grandmaison, *Coloniser, Exterminer. Sur la guerre et l'État colonial*, Fayard, 2005; C Elkins, *Britain's Gulag: The Brutal End of Empire in Kenya* (Cape, 2005).

[10] M Clodfelter, *Warfare and Armed Conflicts: a Statistical Reference to Casualties and Other Figures, 1500–2000* (McFarland, 2002) 266.

[11] I Arreguin Toft, *How the Weak Win Wars: a Theory of Asymmetric Conflict* (Cambridge University Press, 2005) 48 ff.

[12] A Horne, *A Savage War of Peace: Algeria 1954–1962* (Viking Press, 1978).

[13] See R Pankhurst, 'Italian Fascist War Crimes in Ethiopia: A History of Their Discussion, from the League of Nations to the United Nations (1936–1949)' (1999) 6 *Northeast African Studies* 83.

[14] W Eckhardt, 'Civilian deaths in wartime' (1989) 20 *Bulletin of Peace Proposals* 89.

[15] See M Shaw, *War and Genocide* (Polity Press, 2003).

[16] J-P Sartre, *On Genocide, and a Summary of the Evidence and the Judgements of the International War Crimes Tribunal* (A El Kaïm-Sartre, ed) (Beacon Press, 1968) 60.

The relationship between civilians, armed conflicts and legal structures began to change with the rise and evolution of the nation-states, after the revolutions and the wars taking place between the end of the eighteenth and the beginning of the nineteenth century. This process accelerated intensely between 1850 and 1950, that is the 100 years in which interstate armed conflicts became for the first time in history 'total wars'.[17] The boundaries that separated civilians from soldiers, combatants from non-combatants, and frontline from home began to blur and sometimes, as in anti-colonial wars and contemporary asymmetrical conflicts, largely vanished.[18]

A variety of reasons explains this shift. These include: the technological advances bringing combat far into the enemy's rear area; mass mobilisation; the increasing synergy between war and industrial production; and ideologies identifying specific categories of civilians as enemies of 'the society', declaring violence against them a political necessity, if not a patriotic duty. Nevertheless, the early twentieth century also saw the rise of efforts to protect non-combatants in wartime, to legally classify them as civilians, and to attach to this status a wide range of protections. Severe constraints on the waging of war, the means and the methods of warfare have since been codified in the international legal realm.[19]

After the rise of *ius in bello*, military strategy was forced to subvert the antique saying contending that '*moderation in war is a form of imbecility*',[20] and war started to be seen as something very different than a space to unleash the destructive potential of organised armed forces. Thus, international humanitarian law (IHL) has transposed into the legal realm the growing belief that distinction, moderation, 'surgical' precision in attacks and minimisation of civilian harm are virtues in war. In other words, humanitarian law projected the Enlightenment belief in rationality, and rational restraints, into the most irrational human activity. A process of 'rationalisation' of war,[21] successfully limiting the atrocities of wartime and contributing to the affirmation of the respect of civilians and human dignity, even in war, as a universal value. In extreme synthesis, this is the traditional conception about the progressive development of the laws of armed conflicts. However, not all authors have agreed with this view, according to which IHL is generally looked at as a politically neutral legal field, contributing to the progress and civilisation of mankind as a whole, and universally advancing the respect for human

[17] The first use of the expression in the modern meaning is usually attributed to a publication of the German general Erich Ludendorff' in his World War I memoir, *Der Totale Krieg*. The concept of 'total war' is often used to describe a war which is unrestricted in terms of the weapons used, the territory or combatants involved, or the objectives pursued, especially one in which the accepted rules of war are disregarded. In this book, it is used in a narrower meaning, designing the armed conflicts in which the whole infrastructure of the state is invested into the war effort.

[18] As explained by AR Seipp, 'Civilians', *Oxford Bibliography on Military History*, at www.oxfordbibliographies.com.

[19] ibid.

[20] 'The essence of war is violence. Moderation in war is imbecility': JA Fisher, *Memories and Records* (first published 1919) (Hard Press, 2012) 211, emphasis added.

[21] JL Martin, 'The Objective and Subjective Rationalization of War' (2005) 34 *Theory and Society* 229.

dignity in wartime. Leading literature has increasingly unveiled, on the contrary, the contingent histories of the laws of war, and the imprint of imperial and colonial powers on its categories.[22] Once rediscovered, the inherently political constitutive elements of the laws of war enable critical scrutiny.

1.2. International Humanitarian Law as *Koinè*, and its 'Dark Sides'

> Compared to the brutality of religious and factional wars, which by nature are wars of annihilation wherein the enemy is treated as a criminal and a pirate, and compared to colonial wars, which are pursued against 'wild' peoples, European *war in form* signified the strongest possible rationalisation and humanisation of war. Both belligerents had the same political character and the same rights; both recognised each other as States. As a result, it was possible to distinguish an enemy from a criminal. Not only was the concept of enemy able to assume a legal form, but the enemy ceased to be someone 'who must be annihilated'. *Aliud est hostis, aliud rebellis* [It is one thing to be an enemy, another to be a rebel]. A peace treaty with the vanquished party thus became possible. In this way, European international law succeeded in bracketing war, with the help of the concept of 'state'. … An international legal order, based on the liquidation of civil war and on the bracketing of war (in that it transformed war into a duel between European States), actually had legitimated a realm of relative reason. The equality of sovereigns made them equally legal partners in war and *prevented military methods of annihilation*.[23]

With these words Carl Schmitt 'indicted' the post-1945 efforts to outlaw and punish the waging of aggressive war, maintaining that the formalisation of war as legitimate means to solve international disputes allowed European international law to contain enmity between states. The controversial German philosopher condensed in these lines one of the most debated criticisms against liberal universalism and the new features of the laws of war after World War II. In Schmitt's view[24]

[22] The debate around the role and primacy of the Lieber Code in comparison to other early codifications exemplifies many of these disagreements; see eg M Curti, 'Francis Lieber and Nationalism' (1941) 4 *Huntington Library Quarterly* 265; recently, see A Gurmendi, 'Latin Lieber: Uncovering the History of the Treaty on the Regularisation of War' *Opinio Juris*, 10 June 2022, at opiniojuris.org/2022/06/10/latin-lieber-uncovering-the-history-of-the-treaty-on-the-regularisation-of-war. See more comprehensively on the influence of more powerful states on the codification of the fundamental categories of the laws of war, S Moyn, *Humane. How the United States Abandoned Peace and Reinvented War* (Macmillan, 2021) 163 ff; B Van Dijk, *Preparing for War* (Oxford University Press, 2022); and K Nabulsi, *Traditions of War: Occupation, Resistance and The Law* (Oxford University Press, 1999).

[23] C Schmitt, *Der Nomos der Erde im Völkerrecht des Jus Publicum Europaeum* (Duncker & Humblot, 1950); GL Ulmen (trs), *The Nomos of the Earth in the International Law of the Jus Publicum Europaeum* (Telos Press, 2006) 142, emphasis added.

[24] See D Dyzenhaus, *Legality and Legitimacy: Carl Schmitt, Hans Kelsen, and Hermann Heller in Weimar* (Oxford University Press, 1999) 39 ff.

(influenced by highly debatable political motives),[25] the affirmation of humanitarianism, the legal attempts to outlaw aggressive wars and to identify those who wage them as international 'criminals' were rapidly and dramatically eroding the achievements of the legal order that had allegedly assured to European powers centuries of mutually recognised entitlements successfully limiting armed conflicts and their destructive potential. After the order of the *Jus Publicum Europaeum* had put 'war in form', prompting conflicting states to recognise each other as *justi hostes* (just enemies) and to wage legitimate, formalised wars, the criminalisation of war – according to Schmitt – was instead dangerously conflating the concept of enemy and the concept of criminal. With such a conflation, international law would have enabled hegemonic world powers to seize the concept of humanity, and deprive any enemy of this quality, paving the way for total wars of mutual annihilation. As he clarified in another famous passage:

> Humanity as such cannot wage war because it has no enemy, at least not on this planet. The concept of humanity excludes the concept of the enemy, because the enemy does not cease to be a human being-and hence there is no specific differentiation in that concept. That wars are waged in the name of humanity is not a contradiction of this simple truth; quite the contrary, it has an especially intensive political meaning. When a state fights its political enemy in the name of humanity, it is not a war for the sake of humanity, but a war wherein a particular state seeks to usurp a universal concept against its military opponent. At the expense of its opponent, it tries to identify itself with humanity in the same way as one can misuse peace, justice, progress, and civilisation in order to claim these as one's own and to deny the same to the enemy. The concept of humanity is an especially useful ideological instrument of imperialist expansion, and in its ethical-humanitarian form it is a specific vehicle of economic imperialism. Here one is reminded of a somewhat modified expression of Proudhon's: *whoever invokes humanity wants to cheat.* To confiscate the word humanity, to invoke and monopolise such a term probably has certain incalculable effects, such as denying the enemy the quality of being human and declaring him to be an outlaw of humanity; and a war can thereby be driven to the most extreme inhumanity.[26]

Considering the decades of the war on terror, Schmitt's warnings appeared to observers particularly prescient. International law in the last few decades has effectively provided a platform for hegemonic powers to transform narratives deployed to impose their unilateralism into normative theories justifying wars in violation of international law, as happened with the concept of preventive self-defence, or humanitarian military intervention.[27] Similarly, large rival powers have tried to

[25] See G Balakrishnan, *The Enemy. An Intellectual Portrait of Carl Schmitt* (Verso, 2000). see also JW Müller, *A Dangerous Mind: Carl Schmitt in Post-war European Thought* (Yale University Press, 2003).

[26] C Schmitt, *Der Begriff des Politischen*, Duncker & Humblot, 1932, G Schwab (trs), *The Concept of Political* (University of Chicago Press, 2007) 54.

[27] See R Gordon, 'Saving Failed States: Sometimes a Neo-colonialist Notion' (1997) 12 *American University International Law Review* 903; *contra*, see T Nunan, 'The Anti-Colonial Origins of Humanitarian Intervention', Jadaliyya, 15 September 2016, at www.jadaliyya.com/pages/index/25107/

mobilise analogue concepts to justify aggressive wars of territorial conquest, such as the ongoing Russian invasion of Ukraine.[28]

In the contemporary geopolitical arena, discourses on the protection of civilians in times of war are increasingly degraded to rhetorical devices at the disposal of the powers in conflict, useful to assert alleged *universal* functions behind one's own military actions. Moreover, these alleged universal functions were increasingly employed to justify the indiscriminate character of attacks occurring in the context of the hostilities thus commenced, in which the centrality of non-state actors and guerrilla warfare has blurred the legal dichotomy between civilians and combatants,[29] and with it the protective red lines drawn by IHL around the former. In these discourses and narratives, civilian casualties become an unfortunate necessity – that has to be accepted – of military actions that aim to 'protect' states and citizens from terrorist organisations, or cruel governments, in a paradoxical inversion in which a universal value – that is protecting civilians – grounds the moral admissibility of its 'circumstantial' opposite: the killing or mass killing of civilians.

In its most extreme form, this logic, when transposed into military ethics and strategic thinking, even arrived at the extremes of contending that in order to prioritise the protection of its own citizens' lives (whether civilians or combatants), an army 'has to give preference to saving the life of a single citizen even if the collateral damage caused in the course of protecting him or her is *much higher* in number'.[30]

When confronting such arguments, the ethics of which appear entirely irreconcilable with the fundamental protective principles of contemporary law of armed conflicts, analysts should not forget that, in structuralist terms, international law, humanitarian law and human rights, before being legal subjects, are 'orders of the discourse'.[31] In this light, many authors have pointed out a new phenomenon that arose in the first years of the new millennium: the transformation of these discourses in a common language of the world, a *κοινή*, or *lingua franca*, broadening, become universal, and symmetrically losing profundity and effectiveness. A language, in other words, that progressively subsumes, and is appropriated by,

the-anti-colonial-origins-of-humanitarian-intervenn; A Orford, Reading *Humanitarian Intervention: Human Rights and the Use of Force in International Law* (Cambridge University Press, 2003; H Duffy, *The 'War on Terror' and the Framework of International Law*, 2nd edn (Cambridge University Press, 2015).

[28] See eg M Milanović, What is Russia's Legal Justification for Using Force against Ukraine? *EJILTalk!*, 24 February 2022.

[29] See MN Schmitt, 'Asymmetrical Warfare and International Humanitarian Law' (2007) 62 *Air Force Law Review* 1; W Heintschel Von Heineg and V Epping (eds), *International Humanitarian Law Facing New Challenges. Symposium in Honour of Knut Ipsen* (Springer, 2007).

[30] A Kasher and A Yadlin, 'Assassination and Preventive Killing' (2005) 25 *SAIS Reiew. of International Affairs* 25, emphasis added.

[31] See Foucault, *L'Ordre du Discourse* (Gallimard, 1971), trs by R Swyer as 'Orders of Discourse. Inaugural Lecture Delivered at Collège de France' (1971) 10 *Social Science Information* 7. Consulted in Italian, *L'Ordine del Discorso e Altri Interventi* (trs by E Fontana et al) (Einaudi, 2017).

the most diverse range of actors and powers of the global arena, be they dominant or dominated, colonisers or colonised, hegemonic or subaltern, authoritarian or liberal. The more the light brought by human rights broadens, the more their shadow sides emerge.[32]

Human rights and humanitarian law advance axiomatic claims of universalism, but universalism brings with it a tendency towards de-politicisation and the removal of the adversarial dynamics from which human rights and humanitarian legal protections themselves have arisen. Universalism, in fact, abstracts the *human* within the treaties from the field of tensions in which, instead, human groups exist and operate as historical and political subjects. The more one tries to expand the universalist implications of these rights and their supposed neutrality, the greater the risk of transforming the human rights language into a kaleidoscope of particularistic translations and claims, aimed precisely at *universalising* specific and rather partial interests.[33] Within this tendency, depending on who in a determined context acts as 'translator', the concepts of abuse, perpetrator and victim become dramatically interchangeable.[34]

Schmitt, from his anti-liberal perspective, denounced the dangers of universalist humanitarianism as early as the 1930s, when he composed his inflamed essays against liberal humanists, accusing them of being carriers of a theory of 'neutralization and de-politicization',[35] based on the allegedly flawed attempt to dissolve the legitimate enmity that lies behind any political order.

1.3. Civilians in the Interstate Warfare of the *Jus Publicum Europaeum*

It is legitimate to ask if the diagnosis of Schmitt was accurate, and historically proven. What was this 'nomos' evoked by the philosopher and preceding post-World War II international law and modern IHL?

In this regard, it is worth recalling the indications of Koskenniemi. When reflecting on how to read Schmitt's views today, he suggested that

> his nomos is not at all derived from what takes place in the international social world but from a political theology conceived in support of domestic absolutism. As abstract sovereigns, units of the international system, European States of course varied in influence and were engaged in often fierce rivalries. But fluctuations between Spanish,

[32] See the collected essays in AAVV, *Il lato oscuro dei diritti umani*, M Meccarelli, P Palchetti, and C Sotis (eds), (Carlos III University of Madrid, CC, 2014).

[33] See N Gordin and N Perugini, *The Human Right to Dominate* (Oxford University Press, 2015).

[34] The reflection is more extensively articulated in L Daniele, *Penal populism and the BDS movement after Security Council Resolution 2334* (Open Democracy, 30 January 2017), at www.opendemocracy.net/en/penal-populism-and-bds-movement-after-security-council-res-2334.

[35] See in particular C Schmitt, *Political Theology. Four Chapters on the Concept of Sovereignty*, G Schwab (trs) (University of Chicago Press, 1988).

> Dutch, and French 'epochs' failed to change the character of the *jus publicum europaeum*, which lay not in the identity of the leading power but in how the identity of the units – including the leading power – was conceived … This was a system of States … for avoiding domestic chaos and civil war. 'In the struggle of opposing interests and coalitions, absolute monarchy made the decision and thereby created the unity of the state' … The Schmittian view of European public law, whatever its virtues, is of an order between sovereigns that are absolute in the sense that their sovereignty involves the pre-legal decision that both grounds the domestic order and safeguards control of the international realm.[36]

Therefore, the challenge is to understand whether the wars between European monarchies were effectively and historically as 'bracketed' and 'limited' on the battlefield as they were in Schmitt's theory. In other words, is it true that before IHL the continent was theatre of a successful juridical limitation of inter-state wars? Did the legitimate and *non-discriminatory* enmity between states in war limit the hardships and sufferings for civilians in wartimes? Views such as 'The Nomos of the Earth' seem focused on a state-centric conceptualisation of warfare, with little attention dedicated to the concrete destiny of civilians and soldiers *hors de combat* caught up in the armed conflicts waged under the aegis of the *Jus Publicum Europaeum*.

Only more recently has the literature tried to systematise an aetiological theory of the victimisation of civilians in war, with interstate warfare in the early modernity being empirically observed in relation to its immediate impact on civilians. Several of these studies have also condensed datasets on mass civilian killings in the interstate wars waged between the late nineteenth century and the first decades of the twentieth. As it has been argued by scholars analysing the organised killing of non-combatants in conflicts between 1816 and 2003, civilian victimisation can be distinctly observed in these conflicts as 'military strategy in which civilians are either targeted intentionally or force is used indiscriminately such that tens of thousands of civilians are killed'.[37]

Beyond data observation, there are striking 'qualitative' accounts of the traditional warfare in interstate wars waged during the aegis of the *ius gentium*. A seminal work symbolising the birth of the movements leading to the codification of modern IHL is precisely an account of a battle fought during the times and under the legal realm celebrated by Schmitt: 'A Memory of Solferino' by the Swiss businessman Jean Henry Dunant. In this book, Dunant recounts his direct experience of the battle of Solferino and San Martino, a crucial clash during the Second Italian War of Independence and, notably, last major battle in history where the armies were under the personal command of their monarchs: on the one hand, the Franco-Sardinian alliance led by Napoleon III and Victor Emmanuel II; and, on the other, the Austrian Army led by Emperor Franz Joseph I.

[36] M Koskenniemi, 'International Law as Political Theology. How to Read *Nomos der Erde*?' (2004) 11 *Constellations* 8.

[37] AB Downes, *Targeting Civilians in War* (Cornell University Press, 2012) 44.

Dunant wrote:

> Whole divisions threw off their knapsacks in order to be able to charge the enemy more freely with fixed bayonets. As one battalion is repulsed, another immediately replaces it. Every mound, every height, every rocky crag, is the scene of a fight to the death; bodies lie in heaps on the hills and in the valleys. Here is a hand-to-hand struggle in all its horror and frightfulness; Austrians and Allies trampling each other under foot, killing one another on piles of bleeding corpses, felling their enemies with their rifle butts, crushing skulls, ripping bellies open with sabre and bayonet. No quarter is given; it is a sheer butchery; a struggle between savage beasts, maddened with blood and fury. Even the wounded fight to the last gasp. When they have no weapon left, they seize their enemies by the throat and tear them with their teeth. … The fury of the battle was such that in some places, when ammunition was exhausted and muskets broken, the men went on fighting with stones and fists. The Croats finished off every man they encountered; they killed the Allied wounded with the butts of their muskets; the Algerian sharpshooters too, despite all their leaders could do to keep their savagery within bounds, gave no quarter to wounded Austrian officers and men, and charged the enemy ranks with beastlike roars and hideous cries.[38]

The brutality in this description of the last battle fought under the aegis of the *Jus Publicum Europaeum* seems to clash with the idealised representation of Schmitt. In other words, the description of Dunant efficaciously represents the carnages of pre-IHL warfare, in which still no system of care for the wounded, the sick and the shipwrecked existed, and no body of norms had yet codified the principle of military necessity. As a consequence, no legal provisions could have been claimed to protect from killing soldiers *hors de combat*, nor to avoid the infliction of unnecessary suffering and superfluous injuries. Only nine years later, in 1868, was the idea that warfare should be guided by strict military necessity, for the first time, acknowledged in an international legal text: the 'Saint Petersburg Declaration Renouncing the Use, in Time of War, of Explosive Projectiles Under 400 Grammes Weight'. The declaration, establishing a notion that would have then influenced all the successive developments of IHL, stated that:

> the only legitimate object which States should endeavour to accomplish during war is to weaken the military forces of the enemy; … for this purpose it is sufficient to disable the greatest possible number of men; … this object would be exceeded by the employment of arms which uselessly aggravate the sufferings of disabled men, or render their death inevitable.[39]

On the other hand, Dunant also speaks of a time in which warfare was still a matter of frontal clashes between infantries and cavalries on an open battlefield, distant from guerrilla tactics, and from technological developments of weaponry

[38] JH Dunant, *A Memory of Solferino* (American Red Cross, 1939, 1959), reprinted by the ICRC (2010) 19 and 21.

[39] Declaration Renouncing the Use, in Time of War, of Explosive Projectiles Under 400 Grammes Weight. Saint Petersburg, 29 November / 11 December 1868, at ihl-databases.icrc.org/ihl/WebART/130-60001?OpenDocument.

that have radically altered the contemporary spatial, temporal, strategic and – consequently – ethical dimensions of warfare. It is intuitive to understand that in the typology of battles as described by Dunant, the involvement of civilians in war was an extremely limited phenomenon, since the birth and consolidation of the nation-states, entrusting different functions to different bureaucratic bodies, had already led to a high degree of professionalisation of war.[40]

This is the main reason why accounts of battles of the 1800s, as Dunant's, although shedding light on the problem of soldiers *hors de combat* and the absence of any healthcare system for the wounded and sick, still did not dwell on the problem of civilians in war.[41] It is therefore opportune to analyse more closely the issue of the involvement of civilians in war, and to examine some of the most important studies that have articulated a theoretical and historical systematisation of this issue. Firstly, and briefly, these shall be analysed from the point of view of the active participation of civilians in hostilities, and its impact on the developing categories of IHL. Secondly, and more closely, it shall be analysed from the perspective of the victimisation of civilians in war, seeking to understand if and how the killing of the unarmed, through the ages, has been justified under certain conditions and functionalised to pursue specific strategic purposes.

1.4. Civilian Resistance at the Origins of the Civilians/Combatants Legal Dichotomy

One of the basic cornerstones of IHL, as mentioned, is the idea that the only acceptable action in armed conflicts is to weaken the military potential of the enemy. This conceptual axiom implies the necessity to define, on the one hand, who and what must be deemed to be part of this military potential, entitled to participate directly in the hostilities and, correlatively, to be a potential target of lawful attacks (combatants and military objectives); on the other hand, it is equally necessary to identify who and what is not comprised in this sphere, and has to be protected from attacks and shielded as much as possible from the consequences of hostilities, with the corollary that the subjects thus identified cannot claim the right to directly participate in the hostilities, with very few exceptions (civilians and civilian objects).[42]

[40] C Townshend (ed), *The Oxford History of Modern War*, 2nd edn (Oxford University Press) 2005.

[41] Increasingly, however, historical studies are starting to dedicate attention to the problem of civilians in the age of monarchies; see E Charters, E Rosenhaft and H Smith (eds), *Civilians and War in Europe 1618–1815* (Liverpool University Press, 2012); in particular, see, in the same volume, C Horstr, 'Restricted Violence?: Military Occupation during the Eighteenth Century', 118–28.

[42] See M Sassoli, AA Bouvier and A Quintin, *How does Law Protect in War? Cases, Documents and Teaching Materials on Contemporary Practice in International Humanitarian Law*, 3rd edn, Vol I (ICRC, 2001) 75, and N Melzer, *International Humanitarian Law: A Comprehensive Introduction* (ICRC, 2016) 17.

The dividing line between the two categories has developed over time, reflecting the radically conflicting interests between, on the one hand, powerful states that wanted a strict definition of clearly identified combatants, confident in the overwhelming potential of their regular armies, and, on the other, weaker states, fearing invasions or colonial subjugation, interested in maintaining the option to use additional resources flexibly and to continue the hostilities even when their military potential was outweighed, or their territory was under enemy control (materially impossible for lesser military powers without engaging in mass mobilisations and recurring to unconventional methods of warfare).[43]

Only seldomly has the literature dealt with the political and ideological options of the first international discussions and drafting of treaties concerning the protection of civilians.[44] Even more rarely has it been underlined how crucial the unequal military potential of states has been in shaping the boundaries of the legal definitions of civilians and combatants as we know them today. These aspects were explicitly revealed after World War II, when – during the drafting of the 1949 Geneva Conventions – different states' interests on this matter emerged more clearly, since large scale military resistance conducted by civilians had emerged as a new feature of war.[45] As noted by Masson, military strategists, before, during and after World War I did not concern themselves with method of guerrilla warfare, either at military academies or in the literature.[46]

However, the first glimpses of the problems surrounding the principle of distinction between civilians and combatants started to twist the minds of lawmakers following the first international convention dealing with the laws and customs of war, namely the Hague Convention on the Laws and Customs of War on Land of 1899. The central problem engaging the drafters of the Hague Convention, as it has been noted, was not the protection of civilians, but defining what types of combatants the law had to cover, or better, to legitimise.[47]

Diametrically opposed to the way in which the legal debate is constructed today – how to protect civilians – the legal controversies were centred on the issue of which claims of combatancy the law should have acknowledged, in particular in cases of invasions, occupations and annexations, confronted by armed resistance.

The difficulties in finding common ground resulted in the Hague Regulations conspicuously and consciously skating over the problem of privileged belligerency; indeed, the real knots on these problems emerged 25 years before the Hague Regulations (and 100 years before the adoption of the Protocols Additional to

[43] ibid.

[44] An excellent historical analysis of this issue can be found in HM Kinsella, *The Image Before the Weapon. A Critical History of the Distinction Between Combatant and Civilian* (Cornell University Press, 2011).

[45] See B Van Dijk, *Preparing for War* (Oxford University Press, 2022) 157–95.

[46] P Masson, *Une guerre totale 1939–1945: Stràtegies, moyens, controverses* (Tallandier, 1990) 314–15.

[47] See K Nabulsi, *Evolving Conceptions of Civilians and Belligerents: One Hundred Years after the Hague Peace Conferences* in S Chesterman (ed), *Civilians in War* (Lynne Rienner, 2001) 9–24.

the 1949 Geneva Conventions), with the first attempt to introduce notions of legitimate guerrilla warfare in case of conflicts of national self-defence at the Brussels Conference of 1874. One proposal was for a codification of the 'laws and customs of war on land'.[48]

This 'Brussels Declaration', which never entered into force, was strongly influenced by the Lieber Code, while also delineating new protections. Shaped also by these earlier drafts, and by the St Petersburg Declaration of 1868, the 'Convention with Respect to the Laws and Customs of War on Land' with annexed Regulations was adopted in 1899. As explained by Kalshoven and Legveld:

> The Regulations on Land Warfare provide rules concerning all aspects of land warfare on which the contracting States had been able to agree, such as: the types of armed forces that were recognised as 'belligerents'; the treatment of prisoners of war; restrictions on the adoption of means and methods of waging war, including some basic though fragmentary rules on the protection of civilian populations – notably a prohibition to bombard undefended towns – and cultural objects; restrictions on the behaviour of an occupying power.[49]

Four issues discussed in the conference were particularly illustrative of the different political options bearing upon the rules to be adopted: the definition of occupation; the permitted army methods in occupied territories; the question of legitimate combatancy; and the problem of the *levée en masse*.[50]

The definition of occupation was linked to the problematic detection of criteria and conditions to legally identify its commencement. For an invading army, the sooner an overrun territory was declared occupied, then the more rapidly that army could be recognised as the occupying power, with all the prerogatives which that entailed. Some delegations claimed that the simple act of declaring a territory occupied was sufficient to legally consider that an occupation had begun, thus requiring the passive acceptance of the population. Others argued that, on the contrary, precise conditions had to be met: the population had firstly to be subdued, and the occupation had to be considered as continuing until a foreign army was required to maintain control of the land. The longer the thresholds for occupation as a legal status were delayed, the more the citizens could claim the right to bear weapons to defend the independence of their country.[51]

The second problem was constituted by the permitted methods of maintaining a military occupation, such as reprisals and requisitions. Reprisals were largely used to punish hostile acts committed by the population under occupation, and the legal

[48] *Project of an International Declaration concerning the Laws and Customs of War*, Brussels, 27 August 1874, full text available at ihl-databases.icrc.org/en/ihl-treaties/brussels-decl-1874.

[49] F Kalshoven and L Zegveld, *Constraints on the Waging of War. An Introduction to International Humanitarian Law*, 4th edn (Cambridge University Press, 2011) 10–11.

[50] See TE Holland, *A Lecture on the Brussels Conference of 1874, and Other diplomatic attempts to Mitigate the Rigors of Warfare*, in *Lectures 1874–84* (Oxford University Press, 1876) 5–7.

[51] See M Zwanenburg, 'The Law of Occupation Revisited: the Beginning of an Occupation' (2007) 10 *Yearbook of International Humanitarian Law* 99.

dialectic about this point was particularly adversarial, adopting opposing views. There were those who advocated for the complete abolition of these practices, in favour of a full recognition of the right of resistance; those who, on the contrary, considered these practices a military necessity and thus a lawful means to keep control over the occupied territory; and, finally, those who accepted a limited use of reprisal if they maintained a degree of respect of human dignity.[52] Occupying armies typically used levies and requisitions as further methods of punishment, and opinions were deeply divided over their appropriate use. Intuitively, armies and occupying states insisted on a free hand in their application, whereas representatives of nations likely to be invaded argued that they should have been used more sparingly.[53]

The third problem was the question of legitimate combatancy. In the traditional laws of war only professional soldiers were granted belligerent status. The privilege had historically served the interests of the warrior aristocracy, as Michael Howard notes.[54] Accordingly, all civilians who participated in hostilities were considered outlaws and in the words of the draft of the Brussels Conference, those civilians 'were to be delivered to justice'.[55]

Those contesting this principle, supported by the smaller and weaker states seeking to reinforce their possibilities of defence against foreign invasions, argued that all citizens who bore arms for the nation were legitimate combatants.[56]

A last debate centred on the concept of the *levée en masse*. As one jurist later remarked,

> all that can be learnt from the precedents of Napoleonic wars is that each belligerent, when invaded, appealed to the peasantry to rise and expel the invader, without caring how much they suffered, provided they did some harm to the enemy; but whenever the same nation became in its turn an invader, it did not scruple to treat the enemies' peasants as brigands.[57]

Stronger countries sought to restrict in several ways the conditions for considering an uprising to be legitimate, in particular requiring its necessary organisation

[52] See F Kalshoven, *Belligerent Reprisals* (Sijthoff, 1971); and S Darcy, 'Retaliation and Reprisals' in M Weller (ed), *Oxford Handbook on the Use of Force in International Law* (Oxford University Press, 2013) 879–96.

[53] See E Stowell 'Military Reprisals and the Sanctions of the Laws of War' (1942) *American Journal of International Law*, 36, 643 ff.

[54] M Howard (ed), *Restraints on War. Studies in the Limitation of Armed Conflict* (Oxford University Press, 1979).

[55] *Project of an International Declaration concerning the Laws and Customs of War* (n 48).

[56] The resulting Art 9 of the Declaration (n 48) stated: 'The laws, rights, and duties of war apply not only to armies, but also to militia and volunteer corps, fulfilling the following conditions: 1. That they be commanded by a person responsible for his subordinates; 2. That they have a fixed distinctive emblem recognizable at a distance; 3. That they carry arms openly; and 4. That they conduct their operations in accordance with the laws and customs of war. In countries where militia constitute the army, or form part of it, they are included under the denomination "army".'

[57] H Droop, 'On The Relation Between an Invading Army and the Inhabitants, and the Condition Under Which Irregular Troops are Entitled to the same Treatment as Regular Soldiers' *Papers Read before the Juridical Society* (Wildy Sons, 1871) 722 (cited in Nabulsi, n 22).

under responsible military command. Legitimacy and the uprising itself had also to be limited temporally and spatially: it could have been launched only at the approach of the invader army and only in territories not yet subjected to occupation.[58] In sum, the custom and practice of distinction between civilians and combatants emerged from a different historical source than that asserted by the first humanitarian lawyers: the ancient *privileges* of soldiers. Indeed, as it has been noted,

> the legal norm claimed as its purpose (and its customary antecedents) the protection of civilians from the brunt of the battle. Yet it connected the privileges that accrued to the protection of civilians with a correlative duty of passivity on their part.[59]

The assumption was clear:

> [T]he right of the non-combatant population to protection for their persons and property, the limits and extent of which right we have hitherto been discussing, necessarily involves on the part of those who have obtained this protection on the fate of their being non-combatant a corresponding duty of abstaining from all further hostilities against the invaders.[60]

It can be observed that some of the most active publicists of the laws of war in the nineteenth century, while denying the existence of the *levée en masse*, added an emphatic moral condemnation of those civilians who crossed the sacred line of combatancy and took up arms.[61]

In conclusion of this section, as argued by Karma Nabulsi,

> international law in the nineteenth century, both in its structure and practitioners, was broadly liberal in its political assumptions, and underpinning in its attachment to law, order, political stability, hierarchy, continuity, and tempered progress. Yet there is

[58] The compromise was codified in Art 10 'The population of a territory which has not been occupied, who, on the approach of the enemy, spontaneously take up arms to resist the invading troops without having had time to organize themselves in accordance with Article 9, shall be regarded as belligerents if they respect the laws and customs of war.'

[59] *cf* Nabulsi (n 22) 16.

[60] Droop (n 57) 713.

[61] « *Ce qu'il faut souhaiter c'est que, à l'avenir, les peuples libres aient assez de constance et de prévoyance pour se donner une forte organisation militaire, basée sur la participation égale de tous à la défense de la patrie. C'est là pour eux un devoir, non-seulement national, mais humanitaire. Car plus la guerre sera conduite de part et d'autre par des troupes régulières et disciplinées, moins l'humanité aura à souffrir. … Nous croyons au contraire avec le Dr Arnold: 'Que c'est le strict devoir de tout gouvernement, non-seulement de ne pas encourager une guerre aussi irrégulière de la part de la population, mais de la réprimer avec soin et de n'opposer à l'ennemi que ses troupes régulières, ou des hommes régulièrement organisés et agissant sous des officiers autorisés, qui observeront les règles que l'humanité prescrit dans une guerre régulière. Et ce que l'on appelle les insurrections patriotiques, ou les soulèvements irréguliers de toute la population pour harasser une armée envahissante, devrait toujours être condamné, sans distinguer par qui ou contre qui ce moyen est employé, – comme tine ressource d'une efficacité restreinte et douteuse, mais d'une atrocité certaine, et comme la plus terrible des aggravations aux maux de la guerre* »: G Rolin-Jaequemuns, 'Second essai sur la Guerre Franco-Allemande dans ses rapports avec le droit international pour faire suite à la guerre actuelle dans ses rapports avec le droit international' in *Revue de Droit International et de Législation Comparée* (1871) II, 26–27, at gallica.bnf.fr/ark:/12148/bpt6k6112194r/f4.image.

> much evidence that the early founders of the laws of war – those who created the Hague Regulations, rather than international lawyers in general – held strongly conservative, even reactionary views.[62]

These jurists played a crucial role in constructing modern *ius in bello*, and in many cases behind their position there was a clear intent 'to limit the rights of belligerency to a particular class of participant, the soldier, and to exclude all other from the right to become actively involved in war'.[63]

1.5. Civilians at War, the Partisan, and the Problem of Guerrilla Warfare

Importantly, the titularity to participate in the hostilities has been one of the fields of contestation *par excellance* of the whole process of codification of the laws of war in modernity, in reflection of precise historical events. Many scholars have focused on the role of the civilian participating in the hostilities on both European and colonisation/de-colonisation battlefields.[64]

Examples of irregular warfare defined as '*guerrilla*' can be traced back to the Spanish Guerrilla War (1808–1813) against the Napoleonic occupation.[65] As it has been noted,

> The salient point of the Spanish partisan's situation in 1808 was – he wrote – that he took the risk of fighting on his home soil [*Heimatboden*], while his own king and the royal family hadn't yet decided who the real enemy was.[66]

Irregular fighting against states' regular forces, however, was not the only form of civilian participation in organised hostilities. Between the ancestor of contemporary counterinsurgency tactics, appropriating irregular warfare as tactics of states' apparatuses, there are old forms of civilian mobilisation in war in order

[62] Nabulsi (n 22) 14.

[63] ibid, 15.

[64] See eg A Cassese, 'The status of rebels under the 1977 Geneva Protocol on non-international armed conflicts' (1981) 30 *International & Comparative Law Quarterly*, 416; E Crawford, *The Treatment of Combatants and Insurgents under the Law of Armed Conflict* (Oxford University Press, 2010); B Clarke, 'The juridical status of civilian resistance to foreign occupation under the law of nations and contemporary international law' (2005) *University of Notre Dame Australia Law Review*, 1. Again of crucial importance on the theoretical implications of the problem of partisanship and guerrilla fighting, C Schmitt, *The Theory of the Partisan. A Commentary/Remark on the Concept of the Political* (trs AC Goodson from *Theorie des Partisanen. Zwischenbemerkung zum Begriff des Politischen*, Duncker & Humblot, 1963) (Michigan State University Press, 2004).

[65] The word 'guerrilla' (the diminutive of Spanish *guerra*, 'war') itself stems from the Duke of Wellington's campaigns during the Peninsular War (1808–14), in which Spanish and Portuguese irregulars, or *guerrilleros*, helped drive the French from the Iberian Peninsula (see R Brown Asprey, *War In The Shadows: The Guerrilla in History* [first published 1975, William Morrow and Co Pub], 2nd edn (iUniverse, 2004).

[66] Schmitt (n 64) 4.

to resist foreign invasion. Prussia was the first state to officially embrace guerrilla warfare against the French invasion, with the *Landsturm* edict of 1813. This created for all males aged 15–60 who were capable of serving in the military, and not already in the army, an out-and-out obligation to resist foreign invaders by all means. The edict explicitly recommended the use of various kinds of weapons, including axes, pitchforks, scythes or shotguns, and encouraged Prussians to disobey the orders of the invader, and to make of themselves a factor of exasperation for the Napoleonic troops. The edict also asserted that was better to risk the dangers caused by the fury of a population in arms, rather than letting the enemy have control over the nation. This edict was indicated by legal theorists as a *Magna Carta* of partisanship.

Furthermore, while the Spanish Guerrilla War was fought mainly by a coalition of peasants and the lower clergy, the Prussian embracement of partisanship was accompanied and sustained by high intellectual elaboration.[67] Partisanship and guerrilla fighting, in fact, became the topic of military reflections, as in the case of von Clausewitz's *Vom Kriege*.[68] This elaboration also constituted the basis for the rediscovery of the partisan which occurred in the twentieth century, with the works of the revolutionaries and communist leaders. Lenin inserts the partisan in his theory about internationalist class struggle and acknowledges his importance in it.[69] Stalin sustains the necessity of partisanship mobilisation both in the defence against foreign occupation and in the struggle for the communist revolution. More comprehensively, Mao Tse-tung framed the figure of the partisan as key actor against Japanese occupation, the Chinese nationalists and Western colonialism.[70]

From the legal point of view, the features of partisanship are crucial to understanding the challenge that guerrilla warfare poses for the categorisations stemming from the law of armed conflict. The partisan does not wear a uniform, knowingly and willingly disguise himself as a civilian, and of course does not display his weapon openly. Clearly, this constitutes a radical challenge for the basic assumptions of IHL, structurally centred upon a crucial pillar: the fundamental distinction between combatants and civilians. In order to render the distinction practically feasible, in fact, the laws of armed conflict assume that any combatant has the duty to carry arms openly, wear a distinctive emblem, and operate under a chain of command, and all the civilians, to enjoy their legal protection, have the duty to abstain from acts of warfare.

[67] See M Rink, 'The German Wars of Liberation 1807–1815: The Restrained Insurgency' in B Huser (ed), *Small Wars and Insurgencies in Theory and Practice, 1500–1850* (Routledge, 2016) 828–42.

[68] C Von Clausewitz, *Vom Kriege* (first published 1832, Dümmlers Verlag), tr by M Howard and P Paret (Princeton University Press, 1989).

[69] V Lenin, 'Der Partisanenkampf', *Sämtliche Werke*, 2nd edn, v 10, 1930; B Forgàcs, 'Mao and Giap on Partisan Warfare (2019) 18 *Academic and Applied Research in Military and Public Management Science* 31.

[70] Schmitt (n 64) 32.

Partisanship, therefore, not only challenges regular armies from the strategic and military point of view, but also erodes the fundamental components upon which the first IHL prescriptions were built. At the same time, the partisan, even if fighting along the edges of legality, remains firmly distinguished by the common bandit, the criminal and the pirate:

> the partisan has an enemy and 'risks' something quite different from the blockade-breaker and the transporter of contraband. He risks not only his life, like every regular combatant. He knows, and accepts, that the enemy places him outside law, statute, and honour'.[71]

According to Crawford, however, *ius in bello* at the end of the 1940s produced a partial legalisation of what was considered before to be an outlaw ('the inclusion of resistance fighters in the [Geneva] Conventions was considered a substantial broadening of the category of combatant and brought persons traditionally considered … bandits within the ambit of Geneva protection').[72]

In contemporary *ius in bello*, the guerrilla fighter is at the same time partially accepted and relatively formalised internationally as entitled to participate in hostilities when fighting for national liberation (and organised in structures with army-like features), while on the other it remains a criminal for the enemy states' legislation, since the latter are legitimised to target and take repressive measures against the armed civilian participating in the hostilities. This is partly a consequence of the innovations of the Geneva Convention of 1949, in which, given certain conditions, organised resistance movements began to be considered as equivalent to combatants (orientation that was consolidated by the 1977 Additional Protocol I and II to the Conventions).[73]

However, the friction surrounding the legal classification of legally unqualified fighters also elucidates a more general issue: the participation of civilians in the hostilities continuously redefines the border of the legal categories, since their status varies from situation to situation, and from moment to moment, as the essence of partisan warfare is to fight in the shadows and to move disguised as civilian. The partisan, in other words, to compensate his military disadvantage, has to move intrepidly not only into the enemy's rear, but through the confines of the law itself. As Werner explains,

> the combination of the partisan's intense political commitment with his irregular mode of fighting has an immediate effect on the possibilities for international law to contain and limit war. Contemporary laws of armed conflict, after all, are still predominantly based on the idea of conventional enmity, as well as on the imagery of the regular army

[71] ivi, 20.

[72] E Crawford, *Treatment of Combatants and Insurgents under the Law of Armed Conflict* (Oxford University Press, 2010) 52 ff.

[73] See Cassese (n 64).

> that distinguishes itself from the civilian population. … A state-centric body of law is by definition unable to regulate irregular warfare.[74]

At the same time, the ability of any armed resistance movement to become mass, to oppose stronger, better armed, and more structured armies, outsmarting their warfare, depends inevitably on the capacity to generate lines of indistinction between armed and unarmed elements.[75]

Guerrilla warfare, partisan armed struggle and civilians' participation in hostilities can in principle trigger cycles of insurgency and counterinsurgency, both pushing to break free from the confines of conventional and legally contained (and containable) enmity.[76]

The most recent tensions challenging the normativity of legal categories are far from being an exclusive product of irregular warfare. The intense scholarly debates about phenomena such as targeted killing[77] or civilians' direct participation in the hostilities,[78] as well as the supposed necessity for new categorisations of the subjects involved in armed conflict (eg so-called 'unlawful combatants'),[79] demonstrate an unprecedent pressure on basic IHL categories in contemporaneity coming from state powers. The war on terror has shown beyond doubt that pressure against IHL categories does not come from the reality of battlefields alone, nor by increasingly irregular fighting in asymmetrical conflict, but is actively advocated for by states.[80] Not fortuitously, since 2001 until today, scholars have repeatedly emphasised how hegemonic states' approaches have eroded the protective purposes of the laws of war.[81]

[74] W Werner, 'Rereading The Theory of the Partisan' (2009) 1 *Amsterdam Law Forum* 130.

[75] See also N Perugini, 'Decolonizing the Civilian in Third World National Liberation Wars' (2024) 52 *Millennium: Journal of International Studies* 252.

[76] 'The four Geneva Conventions of 12 August 1949 are the work of a humane conscience, and a humanitarian development that deserves our admiration. While they not only permit the enemy a share of humanity but even of legitimacy in the sense of recognition [Gerechtigkeit im Sinne der Anerkennung], they remain grounded in classical international law and its tradition without which such a work of humanity would have been unlikely. Their basis remains the statist foundation of warfare and the achieved containment of war, with their clear distinctions of war and peace, military and civil, enemy and criminal, state war and civil war. While they, thus, relax these essential distinctions and even question them, they open the door for a kind of war that would knowingly destroy such clear divisions. At that point many carefully formulated compromise-rules [Kompromiß-Normierung] will look like the fragile bridges over an abyss concealing portentous metamorphoses in the concepts of war, peace, and the partisan': Schmitt (n 64) 23.

[77] See AAVV, *Targeted Killings: Law and Morality in an Asymmetrical World*, C Finkelstein and J David Ohlin (eds) (Oxford University Press, 2012); N Melzer, *Targeted Killing in International Law* (Oxford University Press, 2008); G Blum and P Heymann, 'Law and Policy of Targeted Killing' (2010) 1 *Harvard National Security. Journal* 145.

[78] See N Melzer, *Interpretative Guidance on the Notion of Direct Participation in the Hostilities Under International Humanitarian Law* (ICRC, 2009).

[79] M Sassoli and D Reisner, '"Unlawful Combatants": The Law and Whether It Needs to Be Revised' (2003) 97 *Proceedings of the Annual Meeting of the American Society of International Law* 196.

[80] D Rieter and A Stam, *Democracies at War* (Princeton University Press, 2004).

[81] See eg A Cassese, 'Terrorism is also Disrupting Crucial Legal Categories of International Law' (2001) 12 *European Journal of International Law* 993; N Quenivet, 'The "War on Terror" and the Principle of Distinction in International Humanitarian Law' (2010) 3 *Colombian Yearbook of*

1.6. Civilian Victimisation in Contemporary Wars. Notes for an Aetiological Enquiry: Why do Liberal Democracies Strike Non-Combatants?

Civilian victimisation in war, as briefly mentioned, is anything but a new phenomenon. Since ancient times, the mass killing and targeting of civilians, as well as indiscriminate use of force, seem to be constant features of conflict.

Over the past three centuries, civilians are reckoned to have constituted half of all war-related victims. I n the twentieth century alone, it is estimated that 43–50 million non-combatants lost their lives due to wars and their consequences.[82] To mention some examples, during World War I, the British-led blockade of the Central Powers caused widespread malnutrition and disease, and played a major role in the nearly one million deaths among the civilian population of Germany and Austria-Hungary. Before and during World War II, Nazi Germany exterminated more than six million Jewish civilians, while Allied bombings were estimated to have killed more than 300,000 German civilians and more than 200,000 Japanese.[83] The percentage of civilian deaths (often framed as 'casualties' or 'collateral damage' in the aseptic language of military professionalism), in addition, increased dramatically in modern asymmetrical conflicts, today constituting the overwhelming majority, when not the quasi-totality, of war-related loss of life.[84] According to a contested statement by the Secretary General of the Council of the European Union, in just the 13 years, from 1990 to 2003, the number people who died in war reached the shocking count of four million, 90 per cent of whom were civilians.[85]

In recent armed conflicts, in Iraq and Afghanistan, and the counterterrorism operations in Pakistan until 2018, the death toll is reckoned to be at least 244,000 civilians.[86] No available dataset, however, calculates accurately the number of

International Law 155, and OA Hathaway, 'How the Erosion of U.S. War Powers Constraints Has Undermined International Law Constraints on the Use of Force' (2023) 14 *Harvard National Security Journal* 336.

[82] W Eckhardt, 'Civilian deaths in wartime' (1989) 20 *Bulletin of Peace Proposals* 89; Clodfelter (n 10) 345 and 396.

[83] See for various estimates BA Valentino, *Final Solutions: Mass Killing and Genocide in the Twentieth Century* (Cornell University Press, 2004); RA Pape, *Bombing to Win: Airpower and Coercion in War* (Cornell University Press, 1996); R Overy, *The Bombers and the Bombed: Allied Air War Over Europe 1940–1945* (Penguin, 2014); A Bellamy, *Massacres and Morality: Mass Atrocities in an Age of Civilian Immunity* (Oxford University Press, 2012) 132–59.

[84] A Roberts, 'Lives and Statistics: Are 90% of War Victims Civilians?' (2002) 52 *Survival, Global Politics and Strategies* 115.

[85] Council of the European Union, *European Security Strategy. A Secure Europe in a Better World*, General Secretariat of the Council, Brussels, 2003, 29, at www.consilium.europa.eu/media/30823/qc7809568enc.pdf.

[86] See NC Crawford and C Lutz, 'Human Cost of Post-9/11 Wars: Direct War Deaths in Major War Zones, Afghanistan & Pakistan (Oct. 2001 – Aug. 2021); Iraq (March 2003 – Aug. 2021); Syria (Sept. 2014 – May 2021); Yemen (Oct. 2002 – Aug. 2021) and Other Post-9/11 War Zones', at watson.brown.edu/costsofwar/figures/2021/WarDeathToll.

civilians who died as an indirect result of these wars, such as due to loss of access to food, water and infrastructure, or war-related diseases, but many hypothesise figures around 800,000.[87] To the frightening resulting figure of 1,044,000 civilian direct and indirect deaths (in the most prudent accounts) in Afghanistan, Pakistan, and Iraq, must then be added the controversial count of the civilian victims of the yrian conflict. In this respect, statistics and data vary,[88] but the UN Special Envoy for Syria estimated in April 2016 that 400,000 civilians lost their lives in the conflict.[89] In other words, in the last 20 years, and according to cautious sources, an aggregative estimate of the civilians killed, or dead from war-related causes, in these four conflicts alone could amount to nearly 1,500,000.

These data demonstrate a staggering collision between common morals and common practice. War has never been limited by so many legal constraints in order to be fought 'humanely' as in the last decades, and the moral stigma attached to the killing of civilians has probably never been so highly recognised in public narratives as it is today. All over the world, the public is – through the vigilance of many NGOs with civilian protection in war as priority mission, or of UN specialised agencies such as the Office for the Coordination of Humanitarian Affairs and the Office of the High Commissioner for Human Rights –increasingly made aware of the civilian death tolls in wars waged around the world.

The protection and defence of civilians during armed conflicts thus represents an elemental strategic commitment on the part of states, armies, and governmental and non-governmental global actors. Yet, even though the protection of civilians is today stronger than ever in the political imagination, civilian victimisation in wartime is as widespread and systematic as it is condemned.[90]

In addition, it might be added that the killing of civilians in war is commonly believed to be a counterproductive strategy: it hardly facilitates the achievement of any state army goals and can strengthen the enemy's consent and approval in its social contexts, with the consequence of reinforcing the population's will to resist and fostering recruitment for active contributions to the hostilities. Studies of the issue have argued that fighting with techniques aimed to spread terror between the civilian population is decisively self-defeating. 'The nation or faction that resorts

[87] ibid. See also for the debate around these estimations, BO Daponte, 'Why Estimate Direct and Indirect Casualties from War? The Rule of Proportionality and Casualty Estimates' in J Asher, D Bank and FJ Scheuren (eds), *Statistical Methods for Human Rights* (Springer, 2008) 51–63; A Hagopian et al, 'Mortality in Iraq associated with the 2003–2011 war and occupation: findings from a national cluster sample survey by the university collaborative Iraq Mortality Study' (2013) 10 *PLoS Medicine*; CL Murray,et al, 'Armed Conflict as a Public Health Problem' (2002) 324 *British Medical Journal* 346.

[88] See M Price, A Gohdes and P Ball, *Updated Statistical Analysis of Documentation of Killings in the Syrian Arab Republic*, Human Rights Data Analysis Group, August 2014, at www.ohchr.org/Documents/Countries/SY/HRDAGUpdatedReportAug2014.pdf.

[89] J Hudson, 'U.N. Envoy Revises Syria Death Toll to 400,000', *Foreign Policy*, 22 April 2016, available at foreignpolicy.com/2016/04/22/u-n-envoy-revises-syria-death-toll-to-400000.

[90] See HM Kinsella, 'Targeting Civilians in War, and Killing Civilians: Method, Madness and Morality in War' (2008) 22 *Ethics & International Affairs* 435.

to warfare against civilians most quickly, most often, and most viciously is the nation or faction most likely to see its interest frustrated and, in many cases, its existence terminated.'[91]

Considering the profound moral stigma of the killing of civilians, its strategic counterproductivity, and the large amount of institutional and scholarly attention and resources dedicated to the fight against civilians' victimisation and impunity for those who perpetrate it, the question therefore arises: why do non-combatants continue to be targeted, and civilians remain the majority of those who lose their lives in war? Different complex answers to this question have emerged in the literature.

Authors developing aetiological enquiries on civilian victimisation have insisted on a fundamental analytical distinction between typologies of civilian victimisation, which can take, on the one hand, the form of arbitrary explosions of violence or revenge inspired by battlefield frenzy or, on the other hand, can represent an out-and-out 'government policy' or 'standing operating procedure'.[92] The notion of 'civilian victimisation', in this light and *stricto sensu*, is only pertinent to cases in which there is a policy or strategy implemented or approved by states, and therefore excluding random or uncoordinated attacks launched by few military units.[93] To be relevant for a legal analysis, in addition, the notion of combatants and civilians employed by aetiological enquiries need to be consistent with the core of the relevant international legal definitions, according to which combatants consist of all organised armed forces, groups and units which are under a command responsible for the conduct of subordinates.[94]

This approach can thus distance itself from the assumption of many just war theorists[95] excluding from the civilian category several subjects not carrying arms (such as ammunitions or military supply chain workers) on the grounds that they contribute to a nation's war-making capacity, since for legal purposes these subjects are not direct participants in the hostilities.[96] In addition, with high relevance for

[91] C Carr, *The Lessons of Terror: A History of Warfare against Civilians*, Random House, 2002, 12 (cited in Downes (n 37) 2; and I Arreguin, 'The [F]utility of Barbarism: Assessing the Impact of the Systematic Harm of Noncombatants in War' Paper, Annual Meeting of the American Political Science Association, Philadelphia, August 2003.

[92] C Browning, *Ordinary Men: Reserve Police Battalion 101 and the Final Solution in Poland* (Harper Perennial, 1993) 160 ff.

[93] Downes (n 37) 14.

[94] See *Protocol Additional to the Geneva Conventions of 12 August 1949, and relating to the Protection of Victims of International Armed Conflicts* (Protocol I), 8 June 1977, 1125 UNTS 3, (AP I), Art 43.

[95] eg M Walzer, *Just and Unjust Wars*, 2nd edn (Basic Books, 1992) 145–46; relatedly, see J McMahan, 'The Ethics of Killing in War' (2004) 114 *Ethics* 693, and ibid, *Killing in War* (Oxford University Press, 2009) 203 ff.

[96] The legal issues posed by arguments sustaining the legality of targeting 'war sustaining capabilities' are assessed inter alia by M Sassoli, 'Legitimate Targets of Attacks Under International Humanitarian Law', *HPCR Policy Brief*, January 2023, 6: 'A military manual substitutes "warfighting or war-sustaining capability" for military action and includes targets that "indirectly but effectively support and sustain the enemy's war-fighting capability". However, to include "war-sustaining capability" means to abandon the limitation to military objectives, and to admit attacks on political, financial (e.g. the main export industry, the stock market or taxation authorities) and psychological

the present analysis, the approach discussed focuses on civilian victimisation only when it presents a sufficient degree of intentionality or systematicity. Accordingly, 'intentional', 'indiscriminate' and 'collateral' civilian targeting can be identified and distinguished in two ways: first – subjectively – through declarations by participants or statements of policy that designate non-combatants as the target of the strategy, or – objectively – through a pattern of repeated attacks over an extended period that kills a high number of civilians, in the order of the tens of thousands; second, an employment of force that is so indiscriminate as to inflict a large amount of damage and death on non-combatants.[97]

Given these premises, studies adopting this angle have examined the area of civilian victimisation through statistical analyses and case studies casting serious doubt on previous theories, traditionally arguing against the willingness of governments to deliberately target civilians in wartime. Among others, Downes challenged previous theories identifying three main decisive factors determining the killing of non-combatants:

1) regime-type factors, especially those who have argued that democratic governments generally exercise much more restraint than non-democratic ones in their treatment of civilians;[98]
2) differences/collision in identity and culture, or the idea of the *barbaric* identity of the adversary, in which civilian victimisation results from the belief that one is fighting an uncivilised enemy;[99] and
3) organisational culture of the military; specifically, according to these authors, these factors are related to situations in which a military's organisational culture dictates a strategy that relies on coercion of the civilian population, typically bringing states to escalate to the killing of non-combatants.[100]

targets, as long as they influence the possibility or the decision (which are two different things) of the enemy to continue the war. Those who suggest a large interpretation of the concept of military objectives mention that targeting of bank accounts, financial institutions, shops and entertainment sites may prove in the long run more destructive than attacks on dual-use targets. If this argument was decisive, in some societies it may be hospital maternity wards, kindergartens, religious shrines or homes for the elderly whose destruction would most affect the willingness of the military or of the government to continue the war.'

[97] Downes (n 37) 15–16.

[98] See, inter alia, B Valentino, P Huth and D Balcch-Lindsay, '"Draining the Sea": Mass Killing and Guerrilla Warfare' (2004) 58 *International Organization* 375; RA Pape, 'The Strategic Logic of Suicide Terrorism' (2003) 97 *American Political Science Review* 343; G Merom, *How Democracies Lose Small Wars: State, Society, and the Failures of France in Algeria, Israel in Lebanon, and the United States in Vietnam* (Cambridge University Press, 2003); RJ Rummel, 'Democracy, Power, Genocide, and Mass Murder' (1995) 39 *Journal of Conflict Resolution* 3; and MJ Engelhardt, 'Democracies, Dictatorships, and Counterinsurgency: Does Regime Type Really Matter?' (1992) 12 *Conflict Quarterly* 52.

[99] See JW Dower, *War without Mercy: Race and Power in the Pacific War* (Pantheon, 1986); B Salter, *Barbarians and Civilization in International Relations* (Pluto, 2002) 35–40; some qualitative examples are provided by Childs (n 6) 102 ff.

[100] IV Hull, *Absolute Destruction: Military Culture and the Practices of War in Imperial Germany* (Cornell University Press, 2005); J Legro, 'Which Norms Matter? Revising the Failure of Internationalism' (1997) 51 *International Organization* 35.

Starting from the last hypothesis, it is argued that it can be trusted when multiple services are competing to make the largest contribution to victory, so as to capture the major share of post-war military expenditures, or when a particular branch or organisation is struggling to achieve independence as a separate service; however, according to the author, arguments based on the military's organisational culture: a) can apply only to the era of professionalised military bureaucracies, which emerged only in the mid/late nineteenth century, while – on the contrary – civilian victimisation has existed since the beginning of recorded history; and b) more importantly, arguments focusing on military organisations as the key factor to explain the transposition of their strategic/tactical preferences into states' policies fails to explain how this can happen when there is civilian control over the military, since it is civilian policymakers that ultimately make decisions.[101]

Against the second theory, it can be noticed that it is not clear what objective and proven differences in identity correlate with civilian victimisation. While it is beyond doubt that colonisation wars framed colonised civilians in racist terms, and that early *ius in bello* contributed to this radically unequal construct,[102] if identity-based theories on civilian victimisation are correct, civilian victimisation should have been much higher and more intense in colonial and imperial wars than in interstate wars. Data analysed by scholarship exploring this issue seem to counter, quantitatively, this hypothesis, showing that civilian victimisation, in figures, does not consistently follow separate patterns in interstate European wars, on the one hand, and colonial or imperial conflicts, on the other.[103] Further research seems needed to verify the viability of this hypothesis (as a separate and independent issue from the evidences of significant racist and colonial roots at the origins of the laws of war).

Finally, and most importantly for the present research, studies confronting data decisively challenges the theories of civilian victimisation centred on the 'regime-type' factor, in particular those assuming that liberal democracies are less likely to kill non-combatants than authoritarian or autocratic regimes. However, literature on democratic regimes at war, and their civilian victimisation highlights the opposite: democracies could be more likely to target non-combatants when the vulnerability of leadership to public opinion dissent makes leaders wary of incurring heavy costs on the battlefield for fear of losing support in the domestic political sphere. This fear constitutes an important factor prompting democratic elites to accept high civilian death tolls of non-combatants to avoid costs or win wars quickly.[104] On this basis, the author identifies two crucial factors of civilian victimisation that appear to consistently have a much higher impact across various conflicts: first, the so-called 'desperation to win', or to achieve victory and

[101] Downes (n 37) 28.
[102] HM Kinsella, 'Settler Empire and the United States: Francis Lieber on the Laws of War' (2023) 117 *American Political Science Review* 629.
[103] ivi, 24–35.
[104] Rieter and Stam (n 80).

minimise costs in long, protracted wars of attrition, in which case civilian victimisation is a coercive strategy meant to sap the morale of an adversary's population or undermine the enemy's ability to fight; second, the so-called 'appetite for territorial conquest', that causes states to use force to subdue or eliminate an adversary's hostile population to gain control over the conquered area.[105]

Analytical study of these factors, in sum, demonstrates that 'states that are less tolerant of costs and in greater need of victory for their institutional and political stability – such as democracies – are likely to be more susceptible to desperation'.[106]

These findings unveil an aspect of crucial importance for this work, both prospectively and retrospectively. Prospectively, they demonstrate that democracies do not structurally possess higher intrinsic defences than other regimes against the risk of victimising civilians in their wars. The decades of the war on terror and its intolerable civilian death tolls have provided overwhelming evidence of this tendency. This illuminates the need to confront interpretations of the legal constraints on warfare trying to bring under the compass of *ius in bello*, against its object and purpose, the killing of civilians and the destructions of civilian objects in military attacks when not fully intentional.[107] Retrospectively, as it has been seen, this tendency of democratic regimes to victimise civilians to the same extent as authoritarian ones in recent decades sheds new light on the continued relevance of the paradigms of victors' justice and of double standards in international legal dynamics, removing any presumed sense of the moral superiority – at least in terms of civilian protection – of liberal democracies.

It has also been demonstrated that the categorisations of the law of armed conflicts itself (starting from the fundamental dichotomy between civilians and combatants) are historically shaped and diachronically revisited by the adversarial arguments and conflicting dialectics between powerful and weak states, with their opposing views on the normative boundaries of legitimate combatancy, means and methods and warfare, occupation, and civilians' participation in the hostilities. Thanks to the scholarship outlining the emerging aetiology of civilian victimisation in wartime (which would of course deserve a separate and specific enquiry), it is possible to assert that from the point of view of the conduct of hostilities liberal-democratic big powers in the contemporary geopolitical arena are no less likely to incur in civilian victimisation in armed conflicts than authoritarian big powers.

This also reinforces the view that there is indeed an urgent necessity to revise the international legal constraints on the waging of war in the current climate

[105] Downes supports his findings with four historical case studies of instances where belligerents have targeted civilians. These look at the blockades imposed by Great Britain and Imperial Germany during World War I; strategic bombing of the Axis countries during World War II; the Boer War of 1899–1902; and Israeli treatment of Arab inhabitants during the 1947–49 war for independence.

[106] Downes (n 37) 28.

[107] See C Jones, *The War Lawyers. The United States, Israel, and Juridical Warfare* (Oxford University Press, 2020), and more extensively on the concepts of intentional and reckless attacks chs 4 and 5 of this volume.

of escalating geopolitical tensions, and readiness to new wars, between liberal democracies and authoritarian regimes. Less military powerful states, as well as emerging powers, might therefore have all the geopolitical interest in reforming and enhancing the legal frameworks protecting civilians in armed conflicts in order to increase their effectiveness, overcome their defects, as well as, by so doing, impose higher legal and political costs, and risks, on big powers' exercises of military supremacy. The progressive development of international criminal law in relation to the punishment of indiscriminate and disproportionate attacks, as a consequence, emerges as both morally and axiologically required to invert the current trends in civilian victimisation, and their impunity, as well as politically feasible to confront the current shockwaves within global peace and the security architecture.

2

Indiscriminate and Disproportionate Attacks in International Humanitarian Law

2.1. The Fundamental IHL Prescriptions Governing Targeting Decisions, between 'Military Necessity' and 'Humanity'

While the whole body of international humanitarian law (IHL) applies in armed conflicts and only in cases of factual circumstances meeting the legal thresholds to be considered an armed conflict, not all of its branches directly regulate combat situations. In order to proceed in the enquiry on indiscriminate and disproportionate attacks it is necessary to look more closely at the segment of IHL that dictates specific prescriptions to regulate the conduct of hostilities. In particular, it is necessary to analyse more closely the law of targeting.

Targeting, as experts suggest, can be summarised very briefly as

> the deliberate application of capabilities against targets to generate effects in order to achieve specific objectives. It is about the application of means (weapons) to affect addressees (people or objects) using a variety of methods (tactics) that create effects contributing to designated goals. Targeting, accordingly, represents the bridge between the ends and the means of warfare.[1]

International rules regulating targeting decisions compose a complex legal framework, worthy of a separate treatise, given the complexity of its categories and the controversies over many of its dictates.[2] Here, instead, the analysis will be limited to its fundamental principles.[3]

The law of targeting is the main area identifying persons, places and objects which can be lawfully attacked in combat situations in order to achieve the

[1] PAL Ducheine, MN Schmitt and FPB Osinga (eds), *Targeting: The Challenges of Modern Warfare* (Springer, 2016) 2.

[2] See, inter alia, WH Boothby, *The Law of Targeting* (Oxford University Press, 2012); I Henderson, *The Contemporary Law of Targeting: Military Objectives, Proportionality and Precautions in Attack Under Additional Protocol I* (Martinus Nijhoff, 2009).

[3] The term 'principles' is used here without any prejudice to the prescriptive content of the relevant norms. 'Principles', from this point of view, is intended here to denote the foundational role of these prescriptions as systematic pillars of the law of targeting.

relevant strategic, operational or tactical objectives pursued by the belligerents. Furthermore, these norms do not only identify who can be considered a target and which objects can be deemed to be military objectives – and thus lawfully attacked – in a static perspective. They also cover the whole targeting process in its dynamic developments on the battlefield: selection of targets, their prioritisation, planning, execution, and post-attack assessment. Decisions on targeting, therefore, 'involve complex operational, strategic, tactical, legal, ethical, and political assessments and need to be flexible to respond to changing circumstances. Because targeting is a dynamic process, the judgment of the commander is critical'.[4] In addition, the law of targeting has important implications for which means and methods of warfare can legitimately be used to pursue the military advantage anticipated, and what measures the belligerents are required to take in order to ensure the protection of specific groups of people and objects, or at least to minimise to the maximum extent feasible the potential damage for those groups deriving from military attacks on legitimate targets.

The development of the branch of IHL regulating the conduct of hostilities did not begin with the First Hague Peace Conference of 1899, to which the name is owned, but few decades earlier, with two codifications constituting a landmark and a model for the subsequent treaties in this area: the Instructions for the Government of Armies of the United States in the Field, General Order n 100,[5] promulgated by President Lincoln during the American Civil War in April 1863; and the subsequent 1868 St Petersburg Declaration Renouncing the Use, in Time of War, of Explosive Projectiles Under 400 Grammes Weight,[6] international treaty constituting the outcome of a diplomatic conference convened upon Russian initiative.

This codification it is best known as 'Lieber Code' since the General Order was drafted by the German jurist Francis Lieber. The Code was technically an internal legal instrument (a military order) destined for use by one party (ie by combatants of one party) in the ongoing civil war in the United States. It was not, therefore, an international, nor a properly humanitarian codification. It served, however, as a model and source of inspiration for successive international efforts to arrive at internationally accepted collections of the laws and customs of war. The code's 157 articles, broken into 10 sections, dealt with a wide range of issues: from martial law to the protection of persons, religion, arts, and sciences; from the treatment of deserters, prisoners of war, partisans, spies and captured messengers to prisoner

[4] As underlined by N Tsagourias, introducing the 'Targeting in International Humanitarian Law' entry in the *Oxford Bibliographies on International Law*, at www.oxfordbibliographies.com/view/document/obo-9780199796953/obo-9780199796953-0142.xml?rskey=jRBzxl&result=141.

[5] Instructions for the Government of Armies of the United States in the Field, General Order n.100 (Lieber Code), adopted 24 April 1863. See D Schindler and J Toman, *The Laws of Armed Conflicts* (Martinus Nihjoff Publisher, 1988) 3–23.

[6] St Petersburg Declaration Renouncing the Use, in Time of War, of Explosive Projectiles Under 400 Grammes Weight, adopted and entered into force 11 December 1868 (St Petersburg Declaration). See Schindler and Toman (n 5) 102.

exchanges and flags of truce; from battlefield booty to the parole, armistice, and assassinations.

With a degree of indulgence toward western-centric approaches to legal history, somehow generalising as sole and necessary origin of international legal categories specific mindsets and contingent declinations emerged as hegemonic throughout history,[7] the Code is commonly identified as 'the first attempt to set down, in a single set of instructions for forces in the field, the laws and customs of war',[8] with authors indicating it as the 'the final product of the eighteenth-century movement to humanize war through the application of reason', offering the 'greatest theoretical contribution to the modern law of war'.[9] Lieber's conception of war and its legal and moral constraints, however, was very distant from what would be identified today as a humanitarian ideal. He had no strong sympathy for the universalism of Enlightenment ideals,[10] nor for Kantian pacifist globalism.[11] In addition, previous legal instruments outside the historical experiences of Global North countries presented in some cases more advanced approaches to civilian protection.[12]

At the same time, it is true that the comprehensiveness of the Lieber Code was *sui generis* and unprecedented at the time, spanning from martial law to the protection of persons, from buildings dedicated to religion, arts and sciences, to the treatment of prisoners of war, deserters and spies, from battlefield booty to

[7] See M Koskenniemi, 'Histories of International Law: Dealing with Eurocentrism' (2011) 19 *Rechtsgeschichte*, 152; A Orford, *International Law and the Politics of History* (Cambridge University Press, 2021) 215–48, A Roberts, *Is International Law International?* (Oxford University Press, 2017) 209–29; A Anghie, *Imperialism, Sovereignty, and the Making of International Law* (Cambridge University Press, 2004) 17–64; N Tzouvala, 'The Specter of Eurocentrism in International Legal History' (2021) 31 *Yale Journal of Law & the Humanities* 427–31.

[8] In these terms, *ex multiis*, C Greenwood, 'Historical Development and Legal Basis' in D Fleck (ed), *The Handbook of International Humanitarian Law*, 2nd edn (Oxford University Press, 2008) § 116, 21. Similarly, see eg M Howard, 'Constraints on Warfare', in M Howard, GJ Andreopoulos and MR Shulman (eds), *The Laws of War: Constraints on Warfare in the Western World* (Yale University Press, 1994) 6.

[9] BM Carnahan, 'Lincoln, Lieber and the Laws of War: The Origins and Limits of the Principle of Military Necessity' (1998) 92 *American Journal of International Law* 212.

[10] See M Curti, 'Francis Lieber and Nationalism' (1941) 4 *Huntington Library Quarterly* 265.

[11] See E Kant, *Perpetual Peace. A Philosophical Project*, first published 1795, translated by M Campbell Smith, 3rd edn (George Allen & Unwin Ltd, 1917); and F Lieber, *Manual of Political Ethics*, 2nd edn, 2 vols, (JB Lippincot, 1890) 2: 430, cited in S Moyn, *Humane. How the United States Abandoned Peace and Reinvented War* (Macmillan, 2021) 48–49.

[12] Relatedly, and as sample of the incidence of Eurocentrism in the framing of the histories of the laws of war, see A Gurmendi, 'Latin Lieber: Uncovering the History of the Treaty on the Regularisation of War' *Opinio Juris*, 10 June 2022, at opiniojuris.org/2022/06/10/latin-lieber-uncovering-the-history-of-the-treaty-on-the-regularisation-of-war, illuminating the advanced humanitarian approach of some of the solutions identified in the 1820 treaty object of the enquiry, little noticed by European scholarship, with few exceptions, see J Basdevant, 'Deux conventions Peu Connues sur le droit de la guerre' (1914) 21 *Revue Générale de Droit International Public* 17. More extensively on this treaty, see A Valencia, *La humanización de la Guerra: Derecho Internacional Humanitario y Conflicto Armado en Colombia* (Ediciones Uniandes, 1992) 25–37. See also, for the Islamic tradition on the constraints on warfare, A Al-Dawoody, *The Islamic Law of War: Justifications and Regulations* (Palgrave Macmillan, 2011).

the parole.[13] The Code, however, was infused with the Clausewitzian views of his author,[14] resulting in a rather broad and all-encompassing declination of the concept of military necessity – that is, 'necessity of those measures which are indispensable for securing the ends of the war' – still far from the humanitarian constraints typical of the contemporary laws of war, and standing out as overarching protected good of the codification.

This approach is evidenced by several emblematic articles, such as those explicitly allowing starvation as legitimate weapon of war,[15] or affirming that 'men live in political, continuous societies, forming organized units, called states or nations, whose constituents bear, enjoy, suffer, advance and retrograde together, in peace and in war', in turning grounding the view that citizens or natives of a hostile country were 'thus an enemy',[16] or allowing 'all direct destruction of life or limb of armed enemies, and of other persons whose destruction is incidentally unavoidable in the armed contests of the war'.[17] As it has been noted in contrast to the emerging vision of European jurists such as Dunant and Moynier, Lieber's 'project shared almost nothing of the aspiration for humane war that Swiss gentlemen breathed deeply across the ocean at the same time'.[18] Despite this distance in spirit and ideals from the aspirations animating other early codifications in the same decades, the Code stated that 'private property, unless forfeited by crimes or by offenses of the owner' could have been 'seized only by way of military necessity' for the 'support or other benefit of the army'.[19] Military necessity, therefore, started to emerge as exception to general protections in some provisions, while overall being framed as the ultimate rule admitting some limits in others. '[T]he principle … that the unarmed citizen is to be spared in person, property, and honor' was still rigorously relative, contained by what 'the exigencies of war will admit'.[20]

[13] *Instructions for the Government of Armies of the United States in the Field, General Order n.100* (Lieber Code), adopted 24 April 1863. See Schindler and Toman (n 5) 3–23.

[14] Moyn (n 11) 163.

[15] War is not carried on by arms alone. It is lawful to starve the hostile belligerent, armed or unarmed, so that it leads to the speedier subjection of the enemy (Art 17 Lieber Code).

[16] The citizen or native of a hostile country is thus an enemy, as one of the constituents of the hostile state or nation, and as such is subjected to the hardships of the war (Art 21 Lieber Code).

[17] 'Military necessity admits of all direct destruction of life or limb of armed enemies, and of other persons whose destruction is incidentally unavoidable in the armed contests of the war; it allows of the capturing of every armed enemy, and every enemy of importance to the hostile government, or of peculiar danger to the captor; it allows of all destruction of property, and obstruction of the ways and channels of traffic, travel, or communication, and of all withholding of sustenance or means of life from the enemy; of the appropriation of whatever an enemy's country affords necessary for the subsistence and safety of the army, and of such deception as does not involve the breaking of good faith either positively pledged, regarding agreements entered into during the war, or supposed by the modern law of war to exist. Men who take up arms against one another in public war do not cease on this account to be moral beings, responsible to one another and to God' (Art 15 Lieber Code).

[18] Moyn (n 11) 163.

[19] And adding: 'If the owner has not fled, the commanding officer will cause receipts to be given, which may serve the spoliated owner to obtain indemnity' (Art. 38 Lieber Code).

[20] Art 22 Lieber Code.

A different conceptual background, instead, was laid down with the other early codification mentioned. In 1863 the Russian army had obtained a rifle bullet which exploded on contact with a hard surface and whose primary utility was to blow up ammunition wagons. The projectile was later modified to also explode on contact with softer surfaces, including human tissue. The result was a range of bullets causing wounds far greater than those associated with all other rifle bullets in use at the time. Conscious that such injuries exceeded what was needed to put an enemy soldier out of combat, and predicting an imminent arms race (which would have diminshed diplomatic relations with neighbouring countries), Russian Emperor Alexander II convened a conference to prohibit this type of projectile by international agreement.[21] The outcome was the St Petersburg Declaration prohibiting the use in international armed conflicts of any projectile of a weight below 400 grams. The Declaration outlined a principle which is still a core premises of contemporary IHL and the law of targeting. It stated:

> [T]he progress of civilization should have the effect of alleviating as much as possible the calamities of war; … the only legitimate object which States should endeavour to accomplish during war is to *weaken the military forces of the enemy*; […] for this purpose *it is sufficient to disable the greatest possible number of men*; … this object would be exceeded by the employment of arms which *uselessly aggravate the sufferings* of disabled men, or render their death inevitable; the employment of such arms would, therefore, be contrary to the laws of humanity.[22]

Here the approach significantly diverges from that of the Lieber Code: it is not the military necessity that limits the extent of the constraints on the means of warfare, but rather the definition – and rationalisation – of the legitimate necessity, in opposition to illegitimate, that becomes the teleological point of reference determining the legality of the means and methods of combat. Another crucial aspect of this codification is that, from that moment on, the law of armed conflicts was organised around the need to strike a balance between two polarities which the Declaration started to outline: on the one hand, the 'principle of military necessity', permitting the complex of measures which are actually necessary to accomplish a legitimate military purpose and are not otherwise prohibited by IHL, and, on the other, the 'principle of humanity', implying the whole set of humanitarian considerations seeking to limit suffering and destruction in warfare, both in terms of protection of specific groups of people or objects from attacks, and in terms of constraints on the means and methods to attack combatants in order to achieve specific military goals. Where the same military advantages can be achieved through less harmful means, considerations of humanity would require the use of such means.

[21] See C Samwer et al (eds), *Mémoire sur la suppression de l'emploi des balles explosives en temps de guerre', Nouveau recueil général de traités, conventions et autres transactions remarquables, servant à la connaissance des relations étrangères des puissances et états dans leurs rapports mutuels*, vol 18 (Librairie de Dieterich, 1873) 458.

[22] St Petersburg Declaration (n 6) (emphases added).

As explained by Melzer:

> IHL is based on a balance between considerations of military necessity and of humanity. On the one hand, it recognises that, in order to overcome an adversary in wartime, it may be militarily necessary to cause death, injury and destruction, and to impose more severe security measures than would be permissible in peacetime. On the other hand, IHL also makes clear that military necessity does not give the belligerents *carte blanche* to wage unrestricted war. Rather, considerations of humanity impose certain limits on the means and methods of warfare, and require that those who have fallen into enemy hands be treated humanely at all times.[23]

This also reflects an operative necessity of the law of armed conflicts. As underlined by Kolb and Hyde:

> If only the principle of humanity was recognised, the LOAC rules that would exist would not be considered practicable by the military branch. Such rules would be worthless in the context of the hostile environment of armed conflict; they would, to some extent, be in direct contradiction with the fact that armed conflict, the subject they seek to regulate, implies destruction, killing and injury.[24]

On the other hand, if considerations of military necessity were the only ones overseeing the *ratio* of IHL norms and the organisation of their systematic, these norms could not impede the overexpansion of military needs as to encompass every person and object indirectly or even remotely contributing to the war effort of an enemy armed force. Dinstein relatedly contends that:

> Some people, no doubt animated by the noblest humanitarian impulses, would like to see zero-casualty warfare. However, this is an impossible dream. … As long as it is waged, humanitarian considerations cannot be the sole legal arbiters of the conduct of hostilities. The law of international armed conflict can and does forbid some modes of behaviour, with a view to minimizing the losses, the suffering, and the pain. But it can do so only when there are realistic alternatives to achieving the military goal of victory in war. Should nothing be theoretically permissible to a belligerent engaged in war, ultimately everything will be permitted in practice – because the rules will be ignored.[25]

This statement illuminates an important condition for the respect of the laws of war: the need for a realistic approach to the objective of governing warfare. Rules of warfare, in fact, would be impracticable for combatants should they radically impede the pursuit of victory; on the other hand, however, this approach has its risks, as it seems to imply that the normative force of IHL rules can be effective only when abiding to those rules does not hamper the pursuit of victory. On the contrary, respect for the rules governing the means and methods of warfare cannot be framed as a variable dependent on the achievement of military goals, as there

[23] N Melzer, *International Humanitarian Law: A Comprehensive Introduction* (ICRC, 2016) 17–18.
[24] R Kolb and R Hyde, *An Introduction to the International Law of Armed Conflicts* (Hart Publishing, 2008) 43.
[25] N Dinstein, *The Conduct of Hostilities Under the Law of International Armed Conflicts* (Cambridge University Press, 2004).

are many situations in which the military goals pursued are in themselves unlawful under IHL. There are also many circumstances where the protective legal red lines IHL draws around protected persons and/or objects must be respected, even (and particularly) when this respect could be detrimental for the pursuit of military advantage.

Beyond the early codifications mentioned, the balance between military necessity and humanity constituting the conceptual premise of the St Petersburg Declaration, and identifying the values still weighed and balanced by the IHL scales as a whole, runs on two parallel binaries in contemporary treaties. Alongside the principles governing targeting decisions in order to protect civilians or civilian objects from attacks and their effects, in fact, IHL prohibits the 'employ[ment of] weapons, projectiles and material and methods of warfare of a nature to cause superfluous injury or unnecessary suffering'.[26] Actualising the principles outlined in the 1868 St Petersburg Declaration, these norms prohibit the needless infliction of harm to enemy combatants, in that it would be greater than necessary to achieve legitimate military objectives. The meaning of the terms 'superfluous injury' and 'unnecessary suffering' remains subject to interpretative controversies. There are, however criteria commonly used to assess the level of suffering. In particular, there are three indexes commonly considered: i) the intensity of the pain; ii) the degree of permanent disability; and iii) the likelihood of death.

Suffering, in addition, must be considered the product of both physiological and psychological elements.[27] There are two main normative references for these rules. Article 23 of the Regulations Respecting the Laws and Customs of War on Land, annexed to the 1907 Hague Convention IV, states:

> [I]t is especially forbidden:
>
> (a) To employ poison or poisoned weapons;
> (b) To kill or wound treacherously individuals belonging to the hostile nation or army;
> (c) To kill or wound an enemy who, having laid down his arms, or having no longer means of defence, has surrendered at discretion;
> (d) To declare that no quarter will be given;
> (e) To employ arms, projectiles, or material calculated to cause unnecessary suffering;
>
> …
>
> (g) To destroy or seize the enemy's property, unless such destruction or seizure be imperatively demanded by the necessities of war.[28]

[26] Art 35(2) *Protocol Additional to the Geneva Conventions of 12 August 1949, and relating to the Protection of Victims of Non-International Armed Conflicts (Protocol II)*, adopted 8 June 1977, entered into force 7 December 1978, 1125 UNTS 609 (AP I).

[27] See R Scott, 'Unnecessary Suffering? – A Medical View' in MA Meyer (ed), *Armed Conflict and the New Law* (British Institute of International and Comparative Law, 1989) 277 ff.

[28] Hague Convention (IV) *Respecting the Laws and Customs of War on Land and Its Annex: Regulations Concerning the Laws and Customs of War on Land*, adopted 18 October 1907 ('Hague Convention IV').

Article 35(2) of the 1977 Additional Protocol I to the Four Geneva Conventions affirms: 'It is prohibited to employ weapons, projectiles and material and methods of warfare of a nature to cause superfluous injury or unnecessary suffering.'[29]

Whilst originally developed to outlaw specific means of warfare (weapons), therefore, the prohibition of superfluous injury and unnecessary suffering now applies also to methods of warfare (ie the way in which weapons are used).

This articulation of the prohibition is also reflected in rule 70 of the International Committee of the Red Cross study on Customary IHL,[30] and recognised by the International Court of Justice (ICJ) as being part of customary law. As stated by the ICJ:

> The cardinal principles contained in the texts constituting the fabric of humanitarian law are the following. … According to the second principle, it is prohibited to cause unnecessary suffering to combatants: it is accordingly prohibited to use weapons causing them such harm or uselessly aggravating their suffering. In application of that second principle, States do not have unlimited freedom of choice of means in the weapons they use. … In conformity with the aforementioned principles, humanitarian law, at a very early stage, prohibited certain types of weapons either because of their indiscriminate effect on combatants and civilians or because of the unnecessary suffering caused to combatants, that is to say, a harm greater than that unavoidable to achieve legitimate military objectives. If an envisaged use of weapons would not meet the requirements of humanitarian law, a threat to engage in such use would also be contrary to that law. [T]hese fundamental rules are to be observed by all States whether or not they have ratified the conventions that contain them, because they constitute intransgressible principles of international customary law.[31]

If the prohibition of superfluous injury and unnecessary suffering applies to the selection of means and methods of warfare in order to protect combatants from harm that would go beyond that strictly necessary for the achievement of legitimate military objectives, what needs now to be analysed more closely is the other crucial formant of the normative fabric of IHL mentioned by the ICJ, that is the complex of principles regulating targeting decisions in order to protect civilian and civilian objects from attacks and their consequences.

These are the principles of distinction, proportionality and precaution. The application of these three principles can be, at first approximation, synthesised in their operational meaning as follows:

I. Only combatants and military objectives precisely identified may be attacked, always distinguishing to the maximum extent possible civilians and civilian objects from combatants and military objectives.

[29] Protocol Additional to the Geneva Conventions of 12 August 1949, and relating to the Protection of Victims of International Armed Conflicts (Protocol I), adopted 8 June 1977, entered into force 7 December 1978, 1125 UNTS 3.

[30] See JM Henckaerts and L Doswald-Beck, *Customary International Humanitarian Law. Volume I: Rules* (Cambridge University Press, 2005) 237 ff.

[31] *Legality of the threat or use of nuclear weapons*, Advisory Opinion, ICJ Rep 1996, 8 July 1996, §§ 78–79.

II. Even attacks directed at lawful targets are prohibited if they may be expected to cause incidental harm to civilians and/or civilian objects which would be excessive in relation to the concrete and direct military advantage anticipated.
III. Even when an attack directed at a lawful target cannot be expected to have an excessive incidental impact on civilians or civilian objects, all feasible precautionary measures must be taken to avoid, or in any event to minimize this impact.[32]

The implications of these prescriptions need to be analysed distinctly, in relation to each principle. To the three principles of distinction, proportionality and precaution is entrusted the operational concretisation of the need to strike the balance, in practice, between military necessity and humanity in combat situations. In this area, considerations of humanity imply first and foremost the absolute immunity of civilians and civilian objects from direct attacks, and their protection from excessive incidental consequences of the attacks themselves.

2.1.1. Distinction

The idea of civilians' immunity from attacks has antique roots and has gradually developed since ancient civilisations,[33] through warriors' ethics and honour,[34]

[32] See M Sassoli, A Bouvier and A Quintin, *How does Law Protect in War? Cases, Documents and Teaching Materials on Contemporary Practice in International Humanitarian Law*, 3rd edn, Vol I (ICRC, 2001) Pt I, Ch 9, 4.

[33] 'The Sumerians regarded war as a state governed by the law, which was started by a declaration of war and terminated by a peace treaty. War was subject to specific rules which, inter alia guaranteed immunity to enemy negotiators. Hammurabi King of Babylon (1728–1686 BC) wrote the 'Code of Hammurabi' for the protection of the weak against oppression by the strong and ordered that hostages be released on payment of a ransom. The law of the Hittites also provided for a declaration of war and for peace to be concluded by treaty, as well as for respect for the inhabitants of an enemy city which has capitulated. The war between Egypt and the Hittites in 1269 BC, for instance, was terminated by a peace treaty. In the 7th century BC, Cyrus I, King of the Persians, ordered the wounded Chaldeans to be treated like his own wounded soldiers. The Indian epic Mahabharata (c 400 BC) and the Laws of Manu (after the turn to a new era) already contained provisions which prohibited the killing of a surrendering adversary who was no longer capable of fighting; forbade the use of certain means of combat, such as poisoned or burning arrows; and provided for the protection of enemy property and prisoners of war. The Greeks, in the wars between the Greek city-states, considered each other as having equal rights and in the war led by Alexander the Great against the Persians, respected the life and dignity of war victims as a prime principle. They spared the temples, embassies, priests and envoys of the opposite side and exchanged prisoners of war. For example, the poisoning of wells was proscribed in warfare. The Romans also accorded the right to life to their prisoners of war. However, the Greeks and Romans both distinguished between those peoples whom they regarded as their cultural equals and those whom they considered to be barbarians': C Greenwood, 'Historical Development and Legal Basis' in D Fleck (ed), *Handbook of International Humanitarian Law*, 2nd edn (Oxford University Press, 2008) 16.

[34] 'The 'Bushi-Do', the medieval code of honour of the warrior caste of Japan, included the rule that humanity must be exercised even in battle and towards prisoners of war. In the 17th century the military tactician Sorai wrote that whoever kills a prisoner of war shall be guilty of manslaughter, whether that prisoner had surrendered or fought 'to the last arrow' (ibid).

religious universalisms[35] and chivalry.[36] Recent literature has debated and criticised the traditional conception of the development of this distinction, demonstrating how – from scholastic philosophers to modern international lawyers – discourses of gender, civilisation and innocence have characterised as intrinsic what is often an arbitrary line between legitimate and illegitimate targets of violence during war, drawn in such a way as to serve the interests of the dominant classes or military powers at any given historical moment.[37] It is with the Enlightenment, however, that the idea of civilians' protection in wartime found a more stable systematisation. It was in particular Jean-Jacques Rousseau, in the second half of the eighteenth century, who developed the idea according to which war did not constitute a confrontation between peoples, but between states and their rulers (so called 'sovereign's war').[38] It is worthy in this respect to quote in full Rousseau's reflection:

> Grotius and others derive from war another origin for the supposed right of slavery. The victor having, according to them, the right of slaying the vanquished, the latter may purchase his life at the cost of his freedom; an agreement so much the more legitimate that it turns to the advantage of both. But it is clear that this supposed right of slaying the vanquished in no way results from the state of war. Men are not naturally enemies, if only for the reason that, living in their primitive independence, they have no mutual relations sufficiently durable to constitute a state of peace or a state of war. It is the relation of things and not of men that constitutes war; and since the state of war cannot arise from simple personal relations, but only from real relations, private war – war between man and man – cannot exist either in the state of nature, where there is no settled ownership, or in the social state, where everything is under the authority of the laws. … War, then, is not a relation between man and man, but a relation between State and State, in which individuals are enemies only by accident, not as men, nor even as citizens, but as soldiers; not as members of the fatherland, but as its defenders. In short, each State can have as enemies only other States and not individual men, inasmuch as

[35] 'In the Middle Ages feud and war were governed by strict principles. The principle of protecting women, children, and the aged from hostilities was espoused by St Augustine. The enforcement of respect for holy places (Truce of God) created a right of refuge, or asylum, in churches, the observance of which was carefully monitored by the Church. The knights fought according to certain (unwritten) rules. The rules of arms were enforced by the arbiters of tribunals of knights. Those rules applied only to knights, not to the ordinary people. The enemy was frequently regarded as an equal combatant who had to be defeated in an honourable fight. It was forbidden to start a war without prior notification. … Islam also acknowledged the essential requirements of humanity. In his 108 orders to his commanders, the first caliph, Abu Bakr (about 632), stipulated for instance the following: "The blood of women, children and old people shall not stain your victory. Do not destroy a palm tree, nor burn houses and corn fields with fire, and do not cut any fruitful tree. You must not slay any flock or herds, save for your subsistence." However, in many cases Islamic warfare was no less cruel than warfare by Christians. Under the reign of leaders like Sultan Saladin in the twelfth century, however, the laws of war were observed in an exemplary manner. Saladin ordered the wounded of both sides to be treated outside Jerusalem and allowed the members of the Order of St. John to discharge their hospital duties' (ibid).

[36] See T Gill, 'Chivalry: A Principle of the Law of Armed Conflicts?' in M Matthee et al (eds), *Armed Conflict and International Law: In Search of the Human Face* (TMC Asser Press, 2013) 33 ff.

[37] HM Kinsella, *The Image Before the Weapon: a Critical History of the Distinction Between Combatant and Civilian* (Cornell University Press, 2011).

[38] As noted by M Bothe, 'Targeting' (2003) 78 *International Law Studies* 135, 173. See W Grewe, *The Epochs of International Law* (M Byers tr and rev) (De Gruyter, 2001) 201 ff.

> it is impossible to claim any true relation between things of different kinds. … The aim of war being the destruction of the hostile State, we have a right to slay its defenders so long as they have arms in their hands; but as soon as they lay them down and surrender, ceasing to be enemies or instruments of the enemy, they become again simply men, and no one has any further right over their lives. Sometimes it is possible to destroy the State without killing a single one of its members; but war confers no right except what is necessary to its end. These are not the principles of Grotius; they are not based on the authority of poets, but are derived from the nature of things, and are founded on reason.[39]

It is from this theoretical footprint that the modern principle of distinction started to develop its contemporary lineaments, through the intellectual and historical movements of the nineteenth and twentieth centuries discussed, and owing much philosophical influence to the jurists of the Enlightenment. Today, the principle can be considered the main cornerstone of IHL, pillar of all the rules of warfare whose purpose is the protection of civilians and civilian objects.

Legally, the principle of distinction is highlighted in Article 48 of the 1977 Additional Protocol 1 to the Geneva Conventions, titled 'Basic Rule', and stating:

> In order to ensure respect for and protection of the civilian population and civilian objects, the Parties to the conflict shall *at all times* distinguish between the civilian population and combatants and between civilian objects and military objectives and accordingly shall direct their operations *only* against military objectives.[40]

As the other principles governing targeting, crucially, distinction has attained the status of customary international law. As recalled above, the ICJ affirmed that the distinction constitutes one of the 'cardinal principles contained in the texts constituting the fabric of humanitarian law' and also one of the 'intransgressible principles of international customary law'.[41]

The customary nature of the principle is also acknowledged in rules one and seven of the ICRC Customary IHL study, which state:

> The parties to the conflict must at all times distinguish between civilians and combatants. Attacks may only be directed against combatants. Attacks must not be directed against civilians.[42]

[39] J-J Rousseau, 'The Social Contract' in *The Social Contract and The First and Second Discourses* (ed by Susan Dunn) (Yale University Press, 2002) 160.

[40] Protocol Additional to the Geneva Conventions of 12 August 1949, and relating to the Protection of Victims of International Armed Conflicts (Protocol I), adopted 8 June 1977, entered into force 7 December 1978, 1125 UNTS 3 (emphases added).

[41] 'The cardinal principles contained in the texts constituting the fabric of humanitarian law are the following. The first is aimed at the protection of the civilian population and civilian objects and establishes the distinction between combatants and non-combatants; States must never make civilians the object of attack and must consequently never use weapons that are incapable of distinguishing between civilian and military targets. … Further these fundamental rules are to be observed by all States whether or not they have ratified the conventions that contain them, because they constitute intransgressible principles of international customary law' (ICJ, *Legality of the threat or use of nuclear weapons, Advisory Opinion*, ICJ Rep 1996, 8 July 1996, §§ 78–79).

[42] Henckaerts and Doswald-Beck (n 30) 3.

And:

> The parties to the conflict must at all times distinguish between civilian objects and military objectives. Attacks may only be directed against military objectives. Attacks must not be directed against civilian objects.[43]

A decisive consequence of this status between the sources of international law is that distinction, together with the other two principles governing targeting, is a cogent principle not only in international armed conflicts, as entailed in the treaty provisions of Additional Protocol I, but also in non-international armed conflicts (or armed conflicts not of an international character), and in hybrid conflicts (or armed conflicts of mixed character, where two or more states' armed forces are involved in protracted armed violence both against each other, and against one or more organised non-state armed groups), in which it is applicable in full. This status complements the provision of Article 13 of the 1977 Additional Protocol II to the Geneva Conventions, which affirms:

> The civilian population and individual civilians shall enjoy general protection against the dangers arising from military operations. … The civilian population as such, as well as individual civilians, shall not be the object of attack.[44]

The customary principle of distinction, therefore, extends to all the typologies of armed conflicts the intransgressible prescription to attack only combatants and military objectives, and thus posing an absolute prohibition against directly attacking civilians and civilian objects.

The principle of distinction, however, would be worthless without previously defining and identifying who is a civilian and who is a combatant, as well as what is a military objective.

In IHL civilian status is negatively defined by Article 50 of Additional Protocol I, which indicates as civilians all those who do not qualify either for the combatant[45] or prisoner of war[46] status. The article makes also clear that 'In

[43] ibid, 25.

[44] *Protocol Additional to the Geneva Conventions of 12 August 1949, and relating to the Protection of Victims of Non-International Armed Conflicts (Protocol II)*, adopted 8 June 1977, entered into force 7 December 1978, 1125 UNTS 609.

[45] '1.The armed forces of a Party to a conflict consist of all organized armed forces, groups and units which are under a command responsible to that Party for the conduct of its subordinates, even if that Party is represented by a government or an authority not recognized by an adverse Party. Such armed forces shall be subject to an internal disciplinary system which, inter alia, shall enforce compliance with the rules of international law applicable in armed conflict. 2. Members of the armed forces of a Party to a conflict (other than medical personnel and chaplains …) are combatants, that is to say, they have the right to participate directly in hostilities. 3. Whenever a Party to a conflict incorporates a paramilitary or armed law enforcement agency into its armed forces it shall so notify the other Parties to the conflict' (Art 43 AP I).

[46] 'A. Prisoners of war, in the sense of the present Convention, are persons belonging to one of the following categories, who have fallen into the power of the enemy: (1) Members of the armed forces of a Party to the conflict as well as members of militias or volunteer corps forming part of such armed forces. (2) Members of other militias and members of other volunteer corps, including those of organized resistance movements, belonging to a Party to the conflict and operating in or outside their own territory, even if this territory is occupied, provided that such militias or volunteer corps, including

case of doubt whether a person is a civilian, that person shall be considered to be a civilian'.[47]

In order identify who is civilian it is therefore necessary to define combatancy. Combatants are, firstly, all members of the armed forces of a party to an international armed conflict. Membership of the armed forces, however, is not synonymous with combatancy. Medical and religious personnel of the army assigned to exclusively humanitarian functions, in fact, are not combatants. On the other hand, members of the armed forces not assigned to combat functions, such as military personnel assigned to various non-combat duties in military bases, but able to assume them in case of need, remain combatants. Importantly, there can be subjects entitled to combatant status even if they are not member of organised armed forces, as it is in the case of 'inhabitants of a non-occupied territory, who on the approach of the enemy spontaneously take up arms to resist the invading forces, without having had time to form themselves into regular armed units, provided they carry arms openly and respect the laws and customs of war'.[48] The civilian armed uprising against an approaching invader is known as *levée en masse*. As noted in the scholarship, this is the only case in which weapon-bearers may be regarded as combatants without being members of the armed forces.[49]

Decisively, the main feature of the combatant status is that those who are entitled to it 'have the right to directly participate in hostilities. If they fall into enemy hands, they become prisoners of war who may not be punished for having directly participated in hostilities'. At the same time, combatants have the obligation to

such organized resistance movements, fulfil the following conditions: (a) that of being commanded by a person responsible for his subordinates; (b) that of having a fixed distinctive sign recognizable at a distance; (c) that of carrying arms openly; (d) that of conducting their operations in accordance with the laws and customs of war. (3) Members of regular armed forces who profess allegiance to a government or an authority not recognized by the Detaining Power. (4) Persons who accompany the armed forces without actually being members thereof, such as civilian members of military aircraft crews, war correspondents, supply contractors, members of labour units or of services responsible for the welfare of the armed forces, provided that they have received authorization from the armed forces which they accompany, who shall provide them for that purpose with an identity card similar to the annexed model. (5) Members of crews, including masters, pilots and apprentices, of the merchant marine and the crews of civil aircraft of the Parties to the conflict, who do not benefit by more favourable treatment under any other provisions of international law. (6) Inhabitants of a non-occupied territory, who on the approach of the enemy spontaneously take up arms to resist the invading forces, without having had time to form themselves into regular armed units, provided they carry arms openly and respect the laws and customs of war. B. The following shall likewise be treated as prisoners of war under the present Convention: (1) Persons belonging, or having belonged, to the armed forces of the occupied country, if the occupying Power considers it necessary by reason of such allegiance to intern them, even though it has originally liberated them while hostilities were going on outside the territory it occupies, in particular where such persons have made an unsuccessful attempt to rejoin the armed forces to which they belong and which are engaged in combat, or where they fail to comply with a summons made to them with a view to internment. (2) The persons belonging to one of the categories enumerated in the present Article, who have been received by neutral or non-belligerent Powers on their territory and whom these Powers are required to intern under international law, without prejudice to any more favourable treatment which these Powers may choose to give …' (Art 4 GC III).

[47] Art 50(1) AP I.

[48] Art 13(6) GC I.

[49] Melzer (n 23) 81.

respect IHL, including the important duty of distinguishing themselves from the civilian population. 'If they violate International Humanitarian Law they must be punished, but they do not lose their combatant status and, if captured by the enemy, remain entitled to prisoner-of-war status, except if they have violated their obligation to distinguish themselves.'[50]

Whereas combatants cannot be punished for exercising their duty – that is actively contributing to the armed hostilities – persons who take a direct part in the hostilities on a continuous and organised basis without being entitled to do so can face penal consequences. They do not have the right to prisoner-of-war status (but they have a legitimate claim to certain fundamental guarantees established in Article 75 AP I, such as the right to humane treatment and a proper judicial procedure before an impartial and regularly constituted court).[51]

Direct participation in the hostilities is thus the right and duty of the combatants. On the other hand, the concept is crucial to understand the extent of civilians' immunity from direct attacks. For the civilians, in fact, direct participation in the hostilities (DPH) constitutes a transformative course of conduct which leads to their loss of protection from direct attacks. As stated in Article 51(3) of AP I, those who qualify as civilians are entitled to protection against attacks 'unless and for such time as they take direct part in the hostilities'.

It is therefore decisive to understand what the components of this course of actions are, whose consequence is the possibility to lawfully target the civilians who engage in it. DPH refers to specific hostile acts carried out by individual

[50] Sassoli, Bouvier and Quintin (n 32) 87.

[51] '3. Any person arrested, detained or interned for actions related to the armed conflict shall be informed promptly, in a language he understands, of the reasons why these measures have been taken. Except in cases of arrest or detention for penal offenses, such persons shall be released with the minimum delay possible and in any event as soon as the circumstances justifying the arrest, detention or internment have ceased to exist. 4. No sentence may be passed and no penalty may be executed on a person found guilty of a penal offense related to the armed conflict except pursuant to a conviction pronounced by an impartial and regularly constituted court respecting the generally recognized principles of regular judicial procedure, which include the following: (a) the procedure shall provide for an accused to be informed without delay of the particulars of the offense alleged against him and shall afford the accused before and during his trial all necessary rights and means of defence; (b) no one shall be convicted of an offense except on the basis of individual penal responsibility; (c) no one shall be accused or convicted of a criminal offense on account of any act or omission which did not constitute a criminal offense under the national or international law to which he was subject at the time when it was committed; nor shall a heavier penalty be imposed than that which was applicable at the time when the criminal offense was committed; if, after the commission of the offense, provision is made by law for the imposition of a lighter penalty, the offender shall benefit thereby; (d) anyone charged with an offense is presumed innocent until proved guilty according to law; (e) anyone charged with an offense shall have the right to be tried in his presence; (f) no one shall be compelled to testify against himself or to confess guilt; (g) anyone charged with an offense shall have the right to examine, or have examined, the witnesses against him and to obtain the attendance and examination of witnesses on his behalf under the same conditions as witnesses against him; (h) no one shall be prosecuted or punished by the same Party for an offense in respect of which a final judgement acquitting or convicting that person has been previously pronounced under the same law and judicial procedure; (i) anyone prosecuted for an offense shall have the right to have the judgement pronounced publicly; and (j) a convicted person shall be advised on conviction of his judicial and other remedies and of the time-limits within which they may be exercised … (Art 75 AP I).

civilians as part of the conduct of hostilities between parties to an armed conflict. As explained by Melzer, in order to qualify as direct participation in the hostilities, an act must meet, cumulatively, three criteria:

- firstly, 'the act must be likely to adversely affect the military operations or military capacity of a party to an armed conflict or, alternatively, to inflict death, injury, or destruction on persons or objects protected against direct attack (threshold of harm);'
- secondly, 'there must be a direct causal link between the act and the harm likely to result either from that act, or from a coordinated military operation of which that act constitutes an integral part (direct causation);'
- finally, 'the act must be specifically designed to directly cause the required threshold of harm in support of a party to the conflict and to the detriment of another (belligerent nexus).'[52]

These cumulative criteria exclude from the scope of the notion of DPH:

1) hostile acts causing scarcely significant and negligible harm to one party to the conflict;
2) acts which only indirectly or randomly bring about harmful consequences for one of the belligerents; and
3) acts of hostility isolated and disconnected from the concerted military efforts of one party.

As for the consequences of the direct participation in the hostilities, since it can vary in intensity and duration, modalities governing the loss of protection differ. Civilians directly participating in hostilities do not cease to be part of the civilian population. Their protection against direct attack, however, is temporarily suspended, but only for the duration of each specific act amounting to DPH. As a consequence, this specificity and temporariness 'necessarily entails that civilians lose and regain protection against direct attack in parallel with the intervals of their engagement in direct participation in hostilities'. IHL, in other words, reactivates civilians' protection from attacks each time the engagement in a specific hostile act terminates. 'Until the civilian in question again engages in a specific act of direct participation in hostilities – has been underlined – the use of force against him or her must comply with the standards of law enforcement or individual self-defence.'[53]

A different mechanism, instead, should descend from DPH parameters in case of individuals becoming members of organised armed groups of a non-state party to an armed conflict, and serving continuous combat functions therein.

[52] N Melzer, *Interpretative Guidance on the Notion of Direct Participation in the Hostilities Under International Humanitarian Law* (ICRC, 2009) 46.

[53] ibid, 70. Contra, see MN Schmitt, 'The Interpretive Guidance on the Notion of Direct Participation in Hostilities: a Critical Analysis' in MN Schmitt (ed), *Essays on Law and War at the Fault Lines* (TMC Asser Press, 2011) 513–46.

Those persons would not qualify for the 'privileged', legally qualified combatancy described above, but at the same time cannot be considered civilians and remain protected. For those individuals, the loss of protection against direct attacks is more durable and lasts for the whole duration of the membership to the armed unit, as long as they serve continuous combat functions, and can be restored only if there is a clear disengagement from these functions and/or from the group.[54] This interpretation of the notion of DPH prevents the mobilisation of the controversial concept of 'unlawful combatants' developed during the war on terror, of no specific IHL significance, and eroding its civilian protection purposes.[55]

Thus combatants and civilians directly participating in the hostilities constitute lawful human targets during military operations, insofar as the choice of the means and methods of warfare is strictly guided by the targeting principles and does not cause superfluous injury and unnecessary suffering to enemy belligerents. It is now necessary to analyse how the principle impacts the legality of another category of potential targets, that is 'objects' – in other words non-human targets.

The first necessary operation to unpack the implications of the principle of distinction from this point of view is to define civilian objects and military objectives.

Civilian objects are negatively defined by Article 52(1) AP I as all objects that are not military objectives. The article also imposes that 'In case of doubt whether an object which is normally dedicated to civilian purposes, such as a place of worship, a house or other dwelling or a school, is being used to make an effective contribution to military action, it shall be presumed not to be so used.'[56] It is therefore necessary to identify military objectives.

The first important point is that under IHL military objectives are not such on the basis of their intrinsic and immutable character, and the law does not provide exhaustive, exemplificatory lists of military objectives. On the contrary, objects 'become military objectives according to their use by the enemy or potential use by the attacker'.[57] The qualification of military objectives, therefore, remains circumstantial. The non-categorical nature of this status determination for objects also remains crucial in order not to incentivise armed units to place themselves in protected objects, with the scope of shielding themselves from attacks (conduct which, under certain conditions, can infringe the IHL prohibition on the practice

[54] See eg G Corn and C Jenks, 'Two Sides of the Combatant Coin: Untangling Direct Participation in Hostilities from Belligerent Status in Non-International Armed Conflicts' (2011) 33 *University of Pennsylvania Journal of International Law* 313; K Dörmann, 'The legal situation of 'unlawful/unprivileged combatants' (2003) 85 *International Review of the Red Cross* 45; D Akande, 'Clearing the Fog of War? The ICRC's Guidance on Direct Participation in Hostilities' (2010) 59 *International and Comparative Law Quarterly* 180.

[55] See *ex multiis* F Mégret, 'From "Savages" to "Unlawful Combatants": A Postcolonial Look at International Humanitarian Law's Other' in A Orford (ed), *International Law and Its Others* (Cambridge University Press, 2006) 265–317; and M Sassoli, 'Query: Is There a Status of "Unlawful Combatant"?' (2006) 80 *International Law Studies* 57.

[56] Art 52(3) AP I.

[57] Sassoli, Bouvier and Quintin (n 32) ch 9, 4.

of human shielding).[58] All objects, therefore, can potentially become military objectives under certain conditions. Specially protected objects, however, have an additional layer of protections (for example, dams, dikes and hospitals) which may not be used by those who control them for military action and should therefore never become military objectives. However, if this happens, these objects can be attacked only under restrictive conditions.[59]

Use or potential and imminent use by the enemy for military purposes is thus the key to understanding whether or not an object may be considered a military objective. In order to determine if an attacker can make this identification, IHL normative guidance is essential. The most important provision in this regard is Article 52(2) of AP I, on customary rank,[60] stating:

> Attacks shall be limited strictly to military objectives. In so far as objects are concerned, military objectives are limited to those objects which by their nature, location, purpose or use make an effective contribution to military action and whose total or partial destruction, capture or neutralization, in the circumstances ruling at the time, offers a definite military advantage.

Article 52, in other words, requires the fulfilment of a 'two-pronged test'.[61] In order to identify an object as military objective, in fact, it is necessary, first, that the object, in the circumstances ruling at the time, makes an effective contribution to military action. Second, it is necessary that the attack on the object offers a definite military advantage (not to be confused with the concrete and direct military advantage considered under proportionality and precautions in attacks).[62]

If these requirements are both simultaneously,[63] or at least – according to some authors – cumulatively[64] met, it is possible to qualify a non-human target as a legitimate military objective.

It is important, thus, to summarise the main features of the two, complementary profiles of the assessment. The first part of the test requires an effective contribution to the military action of the enemy forces, which is legally relevant on one of

[58] See SB De Belle, 'Chained to Cannons or Wearing Targets on Their T-shirts: Human Shields in International Humanitarian Law' (2008) 90 *International Review of the Red Cross* 883; and R Geiss and JG Devaney, 'Zealots, Victims and Captives: Maintaining Adequate Protection of Human Shields in Contemporary International Humanitarian Law' (2017) 47 *Israel Yearbook on Human Rights* 11.

[59] See Art 19 GC IV and Art 56(2) AP I.

[60] See Henckaerts and Doswald-Beck (n 30) Rule 8.

[61] H Robertson, 'The Principle of Military Objective in the Law of Armed Conflict' (1997–98) 35 *United States Air Force Journal of Legal Studies* 48.

[62] Henderson (n 2) 51.

[63] Y Sandoz, C Swinarski and B Zimmermann (eds), *Commentary on the Additional Protocols of 8 June 1977 to the Geneva Conventions of 12 August 1949* (ICRC (Martinus Nijhoff Publishers, 1987) 635.

[64] M Sassoli, 'Legitimate targets of attacks under international humanitarian law' *Harvard Programme on Humanitarian Policy and Conflict Research Policy Brief* (2003), at hhi.harvard.edu/publications/legitimate-targets-attacks-under-international-humanitarian-law.

four possible grounds: nature, location, purpose or use of the object. 'Nature' refers to the object's intrinsic character. 'Location' acknowledges that an object may be a military objective simply because it is situated in an area that renders it functional to military action (eg a bridge). 'Purpose' refers to the enemy's intended imminent use, based on reasonable belief. 'Use' refers to the actual function of the object for those who control it.[65]

Military objectives, therefore, are all those structures which are squarely involved in the military endeavour of the enemy, making an effective contribution to the military operations on the basis of their relevance at a given time, considering the strategic conditions of a specific combat situation.

In the past, almost boundless interpretations of what constitutes a military objective have been adopted, such as under those views contemplating as military objectives 'any objectives which will contribute effectively towards the destruction of the enemy's means of resistance and the lowering of his determination to fight'.[66] The idea of including into the concept of military objectives the endeavour to break the enemy's determination to pursue its goals has, more recently, prompted world military powers such as the United States to expand the concept of military objectives and introduce that of 'war-sustaining capabilities', included, for example, the economic infrastructure used to generate revenue for an enemy's armed forces.[67] Such a view, however, gives rises to the risk of considering every activity, even indirectly or remotely connected with the military action, as sustaining the war effort.[68] As noted in the literature, 'if the intention directly to influence the enemy population's determination to fight were recognised as a legitimate objective for military force, then no limit to warfare would remain'.[69]

On the contrary, the formula adopted by Article 52 AP I represents a 'return to the restrictive definitional approach of the Hague Rules of Air Warfare, with the corresponding purpose of repressing the subsequent (and extremely broad) construction of military objectives favoured by the proponents of strategic air warfare',[70] or – more recently – of the so-called 'axiological targeting', whose aim is to force behavioural shifts in the belligerent leadership.[71]

As for the second part of the test, the object's 'total or partial destruction, capture or neutralization, in the circumstances ruling at the time', must offer a 'definite military advantage'.

[65] Sassoli, Bouvier and Quintin (n 32) ch 9, 5.

[66] C Webster and N Frankland, *The Strategic Offensive Against Germany 1939-1945*, Vol I, 34–51 (HMSO, 1961) cited in W Hays Parks, 'Air War and the Law of War' (1990) 32 *The Air Force Law Review* 138.

[67] R Goodman, 'The Obama Administration and Targeting "War-Sustaining" Objects in Non-international Armed Conflict' (2016) 110 *American Journal of International Law* 663.

[68] APV Rogers, *Law on the Battlefield* (Oxford University Press, 2013) 70–71.

[69] S Oeter, 'Methods and Means of Combat' in D Fleck (ed), *Handbook of International Humanitarian Law*, 2nd edn (Oxford University Press, 2008) 180.

[70] ibid.

[71] P Kam, 'What Should We Bomb? Axiological Targeting and the Abiding Limits of Airpower Theory' (2004) 18 *Air & Space Power Journal* 25.

If the first profile of the test refers to an objective parameter – that is the contribution, or potential contribution, of the object to the military endeavour of the enemy – the second adds a more subjective criterion, since the 'definite military advantage' has to be framed and evaluated within the military purposes of the attacking state and in the light of its tactical and strategic goals (all admissible insofar as they comply with relevant IHL requirements).[72]

The subjective and relative features of the wording of Article 52 make of the definite military advantage one of the most debated concepts in the scholarship. As affirmed by Oeter, the abstract definition laid down in Article 52(2) AP I has a

> distinct advantage over the lists of admissible military objectives ..., namely the flexibility of its practical implementation, preserved by the abstraction of the formula. However, the same abstraction can be a disadvantage, in that it leaves a wide margin of interpretation which allows belligerents to construe it with completely different results according to their particular interest.[73]

Dinstein also underlines this problem, noting that 'it is regrettable that the wording is abstract and generic, and no list of specific military objectives is provided (if only on an illustrative, non-exhaustive, basis)' and suggesting 'that only a composite definition – combining an abstract statement with a non-exhaustive catalogue of concrete illustrations – can effectively avoid vagueness, on the one hand, and overcome the built-in inability to anticipate future scenarios, on the other'.[74]

Notwithstanding its margins of indeterminacy, however, the wording of Article 52 clearly signals the necessity of a 'a concrete and perceptible military advantage rather than a hypothetical and speculative one'.[75] On the same line, the advantage must have a specifically military character, and cannot be merely political, or psychological, as would be the case for attacks aiming at enemy's war sustaining capabilities broadly considered.

Having outlined the fundamental boundaries of the principle of distinction, in respect to both civilians and combatants, on the one hand, and civilian objects and military objectives, on the other, it is possible to proceed analysing the other two principles regulating targeting, that is proportionality and precaution.

2.1.2. Proportionality

The foundation of the modern idea of proportionality in *ius in bello* does not precisely follow the same historical development of the principle of distinction. Proportionality, in fact, even if deriving from ancient traditions of chivalry

[72] ibid, 182.
[73] Henderson (n 2) 64.
[74] Dinstein (n 25) 84.
[75] M Bothe, KJ Partsch and WA Solf (eds), *New rules for victims of armed conflicts: commentary on the two 1977 protocols additional to the Geneva Conventions of 1949*, 2nd edn (Brill Nijhoff, 2013) 325.

and warrior ethics, only began to find a robust legal declination in the late modernity.

Before the First World War the principle of proportionality, 'encapsulated in the notion that the choice of methods to injure the enemy was not unrestricted, was accepted as a basic precept to be balanced against the dictates of military necessity. … Its relevance was mainly confined to combatants.'[76] This significantly changed after World War I and the Spanish Civil War became theatres of aerial bombardment as primary method of warfare. This development shifted jurists' attention to the unprecedented extent of civilian casualties, and their relationship with the legal boundaries of the notion of military necessity. The existing regulation focused rather on land bombardment, governed by the Hague Conventions.[77] In this system, there was no explicit prohibition of indiscriminate bombardment of military defended targets. Aerial warfare exponentially increased the vulnerability of civilians, who became potential 'collateral damage' of attacks on a much larger scale than before. With this shift, the primary focus of proportionality became to prevent excesses in the civilian losses, even when civilians were not targeted, but nonetheless impacted and killed in the course of aerial attacks on lawful military objectives. Aerial warfare, in other words, determined a progressive switch of focus of the principle, from the protection of combatants against superfluous injuries and unnecessary sufferings, to the protection of civilians from the unprecedented impact of the new methods of warfare. As duly noted by Gardam:

> Proportionality offered a method of mitigating the severity of this impact. The norm of non-combatant immunity itself came under great pressure and the balance between military necessity and civilian losses was increasingly difficult to determine. It was one thing to accept the need to protect non-combatants from attack when compliance with this rule did not significantly interfere with military effectiveness. But the requirement that civilian losses be in some way proportionate to the military advantage decreased the effectiveness of means and methods of attack such as aerial bombardment.[78]

The core of this issue lasts into the present day, and the reluctance of air powers to be constrained by strict assessments to be undertaken even in relation to the incidental consequences of military attacks continues to generate controversies over proportionality. It is important, therefore, to understand the main legal features of proportionality under IHL and terms of the controversies over their significance.

[76] J Gardam, 'Proportionality and Force in International Law' (1993) 87 *American Journal of International Law* 391, 396, referring to the idea that 'Apart from the case in which there is no question of punishing an enemy, the whole may be summed up in this general rule: All acts of hostility which injure the enemy without necessity, or which do not tend to procure victory …, are unjustifiable, and as such condemned by the natural law': in E De Vattel, *Droit Des Gens*, Fenwick (tr), first published 1758 (Carnegie Institution of Washington, 1916) 294–95.

[77] BM Carnahan, 'The Law of Air Bombardment in its Historical Context' (1975) 17 *Airforce Law Review* 39.

[78] Gardam (n 76) 400.

If the principle of distinction regulates the decision about whether or not an object is a military objective and therefore can be legitimately attacked, the principle of proportionality affects the decision about whether or not, or in which way, to attack an already identified lawful military objective. In other words, 'given that direct attacks against civilians and civilian objects are already prohibited, the proportionality evaluation is relevant only when attacks are directed against lawful targets'.[79]

This relation between distinction and proportionality, as will be shown, remains a crucial coordinate, and a cornerstone for systematic interpretations of the law of targeting, seen as set of coherent prescriptions to be respected cumulatively, as well as in logical and operational sequence.

The rules concerning the assessment necessary to qualify a human target as a lawful one have been already mentioned. Those concerning the assessment necessary to qualify an object as a military objective, as seen above, are contained in Article 52(2) AP I. However, the fact that a lawful human target or a military objective has been properly identified as such, and as the exclusive target of attack, does not preclude the possibility that civilians or civilian objects will be hit.[80] Proportionality thus guides decision-makers about whether or not, in certain conditions and given limited tactical choices, attacking a military objective, or attacking it with the means available in that given circumstance, will cause excessive incidental harm to civilians or civilian objects. Depending on the outcome of this assessment, the prescription either affects the means and methods of warfare that may be lawfully used to attack a legitimate military target, or even effectively prohibit an attack from being launched, if the attack's harmful consequences on civilians or civilian objects may be expected to be excessive.

The principle of proportionality is enshrined in Article 51(5)(b) AP I, which prohibits

> attacks which may be expected to cause *incidental* loss of civilian life, injury to civilians, damage to civilian objects, or a combination thereof, which would be excessive in relation to the concrete and direct military advantage anticipated.

Article 57(2)(a)(iii) also reiterates, in relation to precautions, that:

> Those who plan or decide upon an attack shall … refrain from deciding to launch any attack which may be expected to cause incidental loss of civilian life, injury to civilians, damage to civilian objects, or a combination thereof, which would be excessive in relation to the concrete and direct military advantage anticipated.

Even if not specifically codified in general IHL treaty provisions regulating non-international armed conflicts, proportionality is a customary rule of IHL, and as such is applicable in all types of armed conflicts.[81]

[79] Melzer (n 23) 101.
[80] Dinstein (n 25) 119.
[81] See Rule 14, Proportionality in attack, in Henckaerts and Doswald-Beck (n 30) 46.

The principle of proportionality substantially brings into the regulations of the targeting practices, and articulates from the operational point of view, the need to strike a balance between consideration of humanity and military necessity. As can be inferred from the above-mentioned provisions, in fact, the principle of proportionality requires a comparative evaluation of the 'weight' of two prospective, and antagonistic elements: *concrete and direct* military advantage, *anticipated*, on the one hand, and *expectable* incidental civilian harm, on the other.

First, the expression 'concrete and direct' underlines that the military advantage referred to in the article has to be substantial and close. As a consequence, advantages which are hardly perceptible, or which would only appear in the long term, or speculative advantages, should not be part of the proportionality test.

Several scholars discuss this wording of the article. Bothe sustains that 'concrete' is best interpreted as 'specific and perceptible', whilst 'direct' implies that no other agency is required to bring the advantage about.[82] Hays Parks criticises interpretations like Bothe's as being too narrow, because they would disregard the long-term benefits of the attacks.[83] This criticism, however, risks to bring under IHL a potential balance between significant incidental civilian harm and remote military advantages. Fenrick affirms that the concept of 'attack' envisages action against several military objectives, but also underlines that the wording of AP I fails to explain 'how the boundaries are to be set geographically or chronologically so that a determination of military advantage can be made'. If an aerial bombardment is considered – according to the author – the degree of military advantage derived from operations

> will obviously vary depending on whether one focuses on the results of a day's operations, a week's, a campaign's, or a war's operations. Similarly, one side of the equation will vary depending on whether one considers military advantage to be the advantage derived from bombarding one particular military objective, all objectives of a similar type, or all objectives in general.[84]

Furthermore, an attack will usually always create some advantage, but the legal admissibility of this advantage will depend on factors such as the location of the objective or its current or potential use. The balancing judgement that must be made in observance of proportionality, in fact, is always relative and contextual. As Kolb and Hyde underline, 'an object that, when considered in the abstract, serves a military purpose may not be attacked, under the given definition, if a definite military advantage will not be gained by its destruction'.[85] The example used by the authors is that of a military aircraft escaping from the combat area towards a third state in order to surrender. In this case the aircraft would not be liable to attack,

[82] M Bothe, KJ Partsch and WA Solf, *New Rules For Victims of Armed Conflicts: Commentary on the Two 1977 Protocols Additional to the Geneva Conventions of 1949* (Martinus Nijhoff, 1982) 360.

[83] W Hays-Parks, 'Air War and the Law of War' (1990) 32 *Air Force Law Journal* 41.

[84] W Fenrick, 'The Rule of Proportionality and Protocol in Conventional Warfare' (1982) 98 *Military Law Review* 91.

[85] Kolb and Hyde (n 24) 131.

simply because it will make no further contribution to the war.[86] In sum, there is no objective measure or indicator of the concrete and direct character of the military advantage which could be valid irrespective of the circumstances ruling at the time of the attack.

The other end of the proportionality 'equation' is constituted by the 'expected incidental civilian loss of life, injury to civilians, damage to civilian objects, or a combination thereof'. These harmful consequences on civilians of lawful attacks, insofar as they are 'proportionate', are usually identified with the notion of 'collateral damage',[87] with some crucial differences in most common uses (as section 2.5 will indicate) deviating from the IHL notion of non-excessive incidental civilian harm.

Collateral damage can coincide with the IHL notion of incidental civilian harm in indicating lack of intentionality in causation of civilian harm, which can lawfully occur as a lateral and not sought consequence of an attack on a legitimate military objective, insofar as it is not excessive. An attack under the IHL will, therefore, be lawful, even when launched despite expecting to cause incidental civilian harm, if this harm is proportionate in relation to the concrete and direct military advantage anticipated. As a consequence, it can be entirely legal to target high-value military targets causing significant civilian losses.[88] However, this possibility depends on the unfeasibility of alternatives, ie, it depends on the unavoidability, in the specific circumstances, of the civilian losses. The legality of attacks which may be expected to cause (proportionate) incidental civilian harm is limited by precautions in attack, requiring – as will be discussed – that incidental civilian harm, other than minimised, should also be avoided entirely whenever this is feasible. IHL thus draws narrow margins of legal admissibility of civilian losses, injury to civilians, damage to civilian objects, or their combinations.

Different scholars underline that the roots of the difficulties in the implementation of proportionality, and in its enforcement, might lie precisely in the elusive concept of collateral damage. In modern, asymmetrical, urban warfare, the armed clashes usually involve combatants and civilians directly participating in the hostilities, military objectives located in densely populated civilian areas, or in the vicinity of installations and civilian settlements, as well as industrial plants, and infrastructure installations of dual use. In these contexts, collateral damage appears to observers 'almost inevitable, and often considerable'.[89] However, in contrast to this standpoint, it can be argued that the advancements in technological developments of weaponry reached in the last decades made possible, at least for the armies of developed and powerful countries, an unprecedented level of

[86] ibid.

[87] See critically F Rosén, *Collateral Damage. A Candid History of a Peculiar Form of Death* (Hurst Publishers, 2016).

[88] J Holland, 'Military Objective and Collateral Damage, Their Relationship and Dynamics' (2004) *Yearbook of International Humanitarian Law* 50.

[89] ibid.

precision in attacks. Considering this aspect, collateral damage is not an inevitability that must be assumed in premise. As Rosén notes:

> Collateral damage thrives in decentralised, responsive, risk-saturated warfare. … The fog of war was once about the lack of situational awareness and operational transparency from commanders. Today, it has found a new primary condition as confusion and adrenaline bend the judgement and memory of individual soldier, *who is now more than ever simultaneously combat planner, law interpreter, executor, witness and, not least, his own moral judge*. … To sum up, the category of death and suffering in war we call collateral damage has been reified over the last century, and developments in norms and law have detailed the criteria for when civilian deaths may be counted as collateral damage.[90]

Given the subjective interpretative profiles of both the notions of concrete and direct military advantage anticipated, on the one hand, and of expectable incidental civilian harm, on the other, the key of the proportionality test becomes the circumstantial 'excessiveness' of the latter.

It is in fact the excessiveness of the incidental harm to civilians in comparison to the military advantage, both foreseen prospectively as they will result from the attack, that will determine the legality of the attack itself. The difficulty in comparing civilian damage and military advantage in combat situations can be significant, since it entails an evaluation of two divergent, antagonistic and hardly commensurable factors. In addition, these factors need to be assessed and compared not 'here and now', as they appear while deciding about launching the attack, but – prognostically – as they will foreseeably manifest at the end of the course of action constituting the attack itself.

In this framework of *ex ante* assessments, and required prognostic evaluation, actors enjoy a wide margin of appreciation. Objective standards for the appraisal of expectable incidental civilian harm and the anticipated military advantage are not provided by IHL. In the final result, therefore, it is

> for the competent military commander and the staff planning the operation – who should know best the possible results and repercussions – to assess the consequences of the operation and to ensure its proportionality. Final responsibility is thus laid in the hands of the military, which can act only on the basis of the information available at the time of the decision.[91]

Dinstein argues that 'the whole assessment of what is 'excessive' in the circumstances entails a mental process of pondering dissimilar considerations – to wit, civilian losses and military advantage – and is not an exact science. There is no objective possibility of quantifying the factors of the equation', and the process 'necessarily contains a large subjective element'.[92] Shamash, analysing the same issue, asserts that

> the concept of proportionality requires a constant *ratio* between variables, in this case, between military advantage and collateral damage. These values are viewed as

[90] Rosén (n 87) 21, emphasis added.
[91] Oeter (n 69) 205.
[92] Dinstein (n 25) 122.

sufficiently incommensurable, and the correct relation between them as sufficiently subjective, so as effectively to preclude any consensus.

The author concludes that the determination of what constitutes 'excessive' collateral damage 'is unclear to the point of inapplicability'.[93] Against this conclusion, Gillard asserts that, 'Provided they do what is required to collect information on which to base their assessment, and conduct it in good faith and in a manner that is reasonable', belligerents maintain broad margin of judgement, but excessiveness assumes a higher factual legal consistence, as 'a wide but not indeterminate standard'.[94] Fenrick, reproducing the assumption of inevitability of civilian harm, notes:

> One might conclude … that inclusion of the rule of proportionality in Protocol I is of debatable humanitarian benefit and might even be harmful. This conclusion would be wrong. From a military standpoint, the rule of proportionality is useful as an acknowledgment of the unfortunate inevitability of incidental civilian casualties in war. Rules of engagement which would prohibit incidental civilian casualties would prove unworkable in time of war. Rules of attack which ignore the issue would, at best, have an implied proportionality rule read into them in combat and, at worst, lead commanders to believe that incidental civilian casualties could be ignored. Finally, rules into which an extensive objective proportionality standard has been incorporated might well be too inflexible to be applied in the myriad circumstances of combat. The proportionality rule as incorporated in Articles 51 and 57 of Protocol I may well result in a substantial humanitarian benefit if Protocol I is applied in good faith.[95]

Trying to decrease the subjective margins of appreciations of proportionality assessments, international criminal jurisprudence has developed a general and abstract standard to evaluate the position and choices of those in charge of attacking decisions in relation to proportionality. The ICTY referred to this standard as that of a 'reasonably well-informed person in the circumstances of the actual perpetrator'.[96] This standard was then dismissed in favour of considering not any agent, but a professional figure: that of the military commander.[97] Actual, and

[93] HE Shamash, 'How Much Is Too Much? An Examination of the Principle of Ius in Bello Proportionality' (2005) 2 *Israel Defense Forces Law Review* 103.

[94] EC Gillard, 'Proportionality in the Conduct of Hostilities. The Incidental Harm Side of the Assessment', *Chatham House Research Paper*, December 2018, para 81, at 22, at www.chathamhouse.org/sites/default/files/publications/research/2018-12-10-proportionality-conduct-hostilities-incidental-harm-gillard-final.pdf.

[95] WJ Fenrick, 'The Rule of Proportionality and Protocol in Conventional Warfare' (1982) 91 *Military Law Review* 127.

[96] *Prosecutor v Stanislav Galić*, Case No IT-98-29, Judgment (Trial Chamber), 30 November 2003, para 58.

[97] See eg Final Report to the Prosecutor by the Committee Established to Review the NATO Bombing Campaign Against the Federal Republic of Yugoslavia, at paras 49–50: '49. The questions which remain unresolved once one decides to apply the principle of proportionality include the following: a) What are the relative values to be assigned to the military advantage gained and the injury to non-combatants and/or the damage to civilian objects? b) What do you include or exclude in totalling your sums? c) What is the standard of measurement in time or space? And d) To what extent is a military commander obligated to expose his own forces to danger in order to limit civilian casualties or damage

potentially wrong/unlawful, proportionality assessments could in this way be re-evaluated by judges (in theory) on the basis of the parameter of what a reasonably well-informed commander would have determined in comparison to the one under legal scrutiny.

Even under these auspices, however, proportionality generates critical problems. Scholars, in fact, have contended that the standard reasonable commander does not seem to represent a decisive criterion to compensate the indeterminacy of proportionality. Dill, in particular, has concluded that most military personnel admit that 'in other than atypical "easy cases," two commanders with the same knowledge of fact and of law may reach diverging conclusions about the projected excessiveness of an attack'.[98] In the review of this author, some military commanders found this lack of action guidance problematic, whilst others considered the resulting flexibility (and reduced justiciability) of proportionality a great asset. A third group even denied that the rule required balancing military advantage and incidental loss of civilian life:

> Commanders argued that proportionality demanded that the attacker made sure they had chosen a truly valuable target and did everything possible to minimise expected incidental harm. Adequacy (that the attack will likely produce a military advantage) and necessity (that it is the mildest means to achieve this particular advantage) are indeed conditions of an attack's legality. Of course, they are not sufficient to make an attack proportionate under international humanitarian law.[99]

According to Dill's enquiry, in the understanding of many commanders, proportionality collapsed into necessity, while in other cases the principle's importance was dissolved into the verifications needed in the targeting process to comply with the principles of distinction and precaution. Dill continues:

> Even if military advantage can in principle be expressed in terms of progress towards a moral good – making a proportionality judgement then requires that an attacker gauges the moral import of her ultimate war aims, makes multiple future oriented judgements about how a particular attack furthers their achievement, and assesses the wrongness of harming civilians with presumably varying moral status. Every single one of these steps poses an enormous, possibly prohibitive epistemic challenge.[100]

to civilian objects? 50. The answers to these questions are not simple. It may be necessary to resolve them on a case-by-case basis, and the answers may differ depending on the background and values of the decision maker. It is unlikely that a human rights lawyer and an experienced combat commander would assign the same relative values to military advantage and to injury to noncombatants. Further, it is unlikely that military commanders with different doctrinal backgrounds and differing degrees of combat experience or national military histories would always agree in close cases. It is suggested that the determination of relative values must be that of the 'reasonable military commander'. Although there will be room for argument in close cases, there will be many cases where reasonable military commanders will agree that the injury to noncombatants or the damage to civilian objects was clearly disproportionate to the military advantage gained.'

[98] J Dill, Assessing Proportionality: An Unreasonable Demand on the Reasonable Commander?, Intercross, 11 October 2016, at intercrossblog.icrc.org/blog/r19aesa7v1kylcc5a4hbcwvfx8imus.

[99] ibid.

[100] ibid.

In the opinion of this author, two hermeneutical steps appear fundamental in order to tackle these challenges, valorising objective qualifiers of the civilian harm under the AP I definition of proportionality. The first, as it will be argued, is reading the targeting principles systematically, in their necessary teleological coordination. The second, consequential step is recentralising the largely overlooked and often neglected notion of 'incidentality' of the civilian harm, as systematised by AP I, in order to counter common misconceptions of proportionality, overextending it into the sphere governed by distinction.

2.1.3. Precautions

The principle of precaution completes the framework regulating targeting decisions provided by AP I.

As it has been shown, the principle of distinction regulates decisions about whether or not a precisely and singularly identified human or non-human target is either a combatant, or a military objective, and therefore whether it can be legitimately attacked. Consecutively, the principle of proportionality affects the decision about whether or not, or in which way, to attack an already identified lawful target. The basis of this second assessment is a prognostic comparative assessment of the expected tangible military gain from the attack and the anticipated incidental loss of civilian life, injury to civilians, damage to civilian objects (or a combination therefor). Whenever this civilian harm may be expected to be excessive, the attack – as it has been shown – has to be cancelled.

This process requiring two different stages of assessment, guided respectively by distinction, and the – only when distinction is satisfied – by proportionality, is not sufficient in order to guarantee the legality of attack. The third spectrum of legally required evaluations, in fact, is bound to the obligation to take all the feasible precautions to avoid, or in any event to minimise civilian harm. These mandatory precautions, in the opinion of this author, can be framed in the systematic of the law of targeting as corollary of both distinction and proportionality. In other words, in the process of logically and operationally sequential obligations imposed by the law of targeting, precautions have to accompany both distinction and proportionality assessments, requiring simultaneous precautionary measures.

Prior to AP I, only a small number of treaty provisions included obligations of precautions in attacks, and those were provided only in relation to particular cases. The 1907 Hague Convention IX contained the first articulation of the principle. It stated that if, for military reasons, immediate actions against naval or military objectives located within an undefended town or port were necessary, and no delay could be allowed, the commander of a naval force had to take 'all due measures in order that the town may suffer as little harm as possible'.[101]

[101] Art 2(3) Hague Convention (IX) Concerning Bombardment by Naval Forces in Time of War, adopted 18 October 1907, entered into force 26 January 1910.

The Hague Regulations concerning the Laws and Customs of War on Land annexed to the 1907 Hague Convention IV also included norms on precautions specifically in the context of bombardments and sieges. Article 26 provided the obligation for the officer in command of an attacking force, before commencing a bombardment, to do everything in his power to warn the authorities. Article 27, in the context of sieges and bombardments, required that 'all necessary steps … be taken to spare, as far as possible' certain categories of buildings including hospitals, 'provided they are not being used at the time for military purposes'.[102] Precautionary measures designed to ensure the specific protection of civilian hospitals were also envisaged in the Fourth Geneva Convention (GC IV) relative to the Protection of Civilian Persons in Time of War of 1949. Article 19(1) of GC IV states that the protection applies unless civilian hospitals 'are used to commit, outside their humanitarian duties, acts harmful to the enemy', providing that the protection can only cease 'after due warning has been given, naming, in all appropriate cases, a reasonable time limit, and after such warning has remained unheeded'.[103]

Today, with significant differences, the principle of precaution is enshrined in AP I.

Article 57(2) AP I states:

(a) those who plan or decide upon an attack shall:
  (i) do everything feasible to verify that the objectives to be attacked are neither civilians nor civilian objects and are not subject to special protection but are military objectives within the meaning of paragraph 2 of Article 52 and that it is not prohibited by the provisions of this Protocol to attack them;
  (ii) take all feasible precautions in the choice of means and methods of attack with a view to avoiding, and in any event to minimizing, incidental loss of civilian life, injury to civilians and damage to civilian objects;
  (iii) refrain from deciding to launch any attack which may be expected to cause incidental loss of civilian life, injury to civilians, damage to civilian objects, or a combination thereof, which would be excessive in relation to the concrete and direct military advantage anticipated;

(b) an attack shall be cancelled or suspended if it becomes apparent that the objective is not a military one or is subject to special protection or that the attack may be expected to cause incidental loss of civilian life, injury to civilians, damage to civilian objects, or a combination thereof, which would be excessive in relation to the concrete and direct military advantage anticipated;

(c) effective advance warning shall be given of attacks which may affect the civilian population, unless circumstances do not permit. When a choice is possible between several military objectives for obtaining a similar military advantage, the

[102] Arts 26 and 27 Hague Convention IV.

[103] Geneva Convention (IV) Relative to the Protection of Civilian Persons in Time of War, adopted 12 August 1949, entered into force 21 October 1950.

> objective to be selected shall be that the attack on which may be expected to cause the least danger to civilian lives and to civilian objects.[104]

Rule 15 of the ICRC Customary IHL study affirms that:

> In the conduct of military operations, constant care must be taken to spare the civilian population, civilians, and civilian objects. All feasible precautions must be taken to avoid, and in any event to minimize, incidental loss of civilian life, injury to civilians and damage to civilian objects.[105]

The first obligation imposed by the principle of precaution thus requires that the identification of the target, in particular when it is located at significant distance, has to be precise and careful. Crucial importance, in this process of 'target verification', is assumed by intelligence. Those who plan or decide upon an attack, in fact, will base their decision on the information available. Those in charge of attacking decisions will normally not have personal knowledge of the objective to be attacked and of its exact nature. However, this does not relieve them from responsibility. Careful target verification means also that, in case of doubts (triggering the legal presumption of civilian status), they must call for additional information. Depending on the variable configurations of different combat scenarios, this process might require additional steps. For example, as noted in the literature, 'in the case of long-distance attacks information will be obtained in particular from aerial reconnaissance and from intelligence units, which will of course attempt to gather information about enemy military objectives by various means'. Precautions require thus that evaluation of the information obtained 'must include a serious check of its accuracy, particularly as there is nothing to prevent the enemy from setting up fake military objectives or camouflaging the true ones'.[106]

The situation differs in case of close combat situations on land. In these contexts, evaluation of the nature of objectives will be based on direct information: the commanding officer ordering an attack will generally have information

> supplied by his own troops who are in direct contact with the enemy, and his task will therefore be much easier. … It is clear that a belligerent who accommodates troops in purely civilian buildings, for example, in dwellings or schools, or who uses such buildings as a base for combat, exposes them and the civilians present there to serious danger: even if attacks are directed only against members of the armed forces, it is probable that they will result in significant damage to the buildings.[107]

Furthermore, information that must be gathered before attacking should not be limited solely to the nature of the objective. Several other profiles, in fact, must

[104] Protocol Additional to the Geneva Conventions of 12 August 1949, and relating to the Protection of Victims of Non-International Armed Conflicts (Protocol II), adopted 8 June 1977, entered into force 7 December 1978, 1125 UNTS 609.

[105] Henckaerts and Doswald-Beck (n 30) 52.

[106] Sandoz, Swinarski and Zimmermann (n 63) 681.

[107] ibid.

be known in order to comply with targeting obligations. For example, the conditions in the immediate surroundings of the target, in order to gain a clear picture of the elements to be weighted according to the principle of proportionality. In this context, a particular challenge is posed by the so-called 'emerging targets', for which no advance planning is possible, and which, by their sudden appearance, make it necessary to strike within a very short time, leaving no opportunity to follow long and articulated procedures. However, the principles also apply in these cases, in that even these rapid procedures must leave room for practical precautionary measures.[108]

Another issue strictly related to target verification is the rank of the officials called upon to assume a central role in this process. The wording of the article does not appear completely clear, since it generically refers to those who plan or decide upon an attack. The primary obligation to verify that an object to be attacked constitutes a military objective will invest primarily the higher military echelons, since lower-level officers can hardly possess the necessary overview of the military situation.[109]

> But for their part – it has been argued – senior commanders are not prone to act intuitively: they rely on military intelligence and information gathering done by lower ranks. Despite all the impressive strides made by high technology, the information available may be inaccurate or wrongly interpreted.[110]

This demonstrates the importance of accurate intelligence as a prerequisite for the respect of the law of targeting. Accurate information gathering and respect of the legal framework for targeting are, in other words, inseparable in order to respect the law regulating the conduct of hostilities. No target verification, in fact, or choice of the means of warfare least harmful to civilians is possible, without the best knowledge of the battlefield, of the military objective, and of the circumstances existing at the time of the attack in the specific area which will be subject to its consequence.

Once the centrality of the target verification process is understood, the main interpretative problem with the principle of precaution remains to clarify the meaning of the wording of Article 57 AP I, which – similarly to proportionality – creates precautionary obligations in relative and contextual terms. In particular, the debate centres on the notion of 'feasibility'. Feasibility is clearly a contextual notion, highly dependent on the circumstances and the military and humanitarian considerations applicable at the time of the attack, such as the value and the time constraints for capturing, neutralising or destroying a target; the range, accuracy and radius of impact of available weapons; the conditions limiting

[108] J-F. Quéguiner, 'Precautions Under the Law Governing the Conduct of Hostilities' (2006) 88 *International Review of the Red Cross* 798.

[109] BL Brown, 'The Proportionality Principle in the Humanitarian Law of Warfare: Recent Efforts at Codification' (1976) 10 *Cornell International Law Journal* 145.

[110] Dinstein (n 25) 126.

or enabling higher accuracy of targeting; crucially, the proximity of civilians and civilian objects to target/s; and the availability and feasibility of alternatives.[111] This last point is of particular importance, considering that Article57(3) prescribes that:

> When a choice is possible between several military objectives for obtaining a similar military advantage, the objective to be selected shall be that the attack on which may be expected to cause the least danger to civilian lives and to civilian objects.

An even longer list of circumstantial considerations when taking precautions in the choice between means and methods of attack is offered by the UK Military Manual, which states:

> A commander should have regard to the following factors: a) the importance of the target and the urgency of the situation; b) intelligence about the proposed target – what it is being, or will be, used for and when; c) the characteristics of the target itself, for example, whether it houses dangerous forces; d) what weapons are available, their range, accuracy, and radius of effect; e) conditions affecting the accuracy of targeting, such as terrain, weather, night or day; f) factors affecting incidental loss or damage, such as the proximity of civilians or civilian objects in the vicinity of the target or other protected objects or zones and whether they are inhabited, or the possible release of hazardous substances as a result of the attack; g) the risks to his own troops of the various options open to him.[112]

Determining the exact precautionary measures to be taken when so many factors come into play cannot but give rise to controversy. The reference to the concept of feasibility in construing mandatory precautions requires therefore the identification of certain parameters, or standards of conduct, necessary for the fulfilment of the relevant obligations. A first handhold in this respect is offered by the Harvard Program on Humanitarian Policy and Conflict Research (HPCR) 'Manual on International Law Applicable to Air and Missile Warfare', which discusses these issues in terms of what is 'practicable or practically possible, taking into account all circumstances prevailing at the time, including humanitarian and military considerations'.[113] When taking precautions in attack, armed forces cannot be required to do what would practically result impossible (with the consequences of posing an obligation that would incur in systematic violations). However, at the same time, these norms require more severe constraints than merely doing what is possible.

The extent of the feasibility for the purposes of precaution remains below what would be impossible in the circumstances ruling at the time, but still much above the level of the mere possibility. Concurrently, it must be noted

[111] Sassoli, Bouvier and Quintin (n 32) ch 9, 25.

[112] UK Ministry of Defence, *The Manual of the Law of Armed Conflict* (2004) para 5.32.5.

[113] HPCR (Humanitarian Policy and Conflict Research, Harvard University), *Manual on International Law Applicable to Air and Missile Warfare*, 2009, Definition, Section A, para 1(q), at ihlresearch.org/amw/HPCR%20Manual.pdf.

that precautions in attack under IHL primarily amount to obligations of means, requiring the adoption of certain measures for the obligations to be fulfilled, as opposed to obligations of results. Violations of those norms might be found if no or inadequate precautionary measures have been taken. As Boutruche argues:

> The norms on precautions do not generally carry an obligation of result in that it is not expected that civilians and civilian objects must not be affected at all as a result of attacks. … While effects on civilians do not mean per se that the obligations of precaution have been violated, attacks resulting in significant loss of lives and destruction could provide indication that such obligations might have been violated.[114]

In this respect, the basic challenge raised by the controversies surrounding the concept of feasibility is determining whether, and to what extent, it can leave room for legitimate mistakes. For example, 'a weapon-delivering carrier could experience a failure leading it to divert from its programmed trajectory and to strike objects that the attacking party did not intend to target'.[115]

The answer of part of the scholarship is that the duty to take precautionary measures is satisfied by acting diligently and in good faith to take practicable measures, acknowledging also that agents acting diligently and in good faith may make mistakes.[116] According to Quéguiner,

> a legal assessment of a given situation will allow a clear line to be drawn between a negligent act that is unlawful under international law and a mistake that was made despite the taking of all feasible precautions. The former type of act will engage a state's responsibility (to be distinguished from individual criminal responsibility), while the latter type will not.[117]

Finally, it is important to underline that precautionary measures have to be taken at different stages of the attacks. Following Article 57 AP I, it is possible to identify three groups of obligations in this respect. The first one is the general obligation to take precautions in all stages of attacking procedure; the second includes the measures to be taken to ensure respect for the other material norms of IHL (distinction and proportionality), such as the obligations to verify the objective and to cancel unlawful attacks, when, for instance, the changing circumstances on the battlefield suddenly alter a proportionality assessment that was previously carried out and lead to the decision to launch the attacks (eg a group of children exiting a school and stationing in the immediate vicinity of

[114] T Boutrouche, *Expert Opinion on the Meaning and Scope of Feasible Precautions under International Humanitarian Law and Related Assessment of the Conduct of the Parties to the Gaza Conflict in the Context of the Operation 'Protective Edge'*, Diakonia, 22 February 2015, at www.diakonia.se/en/IHL/News-List/eo-on-protective-edge.

[115] J-F Quéguiner, 'Precautions Under the Law Governing the Conduct of Hostilities' (2006) 88 *International Review of the Red Cross* 810.

[116] WJ Fenrick, 'Targeting and proportionality during the NATO bombing campaign against Yugoslavia' (2001) 12 *European Journal of International Law* 501.

[117] Quéguiner (n 115) 810.

the military objective to be attacked); the third includes measures to be adopted in cases of entirely lawful attacks to avoid entirely, or (in case this is unfeasible) in any event to minimise the effects on civilians and civilian objects, such as the obligation to issue warnings.[118]

Alongside the precautions to be taken by the attacking forces, AP I also dictates precautionary measures that every military commander must take in his or her own territory (to protect his or her same country's nationals) or in the territory under his or her control (known as 'passive precautions'). In particular, as affirmed in Article 58, the Parties to the conflict shall:

> [T]o the maximum extent feasible:
>
> (a) without prejudice to Article 49 of the Fourth Convention, endeavour to remove the civilian population, individual civilians and civilian objects under their control from the vicinity of military objectives;
> (b) avoid locating military objectives within or near densely populated areas;
> (c) take the other necessary precautions to protect the civilian population, individual civilians and civilian objects under their control against the dangers resulting from military operations.

Substantially, the duty to take constant care to spare the civilian population does not bind only the attacking forces but requires also symmetric and complementary precautions to be taken by the defending powers. However, the wording of the article suggests that the compulsory nature of these obligations is stronger for the attacking forces. The precautionary measures, in fact, have to be taken by the defending party only 'to the maximum extent possible' and the defender only has to 'endeavour to remove' the civilian population and 'avoid' locating military objectives nearby. In sum, while all the law of precaution imposes obligations of conduct, rather than of result, for the defending powers these obligations are also mitigated, and it seems to be sufficient that meaningful attempts are made to respect the prescriptions.

In other words, while responsibility for the protection of the civilian population against the effects of hostilities is shouldered by both the attacker and the defender, 'its weight is not equally distributed'.[119]

[118] The obligation to issue warning was intensely debated during the 2014 Israeli offensive in Gaza denominated 'Protective Edge', on occasion of the diffusion, by press agencies, of images documenting the use of the so-called 'roof-knocking' technique, a term used by the Israel Defense Forces (IDF) to describe its practice of dropping non-explosive or low-yield devices on the roofs of targeted civilian homes in the Palestinian territories as a prior warning of imminent bombing attacks to give the inhabitants time to flee the attack. The practice was employed by the IDF during the 2008–2009 Gaza War, Operation Pillar of Defense in 2012 and Operation Protective Edge in 2014 to target the homes of police officers or Hamas political or military leaders. See I Mann, 'Roof Knocking and the Problem of Talking with Bombs', at www.justsecurity.org/31319/roof-knocking-problem-talking-bombs; and J Dill, 'Israel's Use of Law and Warnings in Gaza', at opiniojuris.org/2014/07/30/guest-post-israels-use-law-warnings-gaza.

[119] Sassoli, Bouvier and Quintin (n 32) 28.

2.2. The IHL Prohibitions of Indiscriminate and Disproportionate Attacks under Additional Protocol I

As already shown when discussing the principle of distinction, the protection of the civilian population constitutes one of the oldest layers of evolution of the law of armed conflict in general, and of IHL specifically, and resulted in the consolidation of the prohibition against indiscriminate warfare.

An early codification of the prohibition against indiscriminate warfare is contained in Hague Regulations, Article 25 of which stated:

> The attack or bombardment, by whatever means, of towns, villages, dwellings, or buildings which are undefended is prohibited.[120]

At this stage, however, the provision outlawed indiscriminate warfare only partially, in case of direct attacks on undefended civilian objects. The prohibition today is much more complex, stringent and detailed. The prohibition embodies one of the most important implications of the principle of 'limited warfare' underlying the basic moral assumptions and aspirations of IHL.

The treaty of reference is again the 1977 AP I to 1949 the Geneva Convention.

Before looking at the relevant articles, it is important to note that the provisions of the Additional Protocols codify pre-existing customary law, because the principle of distinction belongs to the oldest fundamental maxims of established customs of war.[121]

Therefore, from this point of view, the customary nature of these rules renders the dividing line between international and non-international armed conflict less incisive, as it does not radically impact the general applicability of the principles of targeting and of the prohibition of indiscriminate means and methods of warfare.

Article 51(4) of AP I states:

> Indiscriminate attacks are prohibited. Indiscriminate attacks are:
> (a) those which are not directed at a specific military objective;
> (b) those which employ a method or means of combat which cannot be directed at a specific military objective; or
> (c) those which employ a method or means of combat the effects of which cannot be limited as required by this Protocol; and consequently, in each such case, are of a nature to strike military objectives and civilians or civilian objects without distinction.

Article 51(4)(a) prohibits attacks which are not directed at specific military objectives, singularly identified. Those in charge of the attacking decision must be sure that the target to be attacked constitutes a military objective according

[120] Hague Convention IV.
[121] See Kinsella (n 37) 53–81.

to the IHL parameters discussed so far. Furthermore, the attacking forces must restrict their action as much as possible to the specific objectives to be targeted, avoiding at all (when possible), or in any event minimising any incidental impact on protected objects and/or protected persons in the vicinity of the target. The attacking force must use all available intelligence, and means of gathering detailed information, to make sure of directing the attack against a genuine military objective. The intelligence must also clarify whether the destruction or neutralisation of the object against which firing or bombardment is being directed is essential.[122] This aspect leads to the clear prohibition of blind fire into portions of territories controlled by the adversary. Substantially, firing without reliable information about the objective, and therefore without a clear idea of the nature of the objective, is absolutely prohibited. Similarly, the old practice of releasing bombs over enemy territory after missing the original objective, common during World War II, constitute a paradigmatic example of indiscriminate warfare under this provision.[123]

Article 51(a) clearly implies that the attacker must direct fire specifically at the identified military objectives. In attacking a certain target, group of targets, objective or compound of objectives (provided these are military objectives), attackers may intend to spread fire power over a certain area, either as 'harassing fire' against the enemy's lines and deployment areas, or as 'interdiction fire' against certain strategic points. Such kinds of 'barrage fire' covering a certain area, and thus bringing a high risk of lack of distinction, 'must fulfil the basic condition of being directed against specific objectives. Accordingly, in these cases the ground area identified as a target must be definable as a military objective *in its entirety*', ie the whole ground sector targeted must in itself and as a whole fulfil the requirements of Article 52 AP I to be considered a military objective. 'It is prohibited to combine clearly separate objectives in one single target area covered by an overall "area bombardment", since such untargeted fire exposes the civilian population and civilian goods in the intermediate zones to risk.'[124] In other words, not only do direct attacks on civilians or civilian objects remain absolutely prohibited, as consequence of the principle of distinction, but also attacks indistinctly targeting areas with a number of lawful targets, included of high military values, as well as protected persons or objects interspersed among the former.

Article 51(4)(b) AP I also prohibits attacks by means or methods of combat which cannot be directed against specific military objectives. The aim of the drafters of the provision was to introduce a legal restraint to limit the use of remotely controlled weapons with extremely low target accuracy, as long-range missiles

[122] Sandoz, Swinarski and Zimmermann (n 63) 151–55.

[123] See R Schaffer, 'American Military Ethics in World War II: The Bombing of German Civilians' (1980) 67 *The Journal of American History* 318; H Boog (ed), *The Strategic Air War in Europe and the War in the West and East Asia, 1943–1944/5, Vol VII, Germany and the Second World War* (Oxford University Press, 2006).

[124] Oeter (n 69) 201.

with rudimentary guidance systems. It has to be recalled that IHL establishes a clear distinction between indiscriminate use of weapons, on the one hand, and use of inherently indiscriminate weapons, on the other. Every weapon, in other words, even a high-precision one, can be employed indiscriminately (eg a semi-automatic rifle can be employed to explode a hail of bullets on combatants escaping a combat area on a road full of civilians, or in a street market, knowingly hitting the combatants and the surrounding civilians alike). Inherently indiscriminate weapons (such as poisonous gases or chemical weapons), conversely, are indiscriminate 'in nature', and as such they are prohibited at all times since their technical characteristics impede any possible use in compliance with the targeting principles.[125]

The specific importance of letter (b) of this provision, therefore, is that of outlawing indiscriminate uses of non-inherently indiscriminate means of warfare.

From this point of view, the ballistics notion of 'circular error probable' (CEP) assumes crucial importance. The CEP is a measure of a weapon system's precision. It is defined as the radius of a circle, centred on the aimpoint, whose boundary is expected to include the landing points of 50 per cent of the rounds. It is, in other words, a median error radius. It is suggested that is not exactly an average, but rather a predictive tool for military planners based on empirical evidence and testing of the weapon.[126] When considering weapons with very high CEP, it is inevitable to conclude that their structural characteristics, together with their operative uses in combat zones in which military objectives are not isolated or distant from civilian areas, leave little doubt as to the indiscriminate nature of an attack carried out through them. The impossibility of targeting a single military objective accurately, in fact, makes it impossible to distinguish between those and civilian objects. Such an attack would therefore be inherently unable to fulfil the requirements of distinction.[127] This profile of unlawfulness, however, remains bound to the circumstances on the ground. It is not possible to rule out in principle, in fact, that solely lawful targets might be located within the CEP radius of a specific weapon, in a specific combat situation.

Historically, an example about means of warfare used as to fall under this prohibition is the German use of V-2 missiles against British cities in World War II.[128] The V-2 was the world's first long-range guided ballistic missile. The missile, powered by a liquid-propellant rocket engine, was developed in Germany as a 'vengeance weapon', assigned to attack allied cities as retaliation for the Allied bombings against German cities. It is commonly recognised that their early guidance systems were

[125] A Cassese, 'The Prohibition of Indiscriminate Means of Warfare' in A Cassese, P Gaeta and S Zappalà (eds), *The Human Dimension of International Law: Selected Papers of Antonio Cassese* (Oxford University Press, 2008).

[126] Ducheine, Schmitt and Osinga (n 1) 91.

[127] For the controversies in relation to the identification of a precise spatial standard, and translation of this standard into a parameter indicating the commission of indiscriminate attacks, see in particular the discussion of the ICTY *Gotovina et al* case (see ch 3, section 3.3.2 of this volume).

[128] See JM Spaight, *Bombing Vindicated* (Geoffrey Bles, 1944) 214–17.

too rudimentary to hit specific targets. More recently, examples of weapons that fall within this category include a series of missiles launched on Iraqi and Iranian cities during the Gulf War, or the Iraqi 'Scud' missiles attacks on Israel in the Kuwait War of 1991.[129] The Scud missile was a direct product of captured wartime German missile technology. Soviet experiments with the V-2 missile led to a 10-year development effort that culminated in the R-11M missile, a liquid-fuelled missile that rode on a tracked transporter erector launcher. The R-11M could launch a conventional high-explosive warhead from up to 167 miles and a heavier nuclear warhead from up to 93 miles. The R-11M was eventually nicknamed 'Scud' by NATO, and as subsequent versions emerged became known as Scud-A. The Scud-A's short range made it a tactical nuclear delivery system. The missile had poor accuracy, with a circular error probability of 1.8 miles. This, and the primitive state of early nuclear weapons development, meant that the Scud, despite being a tactical system, was still equipped with large warheads with a yield of 20–100 kilotons.[130]

However, aside from these clear cases, the extent and reach of the prohibition in Article 51(4)(b) remain subject to controversy. There is continuing debate on what types of attacks are unequivocally prohibited by this provision. Night attacks without adequate targeting equipment seem to fall into this category, as well bombing raids from extremely high altitudes which render the target accuracy too low. Surely, 'blind' weapons such as long-range missiles with inaccurate guidance systems, or minefields laid without mandatory precautions, can be deemed to breach this article.[131]

The provision does not refer only to means of attack which cannot be directed at specific military objectives, mentioning explicitly also methods of attack characterised by the same inability to discriminate. Tactics or orders encompassing tactics which cannot be directed at specific military objectives, therefore, fall entirely under the scope of the prohibition. This could be the case, in urban warfare, of orders intimating to subordinates to shoot at everyone crossing a certain area, or to destroy everything in a certain location that attackers are seeking to gain control of.

The most controversial part of the definition of indiscriminate attacks is that enshrined in Article 51(4)(c), which prohibits attacks employing means or methods whose effects cannot be limited to the military objective. The article also specifies that the prohibition applies to attacks which employ a method or means of combat the effects of which cannot be limited as required by the Protocol itself requires. This refers to a complex set of limitations on the means and methods of warfare, eg the rules on the protection of the environment (Articles 35(3) and 55(1) AP I),[132]

[129] See ND White and H McCoubrey, 'International Law and the Use of Force in the Gulf' (1991) 10 *International Relations* 347.

[130] See K Mizokami, Why the World Still Fears the Scud Missile *The National Interest*, 10 June 2017.

[131] Oeter (n 69) 201.

[132] Respectively stating 'It is prohibited to employ methods or means of warfare which are intended, or may be expected, to cause widespread, long-term and severe damage to the natural environment', and 'Care shall be taken in warfare to protect the natural environment against widespread, long-term

the prohibition of attacks on works and installations containing dangerous forces (Article 56)[133] and the principle of proportionality.

As can be inferred by this cross-reference, the article is particularly concerned with those weapons whose effects are spread over a wide area, such as white phosphorous bombs or other variants of incendiary weapons. Paradigmatically, weapons whose impact is spread over a wide area is constituted by cluster bombs. The use of such weapons in densely populated regions will necessarily trigger disproportionate effects. Accordingly, their use in these contexts must be considered prohibited under Article 51(4)(c).

It is reported that during the Gulf War more than 61,000 cluster bombs were dropped by coalition forces on Iraq and Kuwait;[134] while during the Kosovo Air Campaign, NATO forces allegedly dropped around 1,400 cluster bombs, each containing 147–202 sub-munitions, on targets in Serbia and Kosovo.[135] Cluster

and severe damage. This protection includes a prohibition of the use of methods or means of warfare which are intended or may be expected to cause such damage to the natural environment and thereby to prejudice the health or survival of the population'.

[133] 'Works or installations containing dangerous forces, namely dams, dykes and nuclear electrical generating stations, shall not be made the object of attack, even where these objects are military objectives, if such attack may cause the release of dangerous forces and consequent severe losses among the civilian population. Other military objectives located at or in the vicinity of these works or installations shall not be made the object of attack if such attack may cause the release of dangerous forces from the works or installations and consequent severe losses among the civilian population. 2. The special protection against attack provided by paragraph 1 shall cease: (a) for a dam or a dyke only if it is used for other than its normal function and in regular, significant and direct support of military operations and if such attack is the only feasible way to terminate such support; (b) for a nuclear electrical generating station only if it provides electric power in regular, significant and direct support of military operations and if such attack is the only feasible way to terminate such support; (c) for other military objectives located at or in the vicinity of these works or installations only if they are used in regular, significant and direct support of military operations and if such attack is the only feasible way to terminate such support.

3. In all cases, the civilian population and individual civilians shall remain entitled to all the protection accorded them by international law, including the protection of the precautionary measures provided for in Article 57. If the protection ceases and any of the works, installations or military objectives mentioned in paragraph 1 is attacked, all practical precautions shall be taken to avoid the release of the dangerous forces. 4. It is prohibited to make any of the works, installations or military objectives mentioned in paragraph 1 the object of reprisals. 5. The Parties to the conflict shall endeavour to avoid locating any military objectives in the vicinity of the works or installations mentioned in paragraph 1. Nevertheless, installations erected for the sole purpose of defending the protected works or installations from attack are permissible and shall not themselves be made the object of attack, provided that they are not used in hostilities except for defensive actions necessary to respond to attacks against the protected works or installations and that their armament is limited to weapons capable only of repelling hostile action against the protected works or installations. 6. The High Contracting Parties and the Parties to the conflict are urged to conclude further agreements among themselves to provide additional protection for objects containing dangerous forces. 7. In order to facilitate the identification of the objects protected by this article, the Parties to the conflict may mark them with a special sign consisting of a group of three bright orange circles placed on the same axis, as specified in Article 16 of Annex I to this Protocol of Amended Annex. The absence of such marking in no way relieves any Party to the conflict of its obligations under this Article'.

[134] Human Rights Watch, *Cluster Munitions a Foreseeable Hazard in Iraq* (2003) 5 ff.

[135] Human Rights Watch, *Ticking Time Bombs: NATO's Use of Cluster Munitions in Yugoslavia*, 1 June 1999, at https://www.hrw.org/report/1999/06/01/ticking-time-bombs/natos-use-cluster-munitions-yugoslavia.

bombs were also extensively used during the Israeli offensive in Lebanon in summer 2006.[136]

Some authors have long argued that it is possible to direct cluster munitions at lawful military objectives; according to these scholars, therefore, cluster bombs should not be considered inherently indiscriminate, and will rather be the specific employment of the weapon that can be, or not be, indiscriminate.[137] In contrast, the ICRC, together with the Cluster Munition Coalition, has for several years called upon states to end the use of cluster munitions, even against any military objective when located in populated areas.[138] The debate is today mostly outdated by the adoption of the Convention on Cluster Munitions,[139] ratified by 111 states and signed by 12 additional ones, which prohibits use, production, transfer and stockpiling of cluster munitions. In addition, it establishes a framework for cooperation and assistance to ensure adequate assistance to survivors and their communities, clearance of contaminated areas, risk reduction education and destruction of stockpiles.

It is still subject to debate whether particular conventional rules which refer only to specific categories of weapons are exhaustive, or whether the general rule of Article 51(4)(c) AP I should be seen 'as providing an overriding legal framework which imposes a final limit'.[140] There seems to be no reason to exclude that all the weapons not covered by specific conventional prohibitions, and which present the same characteristics described in Article 51(4)(c), should be considered prohibited under the latter article itself.

Correlatively, there is an ongoing debate in the literature as to whether, in connection with these prohibitions, a positive obligation to use precision ammunitions – when available – can be postulated. Many answer negatively, although many authors recognise that there are moral and legal grounds to do so. As affirmed by Kolb and Hyde, one may ask

> to what extent a belligerent that possesses precision munitions, which if used will limit the number of collateral civilian losses, is bound to use such arms either exclusively or in preference to any non-precision weapons in their arsenal. IHL has not yet developed to the point where it assesses the legality each attack according to the technical capabilities of the weapons available to the belligerent. There is always a danger when exceptions are introduced into the principle of equality of belligerents. However, a belligerent which possesses precision weapons should carefully consider the possibility

[136] Human Rights Watch, *Flooding South Lebanon. Israel's Use of Cluster Munitions in Lebanon in July and August 2006*, 16 February 2008, at www.hrw.org/report/2008/02/16/flooding-south-lebanon/israels-use-cluster-munitions-lebanon-july-and-august-2006.

[137] TJ Herthel, 'On the Chopping Block: Cluster Munitions and the Law of War' (2001) 51 *Air Force Law Review* 229; APV Rogers, *Law on the Battlefield*, 2nd edn (Manchester University Press, 2004).

[138] ICRC, *Cluster munitions: ICRC calls for urgent international action*, Official Statement of 6 November 2006, at https://reliefweb.int/report/serbia/cluster-munitions-icrc-calls-urgent-international-action.

[139] *Convention on Cluster Munitions*, adopted 30 May 2008, entered into force 1 August 2010, UNTS 2688. See also www.clusterconvention.org.

[140] Oeter (n 69) 203.

> of using such weapons in all situations where collateral damages can be expected, even if such weapons are more costly.[141]

On this point, it is self-evident that armies of developed and powerful countries have at their disposal higher technical abilities and advanced technological weaponry to comply with these prohibitions, in comparison to many non-state armed groups or also to less developed countries' armies. As a consequence, interpreters be prompted to attribute a higher burden of 'discrimination' on those forces which can afford high-precision weapons and tactics, with the risk of reducing the expectations of compliance in respect to those armed forces fighting with less advanced or more rudimental means of warfare, somehow eroding the principle of equality of the belligerents. On the other hand, a material consideration of the inequality of the means at disposal of unequally organised and inequivalently equipped forces appears opportune. The relative and contextual character of the obligations descending from the regulations of means and methods of warfare, in fact, renders this consideration possible, if not necessary. Requiring higher standards of good practices to highly organised, well-trained and well-supplied armies of powerful countries, in fact, does not collide with the principle of equality of the belligerents, and does not imply that less organised and poorly supplied forces can escape the obligations discussed in these paragraphs.

As can be seen from the provision analysed, however, the prohibition of indiscriminate attacks – from the acquisition of information, through the different stages of the targeting process, until the choice of the means and methods to be used in the combat – requires a continuous vigilance and lasting effort to limit every aspect and effect of the attacks to accurately identified lawful targets.

The definition of what constitutes an indiscriminate attack in Article 51(4) of AP I is complemented and supplemented by paragraph 5 of the same article, which describes two examples of indiscriminate attacks.

It states:

> Among others, the following types of attacks are to be considered as indiscriminate:
>
> (a) an attack by bombardment by any methods or means which treats as a single military objective a number of clearly separated and distinct military objectives located in a city, town, village or other area containing a similar concentration of civilians or civilian objects;

Article 51(5)(a) spells out the prohibition of so-called 'area bombardment', that is, bombardments combining a number of clearly separate and distinct military objectives located in a built-up area and treating them as one single military objective. As seen above, these bombardments became common in World War II and were also claimed to be lawful by the Allied Powers.[142] At the same time, they

[141] Kolb and Hyde (n 24) 137.

[142] See Spaight (n 128) 272; M Greenspan, *The Modern Law of Land Warfare* (University of California Press, 1959) 336; H Blix, 'Area Bombardment: Rules and Reasons' (1978) 49 *British Yearbook of International Law* 36.

had given rise to harsh debate and firm public criticism in many countries. Given the long debate between states as to the existence of a customary prohibition of area bombardment, Article 51(5)(a) AP I constitutes a significant advancement, since it makes clear that such practices are prohibited.[143] As for the wording of the article, the expression 'bombardment by any method or means' means – according to the IRCR commentary – all attacks by fire-arms or projectiles (except for direct fire of small arms) and the use of any type of projectile. The paragraph caused much debate during the diplomatic conference. In particular, the expression 'clearly separated and distinct', referring to the military objectives, triggered long discussions. The working group elaborating the proposal had given to the committee called to approve the text (Committee III) a choice between various formulations, such as 'widely separated', 'distinct', or – alternatively – an option for the introduction of a final phrase stating 'unless the objectives are too close together to be capable of being attacked separately'. These options were not voted on, and the working group was requested to formulate a proposal that could have gathered general approval. The new draft, approved without amendments, forms the present text of the paragraph.

It is interesting to note that the ICRC had previously proposed – as for the location of the military objectives – the expression 'at some distance from each other'. The phrase was not added as it was feared that it could have encouraged area bombardment, since the attacking forces – considering the weapons available and the circumstances – could have used their margin of appreciation as to whether the individual objectives were to be considered too close.[144] Both the size of the area in which military objectives are located, as well as the distance separating one objective from another, however, are objective and measurable. In case of doubt, the general rule of respect for the civilian population must always be observed. This means that when the distance separating two or more military objectives is sufficient for the attacking forces, taking into account the means available, to strike them separately, the rule has to be fully applied. There are, however, cases in which there is an limited acceptability of area bombardment. For example, this is the case of open areas which are not built up, or have little-to-none civilian presence (eg a remote military stronghold in a desert, or on a mountain), in which attacks may be launched against the whole area if it has been established that only enemy armed forces are located therein. However, in this case it will be the norms prohibiting excessive damage of the natural environment making the difference, and determining whether or not the attack is lawful. Conversely, in a town, village or any other area where the concentration of protected persons/objects and lawful targets is similar, the military objectives may only be attacked separately, avoiding civilian losses or damage.[145]

Generally, bombardment of an area remains limitedly permissible, and subject to stringent requirements, only when the whole area can be considered

[143] Oeter (n 69) 204.
[144] See Sandoz, Swinarski and Zimmermann (n 63) 624.
[145] ibid.

in its entirety a military objective (eg 'a passage or ground sector the whole of which constitutes a military objective, or where several military objectives are so intermingled that they are practically inseparable and thus can only be attacked together').[146] In such cases, proportionality becomes crucial to determine the legality of the attack itself.

Relatedly, the second typology of attacks identified by Article 51(5) as example, among other types, of prohibited indiscriminate attacks, is:

> (b) an attack which may be expected to cause incidental loss of civilian life, injury to civilians, damage to civilian objects, or a combination thereof, which would be excessive in relation to the concrete and direct military advantage anticipated.

In this analysis, as in the majority of the scholarship, this prohibited attack is identified as being disproportionate. In relation to this prohibition all the considerations about the problems of implementation and effectiveness of proportionality already formulated entirely apply.[147]

What needs to be clarified, therefore, is why disproportionate attacks are considered by AP I as a specific type of indiscriminate attacks. In addition, it must be analysed what (if any) bearing the answer to this question has on the way the scholarship construes the relationships between the targeting principle.

The systematic framing of disproportionate attacks as sub-category of indiscriminate attacks is, in fact, dense of crucial implications, and raises the question about what singularly identifies disproportionate attacks from other indiscriminate attacks.

Under the lens of this analysis is the notion of incidentality of the civilian harm, key for identifying the distinctive features of disproportionate attacks, and consequently for identifying the line separating the operative spheres of the principle of distinction and the principle of proportionality, respectively.

Incidentality, in other words, in the perspective of this work, constitutes a systematic cornerstone to interpret the law of targeting as a coherent set of coordinated prescriptions.[148]

2.3. Interplay of the Targeting Principles: In Search of Systematic Coherence

As it has emerged, the prevention of direct attacks on civilians and civilian objects is ensured by the principle of distinction, and its implications.[149] At the same time, it is the prevention of indiscriminate and disproportionate conduct

[146] Oeter (n 69) 204.
[147] See section 2.1.2 above.
[148] See section 2.5 below.
[149] Art 48 AP I.

of hostilities,[150] rather than simply that of direct attacks on protected persons or objects, that requires the cumulative and consecutive respect for the principles governing targeting, in their logical and operation sequence, and coordination.

Only a coordinated reading of the prescriptions analysed so far, in fact, can concur to delineate a systematic of the interplays between the targeting principles.

As it has been shown, the respect for the principle of distinction is paramount in imposing a careful consideration about whether or not an object to be attacked meets the requirements to be considered a lawful target.[151] Mandatory precautions must accompany this first assessment, which must be exercised to the maximum extent possible in ways allowing to avoid entirely incidental civilian harm.[152]

Even when distinction, with its corollary precautions, is fully respected, this absolutely necessary compliance remains insufficient for the legality of the attack, because another assessment is required: it is the difficult balancing operation required by the principle of proportionality,[153] once again complemented by the necessary precautions to avoid or minimise incidental civilian harm.[154] This means that even attacks directed at military objectives precisely identified, and attacked with lawful means or methods, may be nonetheless unlawful if the prognostic evaluation about incidental civilian harm reveals the risk of its 'excessiveness' in comparison to the concrete and direct military advantage anticipated. If those in charge of attacking decisions, when proceeding to carry out this assessment, can foresee this excessiveness, the attack has to be cancelled.

Lastly, under relevant precautions, when changing unforeseen circumstances on the battlefield revert to a proportionality assessment already carried out, even an attack lawfully decided has to be cancelled if it becomes apparent it may cause excessive incidental civilian harm.[155]

The nexus between precautions and distinction, on the one hand, and precautions and proportionality, on the other, is thus a nexus of simultaneity and cumulative respect. As Boutruche underlined,

> the norms on precautions in IHL, notably with regard to norms on precautions in attack, are conceived as a prerequisite for Parties to a conflict to respect other principles and rules on the conduct of hostilities. Indeed, they form part of a coherent regime of norms aimed at the protection of civilians and civilian objects. … However, continues the author '[t]he intrinsic link between the requirement of precautionary measures to be taken and other IHL norms does not mean that the former obligations disappear behind the latter. Such obligations on precautions exist as such and autonomously in addition to the other rules on the conduct of hostilities, placing additional legal constraints when launching an attack.[156]

[150] Art 51(5) AP I.
[151] Arts 52(2) and 43 AP I.
[152] Arts 57(2)(a)(i) and 57(4) AP I.
[153] Arts 51(5)(b) and 57(2)(a)(iii) AP I.
[154] Art 57(2)(a)(ii) AP I.
[155] Art 57(2)(b) AP I.
[156] Boutruche (n 114).

Precautions are thus complementary to distinction, both in terms of target identification and verification of the status of the target, and in the choice of means and methods of attacks, in terms of feasible avoidance of any incidental civilian harm. Precautions are also complementary to proportionality, since they overlap definitionally and materially in the assessment required, in terms of minimisation of an incidental civilian harm which cannot be feasibly avoided.

The nexus between distinction and proportionality, instead, is differently configured. It is a nexus of cumulative, but *consecutive* respect. The obligations to identify a lawful target accurately and singularly, methodically guided by the relevant precautions, need to be fully respected in order to proceed to the subsequent step (both in logical and operational terms) of assessing the foreseeable incidental consequences of the attack. Proportionality, in other words, cannot be considered operative *in concomitance* with distinction, and remains inoperative unless all the relevant obligations to distinguish always and to the maximum extent possible between lawful targets and protected persons and objects have been fulfilled.

2.4. Reframing the Distinction–Proportionality Nexus

It is therefore of the utmost importance to understand how the dividing line between the operative spheres of distinction and proportionality can be drawn under IHL.

Unpacking the systematic implications of the relationship between distinction and proportionality appears indispensable to counter emerging misuses of IHL postulating, paradoxically, the possibility of 'proportionate' attacks on civilians and civilian objects.[157] This tendency can be neatly observed in military discourses construing attacks aimed at destroying residential towers in their entirety as fully compliant with IHL, even when only one segment of this kind of buildings among many is used for some military purpose.[158] In these attacks, the foreseen or even virtually certain preponderant impact on civilians is often misconstrued as 'collateral damage', and as such lawful under IHL. The fundamental dispositive of these misconstructions is the overextension of proportionality into the domain of distinction, with dramatic consequences for the preservation of the civilian protection purposes of IHL. When proportionality is purported to be a principle legalising any entity of civilian harm insofar as the military advantage anticipated justifies this harm, in fact, the systematic coordination of the targeting principles

[157] See more extensively L Daniele, 'Incidentality of the civilian harm in international humanitarian law and its *Contra Legem* antonyms in recent discourses on the laws of war' (2024) 29 *Journal of Conflict and Security Law* 21.

[158] See section 2.4.1.4 below.

(distinction and proportionality in particular) is fundamentally altered, with high military advantages allegedly bringing under the compass of IHL non-incidental civilian killing. This frequent misinterpretation unveils the need for a reconceptualisation of the systematic coordination between the two principles.

As synthesised in an elucidative dialogue imagined by Frederic Mègret, it is true that under IHL it might be 'worse to kill one civilian deliberately than a hundred *collaterally*'.[159] But what does 'collaterally' mean under *ius in bello*? And under what circumstances (if any) is it possible to legally qualify the anticipated killing of 100 civilians as collateral? In order to answer these questions, the attention has to turn to the IHL concept of incidentality, as systematised in the various prescriptions analysed so far.

2.4.1. Incidentality of the Civilian Harm as Systematic Cornerstone of the Law of Targeting

The collateral killing of civilians and the collateral destruction of civilian objects is a *topos* of IHL analyses,[160] converging on the notion of 'collateral damage', and the problem of its legal admissibility. It is important to note that IHL never uses this concept, opting instead for the notion of 'incidentality' of the civilian harm. Only a civilian harm that can be qualified as incidental, in fact, can be balanced by a high military advantages under proportionality assessments.

Literature dedicating specific attention to the incidental harm side of proportionality assessments affirmed that the requirement that the civilian harm must be incidental means that 'it must occur in the course of an attack directed against a military objective'.[161] This temporal understanding of incidentality appears somehow reductionist and sidesteps efforts to illuminate the normative importance of this qualifier. That civilian harm occurs in the course of an attack directed solely against a military objective, in fact, is only sufficient to exclude that the attack was intentionally directed against civilians or civilian objects *as such*. Even in these cases, however, whether the civilian harm expected (even if not pursued) could be considered incidental cannot be assumed and must be the outcome of a circumstantial evaluation by attackers, to be legally assessed by IHL interpreters.

[159] F Megret, 'Overhead Amidst the Bombs' *Opinio Juris*, 28 May 2021, at opiniojuris.org/2021/05/28/overheard-amidst-the-bombs, emphasis added.

[160] See WH von Heinegg, 'Considerations of Necessity under Article 57(2)(a)(ii), (c) and (3) and Proportionality under Article 51(5)(b) and Article 57(2)(b) of Additional Protocol I: Is There Room for an Integrated Approach' in C Kreß and R Lawless (eds), *Necessity and Proportionality in International Peace and Security Law* *Oxford University Press, 2020); A Haque, 'A Theory of Jus in Bello Proportionality' in JD Ohlin, L May and C Finkelstein (eds), *Weighing Lives in War* (Oxford University Press, 2017) 188–216; see also, considering the understanding of 'collateral damage' as adhered to by the United States Department of Defense, Rosén (n 87).

[161] Gillard (n 94) para 21, at 8.

This assessment is imposed and guided by the text of the treaty norms using the qualifier, 'incidental', when interpreted as Article 31 of the Vienna Convention on the Law of Treaties demands ('in accordance with the ordinary meaning to be given to the terms of the treaty in their context and in the light of its object and purpose').[162] The notion is central, in the fact, for the correct understanding of several provisions of AP I, and of the law of targeting at large as a coherent system of coordinated prescriptions.

2.4.2. Incidentality between Distinction and Proportionality

As we have already seen, Article 51(5)(b) prohibits attacks 'which may be expected to cause *incidental* loss of civilian life, injury to civilians, damage to civilian objects, or a combination thereof, which would be excessive in relation to the concrete and direct military advantage anticipated'.[163]

Even if the preferred qualification to designate these prohibited attacks in the literature is that of 'disproportionate' attacks (since they involve an excessive, disproportionate incidental impact on civilians and/or civilian objects), the systematic collocation of this norm in the Protocol deserves consideration.

The Protocol clearly lists these attacks as *species* and *genus*, among other types, of indiscriminate attacks, that is attacks that a) are not directed at a specific military objective; b) employ a method or means of combat which cannot be directed at a specific military objective; or c) employ a method or means of combat the effects of which cannot be limited as required by the Protocol. These indiscriminate attacks (hereinafter 'indiscriminate attacks *stricto sensu*', to distinguish them from disproportionate attacks) are unlawful because they violate the basic rule of distinction, since they either: a) are not directed at a legitimate target singularly identified; or b) employ means or methods of attack that cannot distinguish between lawful and prohibited targets; or c) employ means or methods that, due to their effects, will impact lawful and prohibited targets without distinction.

It is important to note that differentiating lack of distinction and lack of proportionality in attacks on the basis of the attackers' intent/lack of intent to strike civilians is highly problematic. In at least the latter two cases of indiscriminate attacks *stricto sensu*, in fact, attackers can claim that their aim was to strike the lawful targets, and that they did not *intend* to strike the protected persons or objects. Importantly, IHL does not admit this claim, because in each of these cases the attacks are all considered 'of a nature to strike military objectives and civilians or civilian objects without distinction'.[164] The nature of the means or methods employed, therefore, is enough to render irrelevant that attackers only had the

[162] Art 31, Vienna Convention on the Law of Treaties, approved 23 May 1969, entered into force on 27 January 1980, UNTS 1155.
[163] Art 51(5)(b) AP I.
[164] Art 51(4)(c) AP I.

primary purpose of striking lawful objectives, so long as they also accepted, by using those means or methods, to strike protected persons and objects alongside the lawful targets, indistinctly.

Subsequently, in the same article, the Protocol lists examples of indiscriminate attacks. Before disproportionate attacks, Article 51(5) qualifies as indiscriminate those attacks that 'by any methods or means … treat[s] as a single military objective a number of clearly separated and distinct military objectives located in a city, town, village or other area containing a similar concentration of civilians or civilian objects'. This prohibition of area bombardments, as it has been shown, confirms that even when several lawful targets are the objective of the attack, it remains absolutely prohibited to target them through means or methods that involve the indistinct shelling of high concentrations of protected objects or persons interspersed among the lawful targets.

The AP I article then proceeds to outlaw disproportionate attacks as second example of indiscriminate attacks. This choice clearly indicates that the drafters intended the prohibition of disproportionate attacks as a sub-category of the prohibition of indiscriminate attacks. Thus, when attackers anticipate an excessive incidental impact of the attack on civilians or civilian objects, and launch the attack nonetheless, this action assumes an analogous anti-juridical value of those prohibited because not actually 'discriminating' between civilians and combatants, and between civilian objects and military objectives, ultimately blurring the legal red lines separating lawful targets from protected persons and objects.

What needs to be clarified, therefore, is how these attacks differ from other indiscriminate attacks *stricto sensu* in blurring these red lines. Incidentality plays a crucial and overlooked role in this differentiation, as indispensable conceptual tool for identifying the distinctive features of disproportionate attacks.

2.4.3. Incidentality and Precautions

The qualifier 'incidental' is employed three more times in Article 57 AP I, in relation to precautions in attack.

Article 57(2)(a)(iii) prescribes that those who plan or decide upon attacks must 'take all feasible precautions in the choice of means and methods of attack with a view to *avoiding*, and in any event to *minimizing*, *incidental* loss of civilian life, injury to civilians and damage to civilian objects'.[165] Avoiding incidental civilian harm, therefore, irrespective of its entity, must per se be a parameter guiding the tactical choices of attacking forces within the limits of feasibility. Since this feasibility is contextual, it is admitted that avoiding entirely this incidental harm might not be possible in specific circumstances. Also in these cases, however, the norm

[165] Art 57(2)(a)(iii) AP I.

imposes the duty to do everything feasible in order to minimise incidental civilian harm. Importantly, this paragraph of Article 57 AP I prescinds entirely from mentioning the 'excessiveness' of the harm, reinforcing the view that incidental civilian harm, per se, even if not absolutely prohibited, remains *relatively prohibited whenever avoidable.*

Article 57(2)(a)(iii) proceeds to prescribe that attackers must '*refrain* from deciding to launch *any* attack which may be expected to cause' excessive incidental civilian harm. This section, reproducing the wording of Article 51(5)(b), reinforces the prohibition of disproportionate attacks and confers to these attacks an additional layer of illegality, as attacks involving an unlawful failure to take imperative precautions. Article 57(2)(b) also restates the prohibition against disproportionate attacks a third time, in reference to targeting as dynamic process in changing circumstances (subject to variations while the attacking procedures unfold) asserting that 'an attack shall be cancelled or suspended if it becomes apparent' that 'the attack may be expected to cause' excessive incidental civilian harm.

Incidental civilian harm emerges thus as fundamental building block of the targeting prescriptions of AP I.

Combining the aforementioned provisions, incidental civilian harm is to be avoided or minimised even when not excessive. When it is excessive, this incidental harm is unlawful whenever expectable, but also reason not to plan any attack which may be expected to cause it. It is also reason to impose the cancellation of an attack already decided when the excessiveness (expectable) emerges from the changing circumstances ruling at the time when the attack is being launched.

Importantly, every time the Protocol uses the term 'incidental', it does so in reference to each of the four typologies of civilian harm to be avoided/minimised by taking all the feasible precautions, and to be carefully weighed in proportionality assessments, that is: incidental loss of civilian life; injury to civilians; damage to civilian objects; or a combination of these (which cannot alter the incidentality). Incidentality, in other words, categorically qualifies all the types of civilian harm potentially lawful under AP I, without any reference to admissible civilian harm in absence of this qualifier.[166]

2.4.4. A Serious Misconception: 'Balancing' Incidentality with Military Advantage

Crucially, the qualification of incidental, as analysed, can only be interpreted as related to the consequences of the attacks, and as identifying a quality of one or more expectable consequences of the attacks themselves among several.

[166] To confirm this, it can be noted that in Art 85 – the only article mentioning excessive civilian harm in absence of this stated qualifier – explicit reference is made, twice, to the need to interpret it 'as defined in Article 57, paragraph 2 (a)(iii)'; that is, as incidental civilian harm.

Proportionality and precautions require in fact a prognostic evaluation of what the attack *may be expected* to cause. Then, within this range of expectable consequences of the attacks, attackers need firstly to discern between incidental and non-incidental consequences.

Attackers, in other words, before proceeding to other assessments, must make sure that the expected civilian harm falls in the former camp, that of the *side* consequences of the attack.

Only after this step it is possible to weight the expected civilian harm and the military advantage against each other, in the balancing operation required under proportionality.

The United States Department of Defense Law of War Manual, among many others, accepts the importance and function of incidentality of the civilian harm as a qualifier of what can be weighed in proportionality assessment. However, in several passages, the Manual states that proportionality creates obligations to refrain from 'attacks in which the expected harm *incidental to such attacks* would be excessive'.[167] This formulation, unlike that of IHL, declines incidentality as related to 'attacks', generically indicated, and thus potentially encompassing everything these attacks include. In other words, the formulation risks transforming incidentality in a quality that attackers can attribute to the harm relative to *everything* that they can expect as result of the attacks, included, problematically, the anticipated military advantage.

Interpreted in this way, rather than as objective qualifier identifying one of more *consequences* of the attack expectable, in relation and in contrast to other consequences pursued, incidentality becomes an elastic variable dependent on the extent of the anticipated military advantage from the point of view of the attackers.

The common, and serious misconception deriving from such formulation, in other words, is to consider that incidentality of the civilian harm can *in itself* be counter-balanced by the military advantage anticipated. The importance of a concrete and direct military advantage anticipated, however, under IHL has no bearing on any possible counterbalancing of the incidentality of the civilian harm, but only on deciding its excessiveness/non-excessiveness ('which would be excessive in relation to'), and under the previous condition that the harm potentially admissible remains an incidental one.

The fact that this prognostic evaluation is an *ex ante* assessment does not mean that incidentality can be a subjective determination. A reasonably well-informed agent[168] can, and actually must foresee, as a minimum, the consequences of an action in their objective measure, before assigning any value to them.

[167] See eg US Department of Defence Laws of War Manual, 2015 (updated 2023), 2.4.1.2, 61.

[168] 'It is suggested that the determination of relative values must be that of the "*reasonable military commander*". Although there will be room for argument in close cases, there will be many cases where reasonable military commanders will agree that the injury to noncombatants or the damage to civilian objects was clearly disproportionate to the military advantage gained' (Office of the Prosecutor, International Criminal Tribunal for the Former Yugoslavia (ICTY): Final Report to the Prosecutor by the Committee Established to Review the NATO Bombing Campaign Against the Federal Republic

Leaving any interplay with other international legal frameworks aside for the sake of argument, an example can clarify this point. Imagine a police agent who has accepted the risk to hit five bystanders, ultimately killing them, in order to kill an armed criminal behind the bystanders who is threatening to shoot the agent. In no legal system in the world could the police agent legally claim that he anticipated the five deaths to be an incidental consequence of the (assumingly) legitimate killing of the armed suspect, given – for example – the latter's dangerousness and previous criminal records. This could only change, and the claim be legally admissible, if the criminal had eg a grenade in his hands, and his *imminent* action would certainly kill at least as many police officers and bystanders as the persons that are likely to be killed by the police agent targeting the criminal. However, in this second scenario, it is not the subjective value assigned by the agent to the killing of the criminal, due to its arguable dangerousness, that renders the death of five bystanders potentially incidental, but the objective circumstance that the criminal is on the point of throwing a grenade at a higher number of persons than will be killed.

Transposing this factual scenario in a combat situation, there could be no IHL 'incidentality' attributable, for example, to the expected killing of five civilians based on the high value assigned by the commander to the lawful killing of a single, high-ranked combatant. Doing so would disrupt proportionality entirely. The outcome of killing five civilians could only be seen as incidental under a rather objective circumstance; for example, that the combatant targeted is on the point of firing, with a rocket propelled-grenade shoulder launcher, at the attacking commander and his unit of five soldiers crossing an area with many civilians around them. In this case, the pursued consequence of the attack is still that of eliminating a single combatant, but the foreseen consequence of killing five civilians might, to an extent, be considered incidental compared to the consequence of saving the whole unit and all the civilians around them from an imminent, non-speculative, deadly attack. Only under similar stringent circumstances can a specific type of (non-speculative) advantage, encompassing the protection of civilians, contribute to designating the foreseeable loss of life of civilians as an incidental consequence of an attack, as required by IHL.

An entirely different state of affairs, instead, would follow the assertion that a high military advantage proportionately legalises commensurably high civilian killing or destruction of civilian objects, conveniently eclipsing the insistence of AP I on the incidentality of the latter.

of Yugoslavia, para 50); 'The basic obligation to spare civilians and civilian objects as much as possible must guide the attacking party when considering the proportionality of an attack. In determining whether an attack was proportionate it is necessary to examine whether a *reasonably well-informed* person in the circumstances of the actual perpetrator, making reasonable use of the information available to him or her, could have expected excessive civilian casualties to result from the attack' (ICTY, *Prosecutor v Galić*, IT-98-29-T, Judgment and Opinion, 2003, para 58).

Should the military advantage anticipated be unduly 'displaced' from its systematic collocation, and interpreted as value counterbalancing incidentality, rather than the entity of the incidental civilian harm itself, it would dissolve an essential legal qualifier of one of the two values to be balanced against each other, modifying the balancing operation itself, as a whole, and ultimately altering its pivotal function in determining how the scales of IHL stand between humanity and military necessity. This is exactly what interpreters do when proposing that high military advantages 'legalise' under IHL varied degrees of non-incidental civilian harm. This misinterpretation might be, and actually is, useful to aggressive military powers, but is not one of IHL making.

2.4.5. Multi-Component Objects, *Pars Pro Toto* Determinations of Military Objectives and the 'Synecdoches' Capsizing Incidentality

Within the spectrum of legal problems arising in relation to the meaning and function of incidentality under AP I, and relevant customary obligations, multi-component objects and simultaneous civilian and military uses of their various components pose specific challenges. In particular, the challenges arise from military uses of one or few units of such objects (such as an apartment), within a building structure composed by numerous similar units (such as a residential tower), each usable in entirely separate manner from the one used militarily.

It is well known that the determination of military objectives under IHL is not categorical and rather circumstantial, depending on the two tests required by Article 52 AP I. The provision also makes clear that attacks should be '*strictly* limited' to objectives fulfilling this two-pronged test. Military objectives, accordingly, are only those objects which by their nature, location, purpose or use make an effective contribution to military action. In addition, their total or *partial* destruction, capture or neutralisation, in the circumstances ruling at the time, must offer a definite military advantage. This leads normally protected objects to lose their immunity from attacks when, for example, they are used by enemy forces to position themselves inside and launch attacks therefrom. This loss of immunity remains crucial to avoid fighters using protected objects to shield themselves from attacks, which would inevitably descend from an absolute and categorical immunity. However, the loss of immunity is subject to stringent requirements, with Article 52(3) imposing that in case of doubt whether an object which is normally dedicated to civilian purposes is being used to make an effective contribution to military action, it shall be presumed not to be so used.[169] This circumstantial

[169] States, including state parties to AP I, have objected against this presumption, and its customary standing, claiming that only significant measures of doubt trigger the applicability of the presumption itself. However, the drafting history of the provision demonstrates that the intent of the drafters was

determination of the status (civilian or military) of objects, limited by the presumption of civilian status in case of doubts, therefore leaves open the problem of the identification of the physical boundaries of military objectives fulfilling the tests of Article 52 AP I, but located in multi-component objects, such as multi-storey buildings. Frequently in urban warfare Article 52 tests will only be met by one or more segments among several multi-component objects. In the case of multi-storey buildings, for example, it might well be that only one level, or even one flat among dozens, or hundreds, is a military objective under IHL.

Laws of war scholarship in recent years has confronted this issue on several occasions. Most notably, the International Law Association Study Group on the Conduct of Hostilities in the 21st Century discussed the point in its 2016 Final Report, which stated that

> the majority of the SG took the position that if a given floor of a building can be attacked, this does not mean that only that floor is a military objective and that the remaining parts of the building remain civilian objects. When looking at one individual object partly used for military purposes, for example a multi-story building when only the roof or *one apartment* is used for military purposes, today's prevailing understanding of the notion of military objective is that once an object is used in such a way as to fulfil the definition of military objective, the entire object becomes a lawful target.[170]

This majority view is problematic. Its reasoning is understandable in cases of functionally inseparable objects, such as bridges, where attacks limited to component parts, for example a pier, would not achieve any definite military advantage without neutralising the unitary function of the object (unitary function is also what contributes effectively to the military actions of the enemy under Article 52 AP I).

The same reasoning can instead lead to troubling results in cases of functionally separate components of complex objects whose different, separate units can be used by civilians and fighters simultaneously. The Study Group, in fact, implies that no matter how many functionally separate components, levels or flats a residential object might be made of, and no matter how many of its segments continue to serve an entirely and exclusively civilian purpose, the military use of one of them will suffice to 'militarise' the object in its entirety.

The Group concurrently affirms that in this status determination of multi-component objects in case of simultaneous uses, quantitative considerations about how many components of the object are used for military and how many for civilian purposes are irrelevant, indicating that 'for the purpose of identifying whether the object fulfills [in its entirety] the definition of military objective

to limit the loss of immunity when Art 52 tests can be considered fulfilled with a degree of confidence near to certainty. See Bothe, Partsch and Solf (n 75) 358.

[170] ILA Study Group on the Conduct of Hostilities in the 21st Century, 'The Conduct of Hostilities and International Humanitarian Law: Challenges of 21st Century Warfare' (2017) 93 *International Law Studies* 334.

it is irrelevant whether such use amounts to more than 50%'.[171] Whether the status of military objective of the complex structure as a whole can be determined on the basis of secondary military uses of a small, largely minoritarian part of the object, for example five per cent or two per cent of the entire structure, with 95 per cent or 98 per cent of it remaining solely used for civilian purposes, it is not considered. However, the example provided by the group (a multi-storey residential building with just one apartment used militarily) seems to point in this direction. Legally, the two-pronged test of Article 52 is thus projected from the component part or parts of the object fulfilling the test itself, to all its other parts not actually satisfying any of the requirements to be considered a military objective. This includes – as explicitly affirmed by the group – projection of the military objective status from one single apartment on one level of a multi storey building, to all the other levels, each of which contains many apartments, and consequently to all the other apartments in the whole tower building.

The view under scrutiny entails therefore a significant *fictio iuris*, exponentially extended to each functionally separate component of the object that is not a military objective, raising some doubts in terms of compatibility with a provision explicitly affirming in its first sentence that attacks 'shall be limited limited *strictly* to military objectives'.

Authors analysing the implications of these legal issues have contended that, when one flat in a residential tower meets the criteria of a military objective, the 'use of that flat most likely involves relying on electricity, water, or other utility supplies running through the building'. Consequently, it was proposed that it would be

> highly likely that at least some of these shared spaces and services will likewise meet those criteria, at least in certain circumstances. Treating the lobby, the elevator shaft, the hallway, the water pipes, and the electricity cables all as distinct objects for these purposes overlooks the fact that they are merely constituent parts of a larger whole, that is the building in its entirety.[172]

This suggestion underlines the structural connections between separate segments of multi-component objects, trying to highlight their unity. Ultimately, however, under this view the connective elements between apartments become vectors of the same expansive and permissive projection of the military objective tests (under Article 52 AP I) to the many civilian component parts of the larger whole that are only crossed by these connective structural elements, without any impact on their function, nor potential or effective use. A family home on the ground floor of a residential tower, in other words, cannot become an integral part of a military objective because the same electricity cable is used in a flat 15 floors above by a

[171] ibid, 336.

[172] A Sari, 'Israeli Attacks on Gaza's Tower Blocks' *Articles of War*, 17 May 2021, at lieber.westpoint.edu/israeli-attacks-gazas-tower-blocks.

member of an armed group (eg to jam the military communications of an army), let alone the 14 floors separating the two housing units and all the apartments therein.

For these reasons, the ILA Study Group, conscious of the problematic implications of this conception ('whether an object qualifies in whole or in part as a military objective has clear implications for the prohibition of indiscriminate attacks'),[173] makes clear that, despite some disagreement, the majority of the scholars involved reaffirmed that damage to all the other component parts of the object identified as military in its entirety, and obviously foreseeable injury or loss of life between the civilians therein, remain to be factored into proportionality and precautions assessments, which could per se impose that an attack not be launched against the object whenever the civilian harm expected is excessive in comparison to the concrete and direct military advantage anticipated.

The *fictiones iuris* under this view become two, because firstly it is substantially simulated that the all the civilian components of the object that are not military objectives are part of a unique, bigger military objective including them. Subsequently, it is pretended that the harm to all these parts of the objects can remain a supposedly incidental civilian harm to be evaluated under proportionality, even when this harm would obviously be an entirely non-incidental one, at least in all cases in which only one unit of a residential tower among dozens or hundreds is used militarily, whereas the overwhelming majority of the other functionally separate units of the building that will be damaged or destroyed are, factually and legally, civilian objects. This second *fictio* concerning incidentality of the civilian harm in these cases, however, ensures the preservation of an ultimate normative lifeline indispensable to protect the non-military components of the object, such as housing units, and the families potentially therein.

Absent this essential preservation of the applicability of precautions and proportionality assessments, and the need to factor in damage to civilian segments of multi-component objects, the quality of military objective would behave 'virally', spreading from a single unit and 'infecting' hundreds of surrounding walls, living rooms, kitchens, bedrooms, floors and residential buildings as a whole, at this point destroyable in their entirety, de facto neutralising both the prohibitions of indiscriminate and disproportionate attacks.

An elucidative example of the troubling results enabled by the interpretation proposed by the ILA Study Group can be found in the views arriving at the extreme of hypothesising a sort of 'military objectification' not only of all the civilian units structurally surrounding the one used militarily in this kind

[173] ILA Study Group (n 170) 335.

of objects, but also of all the civilians therein, subsumed by this exponentially expanding status of military objective. Authors have recently questioned, in fact, 'whether the civilian elements of the target – either the object itself or the civilians within it – are now *all* considered part of a legitimate military target, or whether they remain in the civilian category, such that proportionality analysis should be applied'.[174] Support for this view is then attributed to Hays Parks,[175] and to Henderson.[176] Henderson, on the other hand, underlining that under IHL an object is either civilian, or a military objective, *tertium non datur*, effectively affirms that 'when a civilian object meets the test for being a military objective then the civilian object itself does not form part of the collateral damage assessment'.[177] However, in this part of his work, the latter author discusses in general what civilian harm can be factored into proportionality assessments, with no mention of multi-component objects, nor of civilians therein, stating only that damage to objects meeting the tests of Article 52 AP I (thus destroyable as lawful military objectives) does not factor in proportionality assessments. As it has been explained, this cannot be the case of functionally separate and numerous segments of multi-component residential buildings exclusively used by civilians.

More recently, authors proposing this expansive reading of Article 52 AP I in case of multi-component objects, and insisting on the exclusion of damage to all their civilian parts from proportionality assessments,[178] have often cited an analysis of the incidental harm side of proportionality obligations, concluding that when a 'civilian object has become a military objective, there does not appear to be any legal basis for taking into account damage to the dual-use object in proportionality assessments'.[179]

The author of this analysis, however, makes clear in the same section that there is a preliminary question to be answered under the guidance of the principle of distinction, that is 'if a particular apartment in an apartment block has become a military objective by virtue of its use, but the other apartments in the block are not used in this manner, is the military objective just the single apartment or the entire block?'.[180] The analysis does not propose an answer to this question, as a question of distinction, and moves on to discuss what constitutes incidental civilian harm in attacks on dual-use objects continuing to serve

[174] A Cohen and G Zlotogorski, *Proportionality in International Humanitarian Law Consequences, Precautions, and Procedures* (Oxford University Press, 2021) 157.

[175] See WH Parks: 'Asymmetries and the Identification of Legitimate Military Objectives' in WH von Heinegg and V Epping, *International Humanitarian Law Facing New Challenges* (Springer, Berlin, 2017) 106–07.

[176] ibid.

[177] Henderson (n 2).

[178] See eg O Pomson, 'Proportionality and Civilian Use of a Military Objective' *Opinio Juris*, 24 June 2021, opiniojuris.org/2021/06/24/proportionality-and-civilian-use-of-a-military-objective.

[179] Gillard (n 94) 35.

[180] ibid.

simultaneous civilian functions, indicating that 'there is general agreement that civilian deaths and injury and damage to civilian objects expected to occur as a result of the impairment of the continuing civilian function must be included in proportionality assessments'.[181]

It seems therefore that several authors have been mobilised in support of an approximation, conflating dual-use objects (that is objects that can be either protected and immune from attacks, or lawful targets depending on their use) and multi-component objects (that is, objects composed of numerous and functionally separate units, each of which is a dual-use object and each of which needs to be legally viewed through the lenses of Article 52 AP I).

In the view of this analysis, the preliminary question about what constitutes a military objective cannot be answered by interpreting Article 52 AP I with a sequence of exponential *fictiones iuris*, projecting its tests 'virally', from one to unlimited numbers of functionally separate units of multi-component objects. Under the principle of distinction, this appears to infringe the prohibition of indiscriminate attacks, circumventing it by construing civilian houses in no way used for military purposes as component parts of military objectives.

In addition, after this circumvention by means of a legal fiction, the views criticised so far also propose to circumvent precaution and proportionality assessments related to the injuring or killing of civilians that may occur and the damage of civilian objects that *will* (certainly) occur by attacking the multi-component objects in their entirety to destroy them.

2.5. Recentralising Incidentality of the Civilian Harm as *Conditio Sine Qua Non* for Proportionality Assessments

As explained above, it is evident that, under Articles 51 and 57 AP I, when the civilian harm contemplated by attackers (to be avoided or minimised per se to the maximum extent feasible), does not possess this essential and legally required characteristic, if it is not an incidental consequence of the attack, it is simply not a type of civilian harm relevant to proportionality. It can be relevant, however, to assess compliance with distinction.

When the civilian harm foreseen is the prevalent result anticipated from the attack, in fact, be it civilian injury, loss of life, damage to civilian objects, or their combination, then it cannot be said that the attack was exclusively directed at singularly identified lawful targets, with means and methods the effects of which were intended to be limited, as AP I requires, to the targets themselves.

[181] ibid.

This conclusion is consistent with the systematic collocation of the prohibition of disproportionate attacks 'among other types' of indiscriminate attacks, that is, those ignoring the red lines IHL draws around protected persons and objects through the basic rule of distinction.

As has been affirmed, in fact, not only are direct attacks on civilians and civilian objects absolutely prohibited, but also those that would strike civilians and combatants, or civilian objects and military objectives, indistinctly.

But what does singularly identify disproportionate attacks from other types of indiscriminate attacks? In each of the prohibitions analysed, disproportion (ie excessiveness of the incidental civilian harm) traverses the legal red lines separating civilians from combatants only:

(1) *indirectly*, because civilians and civilian objects in these cases are not a *direct* target; in itself, however, this aspect does not sufficiently differentiate these attacks from other indiscriminate attacks, such as area bombardments, in which the direct targets are still military objectives, but the means or methods of the attack are such that they will inevitably impact these targets alongside agglomerations of protected objects or persons in densely populated areas. Therefore, disproportionate are those attacks that blur the mentioned red lines not only indirectly; but also
(2) *collaterally*, because they do not contemplate the shelling of high concentrations, let alone of masses, of protected persons and objects alongside the lawful target/s, but rather accept that a foreseeable *side* consequence of the attack will be excessive.

That a civilian harm is foreseen as collateral, therefore, is insufficient to assert its legality, identifying, on the contrary, just the precondition to determine whether proportionality assessments are legally actionable (and relevant).

When the foreseen impact of an attack on civilians ceases to be a side, incidental consequence thereof, and becomes its expected prevalent outcome, the violation has little to do with disproportionate attacks, because protected persons and objects (particularly in cases of virtually certain preponderant civilian harm) become joined to the lawful targets, falling entirely under the scope of the prohibition of indiscriminate attacks.

The misuse of proportionality *deprived of incidentality* to vindicate the legality of these attacks, in addition, becomes evidence of doctrines contemplating the possibility to strike the lawful target/s together with a number of protected persons and/or objects.

When the common misconceptions analysed construe entirely non-incidental civilian harm as proportionate, or even just as potentially proportionate, in other words, they disrupt the interplay between the prescriptions analysed. Only by respecting this interplay, instead, the excessiveness of the incidental civilian harm regains its decisive role, that is of outlawing even *side* consequences of attacks when they excessively affect protected persons and objects.

The necessary incidentality of the civilian harm expected, in this sense, is thus the *conditio sine qua non* to gain access to proportionality assessment under IHL.

This conclusion, in turn, triggers another decisive question: what does it mean that the civilian harm anticipated, to be considered under proportionality, must be a side, incidental, collateral expectable consequence of the attack?

2.6. The Interpretative Auxilium of *Mens Rea* Categories: Incidentality as a Threefold Dividing Line between Distinction and Proportionality

The provisions analysed all mention an incidental civilian harm which 'may be expected', on the one hand, and a concrete and direct military advantage 'anticipated', on the other, referring to the subjective standpoint of attackers and imposing to evaluate these factors, prospectively.

Relatedly, in addition to the prohibitions in Articles 51 and 57 AP I affirms that, when committed 'wilfully', launching an indiscriminate attack 'in the knowledge' that it 'will cause' excessive incidental civilian harm is a greave breach to the system of protections of the Geneva Conventions and the Additional Protocols.[182]

IHL treaties, however, did not establish international criminal liability for grave breaches, instead giving rise to the special obligations of the states parties to enact and enforce penal sanctions to prevent grave breaches in their domestic systems.[183] As a consequence, IHL notions offer limited help in disentangling knots such as how to discern what consequences of an attack can be said to be anticipated, or rather pursued, by attackers, or in what sense an anticipated consequence of the attack can be said to be a primary, or rather incidental/side consequence of the attack itself.

The fact that, per se, IHL leaves these legal problems unaddressed, however, does not mean that they cannot be addressed by interpreters. The domain of subjective approaches to an action and its foreseeable results is, in fact, typically a criminal law domain. At this point of the analysis, therefore, when facing questions about what it means to anticipate a primary or secondary consequence of an attack, it is necessary to refer to the interpretative auxilium of *mens rea* categories.

[182] Art 85(3)(b) AP I.

[183] See the debate on the 60 years of the grave breaches regime and its domestic implications in J.G Stewart (ed), 'The Grave Breaches Regime in the Geneva Conventions: a Reassessment Sixty Years On' (2009) 7 *Journal of International Criminal Justice* 653.

These categories allow, from the point of view of the attacker, the framing of incidentality as a necessary characteristic of the anticipated civilian harm of an attack in a threefold sense. Such a consequence will need to be anticipated as *incidental*:

(1) in relation to, and in contrast to, the main result of the attack *pursued*, from the volitional point of view;
(2) in relation to, and in contrast to, the main result of the attack *foreseeable*, from the cognitive/prognostic point of view of the representation of the consequences of the action; and
(3) in relation to, and in contrast to, the main result – of a military nature – of the attack *objectively*, from the material point of view, which needs as a minimum to be logically distinguishable and preponderant in comparison to the, secondary and indirect, impact on civilians and civilian objects.

Only under these three logical preconditions (volitional, prognostic and objective) can there be a legitimate 'collateral damage' to civilians under IHL. Incidentality is thus the legal key to access proportionality assessments, and an attack will be lawful when the civilian harm expected can be said to be incidental (that is secondary among the foreseen consequences of the attack), *plus* not excessive (in comparison to the concrete and direct military advantage anticipated).

Absent these conditions, debating proportionality appears a rather military-friendly fiction without legal bases, since if:

(a) the civilian harm is expected to be, from the objective point of view, the largely prevalent result of the attack in comparison, quantitatively, to a secondary impact on legitimate (included high value) military targets; plus
(b) the foreseeability of the main result of impact on civilians is so high as to be equivalent to certainty; then
(c) it can be said that this prevalent result of the attack on civilians is substantially pursued, for the simple reason that it is no more a 'collateral' one, and – in addition – it is expected with certainty by the attacking forces.

The prescription of reference in these cases, in other words, is the principle of distinction *alone*, and its violation *precludes to access* the logically subsequent step of assessing proportionality.

In this sense, the requirement of incidentality of the civilian harm cannot be reduced to an entirely subjective determination of the attackers. The objective identifiability of incidentality within the prognostic evaluation of the attackers is thus non-renounceable.

If, in fact, incidentality is deprived of its objective-material meaning, it becomes impossible to draw any line between main and side foreseen consequence of the attack. Following this conception, the only judgement imperatively valid on what is incidental and what is not between the consequences of an attack would be the one of the attacking forces themselves. Take the example of an attack certain to kill many more civilians than a single combatant targeted, eventually of very high rank, under no imminent threat to the life of as many persons. What if the attackers claim that the concrete and direct military advantage anticipated from the elimination of the high-value target was so high as to render this preponderant civilian loss of life 'proportionate'?

If incidentality is deprived of any objective consistence, collapsed into excessiveness/non-excessiveness of collateral damage, rather than framed as its premise, and reduced to an entirely subjective determination, such a claim would be enabled. Even more concerningly, by claiming that the many more civilians killed were an unfortunate, but inevitable and proportionate incidental consequence of the lawful attack, those in charge of the attacking decision would be also enabled to circumvent the prohibition of indiscriminate attacks, using the same claim even to target, for example, by aerial bombardment a large group of civilians as whole, with one or few high ranked combatants among them.

Through just one conceptual distortion, therefore, proportionality would become meaningless, and distinction would blur, morphing from absolute to relative prohibition, limited by the pursuit of high military advantages, in frontal collision with the structure, wording and purpose of Articles 51 and 57 AP I, and of customary IHL itself. In this way, interpreters not only renounce any possible meaning of incidentality, but rather interpretatively abolish it, at the antipode of what is required by the Vienna Convention on the Law of Treaties. Once abolished interpretatively, incidentality finds no way back in proportionality evaluations, transformed in a balancing operation between any measure of anticipated civilian harm and any value assigned to the anticipated military advantage.

The subsequent chapters will demonstrate how this interpretative eclipse of the IHL concept of incidental civilian harm intertwines with the existing deficiencies within the war crimes regime outlined in the Rome Statute of the ICC, resulting in the emergence of the accountability gap objects of this analysis.

The rule of proportionality, as a consequence of the misconceptions unveiled in this chapter, is increasingly mobilised in scholarly analyses, media and political debates depriving it of its essential premise, that is the necessary incidentality of the civilian harm to be considered proportional. Thus, the concept of collateral damage symmetrically expands beyond its legal limits, progressively overstretching the IHL inclination to admit limited margins of civilian harm. Ultimately, this overexpansion of proportionality disrupts the delicate balance between military necessity and civilian protection mandated by this legal framework. Moreover, the emphasis placed by interpreters on military necessity and the acceptance of non-incidental civilian harm as a permissible pave the way for the acceptance of pseudo-legal justifications by armed forces systematically killing masses of civilians and destroying entire cities during hostilities. As a consequence, hegemony on the alleged legality of non-incidental civilian harm consolidates not only in discourses on the laws of war, but also in the practice of armies. International criminal law should therefore intervene in countering this tendency, punishing at the very least the most egregious cases of indiscriminate and disproportionate attacks in situations under scrutiny of the ICC. At this point, however, the defects of the Rome Statute in relation to indiscriminate and disproportionate attacks become crucial, since the statutory regime governing these attacks equips the Office of the Persecutor with, at best, extremely blunt legal tools to successfully prosecute and punish their commission. As it will be shown, it is for these reasons, and in connection to the *mens rea* issues that will be examined, that indiscriminate and disproportionate attacks, unlike direct attacks on civilians, have never been tried in 20 years of ICC activities, until the recent developments in Ukraine and Palestine, despite their systematic commission in various armed conflicts.

While in the first years of the new millennium it was not predictable how the ICC jurisprudence would have confronted this issue, the persistence of this macroscopic accountability gap in relation to unlawful attacks in combat situations after 20 years suggests the need for critical reflection by scholars, practitioners, NGOs and diplomatic communities interested in preventing the killing of civilians in war, by whoever committed. In addition, the current shockwaves highlighting the fragility of the global peace and security architecture, unveiling new evidences of civilian victimisation in ongoing wars, coupled with the growing readiness to new wars amidst escalating geopolitical confrontations, indicate that addressing this gap has never been more urgent.

3

Indiscriminate and Disproportionate Attacks at the Origins of International Criminal Law: From Nuremberg to the ICTY

3.1. Indiscriminate Warfare at the Origins of International Criminal Law

As it has been shown in the previous chapter, international humanitarian law (IHL) does not provide directly for a regime of international criminal liability for the commission of grave breaches. Rather, the Geneva Conventions identified grave breaches as a particular category of violations: those considered so serious that state parties assumed, upon ratification, an obligation to enact domestic penal legislation to prevent their commission and punish those responsible. With this commitment, states also assumed the so called *aut dedere, aut iudicare* obligation, that is, the duty to prosecute or extradite the suspects of relevant serious violations. As a consequence, war crimes law has developed outside the boundaries of international humanitarian law treaties.

Even if the historical development of the laws of war offers many examples of tribunals established to punish certain excesses in the conduct of war,[1] the modern use of criminal law to punish violations of IHL had long been seen by the community of diplomats and international legal practitioners as a matter to be left to the initiative of states.

As explained by Darcy,[2] since the 1874 Brussels Conference adopting the Project of an International Declaration concerning the Laws and Customs of

[1] See TLH McCormack and GJ Simpson (eds), *The Law of War Crimes: National and International Approaches* (Kluwer Law International, 1997); T Meron, *War Crimes Law Comes of Age: Essays* (Oxford University Press, 1998); KJ Heller and GJ Simpson, *The Hidden Histories of War Crimes Trials* (Oxford University Press, 2013); Y Guo, 'The Grave Breaches Regime of the 1949 Geneva Conventions: Origins, Developments and Prospects' in M Bergsmo, C Wui Ling, S Tianying and Y Ping (eds), *Historical Origins of International Criminal Law* – Volume 3 (Torkel Opsahl Academic EPublisher, 2014) 343–88; E Greppi, 'The Evolution of Individual Criminal Responsibility under International Law' (1999) 81 *International Review of the Red Cross* 531.

[2] A Darcy, *Judges, Law and War* (Cambridge University Press, 2014) 265.

War, the delegates declined the invitation to prepare 'a general penal code for crimes'.[3] It was not until the end of World War I that momentum grew in the international community for international war crimes prosecutions. Being the first industrialised, 'total' war (in which all the states' infrastructures were involved in the war endeavours, transforming entire nations into a war-waging machineries), the war became of the deadliest conflicts in human history, with a civilian death toll estimated to be around 6.5 million.[4] Even excluding those who lost their lives due to war-related famine and disease, hundreds of thousands died as a consequence of military attacks and aerial bombardments of indiscriminate nature. In response to the large-scale attacks against civilians committed during the war, international political and legal circles increasingly advocated for international prosecutions in order to punish the most serious violations of the laws and customs of war.[5]

This led to the creation of the Commission on the Responsibility of the Authors of the War and on Enforcement of Penalties at the Paris Peace Conference of 1919. One of the figures attracting the attention of legal practitioners, diplomats and politicians engaged in this effort at the time was the German Kaiser. Wilhelm II was seen both by the victor powers and public opinion as bearing the main responsibility for the outbreak of the war, given the aggressive conduct of Germany. In addition to his chauvinistic rhetoric, historians have long debated his so-called 'Hun Speech', delivered in Bremerhaven, in July 1900, in which the Kaiser addressed German troops who were departing to suppress the Boxer rebellion in China, inciting them to inspire their conduct to the same ferocity which gave Attila's Huns their reputation.[6]

Furthermore, in a letter to Emperor Franz Joseph, Wilhelm explicitly referred to the necessity of adopting 'methods of terror' against the French civilian population, in opposition to humanitarian ones (as required by laws and customs of war), which would, in his view, have prolonged the war for years.[7]

[3] *Correspondence Respecting the Proposed Conference at Brussels on the Rules of Military Warfare*, United Kingdom Parliamentary Papers, Miscellaneous No 1 (1875) [c.-1128] 313–14.

[4] M Clodfelter, *Warfare and Armed Conflicts: a Statistical Reference to Casualties and Other Figures, 1500–2000* (McFarland, 2002).

[5] HH Bellot, 'War Crimes and War Criminals' (1916) 36 *Canadian Law Times* 754; CM Picciotto, 'War Crimes' (1916) 1 *International Law Notes* 69; CA Hereshoft Barlett, 'Liability for Official War Crimes' (1919) 35 *Law Quarterly Review*, 177.

[6] 'Should you encounter the enemy, he will be defeated! No quarter will be given! Prisoners will not be taken! Whoever falls into your hands is forfeited. Just as a thousand years ago the Huns under their King Attila made a name for themselves, one that even today makes them seem mighty in history and legend, may the name German be affirmed by you in such a way in China that no Chinese will ever again dare to look cross-eyed at a German', (cited in J Prenzler (ed), *Die Reden Kaiser Wilhelms II* [*The Speeches of Kaiser Wilhelm II*] (tr T Dunlap, 4 vols, Leipzig nd) vol 2, 209–12; unofficial version reprinted in M Gortemaker, *Deutschland im 19. Jahrhundert: Entwicklungslinien* [*Germany in the 19th Century: Paths in Development*] (Opladen, 1996) Schriftenreihe der Bundeszentrale für politische Bildung vol 274, 357).

[7] 'My soul is torn asunder, but everything must be put to fire and blood. The throats of men and women, children and the aged must be cut and not a tree nor a house left standing. With such methods of terror, which alone can strike so degenerate a people as the French, the war will finish before two months,

Even if distant from and opposed to the call for terrorist methods of warfare, the idea that 'sharp wars are brief', and thus 'the more vigorously [they] are pursued, the better it is for humanity',[8] was central in an important codification, conventionally regarded as decisive in the historical journey of modern law of war: the 1863 Lincoln's General Order No 100, which contains the 'Instructions for the Government of Armies of the United States in the Field', more commonly known as Lieber Code.[9] Reflecting some of the fundamental problems associated with western-centered approaches to legal history,[10] the Code is commonly identified as 'the first attempt to set down, in a single set of instructions for forces in the field, the laws and customs of war'.[11] Some authors describe it as the 'the final product of the eighteenth-century movement to humanize war through the application of reason', offering the 'greatest theoretical contribution to the modern law of war'.[12] Lieber, however, had no strong sympathy for the universalism of Enlightenment ideals,[13] nor for Kantian pacifist globalism.[14] Moreover, legal histories beyond the Global North offered numerous examples of greater protection of civilians in times of war.[15] Nonetheless, the Code was *sui generis* in its attempt

while if I use humanitarian methods it may be prolonged for years' (see C Bingham, *Men and Affairs* (Angus & Robertson, 1967), cited in D Steiger, 'Enforcing International Humanitarian Law Through Human Rights Bodies' in H Krieger (ed), *Inducing Compliance with International Humanitarian Law: Lessons from the African Great Lakes Region* (Cambridge University Press, 2015) 292).

[8] See JD Ohlin, 'Sharp Wars are Brief' in JD Ohlin, L May and C Finkelstein (eds), *Weighing Lives in War* (Oxford University Press, 2017) 58–76.

[9] See JF Witt, *Lincoln's Code, The Laws of War in American History* (Free Press, 2012); RS Hartigan, *Lieber's Code of the Law of War* (Transaction, 1983).

[10] See M Koskenniemi, 'Histories of International Law: Dealing with Eurocentrism' (2011) 19 *Rechtsgeschichte* 152; A Orford, *International Law and the Politics of History* (Cambridge University Press, 2021) 215–48; A Roberts, *Is International Law International?* (Oxford University Press, 2017) 209–29; A Anghie, *Imperialism, Sovereignty and the Making of International Law* (Cambridge University Press 2004) 17–64; N Tzouvala, 'The Spectre of Eurocentrism in International Legal History' (2021) 31 *Yale Journal of Law & the Humanities* 427.

[11] In these terms, *ex multiis*, C Greenwod, 'Historical Development and Legal Basis' in D Fleck (ed), *The Handbook of International Humanitarian Law*, 2nd edn (Oxford University Press, 2008) § 116, 21. Similarly, see eg M Howard, 'Constraints on Warfare' in M Howard, GJ Andreopoulos and MR Shulman (eds), *The Laws of War: Constraints on Warfare in the Western World* (Yale University Press 1994) 6.

[12] BM Carnahan, 'Lincoln, Lieber and the Laws of War: The Origins and Limits of the Principle of Military Necessity' (1998) 92 *American Journal of International Law* 212.

[13] See M Curti, 'Francis Lieber and Nationalism' (1941) 3 *Huntington Library Quarterly* 265.

[14] See E Kant, *Perpetual Peace. A Philosophical Project*, first published 1795, translated by M Campbell Smith, 3rd edn (George Allen &Unwin Ltd, 1917), and F Lieber, *Manual of Political Ethics*, 2nd edn, 2 vols (1890) 430, cited in S Moyn, *Humane. How the United States Abandoned Peace and Reinvented War* (Macmillan, 2021) 48–49.

[15] Relatedly, and as sample of the prevalence of Eurocentrism in international laws of war history, see A Gurmendi, 'Latin Lieber: Uncovering the History of the Treaty on the Regularisation of War' *Opinio Juris*, 10 June 2022, at opiniojuris.org/2022/06/10/latin-lieber-uncovering-the-history-of-the-treaty-on-the-regularisation-of-war, which illuminates the advanced humanitarian approach of some of the solutions identified in the 1820 treaty object of the enquiry, often overlooked by European scholarship (with a few exceptions; see J Basdevant, 'Deux conventions peu connues sur le droit de la guerre' (1914) 21 *Revue Générale de Droit International* 5. More extensively on this treaty, see A Valencia, *La humanización de la Guerra: Derecho Internacional Humanitario y*

to provide a comprehensive catalogue of rules spanning from martial law to the protection of persons, religion, arts and sciences; from the treatment of prisoners of war to deserters and spies; from battlefield booty to the parole.[16] At the same time, the Code was infused with the Clausewitzian views of its author,[17] resulting in a rather broad and all-encompassing declination of the concept of military necessity – defined as 'necessity of those measures which are indispensable for securing the ends of the war' – still far from the humanitarian constraints typical of the contemporary laws of war, and standing out as overarching protected good of the codification. The pre-eminence afforded to 'securing the ends of the war' is evidenced by several emblematic articles, such as those explicitly declaring starvation (included of the 'unarmed') a legitimate weapon of war,[18] or that the citizen of a hostile country was 'thus an enemy',[19] or that 'all direct destruction of life or limb of armed enemies, and of other persons whose destruction is incidentally unavoidable in the armed contests of the war'.[20]

In contrast to the emerging vision of European authors and jurists such as Dunant and Moynier, the Lieber Code 'shared almost nothing of the aspiration for humane war that Swiss gentlemen breathed deeply across the ocean at the same time'.[21] In Europe, these legal concepts took different historical trajectories. While for Lieber the notion of military necessity was open-ended, and functionally identified as set of means to secure the 'ends of the war', only five years later, the 1868 St Petersburg Declaration adopted a much narrower notion of military necessity, proclaiming that 'the only legitimate object which States should endeavour to accomplish during war is to weaken the military forces of the enemy'.[22] The structural difference between these two visions becomes even more apparent through

Conflicto Armado en Colombia (Ediciones Uniandes 1992) 25–37). See also, for the Islamic tradition, A Al-Dawoody, *The Islamic Law of War: Justifications and Regulations* (Palgrave Macmillan, 2011).

[16] *Instructions for the Government of Armies of the United States in the Field, General Order n.100* ('Lieber Code'), adopted 24 April 1863. See D Schindler and J Toman, *The Laws of Armed Conflicts* (Martinus Nihjoff, Publisher 1988) 3–23.

[17] Moyn (n 14) 163.

[18] 'War is not carried on by arms alone. It is lawful to starve the hostile belligerent, armed or unarmed, so that it leads to the speedier subjection of the enemy' (Art 17 Lieber Code; see n 9 above).

[19] 'The citizen or native of a hostile country is thus an enemy, as one of the constituents of the hostile state or nation, and as such is subjected to the hardships of the war' (Art 21 Lieber Code).

[20] 'Military necessity admits of all direct destruction of life or limb of armed enemies, and of other persons whose destruction is incidentally unavoidable in the armed contests of the war; it allows of the capturing of every armed enemy, and every enemy of importance to the hostile government, or of peculiar danger to the captor; it allows of all destruction of property, and obstruction of the ways and channels of traffic, travel, or communication, and of all withholding of sustenance or means of life from the enemy; of the appropriation of whatever an enemy's country affords necessary for the subsistence and safety of the army, and of such deception as does not involve the breaking of good faith either positively pledged, regarding agreements entered into during the war, or supposed by the modern law of war to exist. Men who take up arms against one another in public war do not cease on this account to be moral beings, responsible to one another and to God' (Art 15 Lieber Code).

[21] Moyn (n 14) 163.

[22] Declaration Renouncing the Use, in Time of War, of Explosive Projectiles Under 400 Grammes Weight, Saint Petersburg, 11 December 1868, av, at ihl-databases.icrc.org.

the 1874 Project of an International Declaration Concerning the Laws and Customs of War (Brussels Declaration).[23] The tensions between these opposing conceptions of what is permissible in wartime, and the affirmation of a circumscribed conception of military necessity, excluding civilian populations and infrastructures from it, consolidated in the final acts of the Hague Peace Conferences of 1899 and 1907.

The consolidation and hegemony of humanitarian conceptions of the limits of warfare, in opposition to those inspiring Lieber, created therefore the fertile cultural terrain in Europe for the emergence of the political will to punish indiscriminate warfare at the end of the Great War.

Legally, however, the crux of the 1919 Commission on the Responsibility of the Authors of the War and on Enforcement of Penalties was that – despite the demands for justice in public opinions – there was no existing international convention criminalising the waging of aggressive war, nor directly criminalising at the international level serious violations of the laws and customs of war codified at the time. It has to be noted that at this stage of the development of the international legal order, subjects of international law, in the positive law of the treaties as well as in the mindset of lawyers, diplomats and statesmen, were still the states themselves, not the individuals. Consistent with this theoretical framework is the fact that even the forms of accountability that were enshrined in the existing humanitarian conventions were still configured as implying state responsibility, giving rise to liability for compensation. For example, Article 3 of the Hague Convention (IV) Respecting the Laws and Customs of War on Land of 1907 ('Hague Convention IV') stated that 'A belligerent party which violates the provisions of the said Regulations shall, if the case demands, be liable to pay compensation. It shall be responsible for all acts committed by persons forming part of its armed forces.' For this reason the United States, during the proceedings of the 1919 Commission on the Responsibility of the Authors of the War and on Enforcement of Penalties, contended that there was 'no international statute or convention making a violation of the laws and customs of war – not to speak of the laws of principles of humanity – an international crime, affixing a punishment to it, and declaring the court which has jurisdiction over the offence'.[24] Nevertheless, the United States position remained minoritarian. The majority of the Commission, in light of the gravity of the violations of the laws and customs of war committed, recommended the opening of trials. The Commission, expressing disconcert for the brutality of indiscriminate means and methods of warfare, affirmed:

> In spite of the explicit regulations, of established customs, and of the clear dictates of humanity, Germany and her allies have piled outrage upon outrage. Additions are

[23] Project of an International Declaration concerning the Laws and Customs of War. Brussels, 27 August 1874, av, at ihl-databases.icrc.org.

[24] 'Annex II. Memorandum of Reservations Presented by the Representatives of the United States to the Report of the Commission on Responsibilities', 4 April 1919, reprinted in (1920) 14 *American Journal of International Law* 127, 145–46.

> daily and continually being made. … It is impossible to imagine a list of cases so diverse and so painful. Violations of the rights of combatants, of the rights of civilians, and of the rights of both, are multiplied in this list of the most cruel practices which primitive barbarism, aided by all the resources of modern science, could devise for the execution of a system of terrorism carefully planned and carried out to the end. Not even prisoners, or wounded, or women, or children have been respected by belligerents who deliberately sought to strike terror into every heart for the purpose of repressing all resistance. Murders and massacres, tortures, shields formed of living human beings, collective penalties, the arrest and execution of hostages, the requisitioning of services for military purposes, the arbitrary destruction of public and private property, the aerial bombardment of open towns without there being any regular siege, the destruction of merchant ships without previous visit and without any precautions for the safety of passengers and crew, the massacre of prisoners, attacks on hospital ships, the poisoning of springs and of wells, outrages and profanations without regard for religion or the honour of individuals, … the methodical and deliberate destruction of industries …, constitute the most striking list of crimes that has ever been drawn up to the eternal shame of those who committed them. The facts are established. They are numerous and so vouched for that they admit of no doubt and cry for justice.[25]

While, tragically, the world continues to witness similar conduction of hostilities more than 100 years later, the indiscriminate nature of German means and methods of warfare, in sum, was felt to be the unforgivable violation demanding punishment. The relevant trials, according to the Commission, should have taken place through the creation of an international 'High Tribunal'. Such tribunal, importantly, should have not been bound to respect immunity for heads of state. The Commission affirmed:

> If the immunity of a sovereign is claimed to extend beyond the limits above stated, it would involve laying down the principle that *the greatest outrages against the laws and customs of war and the laws of humanity, if proved against him, could in no circumstances be punished. Such a conclusion would shock the conscience of civilized mankind* [emphasis added][26]

[25] 'Commission on the Responsibility of the Authors of the War and on Enforcement of Penalties. Report Presented to the Preliminary Peace Conference', 29 March 1919, reprinted in (1920) 14 *American Journal of International Law*, 113–14.

[26] Adding 'In view of the grave charges which may be preferred against – to take one case, the ex-Kaiser – the vindication of the principles of the laws and customs of war and the laws of humanity which have been violated would be incomplete if he were not brought to trial and if other offenders less highly placed were punished. More-over, the trial of the offenders might be seriously prejudiced if they attempted and were able to plead the superior orders of a sovereign against whom no steps had been or were being taken. There is little doubt that the ex-Kaiser and others in high authority were cognizant of and could at least have mitigated the barbarities committed during the course of the war. A word from them would have brought about a different method in the action of their subordinates on land, at sea and in the air. We desire to say that civil and military authorities cannot be relieved from responsibility by the mere fact that a higher authority might have been convicted of the same offence. It will be for the court to decide whether a plea of superior orders is sufficient to acquit the person charged from responsibility' (ibid, 116–17).

The Treaty of Versailles, as a result, included Article 227, stating:

> The Allied and Associated Powers publicly arraign William II of Hohenzollern, formerly German Emperor, for a supreme offence against international morality and the sanctity of treaties. A special tribunal will be constituted to try the accused, thereby assuring him the guarantees essential to the right of defence …[27]

This article, still situated at the intersection between law and morality, and deriving the former from the latter, constitutes the first institutional attempt to create an international criminal tribunal to punish a head of state responsible of atrocity crimes. In legal history, this attempt assumes a distinct importance, as criminal justice had been one of the most self-contained domains of domestic legal systems, since the Enlightenment and the affirmation of the democratic theory of sovereignty, resulting in the contemporary conception of the right of states' to punish 'in the name of the people', to preserve the social contract. This first attempt to punish internationally projects for the first-time this *ius puniendi*, the right to punish, in the supranational sphere via treaty provision.

The ultimate outcome of this process, however, was very far from what was originally envisaged by the drafters of the Treaty. In an emblematic antecedent of the highly problematic issues of complementarity and domestic cooperation faced 90 years later by international criminal tribunals (still, today, entirely reliant on the collaboration of national law enforcement systems to give effect to their orders, first of all arrest warrants and surrender of the person charged with international crimes),[28] the Netherlands refused to extradite Wilhelm. As a result, national prosecutions came about in the form of the Leipzig trials,[29] based mostly on German law, with 'prosecutions of only a small group of perpetrators, light sentences, and limited references to international law, the precedential value of the judgments has been seen as weak'.[30]

3.1.1. The Axis's Indiscriminate 'Total War': War Crimes in Nuremberg

Far more effective and impactful on the successive development of international law, instead, was the institution and the judgments of the Nuremberg International Military Tribunal, and of the Tokyo International Military Tribunal

[27] Treaty of Versailles, 28 June 1919, *Avalon Project – Documents in Law, History, and Diplmacy*, at avalon.law.yale.edu/imt/partvii.asp.

[28] See ICC, *The Prosecutor v Omar Hassan Ahmad Al Bashir*, Decision on the Prosecutor's Request for a Finding of Non-Compliance Against the Republic of the Sudan, ICC-02/05-01/09-227, PTC II Decision, 9 March 2015.

[29] D Kramer, 'The First Wave of International War Crimes Trials: Istanbul and Leipzig' (2006) 14 *European Review* 441.

[30] Darcy (n 2).

for the Far East (IMTFE), after the genocidal mass atrocities of World War II shook the conscience of the world once again.

The idea of prosecuting major war criminals of the Axis after World War II may appear straightforward from the point of view of contemporary observers. In fact, it was at the time highly contentious. Indeed, in different countries vast sectors of the public opinion embraced the possibility of the extra-judicial execution of Nazi leaders most responsible for mass atrocities.[31] It was only thanks to the growing consent around the concept of sending a message of restored 'civilization' through accountability, particularly to future generations, that the calls for prosecution of those responsible for atrocity crimes prevailed.[32] Thus the four main Allies undertook, through the London Agreement of 1945, the creation of the International Military Tribunal (IMT) 'for the just and prompt trial and punishment of the major war criminals of the European Axis'.[33]

Article 6 of the IMT Charter defined the material jurisdiction of the Tribunal, stating:

> The following acts, or any of them, are crimes coming within the jurisdiction of the Tribunal for which there shall be individual responsibility:
>
> (a) Crimes Against Peace: namely, planning, preparation, initiation or waging of a war of aggression, or a war in violation of international treaties, agreements or assurances, or participation in a common plan or conspiracy for the accomplishment of any of the foregoing;
> (b) War Crimes: namely, violations of the laws or customs of war. Such violations shall include, but not be limited to, murder, ill-treatment or deportation to slave labor or for any other purpose of civilian population of or in occupied territory, murder or ill-treatment of prisoners of war or persons on the seas, killing of hostages, plunder of public or private property, wanton destruction of cities, towns or villages, or devastation not justified by military necessity;
> (c) Crimes Against Humanity: namely, murder, extermination, enslavement, deportation, and other inhumane acts committed against any civilian population, before or during the war; or persecutions on political, racial, or religious grounds in execution of or in connection with any crime within the jurisdiction of the Tribunal, whether or not in violation of the domestic law of the country where perpetrated.[34]

Specifically, the war crimes charges can be found in count three of the indictment. Count three showed how indiscriminate warfare, alongside a number of other

[31] See D Bloxham, 'From the International Military Tribunal to the Subsequent Nuremberg Proceedings: The American Confrontation with Nazi Criminality Revisited' (2013) 98 *History* 567; RH Jackson, 'Nuremberg in Retrospect: Legal Answer to International Lawlessness' in G Mettraux (ed), *Perspectives on the Nuremberg Trial* (Oxford University Press, 2008) 354–71.

[32] UN War Crimes Commission, *History of the United Nations War Crimes Commission and the Development of the Laws of War* (HM Stationery Office, 1948) 87–104.

[33] 'Charter of the International Military Tribunal' in *Nuremberg Trial Proceedings* vol I, 'The Avalon Project – Yale Law School', at avalon.law.yale.edu/imt/imtconst.asp.

[34] ibid.

atrocities, and few years after the Leipzig failure, returned at the roots of international criminal justice. The count stated:

> All the defendants, acting in concert with others, formulated and executed a Common Plan or Conspiracy to commit War Crimes as defined in Article 6 (b) of the Charter. This plan involved, among other things, the practice of 'total war' including methods of combat and of military occupation in direct conflict with the laws and customs of war, and the commission of crimes perpetrated on the field of battle during encounters with enemy armies, and against prisoners of war, and in occupied territories against the civilian population of such territories.[35]

The same count included several actions planned and executed on a large-scale and systematic basis, including murder and ill-treatment of the civilian population in occupied territories and on the high seas. Curiously, 'genocide' was only mentioned in this count, and was therefore considered as a typology of war crime.[36] The crimes charged, in addition, included deportation for slave labour and other criminal purposes, plunder of public and private property, exaction of collective penalties, forcing civilians of occupied territories to swear allegiance to the occupying power, and Germanisation and spoliation of occupied territories. Most of these offences were inserted in the frame of the wilful extermination of civilians orchestrated and carried out by the high authorities of the Reich. Of higher relevance to the subject matter of this book, as more closely related to IHL and to combat situations, was the count of 'wanton destruction of cities, towns and villages and devastation not justified by military necessity'.[37] This count, however, was not articulated with much legal analysis, but rather supported by listing episodes in which this conduct was committed, and concluding that:

> The defendants wantonly destroyed cities, towns, and villages and committed other acts of devastation without military justification or necessity. These acts violated Articles 46 and 50 of the Hague Regulations, 1907, the laws and customs of war, the general principles of criminal law as derived from the criminal laws of all civilized nations, the internal penal laws of the countries in which such crimes were committed, and Article 6 (b) of the Charter.[38]

Even the Judgment of the IMT did not provide much legal guidance on war crimes, simply enumerating a vast range of conducts, stemming from the deliberate

[35] 'Indictment – Count Three' in *Nuremberg Trial Proceedings* vol I (n 33).

[36] 'They conducted deliberate and systematic genocide, viz., the extermination of racial and national groups, against the civilian populations of certain occupied territories in order to destroy particular races and classes of people and national, racial, or religious groups, particularly Jews, Poles, and Gypsies and others' (ibid). See also JQ Barrett, 'Raphael Lemkin and "Genocide" at Nuremberg' in C Safferling and E Conze (eds), *The Genocide Convention Sixty Years after its Adoption* (TMC Asser Press, 2010).

[37] 'Indictment – Count Three' in *Nuremberg Trial Proceedings*, vol I (n 33).

[38] ibid.

killing of prisoners of war, to the techniques calculated to spread terror among civilians of the occupied territories. The judgment concluded that:

> The evidence relating to war crimes has been overwhelming, in its volume and its detail. It is impossible for this Judgment adequately to review it, or to record the mass of documentary and oral evidence that has been presented. The truth remains that war crimes were committed on a vast scale, never before seen in the history of war. They were perpetrated in all the countries occupied by Germany, and on the High Seas, and were attended by every conceivable circumstance of cruelty and horror. There can be no doubt that the majority of them arose from the Nazi conception of 'total war', with which the aggressive wars were waged. For in this conception of 'total war', the moral ideas underlying the conventions which seek to make war more humane are no longer regarded as having force or validity. Everything is made subordinate to the overmastering dictates of war. Rules, regulations, assurances and treaties all alike are of no moment, and so, freed from the restraining influence of international law, the aggressive war is conducted by the Nazi leaders in the most barbaric way. Accordingly, war crimes were committed when and wherever the Fuehrer and his close associates thought them to be advantageous. They were for the most part the result of cold and criminal calculation.[39]

Through this segment of the Nuremberg trials, the indiscriminate nature of the Axis warfare could be associated with the concept itself of war crimes, and thus identified as a supreme example of wartime brutality, immorality and systematic criminality. This marked an epochal milestone, commonly identified with the inception of the contemporary international criminal justice, since then inextricably linked to the idea of punishing indiscriminate warfare as inhumane, and against the minimum moral standards of the international community as whole.

3.1.2. Hiroshima, Nagasaki, and the *Einsatzgruppen* Case: At the Origins of Double Standards

While this epochal milestone was achieved, a knot of thorny contradictions emerged from Nuremberg, revolving around the nexus between war and law, victory and defeat, punishment and impunity, which has subsequently affected the development of international criminal law.

The legal contradictions originate from the same problematic nucleus discussed when introducing this work: the post-World War II international military tribunals represented an institutional result of the continuity between military victory and the assumption of law-making, justice-establishing powers. As it will be shown, the victory of the war and the unconditional surrender of Germany were identified as sources of these legislative and jurisdictional powers assumed by the Allies, with the victor powers projecting their will in the international legal realm.

[39] 'The Law Relating to War Crimes and Crimes Against Humanity' in *Judgement of the International Military Tribunal*, The Avalon Project – Yale Law School, at avalon.law.yale.edu/subject_menus/judcont.asp.

The nexus between the victory in war and the law-making process establishing these judicial institutions is indisputable. Indeed, the Nuremberg judges themselves acknowledged that the power to establish it arose from the victory of the war:

> The making of the Charter was the exercise of the sovereign legislative power by the countries to which the German Reich unconditionally surrendered; and the undoubted right of these countries to legislate for the occupied territories has been recognised by the civilised world.[40]

Victor powers, however, had no legislative power over Germany. The London Agreement and the Nuremberg International Military Tribunal (IMT) Charter, in fact, contained no reference to the interim government established in Germany (the Control Council) later in 1945, and the only law concerning the punishment of war criminals enacted by this interim government did not constitute the legal basis for the IMT. As affirmed by Radhabinod Pal, dissenting Indian judge of the IMTFE, the Tribunal could not 'behave in any manner which may justify the feeling that the setting up of the tribunal was only for the attainment of an objective which was essentially political, though cloaked by a juridical appearance'.[41]

Beyond the foundational legal issues related to the power to establish the international military tribunals, their most problematic implication was the open disregard of the principle of equality before the law, and of equal enforcement of sanctions. This profile constitutes possibly the most controversial aspect of the whole historical experience of the post-World War II international tribunals. Rather than punishing *actions* violating the laws and customs of war (first and foremost indiscriminate bombardments) irrespective of nationality of the perpetrators, the IMTs foundationally aimed at punishing unlawful conduct in war when committed by a particular category of *authors*, that is those belonging the Axis. The London Agreement, in fact, was an agreement for 'prosecution and punishment of the major war criminals of the European Axis'.[42]

If equality of treatment is a basic requirement to consider a prescription as 'law', in its modern meaning, and not as a mere *diktat* of the ruling powers, this is even more important in the domain of criminal law. Equality before penal laws, in fact, is not only crucial from the moral point of view, to assure fairness. It is also essential to maintain criminal justice systems within the boundaries of democracy and the rule of law. From the point of view of penal theory, indeed, it is an indispensable condition for every conception of the function of criminal punishment (whether it is general or special prevention, both in their positive or

[40] IMT, *Judgement, Law of the Charter*, The Avalon Project – Yale Law School, at avalon.law.yale.edu/imt/judlawch.asp.

[41] *International Military Tribunal for the Far East*, The Dissenting Opinion of the Member of India (Justice Pal) 1424.

[42] 'London Agreement of August 8th 1945', *The Avalon Project – Yale Law School*, at avalon.law.yale.edu/imt/imtcharticleasp.

negative declinations)[43] that the same offences are to be treated in the same way, no matter who realises them. Sanctions, in other words, need to be attached to type of offences, not to types of authors. On the contrary, a domestic penal system devoted to the punishment of specific categories of subjects would ultimately violate their human rights by exploiting those subjects as instruments, sanctioned for not possessing the identity and values around which, from time to time, dominant powers intend to shape the culture of a society. In this respect, criminal law becomes a powerful tool to protect dominant ideologies by normalising, separating or even eliminating those whose identity is judged as dangerous or abnormal. '*Criminal law of the author*', for these reasons, is one of the formulas convincingly used by continental penal theorists to summarise the set of features characterising the penal systems of authoritarian and totalitarian regimes (included, paradigmatically, the Nazi regime), aimed at the repression of particular categories of subjects and groups, labelled as enemies.[44]

It has been shown in the previous section that the violation of the established laws and customs of war was central in the conviction of the Nazi leaders for war crimes. In Nuremberg, the egregious violations of these laws by the Axis were represented by the judges as the horrifying, immoral product of a 'total war' doctrine inspiring barbarity and ignoring principles of humanity every time it was advantageous.

Simultaneously, however, one of the victor powers had just launched the most indiscriminate and lethal of all the bombardments of the war: the atomic bombing of Hiroshima and Nagasaki.[45]

The uranium bomb detonated over Hiroshima burnt and levelled around 70 per cent of the city's buildings, included medical facilities. The larger plutonium bomb shelling of Nagasaki three days later razed almost 6.7 square kilometres of the city. 280,000 citizens in Hiroshima and 240,000 in Nagasaki suffered indescribable agony. 140,000 in Hiroshima and 73,000 in Nagasaki died instantaneously or within a few months due to the combined injuries caused by blast wind, radiant heat and ionising radiation. The calculated death rates in 1946 is striking: the bomb killed almost 100 per cent of the population within 500 metres from the impact; 90 per cent of those within 750 metres; 70 per cent

[43] See F Jeßberger and J Geneuss (eds), *Why Punish Perpetrators of Mass Atrocities? Purposes of Punishment in International Criminal Law* (Cambridge University Press, 2020).

[44] These reflections have reacquired actuality and centrality on occasion of the intense European debate around the influential concept of 'Criminal Law of the Enemy' coined by Gunther Jakobs. See G Jakobs, 'Kriminalisierung im Vorfeld einer Rechtsgutsverletzung' (1985) 97 *Zeitschrift für die gesamte Strafrechtswissenschaft* 751; G Jakobs, 'Terroristen als Personem im Reicht? (2005) 117 Zeitschrift für die gesamte Strafrechtswissenschaft 839. L Ferrajoli, 'Il «diritto penale del nemico» e la dissoluzione del diritto penale' (2006) *Questione Giustizia – Verso un diritto penale del nemico?* (monographic number) 797 ff; D Salas, *La volonté de punir. Essai sur le populisme pénal* (Pluriel, 2005).

[45] JM Yamazaki, *Children of the Atomic Bomb: An American Physician's Memoir of Nagasaki, Hiroshima, and the Marshall Islands* (Duke University Press, 1995). See also www.aasc.ucla.edu/cab/index.html.

of those within 1,000 metres; 50 per cent of those within 1,250 to 1,500 metres; and 30 per cent of those within 2,000 metres.[46] The vast majority of those who lost their lives were civilians, including many children.

> In the proximity of ground zero, human bodies were burned and carbonized by 2000°C of heat ray. At the same time, they were squeezed by blast wind with speeds over 80 meters per second, and irradiated by more than 100 Gray (Gy) of gamma and neutron rays. It is possible to say that they were killed in three ways simultaneously …[47]

The exact mortality figures of the atomic bombs, according to many, will never be exactly determined since chaos and destruction rendered it impossible to reach an acceptably accurate victim count. It is not unlikely, therefore, that the number of victims and injured in Hiroshima and Nagasaki is still underestimated.[48] Furthermore, no single military attack in history has produced similar long-term consequences in terms of leukaemia, cancer and chronic diseases affecting generations of descendants of the survivors.[49]

Considering these features of the atomic attacks, it can be surely concluded that they were in blatant breach of the existing laws and customs of war, which – as it has been seen – were already a rather consolidated body of norms. The prohibition of damage and civilian harm not justified by military necessity, after all, had its origins in a declaration of 75 years before (the St Petersburg Declaration of 1868), and had been articulated and refined with vast international recognition in the Hague Conventions of 1899 and 1907.

In particular, the Regulations Respecting the Laws and Customs of War on Land annexed to the 1907 Hague Convention IV affirmed:

(1) 'The attack or bombardment, by whatever means, of towns, villages, dwellings, or buildings which are undefended is prohibited.'[50]
(2) 'The officer in command of an attacking force must, before commencing a bombardment, except in cases of assault, do all in his power to warn the authorities.'[51]
(3) 'In sieges and bombardments all necessary steps must be taken to spare, as far as possible, buildings dedicated to religion, art, science, or charitable purposes, historic monuments, hospitals, and places where the sick and

[46] See Report of the Manhattan Engineer District of the United States Army, *The Atomic Bombing of Hiroshima and Nagasaki*, 1946, at avalon.law.yale.edu/subject_menus/mpmenu.asp.
[47] M Tomonaga, 'Use of Atomic Bomb in War: Hiroshima and Nagasaki' in B Finh (ed), *Unspeakable Suffering. The Humanitarian Impact of Nuclear Weapons* (RCW, 2013).
[48] Yamazaki (n 45) 309.
[49] For a summary of the debate over these data, see D Listwa, *Hiroshima and Nagasaki: The Long Term Health Effects*, Columbia University of NY, Centre for Nuclear Studies, K=1 Project, at k1project.columbia.edu/news/hiroshima-and-nagasaki.
[50] Art 25 Hague Convention (IV) *Respecting the Laws and Customs of War on Land, and Its Annex: Regulations Concerning the Laws and Customs of War on Land* ('Hague Convention IV'), adopted 18 October 1907, entered into force 26 January 1910.
[51] ibid Art 26.

> wounded are collected, provided they are not being used at the time for military purposes.'[52]

These basic principles were embraced in the Nuremberg IMT Charter, and in the laws enacted by the Control Council in Germany. The war crimes section of both the IMT indictment and judgment, contained several references to the Hague Conventions.[53] These Conventions were so crucial as to lead the judges to consider part of the articles defining the material jurisdiction of the tribunal over war crimes as 'merely declaratory of the existing laws of war as expressed by the Hague Convention'.[54]

This is an important indication that the prohibitions of the existing laws and customs of war, consolidated in the Hague Conventions, were seen by the Allies' judges themselves as the main legal basis of the IMT war crimes jurisdiction. At the same time, these prohibitions were unconvincingly set aside when the subsequent Nuremberg Trials (under Control Council Law n 10)[55] had to deal with the issue of the atomic bombing.

When this section affirmed 'at the same time', or 'simultaneously', the meaning of the expressions has to be taken literally. The London Agreement, in fact, was subscribed on 8 August. The first bomb on Hiroshima was dropped just two days before, 6 August, and the second, on Nagasaki, just 24 hours after the signature of the agreement, on 9 August.

Juridically, the only case in the post-war Nuremberg trials in which judges dealt with the atomic attacks on the Japanese cities was the *Einsatzgruppen* Case (*The United States of America v Otto Ohlendorf, et al*).[56] This was the ninth of 12 trials (distinct from the IMT trial) for war crimes and crimes against humanity, which took place before courts established under the Allies Control Council Law n 10. The peculiarity of this trial was, as asserted in the Judgment, that

> never before have twenty-three men been brought into court to answer to the charge of destroying over one million of their fellow human beings. There have been other trials

[52] ibid Art 27.

[53] In the judgment, for example, it was stated 'Article 49 of the Hague Convention provides that an occupying power may levy a contribution of money from the occupied territory to pay for the needs of the army of occupation, and for the administration of the territory in question. Article 52 of the Hague Convention provides that an occupying power may make requisitions in kind only for the needs of the army of occupation, and that these requisitions shall be in proportion to the resources of the country. These Articles, together with Article 48, dealing with the expenditure of money collected in taxes, and Articles 53, 55 and 56, dealing with public property, make it clear that under the rules of war, the economy of an occupied country can only be required to bear the expenses of the occupation, and these should not be greater than, the economy of the country can reasonably be expected to bear.' (IMT, *Judgement: War Crimes and Crimes Against Humanity – Murder and Ill-treatment of Civilian Population*, at avalon.law.yale.edu/imt/judwarcr.asp#civilian.

[54] ibid.

[55] Control Council Law No 10, *Punishment of Persons Guilty of War Crimes, Crimes Against Peace and Crimes Against Humanity*, ICC Legal Tools Database, at www.legal-tools.org/doc/ffda62/pdf.

[56] *United States of America v Otto Ohlendorf et al*, Judgment, 8–9 April 1948, IV *Trials of War Criminals before the Nurenberg Military Tribunals* (1949) 1.

> imputing to administrators and officials' responsibility for mass murder, but in this case the defendants are not simply accused of planning or directing wholesale killings through channels. They are not charged with sitting in an office hundred and thousands of miles away from the slaughter. It is asserted with particularity that these men were in the field actively superintending, controlling, directing, and taking an active part in the bloody harvest.[57]

Crucially, the trial involved arguments related to the problem of the atomic bombs. The Nazi defendants, in fact, in an attempt to undermine their atrocity crimes, had argued – in reference to Hiroshima and Nagasaki – that the mass killing of civilians of the Nazi regime, including the Shoah, did not differ from razing to the ground entire cities and their civilian populations by means of the atomic bombs. The judges, therefore, were somehow forced to confront the issue. The answer of the judgment was based on a curious attempt to justify the atomic bombings on the basis of military necessity. In particular, the necessity – according to the judges – was that of overcoming the Japanese resistance. The judgement also tried to draw an unconvincing legal equivalence between traditional aerial bombing and the use of the atomic bombs, stating:

> A city is bombed for tactical purposes; communications are to be destroyed, railroads wrecked, ammunition plants demolished, factories razed, all for the purpose of impeding the military. In these operations it inevitably happens that non-military persons are killed. This is an incident, a grave incident to be sure, but an unavoidable corollary of battle action. The civilians are not individualized. The bomb falls, it is aimed at the railroad yards, houses along the tracks are hit and many of their occupants killed. But that is entirely different, both in fact and in law, from an armed force marching up to these same railroad tracks, entering those houses abutting thereon, dragging out the men, women, and children and shooting them.
>
> It was argued in behalf of the defendants that there was no normal distinction between shooting 'civilians with rifles and killing them by means of atomic bombs. There is no doubt that the invention of the atomic bomb, when used, was not *aimed* at non-combatants. Like any other aerial bomb employed during the war, it was dropped to overcome military resistance.
>
> Thus, as grave a military action as is an air bombardment, whether with the usual bombs or by atomic bomb, the one and only purpose of the bombing is to effect the surrender of the bombed nation. The people of that nation, through their representatives, may surrender and, with the surrender, the bombing ceases, the killing is ended'.[58]

In the reflection of the judges, the 'total war' rationale behind the use of nuclear weapons (*in re ipsa*) returns legitimate, and compatible with military necessity, in striking contrast with what the IMT judgement itself had affirmed, setting a completely different, and opposing standard against it. At the same time, the judges imply that weapons like the atomic bomb can be 'aimed'. The nature of the

[57] ibid 142.
[58] ibid 467.

weapon, however, with a blast radius of kilometres, evidently impedes employing it with any ability to circumscribe its devastating effects to combatants and military objectives. Even worse features characterise its long-term, deadly effects. It is also for this reason that successive international legal instruments developed the category of *inherently* indiscriminate weapons, that is weapons which cannot be directed at a specific military objective and/or the effects of which cannot be limited as required by international humanitarian law.[59]

The 'military necessity' of the atomic bombing of Hiroshima and Nagasaki is a myth that has been incessantly reproposed for 75 years,[60] such that scholars have felt compelled to explain why the bombing of Hiroshima would be indisputably illegal today.[61] For decades, year after year military historians actualised variants of what Justice Jackson, chief US Prosecutor in Nuremberg, wrote in 1945 justifying the nuking of Japan. Jackson asserted 'that modern war [had] become more and more a struggle between whole populations, not between armies alone. The issue is which shall be subjugated, and which will survive'.[62] Here, the conceptualisation of war goes back to a pre-Enlightenment declination, preceding its understanding as conflict between state-entities and professional armies, not between peoples.[63]

The consequences of Hiroshima and Nagasaki – even the theoretical consequences – have lived on for several decades into the present day, with new indiscriminate means and methods of warfare employed in contemporary armed conflicts and, not fortuitously, vindication of their righteousness based on frequent references and parallels to the use of the atomic bombs.[64] The atomic

[59] For an accurate reconstruction, see G Nystuen, S Casey-Maslen and AG Bersagel (eds), *Nuclear weapons under international law* (Cambridge University Press, 2014); see also WH Boothby, *Weapons and the law of armed conflict* (Oxford University Press, 2016).

[60] See K McKinney, SD Sagan and AS Weiner, 'Hiroshima and the Myths of Military Targets and Unconditional Surrender', *Lawfare*, 21 August 2020, at www.lawfaremedia.org/article/hiroshima-and-myths-military-targets-and-unconditional-surrender.

[61] K McKinney, SD Sagan, A. Weiner, 'Why the atomic bombing of Hiroshima would be illegal today' (2020) 76 *Bulletin of the Atomic Scientists* 157.

[62] RH Jackson, 'Worst Crime of All' *New York Times Magazine*, 9 September 1945, 9.

[63] Rousseau argued: 'Men, from the mere fact that, while they are living in their primitive independence, they have no mutual relations stable enough to constitute either the state of peace or the state of war, cannot be naturally enemies. War is constituted by a relation between things, and not between persons; and, as the state of war cannot arise out of simple personal relations, but only out of real relations, private war, or war of man with man, can exist neither in the state of nature, where there is no constant property, nor in the social state, where everything is under the authority of the laws. … War then is a relation, not between man and man, but between State and State, and individuals are enemies only accidentally, not as men, nor even as citizens, but as soldiers; not as members of their country, but as its defenders. Finally, each State can have for enemies only other States, and not men; for between things disparate in nature there can be no real relation'. Rousseau, *The Social Contract and Discourses* (tr GDH Cole) (JM Dent & Sons, 1913.

[64] According to a White House transcript, President Biden affirmed: 'It was pointed out to me – I'm being very blunt with you all – it was pointed out to me that – by Bibi – that "Well, you carpet-bombed Germany. You dropped the atom bomb. A lot of civilians died." I said, "Yeah, that's why all these institutions were set up after World War Two to see to it that it didn't happen again – it didn't happen again. Don't make the same mistakes we made at 9/11. There was no reason why we had to be in a war in Afghanistan

bombing of Japan, in other words, reinstalled in history a conception of war as unlimited enmity between entire populations, to be settled by annihilation and unconditional surrender of the vanquished, in direct contrast with the efforts to codify boundaries to 'bracket' all wars, drawing intransgressible legal red lines protecting the unarmed, not only from face-to-face killing but, somehow even more decisively, from indiscriminate bombardments.[65] Not fortuitously, it has been noted how this legacy of legalisation of the atomic bombing resulted in making it difficult not only to prosecute and punish unlawful aerial bombardments,[66] but even to prosecute and punish the crime of genocide,[67] when committed in armed conflicts.

3.1.3. Kelsen's *Privilegium Odiosum* and Radbruch's Second *Verleugnungsformel*: 'Equality, the Core of Justice'

This was not the only setback in Nuremberg. Beyond the issues of war crimes and crimes against humanity adjudication,[68] profound legal problems of this historical

at 9/11. There was no reason why we had to do some of the things we did." (Remarks by President Biden at a Campaign Reception, The White House, 12 December 2023, at www.whitehouse.gov/briefing-room/speeches-remarks/2023/12/12/remarks-by-president-biden-at-a-campaign-reception-5).

[65] Even these attempts were not linear. As explained by van Dijk, the process of codification of the Geneva Conventions saw a struggle around the attempts to limit aerial bombing and blockades. The author unveils how a concerted campaign on the part of a cartel of Western drafters made aerial bombardment regulations disappear from the Conventions, anticipating the *long durée* of a major struggle over whether humanitarian law would become relevant in aerial warfare; see B van Dijk, 'Indiscriminate Warfare: Bombing, Nuclear Weapons, and Starvation' in *Preparing for War: The Making of the 1949 Geneva Conventions* (Oxford University Press, 2022) 197–252.

[66] At the point that De Saussure, in 1971, could ask if there were at all any laws of aerial warfare. See H De Saussue, 'The Laws of Air Warfare: Are There Any?' (1971) 23 *Naval War College Review* 35.

[67] D Moses, 'Why the International Community Made It So Difficult to Prosecute the Crime of Genocide' *DAWN – Middle East and North Africa*, 19 December 2023, at dawnmena.org/why-the-international-community-made-it-so-difficult-to-prosecute-the-crime-of-genocide.

[68] Since the Nazi policy of persecution of minorities and mass-extermination of the Jews started before the outbreak of the war, the Tribunal failed to adjudicate those crimes which preceded the war. Crimes against humanity, in fact, according to the definition of the Charter, had to present the so-called 'war-nexus', that is, they had to be committed 'in execution of or in connection with any crime within the jurisdiction of the Tribunal' (as stated in the IMT Charter, in order to be punished). The Tribunal itself admitted this 'defeat' in the judgment: 'With regard to crimes against humanity, there is no doubt whatever that political opponents were murdered in Germany before the war, and that many of them were kept in concentration camps in circumstances of great horror and cruelty. The policy of terror was certainly carried out on a vast scale, and in many cases was organised and systematic. The policy of persecution, repression and murder of civilians in Germany before the war of 1939, who were likely to be hostile to the Government, was most ruthlessly carried out. The persecution of Jews during the same period is established beyond all doubt. To constitute crimes against humanity, the acts relied on before the outbreak of war must have been in execution of, or in connection with, any crime within the jurisdiction of the Tribunal. The Tribunal is of the opinion that revolting and horrible as many of these crimes were, it has not been satisfactorily proved that they were done in execution of, or in connection with, any such crime. The Tribunal therefore cannot make a general declaration that the acts before 1939 were crimes against humanity within the meaning of the Charter' (The Avalon Project (n 39)).

experience arose from the duties to respect general principles of criminal law governing liberal-democratic models of justice inspired by the rule of law. A first example of these frictions can be seen in the modes of liability. At Article 6, in fact, the Charter stated:

> Leaders, organizers, instigators and accomplices participating in the formulation or execution of a common plan or conspiracy to commit any of the foregoing crimes are responsible for all acts performed by any persons in execution of such plan.[69]

This provision testifies an extremely unrefined development of penal law categories. According to it even mere 'instigators of the formulation of a conspiracy to commit a crime' are responsible for all the crimes committed in execution of this conspiracy. In this way, suspects offering little to no contribution to the material commission of the crimes themselves, and with roles limited to an initial support of a preparatory ideation of the offences, could virtually be held equally responsibility as those who ordered and/or finalised the material commission of the crimes.[70] This configuration seems to border with a nuancing of the fundamental principle of personality of the criminal liability,[71] constituting a milestone in the long historical process bringing criminal justice in Europe into the modern age.

In terms of respect for the general principles of criminal law in liberal-democratic models of criminal justice, the most controversial issue at Nuremberg was without doubt the ex-post facto nature of the law of the Charter and of the Tribunal itself.

Famously, the *nullum crimen sine lege*, or better, *nullum crimen sine proevia lege penali* (no crime without a previous penal law) is one of the most fundamentals tenets of modern penal theory, prescribing the non-retroactivity of criminal punishment; that is to say, the prohibition of penal sanctions on the basis of a law enacted after the time in which the conduct was committed.[72] This principle has

[69] 'Charter of the International Military Tribunal' in *Nuremberg Trial Proceedings*, vol I (n 3).

[70] L Yanev, 'A Janus-Faced Concept: Nuremberg's Law on Conspiracy Vis-à-Vis the Notion of Joint Criminal Enterprise' (2015) 26 *Criminal Law Forum* 419; S Pomorsky, 'Conspiracy and Criminal Organization' in G Ginsburgs and V Kudriavtsev (eds), *The Nuremberg Trial and International Law* (Martinus Nijhoff Publishers 1990) 218; G Fletcher, *Rethinking Criminal Law* (Oxford University Press, 2000) 219; E Van Sliedregt, *Individual Criminal Responsibility in International Law* (Oxford University Press, 2012) 179.

[71] A Ashworth and J Horder, *Principles of Criminal Law*, 7th edn (Oxford University Press, 2013) 27 ff.

[72] This is also why, 25 years before the Nuremberg IMT, the creation of a permanent International Court of Criminal Justice was perceived as unfeasible during the First Assembly of the League of Nations: 'The second recommendation communicated by the Jurists' Committee at The Hague advocates the establishment of a Court of International Criminal Justice, the object of which would be to prosecute crimes committed against international public order. The Third Committee holds that *there is not yet any international penal law recognized by all nations* [emphasis added], and that, if it were possible to refer certain crimes to any jurisdiction, it would be more practical to establish a special chamber in the Court of International Justice. The Committee therefore considers that there is no occasion for the Assembly of the League of Nations to adopt any resolution on this subject' (see *Records of the First Assembly of the League of Nations*, 1920, tenth meeting of the Third Committee, cited in

not only the function of constituting a basic safeguard of the citizen against arbitrary uses of the *jus puniendi* of the state, but it is also a specific rationale in penal theory: only an *existing* law or statute, in fact, allows the subject to orientate his behaviour in conformity with, rather than in violation, of the law. In the absence of an existing norm criminalising a conduct, those responsible for it are unable to foresee the penal consequences of their actions.

The defence counsel of the Nuremberg defendants adopted a motion lamenting the violation of the principle, declaring:

> On several occasions the League had to decide upon the lawfulness or unlawfulness of action by force of one member against another member, but it always condemned such action by force merely as a violation of international law by the State, and never thought of bringing up for trial the Statesmen, generals, and industrialists of the state which recurred to force. … The present Trial can, therefore … not invoke existing international law, it is rather a proceeding pursuant to a new penal law, a penal law enacted only after the crime. This is repugnant to a principle of jurisprudence sacred to the civilized world, the partial violation of which by Hitler's Germany has been vehemently discountenanced outside and inside the Reich. This principle is to the effect that only he can be punished who offended against a law in existence at the time of the commission of the act and imposing a penalty. This maxim is one of the great fundamental principles of the political systems of the Signatories of the Charter for this Tribunal themselves.[73]

The answer of the judges to this challenge was based, on the one hand, on a sort of reduction of the *nullum crimen* to a purely moral principle of justice, superseded by the need for justice, and, on the other, on the assumption that the violations of previous treaties renouncing war (such as the Kellogg–Briand Pact) were somehow 'implicitly' giving rise to international criminal responsibility of those responsible.

More precisely, the judgment stated:

> In the first place, it is to be observed that the maxim *nullum crimen sine lege* is not a limitation of sovereignty but is in general a principle of justice. To assert that it is unjust to punish those who in defiance of treaties and assurances have attacked neighboring States without warning is obviously untrue, for in such circumstances the attacker must know that he is doing wrong, and so far from it being unjust to punish him, it would be unjust if his wrong were allowed to go unpunished. Occupying the positions, they did in the Government of Germany, the defendants, or at least some of them, must have known of the treaties signed by Germany, outlawing recourse to war for the settlement of international disputes; they must have known that they were acting in defiance of all international law when in complete deliberation they carried out their designs of invasion and aggression. On this view of the case alone, it would appear that the maxim has no application to the present facts.

UN Secretary General, Historical Survey of the Question of International Criminal Jurisdiction – Memorandum submitted by the Secretary-General, A/CN.4/7/Rev.1, 1949, at legal.un.org/ilc/documentation/english/a_cn4_7_rev1.pdf).

[73] *Trial of the Major War Criminals Before the International Military Tribunal*, vol I, Official Texts in English Language, Nuremberg, 1947, 168, at www.loc.gov/rr/frd/Military_Law/NT_major-war-criminals.html.

> This view is strongly reinforced by a consideration of the state of international law in 1939, so far as aggressive war is concerned. The General Treaty for the Renunciation of War of 27 August 1928, more generally known as the Pact of Paris or the Kellogg-Briand Pact, was binding on 63 nations, including Germany, Italy, and Japan, at the outbreak of war in 1939. … The question is, what was the legal effect, of this pact? The nations who signed the pact or adhered to it unconditionally condemned recourse to war for the future as an instrument of policy, and expressly renounced it. After the signing of the pact, any nation resorting to war as an instrument of national policy breaks the pact. In the opinion of the Tribunal, the solemn renunciation of war as an instrument of national policy necessarily involves the proposition that such a war is illegal in international law; and that those who plan and wage such a war, with its inevitable and terrible consequences, are committing a crime in so doing.[74]

It is not difficult to identify the contradiction of this line of reasoning, which substantially declared the legality principle inapplicable to the case, while asserting at the same time that the principle itself was not breached, given the existence of the Kellogg–Briand Pact. The Pact, however – as it has been shown – had nothing to do with individual criminal responsibility.

Many jurists and philosophers have, since then, criticised this solution as legally weak and morally unsatisfactory, starting from the jurist who, until that point, stood out as the main theoriser of the necessity of international criminal tribunals: Hans Kelsen.[75] Kelsen noted that when Britain and France resorted to war against Germany, in 1939, they had not been directly attacked. The existing principles of international law, however, provided for a legal justification, because aggressive counter-war could have been seen as a lawful sanction as much as countermeasures and reprisals, if undertaken in response to a violation of a treaty. On the other hand, Kelsen stated:

> Reprisals and war as sanctions are directed against a State as such, and not against the individuals, forming its government. These sanctions constitute collective responsibility, not criminal responsibility of definite individuals performing the acts by which international law is violate. … It can hardly be denied that international law prior to the London Agreement, did not provide punishment of those individuals who performed the acts of an illegal war.[76]

At the same time, Kelsen partially endorsed the reasoning of the IMT judges, stating that the compression of the non-retroactivity principle was, in the case, morally acceptable. According to Kelsen, since the illegal actions for which the London Agreement established individual criminal responsibility were highly immoral, and the persons who committed those acts were aware of their immoral character,

[74] The Avalon Project (n 39).

[75] See H Kelsen, *Peace Through Law* (The University of North Carolina Press, 1944; Garland Publishing, 1973) 71 ff.

[76] H Kelsen, 'Will the Judgment in the Nuremberg Trial Constitute a Precedent in International Law?' (1947) 1 *International Law Quarterly* 153, 157.

then the retroactivity of their punishment could have hardly been considered as absolutely incompatible with justice:

> Justice required the punishment of these men, in spite of the fact that under positive law they were not punishable at the time they performed the acts made punishable with retroactive force. In case two postulates of justice are in conflict with each other, the higher one prevails; and to punish those who were morally responsible for the international crime of the second World War may certainly be considered as more important than to comply with the rather relative rule against ex post facto laws …[77]

Ultimately, Kelsen's reasoning leads right at the centre of a legal theory *vexata quaestio*, that is, the conflicts between positive law and justice, between legal certainty and moral good, and how to solve them.

Among the numerous legal philosophers grappling with the spectrum of problems associated with solving these fundamental contradictions, the German jurist Gustav Radrubch's theory stands out as one of the most convincing in that regard. Radrubch is in fact associated with the famous 'Radbruch formula', which helps to resolve the contrast between law and justice.[78]

The theory was formulated in order to disqualify the binding force of Nazi legislation (in post-World War II domestic adjudications), and its very status as 'law'. The problem giving rise to the theory and its arguments arose when, in 1946, judges were called to adjudicate the conduct of certain German citizens, holding public or judicial office during the Nazi regime, who had committed so-called 'crimes of obedience', included sending people to death in observance of Nazi laws. In particular, the cases concerned: voluntary informers who signalled to the authority authors of trifling violations, punished with the death penalty; the judges who sentenced the defendants to death; and those who carried out the executions.

Facing this scenario, irresolvable by relying entirely on either positivism, or natural law, the great legal theorist tackled the issue of 'statutory lawlessness' and 'supra-statutory law', focusing on radically unjust laws and on how to solve the contrasts between, on the one hand, legal certainty, requiring respect of the validity of the laws, and, on the other hand, justice, requiring the disapplication of unjust laws.

As Radbruch wrote:

> That the law be certain and sure, that it not be interpreted and applied one way here and now, another way elsewhere and tomorrow, is also a requirement of justice. Where there arises a conflict between legal certainty and justice, between an objectionable but duly enacted statute and a just law that has not been cast in statutory form, there is in truth a conflict of justice with itself, a conflict between apparent and real justice. … The conflict between justice and legal certainty may well be resolved in this way: The positive law,

[77] ibid, 165.

[78] G Radbruch, 'Gesetzliches Unrecht und Übergesetzliches Recht', first published in (1946) 1 *Süddeutsche Juristen-Zeitung* 105 (tr BL Paulson and SL Paulson (2006) 26 *Oxford Journal of Legal Studies* 1).

> secured by legislation and power, takes precedence even when its content is unjust and fails to benefit the people, unless the conflict between statute and justice reaches such an intolerable degree that the statute, as 'flawed law', must yield to justice.[79]

In other words, within a limit of tolerable injustice, the conflict between legal certainty and justice has to be solved by assigning prevalence to legal certainty, therefore respecting and applying the 'flawed law' (this is the solution known by penal theorists as the first Radbruch formula). However, if the injustice of the norm becomes intolerable, legal certainty has to succumb to the benefit of justice.

This part of Radbruch's formula is well known. What remained less debated was the second part of the formula, in which the jurist went further, indicating the extreme cases where norms lack even the minimum qualities necessary to be considered law:

> It is impossible to draw a sharper line between cases of statutory lawlessness and statutes that are valid despite their flaws. One line of distinction, however, can be drawn with utmost clarity: Where there is not even an attempt at justice, where *equality, the core of justice*, is deliberately betrayed in the issuance of positive law, then the statute is not merely 'flawed law', it lacks completely the very nature of law.[80]

What appears crucial in this second formula, known as *Verleugnungsformel*, is that the factor that drives injustice beyond tolerability is the wilful betrayal of the core value of justice: the principle of equality, the 'equal treatment of equals'.[81]

Having regard to Radbruch's formulas, it is not unreasonable to argue that the post-war IMTs, by focusing only on a particular category of perpetrator and deliberately negating equality, had reproduced an authoritarian feature. International criminal justice was born in contemporaneity with an 'original sin' of selectivity on the basis of power relations; a selectivity that would have long implicated the functioning of international criminal institutions,[82] through to the present day.

The just punishment of the Nazi war criminals was, in fact, followed by a validation of the legality of the atomic bombing of Hiroshima and Nagasaki, preceding by merely hours the establishment of the first international criminal

[79] ibid 7.

[80] ibid.

[81] 'The supporting theory had been provided by the Nazi ideologue, Alfred Rosenberg, writing in response to the Potempa death sentences: 'People are not alike, and murders are not alike; the murder of the pacifist Jaurès was properly judged in France in a different light than the attempt to murder the nationalist Clemenceau; for it is impossible to subject the patriotically motivated perpetrator to the same punishment as one whose motives are (in the view of the National Socialists) inimical to the people.' The explicit intention from the very beginning, then, was that National Socialist "law" would extricate itself from the essential requirement of justice, namely, the equal treatment of equals. It thereby lacks completely the very nature of law; it is not merely flawed law, but rather no law at all.' (ibid, 8).

[82] See M Damaška, 'What is the Point of International Criminal Justice?' (2008) *Yale Law School, Faculty Scholarshp Series, Paper* 1572, 1/2008.

tribunal punishing individuals for war crimes, including war crimes committed under 'total war' logics condoning indiscriminate warfare.

Justice Jackson himself, chief US Prosecutor at the IMT, noted that transforming the commission by the enemy into an element of international crimes would have deprived the punishment of minimum standards of fairness. As he argued:

> We would think that had no place in any definition because it makes an entirely partisan declaration of law. If certain acts in violation of treaties are crimes, they are crimes whether the United States does them or whether Germany does them, and we are not prepared to lay down a rule of criminal conduct against others which we would not be willing to have invoked against us. Therefore, we think the clause 'carried out by the European Axis' so qualifies the statement that it deprives it of all standing and fairness as a juridical principle.[83]

As a unilateral justice in which 'States made themselves not only legislators but also judges in their own cause',[84] the IMT war crimes law imprinted on the future of international criminal justice the mark of victors' justice. As Kelsen sharply concluded with particular concern to the exclusion from the Tribunals of judges from neutral countries, the IMTs experience had

> the character of a *privilegium odiosum* imposed upon vanquished States by the victors … If the principles applied in the Nuremberg trial were to become a precedent – a legislative rather than a judicial precedent – then, after the next war, the governments of the victorious States would try the members of the governments of the vanquished States for having committed crimes determined unilaterally and with retroactive force by the former. Let us hope that there is no such precedent.[85]

3.2. The ICTY Jurisprudence on Indiscriminate and Disproportionate Attacks as War Crimes

The IMTs, with their controversial legacy, did not elaborate specifically on indiscriminate attacks in combat situations, nor did they clarify the boundaries of the notion as a war crime offence, except in referring to the 1907 Hague Convention IV respecting the Laws and Customs of War on Land as cogent. On the contrary, the ad hoc international criminal tribunals, particularly the International Criminal Tribunal for the Prosecution of Persons Responsible for Serious Violations of International Humanitarian Law Committed in the Territory of the Former Yugoslavia since 1991 (ICTY), almost 50 years later, tackled the issue extensively, with a dense body of jurisprudence producing several breakthroughs in

[83] R Jackson, *International Conference on Military Trials: London 1945, Minutes of Conference Session of July 23*, The Avalon Project – Yale Law School, at avalon.law.yale.edu/imt/jack44.asp.
[84] Kelsen (n 76) 171.
[85] ibid.

transposing the prohibition of indiscriminate and disproportionate attacks in the international criminal justice realm.

The decisive contributions of the ad hoc tribunals to the development of international criminal law, and specifically of war crimes law, followed decades of growing legal debate around international crimes and how to prevent them. International criminal justice, nonetheless, after World War II, remained mostly confined to academic exercises, and did not progress significantly institutionally.

The political climate in the aftermath of World War II, and the subsequent delicate equilibrium of the Cold War, created an impasse of rivalries between the major world powers, entrenching the space for the creation of international criminal tribunals.

The situation changed when, in the early 1990s, international criminal justice regained centrality and support in the international community in response to mass atrocities and large-scale human rights violations taking place in Europe and Africa. For the first time in history, atrocity crimes and genocide received mass media coverage,[86] and were disclosed to the world's public. In response to growing pressure from the public and international non-governmental organisations, in 1993 the Security Council of the United Nations announced its grave concern for the 'continuing reports of widespread violations of international humanitarian law occurring within the territory of the former Yugoslavia, including reports of mass killings'.[87]

With the aspiration to put an end to such crimes and to punish those responsible, and in order to restore stability in the region, the Security Council took the unprecedented step of establishing an international criminal tribunal pursuant to Chapter VII of the Charter of the United Nations: the ICTY).[88] One year later, the same process was followed for the creation of the International Criminal Tribunal for Rwanda (ICTR).[89]

So, in contrast to the IMTs, these ad hoc tribunals arose multilaterally and not from the will of the powers winning the very same war in which the violations to be adjudicated were committed. However, authors debated the existence of a power of the Security Council to establish international criminal jurisdictions on the basis of Chapter VII of the United Nations Charter.[90] Many, in addition, criticised the political reasons behind the creation of the tribunals, assessing it substantially as a countermove of the Security Council to respond to accusations

[86] M Simmons, 'International Criminal Tribunals and the Media' (2009) 7 *Journal of International Criminal Justice* 83.

[87] Security Council Resolution 808 (1993), UN Doc S/RES/808 (22 February 1993).

[88] Security Council Resolution 827 (1993), UN Doc S/RES/827 (25 May 1993).

[89] Security Council Resolution 955 (1994) UN Doc S/RES/955, (8 November 1994).

[90] See inter alia M Mukai, 'Ad hoc Tribunals: the Failure to Contribute to Precedence-Setting for a Universal Model of International Justice' (2009) 3 *Berkeley Journal of International Law* 48; see also A Kenneth, 'The Rise of International Criminal Law: Intended and Unintended Consequences' (2009) 20 *European Journal of International Law* 331.

of passivity and failure to prevent atrocities, by intervening while the Yugoslav wars and the Rwandan genocide were escalating.[91]

3.2.1. Overcoming the IACs–NIACs Dichotomy: The *Tadić* Lesson

Despite the criticisms of the creative interpretation of UN Charter powers, the jurisprudential contribution of the tribunals became a milestone for accountability, albeit problematically construed and, as it will be shown, not matched by the successive development of war crimes law.

These milestones can be seen, firstly, in the beginning of a realignment between the laws governing international and non-international armed conflicts.[92] Historically, IHL developed in times when war was almost completely synonymous with interstate warfare. In addition, governments were reluctant to accept international rules and standards governing internal conflicts, such as civil wars and armed insurgencies. This resulted in a decisive disparity in the number (600:30)[93] of treaty rules applying respectively to international and non-international conflicts. Furthermore, this disparity radically affected the domain of criminal justiciability for the violations of the treaty rules. Traditionally, in fact, national courts interpreting the 1949 Geneva Conventions and their 1977 Additional Protocols, held that the criminalisation of IHL violations was configurable in the sole international armed conflicts, reproducing what was convincingly identified as a 'glaring and preposterous disparity' for the breaches committed in non-international ones.[94]

[91] 'Most observers believe that the Security Council, led by the United States, could have put an early halt to the bloodshed in the Balkans, but that the members of the council lacked the political will to take the necessary measures, such as air strikes and committing troops to a combat situation which had the potential of turning into a quagmire like Vietnam. Consequently, the idea of a war crimes tribunal appealed to the members of the council as a means of countering accusations that they tolerated massive violations of international humanitarian law in the former Yugoslavia and stood by idly while a defenceless Bosnia succumbed to Serb and Croat aggression' (MP Scharf, *Balkan Justice: the Story Behind the First International War Crimes Trial since Nuremberg* (Carolina Academic Press, 1997) xv); see also H Pierre, *Justice in a time of war: the true story behind the International Criminal Tribunal for the former Yugoslavia* (Texas A & M University Press, 2004). As it has convincingly been argued about the foundations of the tribunals, the 'duty to punish rests ultimately on the duty to protect, that invocation of the former implicitly admits failure to discharge the latter' (A Haque, 'Group Violence and Group Vengeance: towards a retributivist theory of International Criminal Law' (2005–2006) 9 *Buffalo Criminal Law Review* 276).

[92] Non-international armed conflicts (NIACs) have constituted the overwhelming majority of the armed conflict in the world since World War II. In 2016, of 48 armed conflicts identified, 36 were classified as non-international (see A Bellal, *War Report 2016*, Geneva Academy of International Humanitarian Law and Human Rights, 2017).

[93] A Kareem, 'The Legal Challenges Raised by the Conduct of Hostilities Against Organized Non-State Armed Groups' in C Marchand (ed), *The Distinction between International and Non-International Armed Conflicts: Challenges for IHL? 38th Round Table on Current Issues of International Humanitarian Law* (Sanremo, 3rd-5th September 2015) (International Institute of Humanitarian Law – Franco Angeli, 2016) 145.

[94] A Cassese, *Cassese's International Criminal Law*, 3rd edn (Oxford University Press, 2013) 71.

The statutes of the two tribunals presented some differences in this matter. The Rwandan genocide took place, for the biggest part, within an internal armed conflict.[95] The ICTR Statute, therefore, established the jurisdiction of tribunal *rationae materiae* over the violations of Common Article 3 of the Geneva Conventions, as well as over those of Article 4 of Additional Protocol II (I).[96] For the first time in history, the legal regime of war crimes was extended to non-international armed conflict.

The Statute of the ICTY, however, did not contain such a provision. According to the ICTY Statute, the material jurisdiction of the Tribunal comprised Grave Breaches of the 1949 Geneva Conventions,[97] and other offences generically qualified by Article 3 of the Statute as 'violations of the laws and customs of war'.[98] Grave Breaches, however, are listed in Article 85 of the 1977 Additional Protocol I (AP I) to the Geneva Convention, applying to international armed conflicts only.

Consequently, the determination about whether and on what legal basis to punish other violations of the laws and customs of war committed in non-international armed conflicts was left to the jurisprudence of the Tribunal.

The landmark decision in this respect was adopted in the seminal *Tadić* judgment, when the ICTY Appeals Chamber faced a motion contesting the lack of subject-matter jurisdiction of the Tribunal over the crimes alleged, on the basis of the non-international nature of the conflict in which they had supposedly been

[95] See *Preliminary Report of the Independent Commission of Experts established in accordance with Security Council Resolution 935 (1994)*, annexed to Letter dated 1 October 1994 from the Secretary-General addressed to the President of the Security Council, UN doc S/1994/1125, 4 October 1994, paras 91–94; see also *Secretary-General's Report on Practical Arrangements for the Effective Functioning of the International Tribunal for Rwanda*, UN doc S/1995/134, 13 February 1995, paras 11–12.

[96] Included, but not limited to: a) Violence to life, health and physical or mental well-being of persons, in particular murder as well as cruel treatment such as torture, mutilation or any form of corporal punishment; b) Collective punishments; c) Taking of hostages; d) Acts of terrorism; e) Outrages upon personal dignity, in particular humiliating and degrading treatment, rape, enforced prostitution and any form of indecent assault; f) Pillage; g) The passing of sentences and the carrying out of executions without previous judgement pronounced by a regularly constituted court, affording all the judicial guarantees which are recognised as indispensable by civilised peoples; h) Threats to commit any of the foregoing acts.'

[97] The Statute mentions explicitly '(a) wilful killing; (b) torture or inhuman treatment, including biological experiments; (c) wilfully causing great suffering or serious injury to body or health; (d) extensive destruction and appropriation of property, not justified by military necessity and carried out unlawfully and wantonly; (e) compelling a prisoner of war or a civilian to serve in the forces of a hostile power; (f) wilfully depriving a prisoner of war or a civilian of the rights of fair and regular trial; (g) unlawful deportation or transfer or unlawful confinement of a civilian; (h) taking civilians as hostages.'

[98] 'The International Tribunal shall have the power to prosecute persons violating the laws or customs of war. Such violations shall include, but not be limited to: '(a) employment of poisonous weapons or other weapons calculated to cause unnecessary suffering; (b) wanton destruction of cities, towns or villages, or devastation not justified by military necessity; (c) attack, or bombardment, by whatever means, of undefended towns, villages, dwellings, or buildings; (d) seizure of, destruction or wilful damage done to institutions dedicated to religion, charity and education, the arts and sciences, historic monuments and works of art and science; (e) plunder of public or private property.'

committed. The defence argued that Article 2 of the ICTY Statute brought under the jurisdiction of the Tribunal only grave breaches of the Geneva Conventions, widely understood to be pertinent only to international armed conflicts. Also, Article 3 of the ICTY Statute, according to the defence, referring generically to 'violations of the laws of war', should have been interpreted as applying only to inter-state conflicts, due to the absence of an explicit mention of internal armed conflicts, a stipulation which was, in contrast, present in other provisions of the Statute, such as Article 5.[99] Therefore, the *a contrario* argument was that, on the basis of a literal interpretation of the provisions of the Statute, there was no individual criminal liability regime applicable to 'other violations of the laws of war' not mentioned in the Statute and committed in an armed conflict not of international character.[100]

The answer of the ICTY judges relied, instead, on a teleological interpretation of the Statute itself. This interpretation was supported by both a persuasive consideration of the historical developments of contemporary IHL, and an attentive and erudite examination of several state practices innovating customary international law in this area.

The Appeals Chamber, presided by Judge Cassese, acknowledged that IHL, until the beginning of the twentieth century, was characterised by a rigid dichotomy between, on the one hand, belligerency – typical of inter-state armed conflict and governed by a well-developed body of international treaty norms and customs, and on the other, insurgency – typical of civil wars and historically regarded by states as a domain to be regulated by national laws punishing rebellions, mutinies and treason, and therefore resisting against the 'intrusion' of international norms in the domestic jurisdictions.[101]

The judges, however, noted that, from 1930, this rigid dichotomy gradually blurred, and numerous and more pervasive international norm applying to internal armed conflicts emerged.

Civil wars, as a matter of fact, had grown in number, intensity, duration and destructive potential, involving the whole population of the states in which they occurred, to the point that their intrinsic differentiation with inter-state wars became questionable. In addition, the increasing political and economic interdependence between states in the international community, and even more so the Cold War setting with its 'proxy wars', prompted many third countries to intervene in these internal conflicts, thus the idea of legal regulations of civil wars as a self-contained domain of domestic jurisdictions, and rather demonstrating

[99] 'The International Tribunal shall have the power to prosecute persons responsible for the following crimes when committed in armed conflict, *whether international or internal in character*, and directed against any civilian population: (a) murder; (b) extermination; (c) enslavement; (d) deportation; (e) imprisonment; (f) torture; (g) rape; (h) persecutions on political, racial and religious grounds; (i) other inhumane acts' (emphasis added).

[100] See *Prosecutor v Tadić*, ICTY Case No IT-94-1-AR72, Decision on the Defence Motion for Interlocutory Appeal on Jurisdiction, 2 October 1995, para 71.

[101] ibid, para 96.

their greater international implications and growing need for international legal attention.

Most of all, however, the ICTY judges emphasised that the 'human rights revolution' in international law[102] demanded a teleological interpretation of IHL as whole, substituting a state-centred approach with a human rights-centred conception, necessarily entailing an expansive application of the humanitarian protections to individual combatants and civilians caught up in armed clashes of all kinds. As they argued:

> *[H]ominum causa omne jus constitutum est* (all law is created for the benefit of human beings). … It follows that in the area of armed conflict the distinction between interstate wars and civil wars is losing its value as far as human beings are concerned. Why protect civilians from belligerent violence, or ban rape, torture or the wanton destruction of hospitals, churches, museums or private property, as well as proscribe weapons causing unnecessary suffering when two sovereign States are engaged in war, and yet refrain from enacting the same bans or providing the same protection when armed violence has erupted 'only' within the territory of a sovereign State? If international law, while of course duly safeguarding the legitimate interests of States, must gradually turn to the protection of human beings, it is only natural that the aforementioned dichotomy should gradually lose its weight'.[103]

For the Appeals Chamber, thus, it is on the basis of 'elementary considerations of humanity' that the rationale for the protection of civilians and civilian objects in wartime, and for the sanctioning of prohibited means and methods of warfare in international armed conflicts, has to be applied to both the typologies of armed conflicts. 'What is inhumane, and consequently proscribed, in international wars – argue the judges – cannot but be inhumane and inadmissible in civil strife'.[104]

The *Tadić* decision, however, was not limited to considerations of humanity. On the contrary, this line of reasoning was sustained by way of examination of a dense body of pronouncements of states, military manuals, national judicial decisions and domestic norms, UN Security Council and General Assembly resolutions,[105] demonstrating that robust state practice and *opinion juris* converged on the thesis of the judges, prompting them to conclude that the emergence of customary IHL norms governing internal armed conflict could 'not be denied', especially in 'areas as the *protection of civilians from hostilities*, in particular from *indiscriminate attacks* (emphases added)'.[106]

However, the problem relative to the jurisdiction of the Tribunal, and the legal basis thereof, over violations of IHL not explicitly mentioned in Article 3 of the Statute remained unresolved.

[102] JP Humphrey, 'The Revolution in the International Law of Human Rights' (1975) 2 *Human Rights* 205.

[103] *Prosecutor v Tadić*, ICTY IT-94-1-AR72, Decision on the Defence Motion for Interlocutory Appeal on Jurisdiction, 2 October 1995, para 97.

[104] ibid, para 119.

[105] ibid, paras 100–26.

[106] ibid, para 127.

For this reason, the Appeals Chamber made recourse to what was to become notorious as the *Tadić conditions*, that is to say, the requirements to be met for an offence against IHL rules (to be prosecuted under Article 3:

(1) the offence must constitute a breach of an IHL treaty rule or, as in the case discussed, customary rule;
(2) the violation must be 'serious', meaning that it must contravene a rule protecting important values, and must involve grave consequences for the victim (the explanation offered by the Chamber on this rule seem to evoke the concept of 'offensiveness' or 'harm' typical of the continental penal law scholarship);[107]
(3) the breach of the rule must entail, under conventional or customary law, the individual criminal responsibility of the person responsible for its violation.

When these conditions are met, the classification of the armed conflict in which the offences are committed becomes immaterial, and a vast range of prohibited conduct not explicitly mentioned in the article also become punishable, namely: violations of the Hague law applicable to international armed conflicts; breaches of the Geneva Conventions other than those classified as 'grave breaches' by the Conventions themselves and their Protocols; violations of Common Article 3 of the Geneva Conventions and of the customary IHL rules applicable to non-international armed conflicts; and violations of conventions binding for the parties to a conflict, even if they did not acquire customary status.

In this way, in sum, not only were the numerous norms regulating conduct of hostilities and means and methods of warfare in inter-state warfare extended to non-international armed conflicts, but also, through the 'bridge' of customary international law, individual criminal responsibility for the violation of those rules was transposed into the legal regime governing those conflicts.[108]

This is the background against which the jurisprudence of the ICTY could progressively interpret the existing legal framework with a degree of flexibility in drawing the boundaries of criminal relevance of indiscriminate and disproportionate attacks.

The identification of the legal contours of indiscriminate and disproportionate attacks as criminal offences, and of their constitutive elements, however, remained highly problematic.

The common trend of the ICTY jurisprudence on the matter is that both disproportionate and indiscriminate attacks, rather than being qualified as war crimes

[107] See, for example, A Baratta, 'Principi del diritto penale minimo. Per una teoria dei diritti umani come oggetti e limiti della legge penale' (1985) 3 *Dei delitti e delle pene* 445; F Bricola, *Teoria generale del reato* (1973) 19 N*ovissimo Digesto Iitaliano* 77; A Cavaliere, 'Riflessioni sul Ruolo dell'Offensività nella Teoria del Reato Costituzionalmente Orientata' in G Giostra and G Insolera (eds), *Costituzione, diritto e processo penale. I quarant'anni della Corte costituzionale* (Giuffré 1998) 135; V Manes, *Il principio di Offensività nel Diritto Penale. Canone di politica criminale, criterio ermeneutico, parametro di ragionevolezza* (Giappicchelli 2005) 160 ff.

[108] See ch 2, sections 2.1.1, 2.1.2 and 2.1.3.

per se, were identified as possible conduct or concurring elements subsumed under two broader war crimes,[109] that is:

(1) *Direct attacks on civilians*. In this context, an indiscriminate or disproportionate attack, according to the judges, could constitute an indicator of the commission of a direct attack on civilians. The judges, in other words, in the relevant cases (analysed below) inferred from the indiscriminate nature of the attack the intention of deliberately – or recklessly accepting the risk of – attacking civilians;

2) *Attacks, the primary purpose of which is to spread terror among the civilian population*, or *crime of terror*. In this context, the indiscriminate or disproportionate nature of an attack could constitute an indicator of the fact that the purpose of the attacks was in fact to terrorise the civilians.

The jurisprudence of the Tribunal on the matter is dense and articulated and deserves closer consideration.

3.2.2. Indiscriminate and Disproportionate Attacks as Conduct Indicating the Intent of the Crime of Terror

The prohibition of military attacks intended to inflict terror to the civilian population has old roots in modern IHL.

The Hague Rules on Air Warfare of 1922, in Article 22, stated that 'any air bombardment for the purpose of terrorizing the civil population or destroying or damaging private property without military character or injuring non-combatants, is forbidden'.[110]

Notably, the two 1977 Additional Protocols to the Geneva Conventions, when affirming the principle of distinction between civilian and combatant, also outlaw attacks designed to spread terror, stating, in Article 51(2) AP I and Article 13(2) AP II that 'Acts or threats of violence the primary purpose of which is to spread terror among the civilian population are prohibited'.[111]

The ICTY Statute did not mention explicitly acts of terror between the conducts punishable as war crimes. However, similarly to what happened for the construction of the crime of direct attacks on civilians, two leading cases discussed attacks intended to cause terror among civilians as crimes comprised in the jurisdiction of the Tribunal, under its Article 3.

[109] See C Ponti, 'The Crime of Indiscriminate Attack and Unlawful Conventional Weapons: The Legacy of the ICTY Jurisprudence' (2015) 6 *Journal of International Humanitarian Legal Studies* 118–46; F Moneta, 'Direct Attacks on Civilians and Indiscriminate Attacks as War Crimes' in M Frulli, M Pedrazzi and F Pocar (eds), *War Crimes and the Conduct of Hostilities: Challenges to Adjudication and Investigation* (Edward Elgar Publishing, 2013) 65.

[110] See HM Hanke, 'The 1923 Hague Rules of Air Warfare' (1991) 3 *International Review of the Red Cross* 139–72.

[111] Arts 51(2) and 13(2) AP I.

In the *Galić* case (discussed in more detail below) the Trial Chamber found that the *Tadić* conditions were satisfied for the crime of terror on the basis of applicable treaty law, therefore there was no need to determine whether the crime was part of customary international law.[112] The Appeal Chamber took a position on the matter, finding that the codification of the relevant prohibition in the Protocols was indeed expression of customary international law.[113]

The Trial Chamber in *Galić* proceeded to specify the elements of the crime of terror, identifying them as, for the *actus reus*, 'acts of violence directed against the civilian population or individual civilians not taking direct part in hostilities causing death or serious injury to body or health within the civilian population'; and, for the *mens rea*, when the offender had:

(1) the general intent of wilfully making the civilian population or individual civilians not taking direct part in hostilities the object of the acts of violence; plus
(2) the specific intent of committing the offence with the primary purpose of spreading terror among the civilian population.[114]

Importantly, the Chamber also found that the actual infliction of terror as a result of the attack is not a constitutive legal element of the offence.[115] It is, in other words, sufficient to launch the attack with the purpose to cause the terror, without the need for the effective terrorisation of the civilian population to eventuate.

In addition, the act of violence can also be a threat of violence, which in some cases can alone be the cause of grave consequences, such as 'extreme fear' among the civilians (for example, a credible threat to bombard indiscriminately a civilian area, which might well determine the serious consequence of mass civilian displacement).[116]

On the other hand, the mental element requires a significantly higher threshold in comparison to what is required for the crime of direct attacks on civilians. The terrorisation of the civilians, in fact, cannot be simply a foreseen consequence of the attack, or a recklessly accepted risk, but it needs to be the 'primary purpose' of the attack itself. As the Chamber states, the concept of 'primary purpose' needs

> to be understood as excluding *dolus eventualis* or recklessness from the intentional state specific to terror. Thus, the Prosecution is required to prove not only that the Accused accepted the likelihood that terror would result from the illegal acts – or, in other words, that he was aware of the possibility that terror would result – but that that was the result which he specifically intended.[117]

[112] *Prosecutor v Galić*, Trial Judgment, ICTY IT-98-29-T, 5 December 2003, paras 69 and 113.
[113] *Prosecutor v Galić*, Appeal Judgment, ICTY IT-98-29-A, 30 November 2006, paras 86–87, 98.
[114] *Prosecutor v Galić*, Trial Judgment (n 112) para 133.
[115] ibid, para 134.
[116] ibid, para 110, fn 179.
[117] ibid, para 136.

For the mental element to be satisfied, it is therefore crucial that the attack was launched or threatened with the *dolus specialis* of causing terror among civilians.

In the *Dragomir Milošević* case, the Trial Chamber drew a distinction between the crime of terror, and the fear that legitimate military attacks can cause in the civilian population. Even in cases in which attacks on combatants may determine 'intense fear and intimidation' among civilians, the *dolus specialis* would not be met when the primary purpose of these military actions would not be to instil fear.[118]

Finally, the Appeal Chamber in the *Galić* case clarified that this special intent of causing terror does not need to be the exclusive, albeit primary, purpose of the attack. The primary purpose of spreading terror can coexist with other objectives. However, insofar as spreading terror among civilians remains the main aim among the various, the crime can be perfected. Determining if this purpose of terrorising civilians is the principal purpose requires consideration of circumstances such as nature, manner, timing and duration of the acts or threats of violence.[119]

Most importantly for the present analysis, the Appeals Chamber also declared that:

> [T]he acts or threats of violence constitutive of the crime of terror shall not be limited to direct attacks against civilians or threats thereof but may include indiscriminate or disproportionate attacks.[120]

In *Dragomir Milošević*, the Trial Chamber even more specifically inferred the intent to terrorise civilians from the use of highly inaccurate weapons, stating that

> the use of the modified air bombs is another clear indication of the Accused's intent to spread terror. The highly destructive force and the psychological effects these bombs had on the civilian population were obvious to anyone. The decision by the Accused to use modified air bombs against civilian targets can, therefore, only be interpreted as demonstrating the intent to spread terror.[121]

For indiscriminate attacks, inferring a terrorising intent does not pose significant difficulties, as such intent can be deduced from the decision to hit with wide-area-impact weapons urban territories with high concentrations of civilians or civilian objects, or by protracted campaigns of shelling and sniping upon civilian areas. On the contrary, deducing a primary purpose of spreading terror among civilians from disproportionate attacks appears much more controversial.

Disproportionate attacks, in fact, are those launched despite foreseeing the causation of excessive incidental civilian harm but aimed, in terms of primary purpose, at legitimate military objectives (at least this appears the only

[118] *Prosecutor v Dragomir Milošević*, Trial Judgment, IT-98-29/1-T, 12 December 2007, para 888.
[119] *Prosecutor v Galić*, Appeal Judgment (n 113) para 104.
[120] ibid, para 102.
[121] *Prosecutor v Dragomir Milošević*, Trial Judgment (n 118) para 970.

meaningful, coherent systemisation of the relationship between disproportionate and indiscriminate attacks).[122] Inferring a primary purpose of terrorisng civilians from disproportionate attacks, therefore, requires substantially to prove that there was an intent to strike a lawful target, although secondary in comparison to the primary purpose of disproportionately affecting civilians, with the aim of terrorising aim. As such, this aspect will be discussed in more detail in relation to the crime of direct attacks on civilians, which, as defined by the ICTY, presents large overlapping with the latter hypothesis.

3.2.3. Indiscriminate and Disproportionate Attacks as Conduct Indicating the Intent of Direct Attacks on Civilians

Between the first occasions in which the ICTY, based on the *Tadić* findings, indicated the elements to be met in order to configure the war crime of direct attacks on civilians (at this stage indicated as crime of 'unlawful attacks on civilians'), the *Blaskić* case stands out.

The Trial Chamber assessed the conduct of hostilities of the forces of the Croatian Defence Council (HVO). Units of the HVO had employed military tactics developed for combat in built-up areas, implying the use of automatic weapons and grenades on a house-by-house basis, in order to clear the enemy from a number of areas within several municipalities in the territory of Bosnia and Herzegovina. The defence argued that the civilian victims of these attacks, even if higher in number than the combatants actually targeted, had to be considered collateral casualties of attacks against legitimate military objectives. The Trial Chamber emphasised, in contrast, the evidence demonstrating that in many cases these tactics encompassed the burning of entire villages,[123] without possible justifications in terms of military necessity.

As for the relevance of the weapons employed, the indictment included a controversial attack on the municipalities of Vitez and Stari Vitez in April 1993, which resulted in a high number of civilian casualties and massive damage to numerous civilian objects. The judges considered the nature of the weapons employed for the attack on these municipalities, and concluded that, being the relevant bombs shot from 'home-made mortars', they could have hardly been directed accurately to lawful targets. The irregular and non-linear trajectory of this artillery made the weapons likely to hit non-military targets to a degree allowing to qualify the mortars as 'blind weapons'.[124]

The Chamber concluded that these attacks were unlawful attacks on civilians and on civilian objects. As for the elements of the relevant crimes, the judges

[122] See ch 2, sections 2.5–2.6.
[123] *Prosecutor v Blaskić*, Trial Judgment, ICTY IT-95-14-A, 29 July 2004, para 406.
[124] ibid, para 512.

indicated that such attacks, to be punishable, needed to meet a result requirement, that was causing 'deaths and/or serious bodily injury within the civilian population or damage to civilian property'. As regards the mental element, the attacks had to be conducted 'intentionally, in the knowledge [or "when it was impossible not to know"] that civilians or civilian property were being targeted not through military necessity'.[125]

Contesting this point, the Chamber made clear 'that the *mens rea* which characterises all the violations of Article 3 of the Statute, as well as the violations of Article 2, is the intentionality of the acts or omissions, *a concept containing both guilty intent and recklessness*' (emphasis added).[126] Intentionality, therefore, was interpreted as including the pursuit of a course of action deliberately disregarding that, in the ordinary course of the events, a certain result of the action (in this case hitting civilians or civilian objects) would have occurred.

Problematically, however, the Chamber caused serious misgivings when stating – in an oxymoron – that 'targeting civilians or civilian property is an offence when not justified by military necessity'.[127] If interpreted literally, this notation seems to imply that there might exist combat situations in which the *direct* targeting of civilians can be considered lawful, if justified by military necessity. From the IHL point of view, this is a contradiction in itself, since military necessity legally operates only when legitimate military objectives are targeted (eventually condoning a 'proportionate', that is incidental plus not excessive civilian harm), and can never justify the targeting of civilians and civilian objects as such.

This knot was disentangled in the leading case in this area, the *Galić* judgment,[128] in which the ICTY both refined the interpretation of the crime of direct attacks on civilians, and for the first time explicitly considered the interpretation of indiscriminate attacks.

The case concerned the military campaign conducted from 1992 by a branch of the military forces of the Republika Srpska, the Sarajevo Romanija Corps (SRK), which had surrounded the city of Sarajevo, against units of the Army of Bosnia and Herzegovina (ABiH), in control of the majority of the areas of city. The campaign of sniping and shelling, conducted in a densely populated area, had killed hundreds of civilians and injured thousands.

The prosecution alleged that many attacks had been deliberately directed against the civilian population, and several witnesses reported civilians being hit while they were attending funerals, or while in ambulances, trams and buses, as well as during shopping or while clearing rubbish from the streets. The defence asserted that the civilian victims were collateral casualties of legitimate military activities.

[125] *Prosecutor v Blaskić*, Trial Judgment (n 123) para 180.
[126] ibid, para 179.
[127] ibid, para 180.
[128] *Prosecutor v Galić*, Trial Judgment (n 112).

The Trial Chamber acknowledged that, given the combat was in an urban area, military targets were not always clearly separated from civilian objects. However, the judgment reinforced the validity of the presumption of civilian status enshrined in IHL, stressing that, for as long as there is doubt as to the status of a person that is going to be attacked, it must be presumed that he or she is a civilian. Importantly, the Chamber also underlined that 'The presence of individual combatants within the population does not change its civilian character.'[129]

The judges then corrected the controversial assertion of the *Blaskić* trial judgment, explicitly stating that the customary prohibition of attacks on civilians could not be 'adequately described' as forbidding 'targeting civilians when not justified by military necessity', since the norm enshrining the prohibition, that is Article 51(2) AP I, makes clear that civilians and the civilian population as such cannot be directly targeted, and does not contemplate any derogation from the rule based on military necessity.[130] The Trial Chamber, in other words, removed any doubt about the *categorical* nature of the prohibition of attack directed at civilians and/or civilian objects.

Crucially for the present analysis, the Trial Chamber continued the discussion of the crime of direct attacks on civilians in *Galić* analysing specifically indiscriminate and disproportionate attacks.

The judges found, first of all, that the prohibition against indiscriminate attacks, that is attacks which strike civilians and combatants, or civilian objects and military objectives, without distinction, is the expression of a well-established rule of customary law applicable in all armed conflicts.

The assertion was supported recalling that since 1922 authoritative sources of interpretation as the Hague Air Warfare Rules enunciated the prohibition on indiscriminate attacks.[131] It was also underlined by the judges as a matter of *opinio juris* that the British Prime Minister, in 1938, concerning the bombing of Barcelona during the Spanish Civil War, had declared at the House of Commons that 'The one definite rule of international law, however, is that direct and

[129] ibid, para 50.

[130] ibid, para 44.

[131] The Hague Air Warfare Rules effectively provided that an air bombardment 'is legitimate *only* when directed *exclusively*' against specific military objectives, that is 'military forces, military works, military establishments or depots, manufacturing plants constituting important and well-known centres for the production of arms, ammunition or characterized military supplies, lines of communication or of transport which are used for military purposes'. In addition, the rules stated that, should any of the aforementioned objectives 'be so situated that they could not be bombed but that an undiscriminating bombardment of the civilian population would result therefrom, the aircraft *must abstain* from bombing'. In these body of rules was also made clear that the bombardments of cities, towns, villages, habitations and buildings can be justified by proportionality only at two conditions: 1) that the bombardment takes place 'in the immediate vicinity of the operations of the land forces', and 2) that there is a 'reasonable presumption that the military concentration is important enough to justify the bombardment, taking into account the danger to which the civilian population will thus be exposed'. See *Rules Concerning the Control of Wireless Telegraphy in Time of War and Air Warfare*, adopted on 19 February 1923 by the Commission of Jurists nominated by the Washington Conference of 1922 on the Limitation of Armaments.

deliberate bombing of non-combatants is in all circumstances illegal'. Different resolutions of the League of Nations and of the United Nations on the same line were also recalled.[132]

After declaring the customary nature of the prohibition, the Chamber seem to construe indiscriminate attacks as conduct from which the war crime of direct attacks on civilians can be inferred.

As stated in the judgment, 'indiscriminate attacks ... *may qualify as direct attacks against civilians*'.[133] It is also recalled that other Chambers of the Tribunal have considered that certain attacks employing weapons that cannot discriminate between military objectives and civilian objects (evoking the IHL concept of 'inherently indiscriminate weapons'),[134] are '*tantamount to direct targeting of civilians*'.[135]

It was not specified under what circumstances and conditions indiscriminate attacks qualify as direct attacks on civilians, but other sections of the judgment referred to the relevance of factors related to target verification, such as:

> [D]istance between the victim and the most probable source of fire; distance between the location where the victim was hit and the confrontation line; combat activity going on at the time and the location of the incident, as well as relevant nearby presence of military activities or facilities; appearance of the victim as to age, gender, clothing; the activity the victim could appear to be engaged in; visibility of the victim due to weather, unobstructed line of sight or daylight.[136]

Furthermore, following the structure of Article 51(5) AP I, the Chamber mentions disproportionate attacks, and classifies them as a *species ad genus* of indiscriminate attacks, stating '*One type of indiscriminate attack violates the principle of proportionality*'.[137] The judges indicate that, once a legitimate military target is identified, the commander has to consider whether striking the target is expected to cause incidental civilian harm excessive in comparison to the military advantage anticipated. If such harm is expected, it is duty of the commander to cancel the attack. For the Chamber, 'certain *apparently disproportionate attacks may give rise to the inference that civilians were actually the object of attack*'.[138] In other words, according to the judges, some of these prohibited attacks, in particular when the disproportion of the expected civilian harm is evident, allow the Chamber, in an analogy with indiscriminate attacks and on a case-to-case basis, in light of the available evidence, to infer that the real intent of the perpetrator was to strike civilians.

[132] *Prosecutor v Galić*, Trial Judgment (n 112) para 57, fn 103.
[133] ibid, para 57 (emphasis added).
[134] See ch 2, section 2.2.
[135] *Prosecutor v Galić*, Trial Judgment (n 112) para 57, fn 101 (emphasis added).
[136] ibid, para 188.
[137] ibid, para 58, emphasis added.
[138] ibid, para 60.

It is therefore essential to understand the elements of the crime of direct attacks on civilians, highlighting their intersection with disproportionate and indiscriminate attacks:

- the *actus reus* consists of 'acts of violence directed against the civilian population or individual civilians not taking a direct part in the hostilities causing death or serious injury to body or health within the civilian population';[139]
- the *means rea* is satisfied with 'wilfully making the civilian population or individual civilians not taking a direct part in hostilities the object of those acts of violence'.[140]

The Chamber dwelled on the mental element for this crime, and adopted the widely agreed interpretation of intent as construed by the majority of the literature in relation to the grave breaches of the Geneva Conventions, according to which 'wilfully' means that:

> [T]he accused must have acted consciously and with intent, i.e., with his mind on the act and its consequences, and willing them ('criminal intent' or 'malice aforethought'); this encompasses the concepts of 'wrongful intent' or 'recklessness', viz., the attitude of an agent who, without being certain of a particular result, accepts the possibility of it happening; on the other hand, ordinary negligence or lack of foresight is not covered, i.e., when a man acts without having his mind on the act or its consequences.[141]

Following this interpretation, the ICTY indicated that even from the international criminal law (ICL) standpoint, launching an attack accepting the possibility – or disregarding the likelihood – of hitting civilians, satisfies the mental element required for the crime of direct attacks on civilians. The perpetrator who recklessly attacks civilians acts 'wilfully'.

This notion of intent includes therefore the continental concept of *dolus eventualis*. The ICTY specifically explains this correspondence between recklessness and *dolus eventualis* in the *Stakić* case, in relation to the crime of murder as a violation of the Statute's Article 3. The Chamber in this judgement stated:

> The technical definition of *dolus eventualis* is the following: if the actor engages in life-endangering behaviour, his killing becomes intentional if he 'reconciles himself' or 'makes peace' with the likelihood of death. Thus, if the killing is committed with 'manifest indifference to the value of human life', even conduct of minimal risk can qualify as intentional homicide. Large scale killings that would be classified as reckless murder in the United States would meet the continental criteria of *dolus eventualis*.[142]

[139] ibid, para 56.
[140] ibid.
[141] Y Sandoz, C Swinarski and B Zimmermann (eds), *Commentary on the Additional Protocols of 8 June 1977 to the Geneva Conventions of 12 August 1949* (International Committee of the Red Cross – Martinus Nijhoff Publishers, 1987) para 3474.
[142] *Prosecutor v Stakić*, Trial Judgment, ICTY IT-97-24-T, 31 July 2003, para 587.

From these definitions of the mental elements, it follows that the burden of proof on the prosecution is to demonstrate, for indiscriminate attacks, that the person in charge of the attacking decision was aware of the civilian status of those that were going to be shelled or hit in the attack. As a consequence, the *mens rea* has to be ascertained evaluating if a reasonably well-informed agent, with the knowledge of the commander at the moment of the attack, would have been aware of the civilian status of the targets. It is the so-called 'reasonable commander' standard,[143] borrowed from the 'reasonable person' standard of criminal law.[144]

In the case of disproportionate attacks, this standard requires a higher mental element, as the prosecution must also prove that the attack was launched wilfully and in the *knowledge* of circumstances giving rise to the expectation of excessive civilian casualties.

The mental element, in other words, is determined, through a *post facto* assessment of the perpetrator's *ex ante* knowledge of the possible results of launching the attack.[145]

These subjective tests bring with them all the problems and the challenges inherent in proving mental elements whose legal characterisation demands a level of stringency contrasting with the blurred fluidity of the psychological stances of the agent/perpetrator toward the different – either foreseen, pursued, or both – consequences of an attack. The high degree of subjectivity of these assessments, therefore. prompted the Tribunal to make recourse, in different cases, to several objective indicators and characteristics of the attacks, in order to infer the intent of indiscriminately or disproportionately attacking civilians, including targeting failures, methods of combat and weapons employed.[146]

These indicators are evaluated through the lenses of the IHL targeting principles, interpreted teleologically, according to their protective purpose.

In the *Kupreskić* case, the ICTY assessed the attack, in 1993, of the village of Ahmici, in central Bosnia, in which in just a few hours 116 Muslim civilians were killed, and hundreds of houses were destroyed. The main focus of the case was the analysis of persecution as a crime against humanity, but in the 'preliminary issues' section of the judgment violations of the laws and customs of war were also discussed. The defence alleged that a number of victims had

[143] See inter alia, I Henderson and K Reece, 'Proportionality under International Humanitarian Law: The Reasonable Military Commander Standard and Reverberating Effects' (2018) 51 *Vanderbilt Journal of Transnational Law* 835; RD Sloane, 'Puzzles of Proportion and the Reasonable Military Commander: Reflections on the Law, Ethics, and Geopolitics of Proportionality' (2015) 6 *Harvard National Security Journal* 299; T Broude, 'Behavioral International Law' (2014) 163 *University of Pennsylvania Law Review* 1129.

[144] See inter alia M Baron, 'The Standard of the Reasonable Person in Criminal Law' in RA Duff et al (eds), *The Structures of Criminal Law* (Oxford University Press, 2011); A Ashworth and J Horder, *Principles of Criminal Law*, 7th edn (Oxford University Press, 2013) 17 ff.

[145] Moneta (n 109) 65.

[146] Following the schematisation of I Bonomy, *Principles of Distinction and Protection at the ICTY* (Torkel Opsahl Academic EPub, 2013) 24 ff.

previously taken up weapons to resist the attack, and therefore had taken direct part in the hostilities. Consequently, the city should have not been qualified as undefended town. In response, the judges hold that it was beyond dispute that 'a large numbers of civilian casualties would have been interspersed among the combatants', and emphasised the 'sacrosanct character of the duty to protect civilians'. Thus, even admitting that the Muslim population of the village was not entirely civilian, but comprised some armed individuals, 'still no justification would exist for widespread and indiscriminate attacks against civilians'. Even during full-scale hostilities, the judges continued, fundamental norms such as those related to the proportionality principle, 'unambiguously outlaw such conduct'. Therefore, attacks directed against legitimate military objectives can still be unlawful if conducted through *indiscriminate means and methods of warfare*, or – as the Chamber states – if carried out 'in such a way as to *cause indiscriminate damage to civilians*'.[147]

Importantly, the Chamber not only qualified both the principles of proportionality and precaution as expression of customary international law, but also clarified that their interpretation has to be guided by 'elementary consideration of humanity'. The reference is to the 'dictates of public conscience' and the 'principles of humanity' of the Martens Clause. The judges, in other words, derive from the Martens Clause a duty to interpret the targeting principles according to it, so as to enhance their rigour, precision and operative function. This extensive interpretation is therefore teleological, explicitly aiming to 'expand the protections accorded to civilians'.[148]

The *Mrkšić* judgment concerned the mistreatment and execution of Croat and other non-Serb individuals taken from the Vukovar Hospital by Serb forces in 1991. Although the indictment did not include the attack against the city of Vukovar and its civilians, and the resulting devastation, the judgment discussed them nonetheless, as matters relevant to establishing elements of the offences charged in relation to the first violation mentioned.

When considering this attack, the Trial Chamber affirmed that duration of the armed clashes, the significant disparity between the different forces engaged in the battle and in their armament and equipment and, most importantly, the nature and the extent of the devastation brought on Vukovar as a whole, were all circumstances leading to the conclusion that 'the Serb attack was also consciously and deliberately directed against the city of Vukovar itself and its hapless civilian population'.[149] The judges underlined in this reflection that the assessment of the methods of the attack as a whole reinforced the conclusion. Furthermore, the

[147] *Prosecutor v Kupreškić et al*, Trial Judgment, ICTY IT-95-16-T, 14 January 2000, para 524 (emphasis added). When talking of 'indiscriminate damage' the Chamber adopts a slight deviation from the IHL terminology, which usually associates the prohibited collateral civilian damage with 'disproportion', rather than with indiscriminate nature.

[148] ibid, para 525.

[149] *Prosecutor v Mrksic et al*, Trial Judgment, ICTY IT-95-13/1-T, 27 September 2007, para 470.

extensive destruction of civilian properties and infrastructure and the number of civilians displaced indicated 'the attack was carried out in an indiscriminate way, contrary to international law. It was an unlawful attack. Indeed, it was also directed *in part* deliberately against the civilian population'.[150]

In the *Strugar* judgment, the ICTY adjudicated an attack which took place during the during the military campaign conducted by the troops of the former Yugoslav People's Army (JNA) in the region of Dubrovnik. The attack consisted of mortar and artillery shelling on the Old Town of Dubrovnik.

The city at the time of this military campaign was theatre of counter-offensives from the Croatian forces against the JNA. Even if in a position and condition of strategic disadvantage, the Croatian forces held several fixed and mobile firing positions across the city. Their tactic was to get close to the JNA targets with mobile mortar units, fire and move away to avoid return fire. Mobile mortar units were moved in and around the newer parts of Dubrovnik. Ample evidence, however, testified that at the time of the attack none of these fixed or mobile units were situated in the Old Town, and reports only indicated that sporadically individuals armed with light weapons were seen crossing the area.[151]

After discussing in detail the weaponry employed and the locations of legitimate military targets in the city, the Chamber concluded that 'there was inadequate direction of the fire of the JNA mortars and other weapons against Croatian military targets. Instead, they fired extensively and without disciplined direction and targeting correction, at Dubrovnik, including the Old Town'. The judges found that the Old Town was extensively targeted by JNA artillery and that no adversary firing points or other military objectives were located or could have been believed to be located in the Old Town. The Chamber found therefore that the intent of the perpetrators was to target civilians and civilian objects in the Old Town.[152] Importantly, the judges added that the presence of certain non-civilian individuals among the targeted population does not change the character of that population. It is sufficient for the elements of the crime a 'predominantly civilian nature' of those targeted.[153]

In the *Dragomar Milošević* case (previously mentioned in relation to the crime of terror and its specific intent) the Chamber analysed, in the context of the siege of Sarajevo, attacks of the SRK with modified air bombs. Each bomb had an explosive charge or a fuel-air mixture weighing 100–250 kilograms. These modified bombs were either dropped from aircraft or attached to rockets fired from ground launch pads and mortars. The Chamber considered the experts' opinions signalling that fuel-air explosions 'cause a lethal wave of overpressure destroying everything and everyone in the blast', and that civilians in the vicinity of the impact areas reported 'blast syndrome'; that is, serious damage to internal

[150] ibid, para 472.
[151] *Prosecutor v Strugar*, Trial Judgment, ICTY IT-01-42-T, 31 January 2005, para 72.
[152] ibid, para 288.
[153] ibid, para 282.

organs, without evident shrapnel wounds or blood.[154] The judges found that once a modified air bomb was launched, its trajectory and flight path could not be guided, and therefore that the bomb could only be directed generally toward an area. In addition, military experts noted that the rockets were mounted under the air bombs unprofessionally, increasing the risks of deviations. As a result, modified air bombs were identified as highly inaccurate weapons with extremely high explosive force.[155] For these reasons, in light of the evidence demonstrating the *indiscriminate nature* of the modified air bombs, in consideration of the knowledge of the SRK of that indiscriminate character, and given the number of civilian deaths and seriously injured, the Trial Chamber found that the SRK was responsible for shelling civilians and civilian areas (in this case, the indiscriminate nature of the weapon allows the judges to infer the intent to terrorise civilians).[156]

On the same line of reasoning, in *Martić* the Trial Chamber analysed the shelling of the city of Zagreb from the SRK. In particular, the judges assessed the legality of repeated attacks on the city by means of Orkan rockets. The areas bombed included the main square of the city, various shopping streets, a school, a village near the Zagreb airport and the airport itself. Five civilians were killed in the attacks and more than 150 were severely injured.

The Chamber again assessed the nature of the weapon employed to reach important conclusions. The M-87 Orkan is a multi-barrelled rocket launcher (MBLR), firing unguided rockets. It is commonly used to target soldiers, as well as armoured vehicles. In the attacks on Zagreb, each rocket was loaded with a cluster warhead containing 288 bomblets, expelled at a height of around one kilometre above the targeted area. At the moment of the impact, every bomblet exploded, releasing 420 steel pellets, each of them lethal in a range of 10 metres. Importantly, at the firing range 50 kilometres from the target area, the weapon displayed a targeting error of one kilometre in any direction.[157] It was from this range that the attacks on the city were launched. The Chamber therefore noted, against the allegations of the defence, that the presence of military targets in Zagreb was 'irrelevant in light of the nature of the M-87 Orkan'. According to the judges – considering that the projectiles were non-guided, that each contained a cluster bomb impacting a wide area, and that the distance between the firing position and the target areas was maximum – it was legitimate to conclude the weapon was incapable of hitting specific targets. The Orkan rocket was therefore considered unsuitable to distinguish between military objectives and civilian objects, particularly in densely populated areas like Zagreb.[158] The attacks were therefore widespread attacks against the civilian population.

[154] *Prosecutor v Dragomir Milošević*, Trial Judgment (n 118) para 94.
[155] ibid, para 97.
[156] ibid, para 912.
[157] *Prosecutor v Martić*, Trial Judgment, ICTY IT-95-11-T, 12 June 2007, para 462.
[158] ibid, para 463.

3.3. Critical Knots in the ICTY Jurisprudence

3.3.1. In Search of Objective Parameters Indicating the Indiscriminate Character of Attacks: The Circular Error Probable

The jurisprudence analysed above, mostly elaborating on the implications of many contingent variables of the attacks under its scrutiny, did not establish a solid and objective legal parameter – going beyond a case-by-case approach – to qualify an attack as indiscriminate.

The efforts of establishing objective indicators of the indiscriminate character of any attack assume a crucial importance. As argued in the previous chapter, military powers, particularly militaries of large, aggressive powers in the international arena, as well as military lawyers, particularly in academic centres of the same big powers, have often exploited the indeterminacy of the balancing test of proportionality in attacks (that is the indeterminacy of the notion of 'excessive' civilian harm) to expand, until the removal of any upper limit, the entity of so-called 'collateral damage' legally tolerable in lawful attacks. This unlimited 'collateralisation', unduly expanding proportionality far beyond its normative lineaments, served the purpose of legitimising the anticipated killing and injuring of entire crowds of civilians, as well as the damage and destruction of entire neighbourhoods, included in single strikes, camouflaged as 'proportionate' attacks.[159] The overexpansion of the notion of proportionality, however, had another effect: by removing limits to killing and destruction that can be presented as always incidental, and never excessive in comparison to certain high military advantages, the notion of indiscriminate attacks becomes meaningless, and never applicable. Any lawful target in the vicinity of crowds of civilians killed or injured, in fact, can at that point trigger claims that the civilian harm, no matter its extent, was 'proportionate' due to a high military advantage being sought. With one distortion, therefore, militaries and authors advancing these misconceptions tend not only to install a presumption of proportionality of attacks killing scores of civilians, but de facto abolish the prohibition of indiscriminate attacks. Establishing objective indicators that allow the determination of the indiscriminate nature of attacks, therefore, becomes crucial for preserving a coherent reading of the nexus between distinction and proportionality (otherwise set to work in reciprocal neutralisation), and more importantly becomes vital for protecting civilians.

Ballistics – the science analysing the impact of projectiles – adopts several notions to measure the precision of weapons systems. Among these notions, of crucial importance is the circular error probable (CEP), also called 'circular error

[159] See F Albanese, L Daniele and N Perugini, 'Humanitarian Camouflage: Israel's Rewriting of the Laws of War to Legitimize the Gaza Genocide' (2024) 12 *Institute of Palestine Studies – Current Issues in Depth* 5.

probability' or 'circle of equal probability',[160] identified as the radius of a circle, centered on a target, that is expected to circumscribe the landing point of half of the rounds of a weapon system shot at the target. It represents, in other words, the median error radius of a weapons system. A CEP of 100 metres, for example, will indicate that if 100 munitions are targeted at the same point, approximately 50 will impact within a circle of a 100-metre radius around that point. The adoption in war crimes adjudications conflicts of a CEP indicating the indiscriminate character of attack was at the centre of a controversial ICTY saga, and problematic legacy, revolving around a specific case.

3.3.2. The *Gotovina* 'Scandal': The 'End of Indiscriminate Attacks'?

A major step for identifying an objective indicator of the indiscriminate nature of attacks was undertaken in the *Gotovina* case, in which the Trail Chamber effectively established a legal standard of indiscriminate targeting, which was then rejected by the Appeal Chamber, with grave legal implications. Shortly after the Appeal Chamber acquittal, a letter by an ICTY judge was leaked to the press, accusing the then President, Judge Meron,[161] to have pressured his peers to acquit the defendant,[162] allegedly in furtherance of US and Israel military interests against setting strict legal standards of conduction of aerial bombardments. According to some scholars, this was 'one of the worst scandals to engulf the ICTY in its history'.[163] The scandal followed the publication of the letter of the Danish judge of the Tribunal, Frederik Harhoff, emailed to 56 of his contacts, in which the judge accused the President of the Tribunal, Judge Theodor Meron, of exercising pressure on his colleagues in order to acquit high-profile defendants such as *Gotovina*. In it, Judge Harhoff explained that

> up until autumn 2012, it has been a more or less set practice at the court that military commanders were held responsible for war crimes that their subordinates committed … But then the court's Appeals Chamber suddenly back-tracked last autumn with the three Croatian generals and ministers in the Gotovina case.[164]

[160] See MN Schmitt, 'Precision Attack and IHL' (2005) 87 *International Review of the Red Cross* 445; S Casey-Maslen (ed), *Weapons Under International Human Rights Law* (Cambridge University Press, 2014).

[161] Who later came back on this controversial acquittal in his 'General Gotovina: A Controversial Acquittal' in T Meron, *Standing Up for Justice: The Challenges of Trying Atrocity Crimes* (Oxford University Press, 2021) 173–82.

[162] M Simmons. 'Hague Judge Faults Acquittals of Serb and Croat Commanders' *New York Times*, 14 June 2013, at www.nytimes.com/2013/06/14/world/europe/hague-judge-faults-acquittals-of-serb-and-croat-commanders.html?smid=tw-share&_r=0.

[163] See M Milanović, 'Danish Judge Blasts ICTY President' *EJILTalk!*, 13 June 2013, at www.ejiltalk.org/danish-judge-blasts-icty-president.

[164] Letter available at a.bimg.dk/node-files/511/6/6511917-letter-english.pdf, annexed to the article of S Andersen, 'Murderers Are Being Allowed To Go Free' *BT Denmark*, 13 June 2013, at www.bt.dk/udland/english-version-murderers-are-being-allowed-to-go-free.

In Harhoff's opinion, after the *Gotovina* and *Perišić*[165] acquittals, the joint criminal enterprise traditionally adopted by the ICTY to convict commanders for war crimes of their subordinates was reduced from the contribution to crimes 'to demanding a *direct intention* to commit the crime (and so not just *acceptance* of the crimes being committed)'.[166] The judge, then, bluntly connected this sudden overturn of the Chamber's legal approach to external political pressures. He stated:

> You would think that the military establishment in leading States (such as USA and Israel) felt that the courts in practice were getting too close to the military commanders' responsibilities.
>
> … Have any American or Israeli officials ever exerted pressure on the American presiding judge (the presiding judge for the court that is) to ensure a change of direction? We will probably never know. But reports of the same presiding judge's tenacious pressure on his colleagues in the Gotovina – Perisic case makes you think he was determined to achieve an acquittal. … Most of the cases will lead to commanding officers walking free from here on.
>
> So the American (and Israeli) military leaders can breathe a sigh of relief. You may think this is just splitting hairs. But I am sitting here with a very uncomfortable feeling that the court has changed the direction of pressure from 'the military establishments' in certain dominant countries … The worst of it is the suspicion that some of my colleagues have been behind a short-sighted political pressure.[167]

Scholars and commentators understood in different ways the implications of the letter, and reached different conclusions about the likelihood of this political pressure from diplomatic circles of powerful countries on the judges,[168] but the suspect of a weakened independency of the Tribunal inevitably arose.[169] The likelihood of these forms of pressure on the Tribunal, directed at cases on the point of establishing an objective legal parameter indicating the indiscriminate nature of attacks, confirms what was asserted when explaining the background of this analysis. Even international criminal justice, in other words, constitutes an especially conflictual field of tensions, not only between different theories and legal approaches, but obviously between the different political economic pressures and interests that might be weakened or empowered by the affirmation of one legal approach over another.

[165] ICTY, Appeals Chamber Acquits and Orders Release of Momčilo Perišić, Press Release, 28 February 2013, at www.icty.org/en/press/appeals-chamber-acquits-and-orders-release-mom%C4%8Dilo-peri%C5%A1i%C4%87.

[166] ibid (emphasis added).

[167] ibid.

[168] See KJ Heller, 'The Real Judge Meron Scandal at the ICTY' *Opinio Juris*, 17 June 2013, at opiniojuris.org/2013/06/17/the-real-judge-meron-scandal-at-the-icty; D Jakobs, 'Some Thoughts on The bombshell Letter by Judge Harhoff at the ICTY' *Spreading The Jam – International Law, International Criminal Law, Human Rights and Transitional Justice*, at dovjacobs.com/2013/06/13/some-thoughts-on-the-bombshell-letter-by-judge-harhoff-at-the-icty.

[169] M Simons, 'Judge at War Crimes Tribunal Faults Acquittals of Serb and Croat Commanders' *New York Times*, 14 June 2013.

In the case mentioned, the focal point of this field of tensions, at the same time a foxhole and trench of the legal struggle for and against accountability of powerful perpetrators, is exactly the intent to be met for the commission of indiscriminate and disproportionate attacks.

The *Gotovina* case concerned a number of crimes allegedly committed by the Croatian military forces (HV) against the Serb population in various municipalities of the Krajina region. The most problematic part of the trial judgment focused on the legality of the HV artillery shelling of the town of Knin.

It was acknowledged that in the area of Knin the HV, in the context of Operation Storm, had identified a number of legitimate military targets of the Serbian Army of Krajina (SVK).

Problematically, however, the HV attacks in the Knin area employed 122mm calibre Grad rockets. Grad rockets are unguided projectiles fired from multiple-barrel launchers. These launchers can fire up to 40 rockets in a very short time lapse toward targets located in a range of 20 kilometres. Grad rockets are considered 'area weapons', firing against several military targets of significant dimension located at distance. Different variables (such as fusing, ballistic and firing technique) influence the extension of the area of impact of the relevant attacks, which include the combined blast radiuses of the individual rockets. The impact area, as a consequence, can be very wide, with a high risk of harming civilians when the weapon is employed against targets located in densely populated areas.[170]

During the attacks under scrutiny, evidence suggested that the HV fired at least 600 projectiles on 4 August 1995 and at least 300 projectiles on 5 August 1995 into the city of Knin.

When considering the means and methods of the attacks, the Trial Chamber considered that 'although MBRLs (Multi-barrel rocket launchers) are generally less accurate than Howitzers or mortars, their use by the HV in respect of Knin on 4 and 5 August 1995 *was not inherently indiscriminate*.'[171]

The problem remained to understand how to determine the accuracy of the HV targeting, and how to consider the shelling of wide areas around the legitimate military targets identified. After analysing the evidence and the experts' opinions submitted, and assessing a variety of complex ballistic factors, the Chamber found that a reasonable interpretation of the evidence was to conclude that:

> [T]hose artillery projectiles which impacted within a distance of *200 metres* of an identified artillery target were deliberately fired at that artillery target.[172]

Thus, a standard was established whereby projectiles impacting the ground within a radius of 200 metres from a legitimate military target could be presumed to have

[170] M Brehm, 'Use of Grad Rockets in Populated Areas: What Lessons from Gotovina?' *EJILTalk!*, 30 July 2014, at www.ejiltalk.org/use-of-grad-rockets-in-populated-areas-what-lessons-from-gotovina.

[171] *Prosecutor v Gotovina et al*, Trial Judgment, ICTY IT-06-90-6, 15 April 2011, para 1987 (emphasis added).

[172] ibid, para 1898 (emphasis added).

been directed at that target itself, while projectiles foreseeably impacting further away from this circular distance from the target were evidence of indiscriminate firing.[173] This parameter was one of the key factors leading the Trial Chamber to convict the defendants, and the first time in the history of ICL a jurisdiction set an effective indicator of the indiscriminate character of attacks, which could have consolidated in a standard transposable in all armed conflicts in populated areas.

The Appeal Chamber, in contrast, rejected the 200 metres margin of error standard, and on this basis also refuted the related joint criminal enterprise that the Trial Chamber had found, deciding by a majority of three to two (dissenting judges Agius and Pocar) to acquit the defendants.

According to the judges, the Trial Chamber findings were not sufficiently supported by the evidence received, and the Chamber 'provided no explanation as to the basis for the margin of error it adopted; this amounted to a failure to provide a reasoned opinion'.[174] The Appeals judges maintained that, absent this standard, it could have not been excluded

> the possibility that all of the impact sites considered in the Trial Judgement were the result of shelling aimed at targets that the Trial Chamber considered to be legitimate. The fact that a relatively large number of shells fell more than 200 metres from fixed artillery targets could be consistent with a much broader range of error. The spread of shelling across Knin was also plausibly explained by the scattered locations of fixed artillery targets, along with the possibility of a higher margin of error.[175]

In other words, without the 200 metres standard, and considering the presence of targets across the various areas bombarded, the evidence assessed in the trial judgment did not conclusively demonstrate or prove, according to the appeal judgment, that indiscriminate attacks had been committed.

While different scholars agreed on the lack of such a standard in existing international law of targeting,[176] the majority of the commentators, as well as the dissenting judges, signalled that the Appeal Chamber itself had failed to indicate an alternative valid standard.

As convincingly argued by Milanović, the majority of the Appeal Chamber failed even to indicate whether the Trial Chamber's error about the 200-metre CEP standard was an *error of law* or an *error of fact*. If seen as an error of law, the majority should have indicated a new legal standard to determine the indiscriminate or lawful character of the shelling of Knin. If seen as an error of fact, the majority should have contested the factual finding of the Trial Chamber only if no other reasonable trier of facts could reasonably indicate that the attack

[173] This finding of the ICTY Trial Chamber has to be read in connection to what has already been explained in relation to the notion of Circular Error Probable (see ch 2, section 2.2).

[174] *Prosecutor v Gotovina at al*, Appeals Judgment, ICTY IT-06-90-A, 16 November 2012, para 61.

[175] ibid, para 65.

[176] See inter alia WB Huffman, 'Margin of Error: Potential Pitfalls of the Ruling in The Prosecutor v. Ante Gotovina' (2012) 22 *Military Law Review* 5.

was indiscriminate.[177] Vallentgoed emphasised that, through the dismissal of the 200-metre standard without identifying any other, the Appeal Chamber majority not only had left unanswered the crucial question of what the correct margin of error actually is, but also 'refused to address critically a plethora of evidence that suggested crimes may have taken place'.[178]

Furthermore, other commentators noted that the Appeal Chamber majority interpreted the role of the 200-metre standard in the Trial judgment as going beyond what the Trial Chamber itself claimed in its reasoning. Considering the relevant paragraphs of the Trial Chamber judgment, according to Clark, the Trial Chamber's reasoning did not apply the standard with a 'black and white metric approach', as the Appeal Chamber judgment asserted. Rather, the Trial Chamber judges 'assessed the legality of attacks in which the projectiles impacted outside of a 200 metres radius on a case-by-case basis'.[179]

Even more concerningly, the approach adopted by the Appeal Chamber, in the absence of an established margin of error, rendered it virtually impossible to classify *any* shelling as indiscriminate, including those far beyond the presumptively legal distance from the target identified. The dissent of Appeal Chamber Judge Pocar in this regard was blunt. In his opinion, the majority's approach was described as 'wholly erroneous and in violation of [the ICTY] standard of review on appeal'. According to Judge Pocar, having found that deducing and applying the 200-metre standard was an error of law, the Appeals Chamber, pursuant to the Tribunal's standard of appellate review, failed to fulfil two separate obligations:

> Having found that the 200 Metre Standard was erroneous and that the Trial Chamber committed an error of law in deriving and applying an incorrect legal standard, the Appeals Chamber had … First, to identify and articulate the correct legal standard and, second, to apply this standard to the evidence contained in the trial record or, in the alternative, to remand the case back to the Trial Chamber to apply the correct legal standard to the evidence. However, in contravention of our well-established appellate standard of review, the Majority followed neither of these requirements.[180]

Even dissenting Judge Agius, despite agreeing on the error of the Trial Chamber in establishing the 200-metre standard, noted in his dissenting opinion that according to the reasoning of the majority:

> [E]ven impacts which were more than 400 metres distant from the nearest military target would still have to be ignored. This conclusion thus allows the Majority to avoid

[177] M Milanović, 'The Gotovina Omnishambles' *EJILTalk!*, 18 November 2012, at www.ejiltalk.org/the-gotovina-omnishambles.

[178] D Vallentgoed, 'The Last Round? A Post-Gotovina Reassessment of the Legality of Using Artillery Against Built-up Areas' (2013) 18 *Journal of Conflict and Security Law* 44.

[179] N Clarke, 'Courting Controversy: The ICTY's Acquittal of Croatian Generals Gotovina and Markač' (2013) 11 *Journal of International Criminal Justice* 399.

[180] *Prosecutor v Gotovina et al*, Appeals Judgment, Dissenting Opinion of Judge Fausto Pocar, ICTY IT-06-90-A, 16 November 2012, para 11.

> considering evidence of any artillery impacts further than 400 metres from the nearest military target, and therefore outside the highest possible range of error given at trial … It thus has the effect of rendering, in the Majority's view, all artillery impacts potentially lawful, when – as I see it – there are clear indications to the contrary. … In my opinion, the Majority is not entitled to effectively raise the margin of error *ad infinitum*, as it does here.[181]

Not fortuitously, some commentators, when analysing the consequences of this judgment, suggested a legacy risking to formalise the 'end of indiscriminate attacks'.[182] Effectively, the tragic setback of the Appeals Chamber majority approach in *Gotovina* was ultimately that of erasing a limited (even if possibly flawed) presumption of unlawfulness, while generating, as a consequence, an unlimited (and undoubtedly flawed) presumption of legality.

Judge Pocar, in his dissenting opinion, asked why the majority, rather than focusing on the contribution of the defendant, and eventually acquitting them on the basis of an insufficient contribution to a liable joint criminal enterprise (JCE), had instead to erase entirely the unlawfulness of the actions under scrutiny. In particular, the judge alluded to impenetrable reasons which may have lain behind the decision of the majority, wondering in his dissenting opinion 'what the majority wanted to achieve by quashing the mere existence of the JCE rather than concentrating on Gotovina's and Markač's significant contributions to the JCE'.[183]

Whichever the scholarly orientations around this issue, it is hard to dispute that denying that the 200-metre error probable could be adopted, while at the same time omitting to identify any alternative, valid standard, changed the history of the development of war crimes law, and did so to the radical detriment of accountability for indiscriminate attacks. Since the *Gotovina* case, in fact, the erosion of the prohibition of indiscriminate attacks in the wars fought since has continued to grow, up to the point of consolidating misconceptions of proportionality in attacks obscuring, or even abolishing the prohibition of indiscriminate attacks.[184]

It is therefore necessary to draw some conclusive critical reflection on the legal solutions devised from this point of view by the ICTY in all the cases mentioned.

[181] ibid, Dissenting Opinion of Judge Carmel Agius, paras 20–21.

[182] M Brehm, 'Use of Grad Rockets in Populated Areas: What Lessons from Gotovina?' *EJILTalk!*, 30 July 2014, at www.ejiltalk.org/use-of-grad-rockets-in-populated-areas-what-lessons-from-gotovina.

[183] *Prosecutor v Gotovina et al*, Appeals Judgment (n 179) para 30.

[184] See L Daniele, 'A lethal misconception, in Gaza and beyond: disguising indiscriminate attacks as potentially proportionate in discourses on the law of war' *EJILTalk!*, 7 November 2023, at www.ejiltalk.org/a-lethal-misconception-in-gaza-and-beyond-disguising-indiscriminate-attacks-as-potentially-proportionate-in-discourses-on-the-laws-of-war; more extensively, expanding on the arguments outlined in ch 2, see L Daniele, 'Incidentality of the Civilian Harm in International Humanitarian Law and its *Contra Legem* Antonyms in Recent Discourses on the Laws of War' (2024) 29 *Journal of Conflict and Security Law* 21–54.

3.3.3. Indiscriminate and Disproportionate Attacks as Reckless Attacks on Civilians, and the Fragility of Case-by-Case Inferences: Back to Victor's Justice?

It is possible, in light of all the cases analysed, to validate the thesis that recklessness stands out as key in the ICTY jurisprudence in relation to war crimes. Had the mental element to be met for the crime of direct attacks on civilians been direct intent (carrying out the action pursuing the realisation of the prohibited result), in fact, then it would have been impossible to punish indiscriminate and disproportionate attacks under this crime.

Intentionally directing attacks against civilians and/or civilian objects *as such*, in fact, is different from identifying legitimate military objectives, and attacking them despite the foreseeable shelling of civilians and/or civilian objects *as well*, in the case of indiscriminate attacks, or incidentally but *excessively*, in the case of disproportionate attacks. Since IHL tolerates incidental civilian casualties or damage to civilian objects when proportionate, ie not excessive in comparison to the concrete and direct military advantage anticipated, it is to be expected that any combatants responsible for civilian deaths, included mass killing of civilians, will always allege that civilians were not the actual target of the attack, and that the real target was a military objective in their vicinity, or was situated among the civilians killed, or simply that the military advantage pursued outweighed the civilian deaths expected. Direct intent as *mens rea* threshold, in other words, obstructs accountability whenever the intent of attackers is to hit *also* lawful targets, particularly targets whose killing or destruction would offer high military advantage. Through recklessness, instead, perpetrators' willingness to kill civilians *as well as* combatants becomes a space of subjective approaches which judges can scrutinise, and infer – on a case-by-case basis, and given the verification of certain objective factors – that the indiscriminate and disproportionate character of the attacks 'hid' in fact an oblique intent, or a reckless willingness to kill civilians and/or destroy civilian objects.

The merit of this approach is that of neutralising the instrumental use of the presence of lawful targets in densely populated areas, or co-location of some combatants among crowds of civilians, to kill and destroy indiscriminately. However, the hermeneutical inference of direct attacks of civilians from the indiscriminate or disproportionate nature of attacks relies on broad margins of discretion, leading to contradictory results.

In support of this argument, it is interesting to compare the findings of the Tribunal in some of the cases previously mentioned, to those formulated in relation to the NATO bombing campaign in Kosovo.

In May 1999, the Chief Prosecutor of the ICTY established a committee to review the allegations of serious violations of the laws and customs of war during the NATO aerial attacks in the region, in order to advise the prosecution to decide whether or not there was a sufficient basis to open a formal investigation into some of these alleged violations.

The review committee was entrusted with the assessment, between others, of attacks strikingly similar to some of those analysed by the Tribunal in its previous jurisprudence.

Between the relevant cases to compare, the *Dragomir Milošević* appears particularly relevant. In relation to dual-use objects controlled by enemy forces, the Trial Chamber was called to adjudicate the legality of the shelling, in June 1995, of a television building in Sarajevo. The Chamber rejected the argument that the TV station, at the time used for the propaganda of one of the warring sides, could be seen as a legitimate military objective, and concluded that the building was a civilian object.[185]

In April 1999, NATO forces launched a missile attack on the Radio Television Serbia station in Belgrade, causing the death of 16 employees. The Final Report of the Review Committed, however, maintained that media stations can be part of a command, control and communications network for military purposes, and in that circumstance, they are military objectives.[186]

Furthermore, in the *Martić* case, the Tribunal concluded that the use of Orkan rockets loaded with cluster warheads for attacks against objects located in populated areas amounted to an indiscriminate attack. Amnesty International denounced specific attacks carried out by NATO with cluster munitions in the Serbian city of Niš, including areas near the central market and the city hospital, causing the deaths of 16 civilians, and injuring 60.[187]

The Review Committee found that cluster ammunitions were effectively used by NATO, but maintained that there was no explicit treaty provision restricting the use of cluster bombs, and that the use of this weaponry can and must comply with the IHL targeting principles. The Committee also referred in the report to the *Martić* case, noting that the Tribunal 'regarded the use of the Orkan rocket with a cluster bomb warhead … as evidence of the intent of the accused to deliberately attack the civilian population'. The Tribunal, according to the Review Committee, reached the conclusion the rocket was used to terrorise civilians, since the attack was inaccurate, the rocket landed in an area with no military objectives nearby, and it was used as an antipersonnel weapon.

However, according to the drafters of the Report, there was no indication that cluster bombs 'were used in such a fashion by NATO'. Without further legal

[185] 'Finally, the Appeals Chamber cannot accept Milošević's argument that the shelling incident could have been a legitimate military action since the TV Building was clearly civilian object. Witnesses testified at trial that there were neither any military targets or activity, nor any ABiH military equipment inside or around the TV Building' (*Prosecutor v Dragomirv Milošević*, Appeals Judgment, ICTY IT-98-29/1-A, 12 November 2009, para 250).

[186] *Final Report to the Prosecutor by the Committee Established to Review the NATO Bombing Campaign Against the Federal Republic of Yugoslavia*, The Hague, 14 June 2000, para 55.

[187] 'The bombs fell on a busy part of town at a time when people were out in the streets and at the market, not protecting themselves in the bomb shelters where they had spent the night. According to a Serbian news source, this was the 14th attack on Niš, the third within 10 hours, and the first to have taken place in daylight hours' (Amnesty International, 'Collateral Damage' or Unlawful Killings? Violations of the Laws of War by NATO during Operation Allied Force', 5 June 2000, 50).

reasoning, the Committee concluded 'that the OTP should not commence an investigation into use of cluster bombs as such by NATO'.[188]

The argumentation appears unstable and circular: rather than demonstrating that the inferential operation of the ICTY in *Martić* (use of the Orkan rocket as evidence of the intent to terrorise civilians by indiscriminately attacking them) was not applicable to the NATO attacks with cluster ammunitions, the Committee drew an antithetical and unsupported inference (lack of intent to terrorise civilians as evidence of a lawful attack), without dwelling on the technical characteristics of the ammunitions used and the presence, or density of presence, of civilians and civilian objects in the targeted areas.

In conclusion, the margin of judicial creativity used by the ICTY judges to bring, through recklessness, indiscriminate and disproportionate attacks under the scope of direct attacks on civilians revealed all its fragility when confronting the doubtful legality, under the same parameters, of the means and methods of warfare of hegemonic Western powers. Simultaneously, in other words, progressive jurisprudence expanded and restricted the contours of war crimes-type offences on the basis of nationality and geopolitical collocation of the suspects. The same inferences that led to the conviction of Serb nationalist commanders for war crimes were declared inapplicable when similarly indiscriminate and comparably disproportionate attacks were launched by NATO, against targets in densely populated areas, and killing civilians.

This consideration further reinforces the hypothesis that more stringent and *written* types of offence are required in order to ensure that punishments for war crimes maintain meaningful functions of general prevention, which are obviously premised on the equal enforcement of war crimes law. Unlimited faith in the variable discretion of judges and institutions, forgets that they, unlike the law, are not general and abstract, but – as any other humane deliberative forum – inherently and inevitably subject to the influence of power relations and the impact of hegemonic conditioning, producing their own common wisdoms.

[188] *Final Report* (n 186) para 27.

4

Indiscriminate and Disproportionate Attacks in Contemporary War Crimes Law: Born to be Blunt?

4.1. Indiscriminate and Disproportionate Attacks as Turning Points for the ICC at 30: Two Alternative Futures for the Court (and Warfare)

The preceding chapter explored how indiscriminate and disproportionate attacks have been conceptualised and defined in international criminal justice. Initially, in the post-World War II International Military Tribunal (IMTs), they were categorised as war crimes committed under the Nazi regime's indiscriminate, total warfare policies. Subsequently, the ad hoc international criminal tribunals (mainly the International Criminal Tribunal for the Prosecution of Persons Responsible for Serious Violations of International Humanitarian Law Committed in the Territory of the Former Yugoslavia; ICTY), established more precise legal boundaries for their prosecution. It is now necessary to discuss the contemporary lineaments of the legal challenges identified by looking the Rome Statute of the International Criminal Court (ICC).

The creation of a permanent international criminal tribunal, the ICC, with potentially worldwide jurisdiction, is one of the most significant developments not only in international law in the last decades, but possibly in the history of legal institutions. By signing and ratifying the 1998 Rome Statute, for the first time, states have voluntarily accepted a complementary, permanent criminal jurisdiction of a supranational institution for crimes committed by their nationals, or on their territory. This profile constitutes a breakthrough in the international legal landscape, in particular considering that criminal justice systems have historically been the most self-contained branch of domestic legal orders, as direct expression of the different legal traditions and criminal policies of the states.[1]

The birth of the ICC was greeted as an unprecedented universalist achievement, promising the affirmation of a season of globalisation of the rule of law,

[1] L Daniele, 'The International Criminal Court between Human Rights and Realpolitik' in G. Oberleitner (ed), *International Human Rights Institutions, Tribunals, and Courts* (Springer, 2018) 355.

and as the beginning of the end of impunity for mass atrocities. An account of the hopeful enthusiasm surrounding the establishment of the Court can be found in the statement of the Secretary General of the UN at the time, Kofi Annan, at the Ceremony for the adoption of the Rome Statute. He began his discourse at the Rome Diplomatic Conference by referring to Cicero's statement discussed in the introduction to this work, and emphasised the breakthrough that the ICC constituted, seen as an epochal achievement in overturning the powerlessness of law in times of war. In particular, he emphasised the importance of this breakthrough in relation to the crimes of the most powerful, in contraposition to the victor's justice critique of the IMTs:

> Two millenniums ago one of this city's most famous sons, Marcus Tullius Cicero, declared that 'in the midst of arms, law stands mute'. As a result of what we are doing here today there is real hope that that bleak statement will be less true in the future than it has been in the past. Until now, when powerful men committed crimes against humanity, they knew that as long as they remained powerful no earthly court could judge them. Even when they were judged … they could claim that this [was] happening only because others have proved *more powerful*, and so are able to sit in judgement over them. Verdicts intended to uphold the rights of the weak and helpless can be impugned as 'victors' justice'.

According to Annan, such accusations had unjustly been made also against the ICTY and the ICTR, since, given their ad hoc basis, the same crimes, committed by different people, or at different times and places, remained unpunished. He concluded:

> Now at last we shall have a permanent court to judge the most serious crimes of concern to the international community as a whole.[2]

It can be seen clearly through this statement, how the equal enforcement of international criminal law was one of the foundational aspirations of the ICC, and one of the reasons why the latter attracted such high hopes of jurists, politicians, diplomats and NGOs convinced that the institution itself would have heralded the dawn of a new era in the prevention of atrocity crimes.

Even more clearly, the Preamble to the Rome Statute itself affirmed numerous, momentous, and perhaps irreconcilable tasks entrusted to the ICC. Going far beyond the objectives of national criminal justice systems, in fact, the ICC aimed to propagate human rights values and reinforce global civil conscience around them, to provide a forum for the voice of victims of international crimes, to produce a reliable historical record of the crimes perpetrated and the context in which they were committed, and to strengthen peace and security of the world.[3]

[2] 'Secretary General Says Establishment of ICC is Major Step in March Towards Universal Human Rights, Rule of Law', UN Press Release L/2890, 20 July 1998, at press.un.org/en/1998/19980720.l2890.html.

[3] Preamble, Rome Statute of the International Criminal Court, 2187 UNTS 90, adopted 17 June 1998, entered into force 1 July 2002, last amended 2010.

As it has been noted,

> the Court appears as a single body with a multiplicity of identities: a criminal court dealing with individual criminal responsibility; a form of restorative justice, which – as a forum for victims to express their views and concerns – contributes to reconciliation; a pedagogic institution strengthening the public sense of accountability for human rights violations; in cases of referrals by the Security Council, an organ of international security with the duty to restore peace between nation-States; a human rights court with the main purpose to protect human dignity; a historian vested with the authority to make an objective record of events; an agency engaging in activities which enhance the effectiveness of national jurisdiction capacity to prosecute serious crimes.[4]

Relatedly, as Damaška puts it,

> the task of fulfilling all these self-imposed demands is truly gargantuan. Unlike Atlas, international criminal courts are not bodies of titanic strength, capable of carrying on their shoulders the burden of so many tasks. Even national systems of criminal justice, with their far greater enforcement powers and institutional support, would stagger under this load.[5]

This overload of goals generated teleological tensions. Trials of political and military leaders, for example, do not necessarily assist de-escalations in armed conflicts and promote peaceful resolutions. Moreover, the idea of producing an accurate historiographical record of the context in which core crimes were committed does not sit well with the normative tools and procedural equipment of the Court, which remains a criminal court called to adjudicate individual criminal responsibilities. A further consideration is the inevitable tension between the pursuit of individual criminal liability and crimes usually characterised by a collective dimension, in terms of both victims and authors, in which main perpetrators, aiders and abettors can be in the hundreds of thousands.[6]

This overload of goals, and of expectations, has been followed by a gradual and growing disenchantment regarding the role of the ICC as a global institution,[7] triggered by a series of retractions of the Court itself from the persisting challenge of adjudicating crimes of agents of the most powerful states in the international arena. Beyond the difficulties faced by the Court in regard to state cooperation and the length of proceedings, the Court became entangled in a strident contradiction between the resounding goals mentioned and the selectivity of

[4] T Mariniello, *The International Criminal Court in Search of its Purpose and Identity* (Routledge, 2014) 16.

[5] M Damaška, 'What is the Point of International Criminal Justice?' Yale Law School, Faculty Scholarship Series, Paper 1572, 1/2008, 331.

[6] M Drumbl, 'Collective Violence and Individual Punishment: The Criminality of Mass Atrocity' (2004) 99 *Northwestern University Law Review* 539.

[7] F Jessberger and J Geneuss, 'Down the Drain or Down to Earth? International Criminal Justice under Pressure' (2013) 11 *Journal of International Criminal Justice* 501, 501–03.

its practice.[8] Selective enforcement in the ICC practice soon became its most discussed profile. Obviously, selectivity is a feature of every criminal justice system, intended to pursue only a fraction of all the offences committed. This is even truer for the Court, whose jurisdiction is only activated when relevant domestic jurisdictions are unwilling or unable to genuinely investigate the relevant alleged crimes. However, in the case of the ICC, the selectivity increasingly eroding its legitimacy is a different one; that is, selectivity of enforcement based on states' power relations and discriminating suspects on the basis of citizenship. The decade-long focus of the Court on African suspects, the controversial decision not to open an investigation into crimes committed in Iraq by UK forces, the Pilatesque decisions delaying the opening of an investigation into the situation in Palestine, as well as the Pre-Trial Chamber (PTC) initial rejection of the former prosecutor's request to open an investigation in Afghanistan, followed by the current prosecutor's 'de-prioritization' of the aspects of the investigations concerning US forces, have all contributed to the growing disillusionment, in the scholarship and global civil society, about the ability of the Court to exert any general-preventive effect against the commission of atrocity crimes by forces and leaders of hegemonic powers.

This chapter demonstrates that the defects of the Rome Statute war crimes provisions punishing violations of the law of targeting lies at the core of these missed opportunities of international criminal justice. These defects, as the chapter shows, impacted the activities of the ICC as much as the conditionalities imposed on the Court by powerful states, such as pressure from Western hegemonic powers and their allies, major donors, on the Court's selection of cases.[9] As was demonstrated in chapter one of this work, in fact, liberal democracies, from the war on terror (directly) to Gaza (indirectly, through their arms transfers and political support) have continued to kill masses of civilians in armed conflicts, often exponentially more than combatants. Nonetheless, no international criminal trial has ever been held against the most responsible actors of the military policies sanctioning this mass killing of civilians as necessary, acceptable or collateral.[10]

As will be shown, the Rome Statute's lack of explicit criminalisation of indiscriminate attacks as war crimes, as well as its problematic definition of the war crime of disproportionate attacks (contained in Article 8(2)(b)(iv), was sufficient to leave this mass civilian victimisation unpunished. In line with the *Gotovina* case, in which the ICTY failed to establish any objective parameter indicating the indiscriminate nature of an attack, it appears that the development of war crimes law punishing the violation of IHL targeting rules suffered a significant setback. In

[8] W Schabas, 'The International Criminal Court at Ten' (2011) 22 *Criminal Law Forum* 493; W Schabas, 'The Banality of International Justice' (2013) 11 *Journal of International Criminal Justice* 545.

[9] D Bosco, 'Discretion and States' Influence at the International Criminal Court: The Prosecutor's Preliminary Examinations' (2017) 11 *American Journal of International Law* 395.

[10] On how the concept of 'collateral damage' has been unlawfully overexpanded to designate the anticipated killing of entire crowds of civilians in attacks, not only disproportionately, but even indiscriminately, see ch 2, sections 2.4 and 2.5.

the first 20 years of the Court's activity, in fact, indiscriminate attacks were never the object of a war crimes conviction, and (even more perplexingly) the war crime of disproportionate attacks was never charged.

While the analysis was being composed, the Office of the Prosecutor of the ICC took a first step in an opposite direction. After the described stage of persisting impunity for the war crimes of hegemonic actors in the international arena, in fact, the Court displayed, antithetically, its full potential against powerful actors after the full-scale Russian invasion of Ukraine of 2022. Western state parties' mobilisation for Ukraine's self-defence, and for justice for Ukrainian victims of international crimes, catalysed an unprecedently robust and swift response, commendable in the view of this author, which culminated first in the issuing of the arrest warrants against the Head of State of the second world nuclear power,[11] and then in the issuing of the first arrest warrants since the entry into force of the Rome Statute based on a charge of the war crime of disproportionate attacks under Article 8(2)(b)(iv) of the Statute.[12] Shortly after the first disproportionate attacks war crime charge in 20 years, the Prosecutor of the ICC requested arrest warrants for the Israeli Prime Minister and Minister of Defence,[13] which included the war crime of intentionally directing attacks against the civilian population, in a war context where indiscriminate attacks appear to have been operationalised as routine method of warfare.[14] For the first time in the history of the ICC, an arrest warrant was requested against members of the executive of a United States key ally.

In other words, around indiscriminate and disproportionate attacks seems to revolve the last chance for a different future of the ICC, as it approaches 30 years since its establishment. After two decades of unpunished realities of mass civilian victimisation in wartime by hegemonic states, and a correspondent loss of legitimacy, the Court finds itself at a crucial turning point. If the ICC wants to survive as an institution recognised by world public opinions as coherent with its mission, it will need to prove itself able to enforce war crimes law equally across the blocks of contraposed states increasing their preparedness for new wars. Only a *super partes* institution applying the law without fear or favour, in fact, can aim to restrain the

[11] 'Situation in Ukraine: ICC judges issue arrest warrants against Vladimir Vladimirovich Putin and Maria Alekseyevna Lvova-Belova', ICC, 17 March 2023, at www.icc-cpi.int/news/situation-ukraine-icc-judges-issue-arrest-warrants-against-vladimir-vladimirovich-putin-and.

[12] 'Situation in Ukraine: ICC judges issue arrest warrants against Sergei Ivanovich Kobylash and Viktor Nikolayevich Sokolov', ICC, 5 March 2024, at www.icc-cpi.int/news/situation-ukraine-icc-judges-issue-arrest-warrants-against-sergei-ivanovich-kobylash-and; and 'Situation in Ukriane: ICC judges issue arrest warrants against Sergei Kuzhugetovich Shoigu and Valery Vasilyevich Gerasimov', ICC, 25 June 2024, at www.icc-cpi.int/news/situation-ukraine-icc-judges-issue-arrest-warrants-against-sergei-kuzhugetovich-shoigu-and.

[13] 'Statement of ICC Prosecutor Karim A.A. Khan KC: Applications for arrest warrants in the situation in the State of Palestine', ICC, 20 May 2024, at www.icc-cpi.int/news/statement-icc-prosecutor-karim-aa-khan-kc-applications-arrest-warrants-situation-state.

[14] See F Albanese, L Daniele and N Perugini, 'Humanitarian Camouflage: Israel's Rewriting of the Laws of War to Legitimize the Gaza Genocide' (2024) 12 *Journal of Palestine Studies – Current Issues in Depth*, at www.palestine-studies.org/en/node/1656283.

conduct of hostilities of the powers currently projected toward mutual destruction to maintain, or appropriate, world dominance. Absent this projection in a new phase of principled pursuit of equal accountability, the Court risks transiting from a stage of withdrawals when challenged by the criminality of the most powerful, to a stage of dominance of double standards. Capitulating to this dominance could be fatal for the Court, which would start to be perceived, as it is already in large sectors of the Global South, as a tool of hybrid warfare by one block of states over another. This is particularly true in a geopolitical context where, increasingly, international criminal law enforcement is systematically invoked by powerful actors as absolute moral duty against enemies, while it is simultaneously and systematically antagonised by the very same actors when probable international crimes are committed by allies.

4.2. Indiscriminate and Disproportionate Attacks in the Rome Statute of the ICC: In Search of Lost Enforcement

At the centre of this crossroads between two opposed futures for international criminal justice, for international law institutions more generally, and for warfare itself (globally), indiscriminate and disproportionate attacks continue to be committed in nearly all the armed conflicts of contemporaneity, albeit at different pace and extents.

The stark increase in indiscriminate and disproportionate attacks in current conflicts, rising again to systematic commission in new wars of annihilation, has been the object of the recent, alarmed attention (among other institutions) of the United Nations Secretary General,[15] and of the Office of the High Commissioner of Human Rights.[16] Such attention further highlights how these unlawful attacks constitute an unaddressed, critical challenge to the international legal order at the times of its highest instability, weakening some of its most foundational tenets. The incessant erosion of the category of the civilian, and of the related legal protections, grown during the decades of the war on terror, culminated in discourses on the laws of war vindicating the righteousness and lawfulness of the mass killing of the unarmed in urban warfare.[17] From this point of view, therefore, the enforcement of war crimes law against unlawful attacks has never

[15] UNSC, 'Protection of civilians in armed conflict, Report of the Secretary-General', 14 May 2024, S/2024/385, at documents.un.org/doc/undoc/gen/n24/110/29/pdf/n2411029.pdf.

[16] OHCHR, 'Indiscriminate and disproportionate attacks during the conflict in Gaza (October – December 2023)', Thematic Report, 19 June 2024, at www.ohchr.org/sites/default/files/documents/countries/opt/20240619-ohchr-thematic-report-indiscrim-disprop-attacks-gaza-oct-dec2023.pdf.

[17] See L Daniele, 'Incidentality of the Civilian Harm in International Humanitarian Law, and its *Contra Legem* Antonyms in Recent Discourses on the Laws of War' (2024) 29 *Journal of Conflict and Security Law* 21.

been more urgent, particularly in light of their normalisation by a number of world powers.

The purpose of the following sections is to explore the Rome Statute targeting war crimes framework critically appraising the likelihood of ensuring accountability for the most serious violations of the IHL targeting prescriptions. A preliminary note is necessary in this regard. Discussing indiscriminate and disproportionate attacks 'in' the Rome Statute, as this chapter does, might draw criticisms, since the Statute itself does not contain any explicit reference to indiscriminate attacks as war crimes. This lack of explicit criminalisation, however, can in no way be interpreted as indifference of the Rome Statute for indiscriminate attacks, as it will be demonstrated.

As it has been argued, indiscriminate attacks are classed under IHL as a *genus* of unlawful attacks subsuming disproportionate attacks as specific typology of prohibited conduct. Punishing the *species* of unlawful attacks while considering their *genus* extraneous to the war crimes regime of the Statute, therefore, would be normatively incoherent. In addition, it appears interpretively unfeasible. Such an interpretation, in fact, would trigger a paradoxical, dangerous consequence: armed actors, under this orientation, would be decisively encouraged to go beyond disproportionate attacks (that is, those launched despite foreseeing clearly excessive incidental civilian harm, but aimed exclusively at lawful targets), and opt for launching rather indiscriminate attacks (that is those targeting both lawful targets and protected persons and objects at once, particularly in densely populated areas). In such cases, they would evade any responsibility for violating intentionally the rule of distinction, the cornerstone of IHL, and risk only the lesser responsibility for knowingly causing clearly excessive incidental civilian harm.

In other words, a legal nonsense: to assess proportionality, in fact, attackers need first to respect the rule of distinction, the logical and normative premise of any proportionality assessment. It is impossible to evaluate whether or not incidental civilian harm would be excessive when the protected civilians and civilian objects are directly shelled, rather than being incidentally impacted by attacks on lawful targets. This interpretation would also force ICC judges to become protagonists of a *fictio iuris* with no legal or factual basis: to adjudicate indiscriminate attacks, they would need to scrutinise the attackers' proportionality assessments, when they have in fact not carried out any.

Other than for its paradoxical consequence, the necessity of an integrated approach around indiscriminate attacks, reading coherently war crimes law in light of their systematic coordination with the IHL targeting principles, finds robust support in the Rome Statute itself. Article 21 of the Statute, in fact, makes clear that the Court shall apply not only the law of the Statute and of the Elements of Crimes, but also 'when appropriate, applicable treaties and the principles and rules of international law'. This reference would have already, in itself, included principles and rules of IHL, as part of international law governing armed conflicts. Nonetheless, the drafters explicitly added the applicability of 'established principles of the international law of armed conflict'. This anchorage is particularly relevant. As a matter of fact, the long list of war crimes in Article 8, within its complex structure, are a 'hodgepodge',[18] with a short definition of each type of offence, and limited guidance offered by the Elements of Crimes, rendering the interpretation and application of these provisions arduous. As it has been argued,

> one would still be at a loss to adequately understand the elements of the individual war crime without referring to international humanitarian law ... Hence, we must examine with regard to each war crime what treaty or customary international humanitarian law rules it is derived from, and what violation of humanitarian law it precisely criminalizes, to determine the material and mental elements of the offense.[19]

Article 21, in other words, not only allows but rather requires an interpretation of the Statute under the guidance of existing IHL rules. From this point of view, the following sections will interpret the targeting war crimes of the Rome Statute – that is those related to violations of the law of targeting – in light of the systematisation of the relationship between the IHL rules of distinction and proportionality already proposed.[20]

4.2.1. The War Crimes Regime of the Rome Statute: Structure of Article 8 and Common Elements

The Rome Statute of the ICC enshrines the discipline related to war crimes in its Article 8. The twofold structure of this article, and the complexity of the resulting discipline, is the result of the delicate legal and political compromises reached during its drafting history.

The mandate to prepare a draft statute for the future court was entrusted in 1989 to the International Law Commission (ILC). Initially, the Commission embraced the view that the draft statute should have primarily contained procedural and organisational regulations, leaving the jurisdiction *rationae materiae* of the court to treaty law. The crimes under the jurisdiction of the future court, in other words, should have been those of international concern identified by the existing treaties. The view of the Commission progressively changed, pressured by the criticism of the states seeing in such a solution a danger of excessive discretion for the court. Thus, the solution adopted for the 1994 Draft Statute was to limit the jurisdiction of the court to four crimes: the crime of genocide; the crime of aggression; crimes

[18] M Bothe, 'War Crimes' in A Cassese, P Gaeta and JRWD Jones (eds), *The Rome Statute of the International Criminal Court: A Commentary* (Oxford University Press, 2002) vol 1, 379.
[19] M Cottier, 'War Crimes' in O Triffterer and K Ambos (eds), *The Rome Statute of the International Criminal Court: A Commentary* (Hart-Nomos, 2015) 317.
[20] See ch 2.

against humanity; and 'serious violations of the laws and customs applicable in armed conflicts'.[21]

In respect to this category of crimes, which later evolved in the present war crimes provisions, the ILC Report added that not all breaches of the laws of war were of sufficient gravity to justify their falling within the jurisdiction of the court. Accordingly, the Draft limited the jurisdiction to 'serious violations'. The term 'serious violations', according to the Commission, was used to avoid confusion with 'grave breaches', since it was held that it does not follow automatically from the classification of conduct as a grave breach (in the Geneva Conventions of 1949 and Additional Protocol I of 1977 (AP I)) that it also constitutes a serious violation.[22] During the subsequent drafting stage, from 1994 to 1998, in the Ad Hoc and Preparatory Committee for the Establishment of an International Criminal Court, this view was progressively abandoned. The Report of the Preparatory Committee recounted that several delegations affirmed that

> grave breaches were by definition serious offences, that any attempt to distinguish between grave breaches would be inconsistent with the obligation to prosecute or extradite, that the seriousness criterion was more appropriate for distinguishing between violations of the laws and customs applicable in armed conflict which varied in gravity.[23]

The grave breaches provisions of the four 1949 Geneva Conventions, consequently, as well as violations listed in Article 23 of the Hague Regulations, widely recognised as expression of customary international law, were included in the draft statute. In contrast, however, the inclusion of other offences based on grave breaches listed in the two 1977 Additional Protocols to the 1949 Geneva Conventions raised intense debate.

A first proposal, including a closed list of war crimes, was advanced by the United States.[24] Interestingly for the present analysis, this US proposal, at the voice 'other serious violations of the laws and customs applicable in international armed conflict within the established framework of international law', did not include war crimes based on unlawful attacks clearly identified by AP I as grave breaches, such as making the civilian population or individual civilians the object of attack,[25] or making civilian structures the object of attacks or reprisals.[26]

[21] ILC, 'Draft Statute for an International Criminal Court with commentaries,' *Yearbook of the International Law Commission*, 1994, vol II, Part Two, Article 20(c), 38, at legal.un.org/ilc/texts/instruments/english/commentaries/7_4_1994.pdf.

[22] ibid, 39–40 (paras 10–11).

[23] Report of the Preparatory Committee on the Establishment of an International Criminal Court, Volume I (Proceedings of the Preparatory Committee during March-April and August 1996), UNGA Fifty-first Session (A/51/22), 20, para 76, at www.legal-tools.org/doc/e75432/pdf.

[24] Proposal submitted by the United States, Working Group on definition of crimes, UN Preparatory Committee on the Establishment of an International Criminal Court, 11–21 February 1997, Doc A/AC.249/1997/WG.1/DP.1 (14 February 1997), at www.legal-tools.org/doc/c5359c/pdf.

[25] See Arts 85(3)(a) and 51(2) AP I.

[26] See Art 52(1) AP I.

Similarly, the US proposal made no mention of launching an indiscriminate attack affecting the civilian population or civilian objects, or launching an attack which may be expected to cause incidental loss of life, injury to civilians, damage to civilian objects, or a combination thereof, which would be excessive in relation to the concrete and direct military advantage anticipated.[27] A more comprehensive draft incorporating a longer list of offences, and more informed by the orientations of the ICRC, was submitted by New Zealand and Switzerland and resulted in the draft eventually forwarded to the Rome Diplomatic Conference.[28]

At the Rome Conference, one of the more controversial profiles of the war crimes debate was the list of war crimes configurable in non-international armed conflicts. Several states represented at the Conference were in fact involved in internal conflicts on their territory and were reluctant to accept a fuller article that included numerous offences criminalised in these situations. In particular, the controversy over the criminalisation of disproportionate attacks and indiscriminate weapons in non-international conflict was so thorny and intense that it threatened to bring the whole negotiation process to an *impasse*.[29] From this point of view, states remained hostile to the efforts of developing a unique framework punishing unlawful attacks in both international and non-international armed conflicts, based on customary IHL, which meanwhile were being pursued by the ICTY. As noted by Cassese,

> insofar as Article 8 separates the law applicable to international armed conflict from that applicable to internal armed conflict, it is somewhat retrograde, as the current trend has been to abolish this distinction and to have simply one corpus of law applicable to all conflicts. It can be confusing – and unjust – to have one law for international armed conflict and another for internal armed conflict.[30]

The compromise reached on these provisions resulted in the actual structure of Article 8 of the Rome Statute (the latest version of the article was amended at the Sixteenth session of the Assembly of States Parties in December 2017, which added to the existing list of crimes the use of biological, fragmentation and laser blinding weapons in non-international armed conflicts).[31]

The structure of Article 8 is therefore divided into three paragraphs, six letters and lists 54 offences.

The first paragraph introduces a contextualisation of these crimes, stating that:

> The Court shall have jurisdiction in respect of war crimes *in particular* when committed as part of a plan or policy or as part of a large-scale commission of such crimes.

[27] See Art 85(3)(b) AP I.

[28] UN Doc A/AC.249/1997/WG.1/DP.2 (14 February 1997).

[29] As recalled by Cottier (n 19) 310 (para 22).

[30] A Cassese, 'The Statute of the International Criminal Court: some preliminary reflections' (1999) 10 *European Journal of International Law* 144, 150.

[31] Resolution on amendments to article 8 of the Rome Statute of the International Criminal Court, Sixteenth session of the Assembly of States Parties, ICC-ASP/16/Res. 4, 14 December 2017.

From this wording it might be inferred that a large-scale commission, or the existence of a plan or policy, are necessary for the adjudication of the violations listed, as contextual elements of the crimes. Unanimously, however, the literature regards such provisions, preceded by 'in particular', as not altering the definition of the offences in the article, that is, as not adding a contextual element for the crimes described in the subsequent paragraphs.[32] As it has been convincingly argued,

> the threshold clause contained in article 8 para. 1 of the Statute must be interpreted in line with article 5 in the sense that individual war crimes which are not committed as part of a plan or policy shall only be prosecuted if they are of such a gravity as to indeed be of concern to the international community as a whole.[33]

A large-scale commission, or the existence of a plan or policy, in other words, are not required profiles of the offences, which can be configured even in case of a single or isolated act of such gravity to grant the Court's attention.

According to some authors, the words 'in particular' suggest that the paragraph should be intended as a practical guideline for the ICC and the prosecutor on what type of war crimes they should primarily focus upon, given the limited resources of the Court and the necessity to select the most egregious offences to be investigated.[34]

Paragraph 2 is articulated into six letters, classifying the different war crime offences according to the type of conflict (international or non-international), in which they are committed.

Paragraph 2(a) criminalises first of all the grave breaches of the four 1949 Geneva Conventions.[35] The grave breaches, and therefore these war crimes, follow the same threshold of existence of an armed conflict established according to Common Article 2 of the Conventions themselves: all interstate armed conflicts, included occupation, regardless of their level of intensity.[36]

Paragraph 2(b) lists 26 war crimes categorised as 'violations of the laws and customs applicable in international armed conflict, within the established

[32] See eg M Klamberg, 'Article 8(1)' in M Klamberg, J Nilsson and A Angotti (eds), *Commentary on the Law of the International Criminal Court: The Statute*, 2nd edn (Torkel Opsahl Academic EPublisher, 2023) vol 1, 179; Bothe (n 18); Cottier (n 19) 312.

[33] A Zimmermann, 'Article 5' in O Triffterer and K Ambos (eds), *The Rome Statute of the International Criminal Court: A Commentary*, 3rd edn (Hart Publishing, 2015) 123.

[34] K Dörmann, 'War Crimes' in O Triffterer and K Ambos (eds), *The Rome Statute of the International Criminal Court: A Commentary*, 3rd edn (Hart Publishing, 2015) 547.

[35] That is: '(i) Wilful killing; (ii) Torture or inhuman treatment, including biological experiments; (iii) Wilfully causing great suffering, or serious injury to body or health; (iv) Extensive destruction and appropriation of property, not justified by military necessity and carried out unlawfully and wantonly; (v) Compelling a prisoner of war or other protected person to serve in the forces of a hostile Power; (vi) Wilfully depriving a prisoner of war or other protected person of the rights of fair and regular trial; (vii) Unlawful deportation or transfer or unlawful confinement; (viii) Taking of hostages.'

[36] See J Pictet (ed), *The Geneva Conventions of 12 August 1949. Geneva Conventions of 12 August 1949: Commentary* (ICRC, 1958) vol IV (Geneva Convention IV), Art 2, 20–21.

framework of international law'. These offences, therefore, are punishable only if committed in the context of an international armed conflict. This paragraph contains the crime of direct attacks on civilians and disproportionate attacks, that will be examined in the next sub-section.

Paragraph (2)(c), (d) and (e), and paragraph 3 of the article concur to define the regime applicable to non-international armed conflicts, inheriting and translating into the Rome Statute some of the ICTY *Tadić* findings, extending the applicability of war crimes to this typology of armed conflict.

Letter 'c' lists grave breaches of Common Article 3 of the four 1949 Geneva Conventions,[37] referring to armed conflicts 'not of an international character'. Letter 'd' reiterates the IHL distinction between, on the one hand, non-international armed conflicts, requiring a threshold of organised armed violence, and, on the other, situations of internal disturbances and tensions, clarifying that the latter do not trigger the applicability of the laws of war and, consequently, do not fall under the war crimes regime of the Statute.

Letter 'e' partially reproduces the content of letter 'b', listing war crimes under a *chapeau* stating, 'violations of the laws and customs applicable in conflicts not of international character, within the established framework of international law'. This letter, even after the 2017 amendments, contains only 15 conducts, compared to the 26 criminalised if committed in international armed conflicts. Inter alia, it does not include a provision criminalising disproportionate attacks.

The common contextual element of all the offences listed in Article 8 of the Statute is the existence of an armed conflict, in IHL terms.[38]

Since all war crimes are criminalised violations of IHL, and IHL only applies to conducts associated with an armed conflict, the *nexus* with an armed conflict is a required element of any war crime. A conduct, in other words, can be considered a war crime only if it presents a sufficient *nexus* with an armed conflict.[39] This nexus must be more tangible than the simple commission of the conduct in times of war. A conduct realised amidst actual armed hostilities, in temporal, geographical and personal (victim or perpetrator) connection with the hostilities themselves,

[37] '(i) Violence to life and person, in particular murder of all kinds, mutilation, cruel treatment and torture; (ii) Committing outrages upon personal dignity, in particular humiliating and degrading treatment; (iii) Taking of hostages; (iv) The passing of sentences and the carrying out of executions without previous judgement pronounced by a regularly constituted court, affording all judicial guarantees which are generally recognized as indispensable.'

[38] See N Melzer, *International Humanitarian Law. A Comprehensive Introduction* (ICRC, 2016) 49–76; M Sassòli, A Bouvier and A Quintin, *How Does Law Protect in War? Cases, Documents and Teaching Materials on Contemporary Practice in International Humanitarian Law*, 3rd edn (ICRC, 2011) vol I, 21–27; D Fleck (ed), *Handbook of International Humanitarian Law*, 2nd edn (Oxford University Press, 2008) 45–78; R Kolb and R Hyde, *An Introduction to the International Law of Armed Conflicts* (Hart Publishing, 2008) 65–73.

[39] For an extensive treatise and critical appraisal of the war nexus, see E Potoleth, *Searching for the 'nexus': A proposal to refine the scope of applicability of international humanitarian law and war crimes law*, (Doctoral Thesis, 2020), at archive-ouverte.unige.ch/unige:154772.

would surely integrate the required link. An act of violence isolated and disconnected from the hostilities, even if committed on the territory of a country at war, would not meet the required *nexus*. Conduct and armed conflict, in other words, have to be closely related. As it was explained by the ICTY in the *Kunarac* Appeals judgment,

> what ultimately distinguishes a war crime from a purely domestic offence is that a war crime is shaped by or dependent upon the environment – the armed conflict – in which it is committed. It need not have been planned or supported by some form of policy. The armed conflict need not have been causal to the commission of the crime, but the existence of an armed conflict must, at a minimum, have played a substantial part in the perpetrator's ability to commit it, his decision to commit it, the manner in which it was committed or the purpose for which it was committed.[40]

This aspect is reflected in the Elements of Crimes of Article 8, stating that 'the conduct took place in the context of and was associated with' an armed conflict.[41]

Another, closely related common element of the crimes under Article 8, requires that 'The perpetrator was aware of factual circumstances that established the existence of an armed conflict.'

The wording of this element opens some problems related to the psychological stance and perception of the perpetrator in relation to the context surrounding the conduct, as well as the *nexus* between the conduct and the war. The interpreter, in fact, might be prompted to think that there is a requirement, for the perpetrator, to be aware of the facts that established legally the existence of the armed conflicts. This could determine the paradox of requiring knowledge of legal thresholds determining the existence of international and non-international armed conflicts. For this reason, and to avert the equivocation, the introductive section of the Elements of Crimes for Article 8 specifies that there is 'no requirement for a legal evaluation by the perpetrator: in relation to the existence of an armed conflict', as well as in respect to 'its character as international or non-international'. Similarly, there is no need for the perpetrator to have 'awareness of the facts that established' the typology of the armed conflict. Conclusively, the introductory section states that 'There is only a requirement for the awareness of the factual circumstances that established the existence of an armed conflict that is implicit in the terms "took place in the context of and was associated with"'.[42]

[40] *Prosecutor v Kunarac et al*, ICTY IT-96-23, Appeals Judgment, 12 June 2002, paras 57–61.

[41] This element recurs in all the war crimes under Art 8, see ICC, Elements of Crimes, *Official Records of the Assembly of States Parties to the Rome Statute of the International Criminal Court, First session*, New York, 3–10 September 2002, ICC-ASP/1/3, part II.B (as updated in *Official Records of the Review Conference of the Rome Statute of the International Criminal Court*, Kampala, 31 May–11 June 2010).

[42] ibid.

4.2.2. The Elements of the Crimes of Direct Attacks on Civilians and Civilian Objects

Article 8(2)(b) of the Rome Statute criminalises 'Other serious violations of the laws and customs applicable in international armed conflict, within the established framework of international law'.

The difference between war crimes and grave breaches has already been discussed. The development of international law in the last decades has witnessed a process of absorption of the conduct subjected to the IHL grave breaches regime into war crimes law, translated as offences under ICL.[43] Article 8(2)(b), however, shows that war crimes law does not cover only the conduct previously qualified as grave breaches in IHL, but as recounted in relation to the ICTY, as well as other serious violations of IHL, under both its treaty and customary components. It is in this sense that the words 'other' and 'serious' in Article 8(2)(b) need to be read. The offences under letter 'b' are other serious violations of the law of international armed conflict adding up to the other serious violations constituted by the grave breaches under letter 'a'.

Article 8(2)(b) contains a list of 26 war crimes (from subsection 'i' to 'xxvi'), punishing the violations of many of the IHL rules on the conduct of hostilities in international armed conflicts, including: the killing of combatants *hors de combat*; the transfer of civilian population of the occupying power into occupied territories; launching attacks against buildings dedicated to religion, education, art, science or against historic monuments; pillaging; subjecting people to mutilations, experiments, rape or sexual slavery and other outrages to personal dignity; using human shields; and employing poisonous or asphyxiating weapons, expanding bullets, and weapons indiscriminate or of a nature to cause superfluous injury or unnecessary suffering.

Among the war crimes codified in the article, none of its sub-paragraphs refer explicitly to indiscriminate attacks. As has been mentioned, this does not mean that indiscriminate attacks cannot be punished, or that their unlawfulness is confined to IHL, without giving rise to profiles of individual criminal liability. In order to understand the point, it is necessary to analyse the crimes punishing the intentional disregard of the IHL targeting prescriptions, starting from the principle of distinction between civilians and combatants, and between civilian objects and military objectives.

Article 8(2)(b)(i) punishes:

> Intentionally directing attacks against the civilian population *as such* or against individual civilians not taking direct part in hostilities.[44]

[43] See ch 2, section 2.5. See also M Divac-Oberg, 'The Absorption of Grave Breaches into War Crimes Law', (2009) 91(873) *International Review of the Red Cross* 163; M Divac-Oberg, 'The Grave Breaches Regime in the Geneva Conventions: A Reassessment' in A Clapham and P Gaeta (eds), *The Oxford Handbook of International Law in Armed Conflict* (Oxford University Press, 2014) 355–78.

[44] Emphasis added.

This war crime has its treaty roots in Article 51(2) AP I dictating that 'The civilian population as such, as well as individual civilians, shall not be the object of attack'. This prohibition, a pillar of IHL, has obviously customary status.[45] Article 85(3) AP I classifies 'making the civilian population or individual civilians the object of attack' as a grave breach, provided that the conduct is committed wilfully and causing death or serious injury to body or health.[46] While this result element characterises the IHL grave breach, during the drafting of the Elements of Crimes of the Rome Statute it was discussed and consciously left out by the delegations. For the crime of direct attacks on civilians to be committed, therefore, it is not necessary that the attack causes death or injury. An attack directed at civilians and not actually shelling them due to failure of the relevant weapon system, for example, would suffice for liability.

The elements of the crime require that:

(1) The perpetrator directed an attack.
(2) The object of the attack was a civilian population as such or individual civilians not taking direct part in hostilities.
(3) The perpetrator intended the civilian population as such or individual civilians not taking direct part in hostilities to be the object of the attack.[47]

It is therefore necessary that the attack was directed by the perpetrator against the civilian population as such, or against individual civilians. These elements reflect the absolute nature of the rule of distinction under IHL, and the related, absolute prohibition to aim at civilians in attacks, which does not tolerate derogations or exceptions. Civilians, in fact, as it has been demonstrated in previous chapters, can never be made the object of attacks. The only situation in which civilians can be targeted is that of civilians actually behaving like fighters; that is, taking a direct part in the hostilities. In relation to this aspect, it is important to note that the loss of protection from attacks in these cases lasts only for the duration of the direct participation; that is, as long as the hostile actions by the civilian continue. Once the direct participation ceases, the relevant person regains protection, and the war crime returns entirely applicable.

The third element of the crime emphasises that the perpetrator 'intends' the civilian population to be object of the attack. Such specification, even if redundant considering the second element, is important to distinguish this war crime from the crime of clearly disproportionate attacks (see below), in which the perpetrator intends only the lawful targets to be the object of the attack but launches it despite knowing that the attack will cause excessive incidental harm to civilians.

[45] See JM Henckaherts and L Doswald-Beck, *Customary International Humanitarian Law. Volume I: Rules*, (Cambridge University Press, 2005) 3 ff; and JM Henckaherts and L Doswald-Beck, *Customary International Humanitarian Law. Volume II: Practice* (Cambridge University Press, 2005) 3–66.

[46] See AP I, Art 85(3)(a).

[47] ICC (n 41) Art. 8(2)(b)(i).

In correlation and analogy with the mentioned provision, Article (8)(2)(b)(ii), punishes:

> Intentionally directing attacks against civilian objects, that is, objects which are not military objectives

This article complements Article 8(2)(b)(i) and reflects Article 52(1) AP I, dictating that 'Civilian objects shall not be the object of attack or reprisals.' For identification of the notions of 'civilian' and 'civilian objects', as well as for the concept of 'attack', all the IHL discipline analysed above remains entirely valid. This discipline defines civilian objects negatively, that is through exclusion. Civilian objects are those which are not military objectives. For the determination of the latter category, IHL does not contain any list of military objectives, nor indicates intrinsic characteristics of objects which, if present, render them attackable. Rather, in line with the 'non-categorical' nature of IHL rules, bound to factual determinations following the reality of the battlefield, the targeting principles require to assess nature, location, purpose or use of every object, in order to determine if it is being used or will be imminently used with prevalent military functions by the relevant party to the conflict. To be considered a legitimate military objective, the object's total or partial destruction, capture or neutralisation, in the circumstances ruling at the time, has to offer a definite military advantage for the attacking party.[48]

It is therefore required to reaffirm what has been already criticised: in the last decades, large sectors of law of war scholarship have excessively dilated the boundaries of IHL, to the point of construing as military objectives in their entirety residential towers where only one flat among hundreds was used militarily. The necessity to reject these 'synecdochical' determinations of the status of military objectives, therefore, assumes even higher importance to preserve the validity of this war crime, and to avoid neutralising its functions whenever one object in multi-component structures made of many is a lawful target.

The elements of the crime, relying on the mentioned IHL categories, require that:

(1) The perpetrator directed an attack.
(2) The object of the attack was civilian objects, that is, objects which are not military objectives.
(3) The perpetrator intended such civilian objects to be the object of the attack.

The emphasis is again on the intent of the perpetrator, who perfects the prohibited conduct in pursuit of the forbidden consequence, which even in this crime does not need to effectively materialise. For this crime, no grave breach provision of AP I indicated the necessity of any threshold of harm, therefore the choice to dismiss a result requirement did not encounter much opposition. Consequently,

[48] For the notion of military objectives, see ch 2, section 2.1.1.

the crime of direct attacks on civilian objects is perfected even if the shelling of the civilian object does not ultimately take place because, for example, the weapon employed suffers a malfunction, and strays from the objective unlawfully targeted.

Direct attacks on civilians, in sum, as well as direct attacks on civilian objects, are undoubtedly configurable in case of *dolus directus* in the first degree, or direct intent; that is, the targeting of the protected persons and/or objects as such, pursuing specifically the injuring or killing of the civilians, or the damage or destruction of the civilian objects. In these cases, the volitional element of the perpetrator is central, legally, and it is prevalent, factually, because the suspect purposefully wills or desires the prohibited result of the action.

However, the crucial issue is whether these crimes are also configurable in other, much more common cases, such as when the perpetrator does not have the *primary* aim of striking civilians. It is entirely possible, in fact, that an attacker assumes an approach of moral indifference toward the mass killing of civilians (eventually civilians of a discriminated national group) and, without desiring or aiming primarily at this result, foresees with certainty they will be directly shelled in attacks (for example because there is a target among them), and engage in the prohibited conduct, nonetheless. In such cases, the volitional element of the perpetrator will be less central, and what would be legally decisive is the cognitive element, that is, for example, the certainty, or near certainty, that attack will directly impact civilians and/or civilian objects.

This legal issue is central to this analysis, as it is inextricably connected to the possibility of applying these crimes to the numerous cases in which perpetrators do not have the intention of targeting *solely* civilians and/or civilian objects. Notably, indiscriminate attacks under IHL fall into this category. In sum, the question for the ICL framing of these attacks is: do the war crimes of direct attacks on civilians and civilian objects only punish the conduct of attackers aiming *exclusively* at unlawful targets?

Such a restriction of the scope of application of the crimes (if one reads the *mens rea* threshold as confined to *dolus directus* in the first degree) would largely neutralise the function of these offences. The crimes would be inapplicable, in other words, whenever some lawful target is involved in the attacking procedures, as it is often the case in urban warfare. Imagine, for example, one, or a few lawful targets interspersed in a dense crowd of civilians, eventually hundreds of civilians, and attackers deciding to shell them all at once, knowingly killing and injuring all. In this case, a direct intent to kill the hundreds of civilians as such might well be missing, and suspects could contend they acted with the primary aim of eliminating the target or targets as a war priority. *Dolus directus* in the first degree would thus be excluded, and the perpetrator, having acted with the certainty of killing *also* all the hundreds of civilians, targeted jointly with the objectives, would remain immune from any liability.

Against all the cases of attacks aiming cumulatively at lawful targets and protected persons and objects, however, the entire IHL targeting framework, already analysed, imposes its intransgressible legal boundaries. It would be paradoxical if the Rome Statute war crimes regime were to be interpreted as remaining indifferent to the commission of attacks unlawful under customary IHL.[49]

4.2.3. Indiscriminate Attacks as Direct Attacks on Civilians and Civilian Objects? The ICC Jurisprudence

It is therefore important to see how the ICC jurisprudence has dealt with the relevance of indiscriminate attacks under the Rome Statute framework.

Since the earliest ICC cases, judges have faced the issue of indiscriminate attacks. In the early stages of the *Katanga* case, PTC I of the Court found that there were reasonable grounds to believe that

> the attack jointly launched by the FRPI and the FNI on the village of Bogoro on or about 24 February 2003 was neither specifically aimed at the civilian population of Bogoro nor at individual civilians not taking direct part in hostilities.[50]

PTC I judges added, with an explicit reference to the type of indiscriminate attacks consisting in area bombardments,[51] that:

> Germain Katanga, and other senior FRPI and FNI commanders planned to launch an indiscriminate attack against the village of Bogoro which was to be targeted as a single military objective, instead of directing the attack to the clearly separated and distinct military objectives located in the village.[52]

The Chamber, after this finding, indicated that the decision over the question of whether criminal liability can arise under Article 8(2)(b)(i) for the launching, or attempted launching, of an indiscriminate attack should have been answered at the confirmation of charges hearing stage.

The relevant decision on the confirmation of charges was the first judicial decision of the ICC indicating, crucially for the present analysis, that indiscriminate attacks fall under the scope of application of the crime of direct attacks on civilians.

In the decision, judges discussed the elements of the relevant crime, and added (crucially for the arguments of this research) that:

> The crime is also committed when the perpetrator launches the attack with two distinct specific aims: (i) to target a military objective within the meaning of articles 51 and 52 of AP I; and simultaneously, (ii) to target the civilian population or individual civilians not taking direct part in the hostilities who reside in the vicinity. In such a case, the crime is committed when an attack is launched against a village which

[49] See ch 2, para 2.3.

[50] *Prosecutor v Katanga* (Decision on the evidence and information provided by the Prosecution for the issuance of a warrant of arrest for Germain Katanga), ICC-01/04-01/07, 6 July 2007, para 40.

[51] ibid, at p 17, fn 51 of the Decision.

[52] ibid, para 40.

> has significant military value because of its strategic location and when the village contains two distinct targets:
>
> (i) the defending forces of the adverse or hostile party in control of the village (that is, when only the defeat of these forces would permit the attacking party to seize control of the village); and
> (ii) the civilian population of the village, if its allegiance is with the adverse or hostile party in control of the village thus leading the attacking forces to consider the "destruction" of that civilian population as the best method for securing control of the village once it has been seized.[53]

As emerges clearly from this *dictum*, the criminal implication of such conduct is the transformation of the entirety of a civilian area, simply because it is controlled by enemy forces and of strategic relevance, in a target as a whole, comprising not only the armed opponents, but also the unarmed civilians residing in the area. Such indication is coherent with the ICTY jurisprudence, which states repeatedly that the presence of combatants amidst a group of civilians does not alter the civilian status of the group, and thus its protection from direct attacks.[54]

Does this mean that armed forces will not be able to target combatants if they are in the vicinity of civilians? As it has been shown, it does not. Importantly, in fact, judges added in the *Katanga* decision:

> This second type of case must be distinguished from the other situations in which an attack is launched with the specific aim of targeting *only* a military objective, albeit with the awareness that incidental loss of life or injury to civilians will or may result from such an attack.[55]

This paragraph traces the dividing line between indiscriminate and disproportionate attacks. Armed forces are not absolutely prohibited from causing incidental harm to civilians and civilian objects in their attacks, insofar as their objectives are only the lawful targets. In these cases, provided that the attackers aimed *exclusively* at combatants, taking the relevant, mandatory precautions, the issue becomes one of the proportionality of the collateral damage, that is, the foreseeable incidental harm to civilians and civilian objects.

This distinction by PTC I judges corresponds to the systematisation of the relationship between distinction and proportionality proposed in this research, confirming that proportionality is operative exclusively when lawful targets were

[53] *Prosecutor v Katanga*, Decision on the confirmation of charges, ICC-01/04-01/07, 30 September 2008, para 273.

[54] *Prosecuto v Tadić*, Judgment, IT-94-1-T, 7 May 1997, para 638, ('it is clear that the targeted population must be of a predominantly civilian nature. The presence of certain non-civilians in their midst does not change the character of the population'); *Prosecutor v Jelisić*, Judgment, IT-95-10-T, 14 December 1999, para 54; *Prosecutor v Kordić and Čerkez*, Judgment, T-95-14/2-T, 26 February 2001, para 180; *Prosecutor v Naletilić and Martinović*, Judgment, IT-98-34-T, 31 March 2003, para 235; *Prosecutor v Blaskić*, Appeals Judgment, IT-95-14-A, 29 July 2004, para 115; *Prosecutor v Galić*, Appeal Judgment, IT-98-29-A, 30 November 2006, para 137.

[55] *Prosecutor v Katanga*, Decision on the confirmation of charges, ICC-01/04-01/07, 30 September 2008, para 274 (emphasis added).

the *sole* objects of direct attacks. The indication by the judges is, therefore, an important reminder that the targeting of civilians and civilian objects (even if jointly with lawful targets) can never be counterbalanced by any military advantage, as it is absolutely prohibited, and extraneous to proportionality assessments in the IHL sense.

In addition to the indications in *Katanga*, ICC judges dealt with the simultaneous targeting of combatants and civilians in the *Mbarushimana* case. In the confirmation of charges decision, the Chamber affirmed

> the war crime of attacking civilians pursuant to article 8(2)(e)(i) of the Statute does not presuppose that the civilian population is the *sole and exclusive* target of the attack. The crime may be perpetrated in any of the two following scenarios:
>
> (i) when individual civilians not taking direct part in the hostilities or the civilian population are the sole target of the attack, or
>
> (ii) when the perpetrator launches the attack with two distinct specific aims: (a) a military objective, within the meaning of articles 51 and 52 of the Protocol Additional to the Geneva Conventions of 12 August 1949 (the AP I); *and simultaneously*, (b) the civilian population or individual civilians not taking direct part in the hostilities.[56]

Again, the Court affirms that targeting both military objectives and civilian objects, and/or combatants and civilians at the same time, falls under the scope of Article 8(2)(b)(i)–(ii). Mbarusihmana's defence argued – as often happens in similar cases – that the civilians killed were lawful collateral damage, and contested the configurability of the crime asserting that more combatants than civilians were killed in the attack. In response to this claim, the PTC judges reaffirmed that the fact that combatants were killed did not exclude the crime of direct attacks on protected persons and objects, and found reasonable grounds to believe that the crime was committed.

Such orientation was also followed in the *Mudacumura* case, where pre-trial judges affirmed:

> The Chamber emphasises that these incidents involve indiscriminate targeting against mixed civilian-military positions. Such attacks do fall within the ambit of article 8(2)(e)(i) of the Statute.[57]

Importantly, two judgments among others tackled specifically the issue of indiscriminate attacks, albeit with some inconsistencies.

In the *Katanga* trial judgment, Trial Chamber II reaffirmed that indiscriminate attacks may constitute direct attacks on civilians, stating:

> The Chamber considers that the crime may be established even if the military operation also targeted a legitimate military objective. It is important, however, to establish that

[56] *Prosecutor v Mbarushimana* (Decision on the confirmation of charges), ICC-01/04-01/10, 16 December 2011, para 142 (first emphasis added).

[57] *Prosecutor v Mudacumura*, Decision on the Prosecutor's Application under Article 58, ICC-01/04-01/12, 13 July 2012, para 38.

> the primary object of the attack was the civilian population or individual civilians. Thus, situations in which the attack is directed against a military objective and civilians are incidentally affected fall outwith article 8(2)(e)(i). It must be noted that indiscriminate attacks – proscribed by a rule of custom – *may qualify as intentional attacks against the civilian population or individual civilians*, especially where the damage caused to civilians is so great that it appears to the Chamber that the perpetrator meant to target civilian objectives.[58]

In the first part of the paragraph, judges refer to civilians as the 'primary object' of the attack, terminology that doesn't provide any clarification, as it could be interpreted as requiring no less than direct intent. It appears from the second part of the paragraph, however, that the judges held that indiscriminate attacks, to be punishable under Article 8(2)(b)(i), need to present a clear lack of distinction, so as to allow the Court to infer that the civilians, or civilian objects, were the direct targets of the attacks, even if jointly with military objectives.

The judgment also added:

> Use of weaponry that has indiscriminate effects may, inter alia, show that the attack was directed at the civilian population or individual civilians. The Chamber notes in this regard that an indiscriminate attack does not, however, automatically constitute an attack against the civilian population under article 8(2)(e)(i), as the subjective element is decisive in respect of the second case.[59]

Read in light of the judicial decisions recalled so far, this passage indicates that judges, on the basis of an assessment of the relevant *mens rea*, need to determine whether the indiscriminate attack was sustained by an intent to target civilians, or whether the intent of the suspect was to target only military objectives. In the opinion of this author, this second case would, in turn, trigger the alternative, potential relevance of Article 8(2)(b)(iv), dealing with disproportionate civilian harm resulting from the attack as incidental consequence. Judges would then be obliged to scrutinise the liability of the suspect under the relevant offence.

Overall, the *Katanga* judgment, while referring to the mental element as a decisive factor for establishing the commission of the crime, omitted to provide more specific indications about which mental element of the suspects launching the indiscriminate attack suffice to perfect the crime of direct attacks on civilians. The problem remains thus open.

Another important judgment in this regard, albeit leaving still unsolved the issue just mentioned, is the one delivered in the (more recent) *Ntaganda* case.

In this judgment, it was affirmed that:

> The crime under Article 8(2)(e)(i) of the Statute may encompass attacks that are carried out in an indiscriminate manner, that is by targeting an area, as opposed to specific objects, or not targeting specific military objects or persons taking a direct part in

[58] *Prosecutor v Katanga*, Judgment, ICC-01/04-01/07, 7 March 2014, para 802 (emphasis added).
[59] ibid.

> hostilities, *so long as the perpetrator was aware of the presence of civilians in the relevant area*. It may also include attacks that are launched *without taking necessary precautions* to spare the civilian population or individual civilians.[60]

Importantly, in case of indiscriminate attacks, the awareness of the perpetrator of the presence of civilians in the area is necessary, and at the same time indicative of a probable intent to target the civilians alongside the lawful targets. Similarly, when civilian areas are attacked without taking mandatory precautions, the circumstance indicates an intent of *also* attacking the civilians and civilian objects.

In conclusion, there appears to be no doubt that indiscriminate attacks, when driven by the intent to target the civilian population, individual civilians, or civilian objects, even if jointly with lawful targets, fall under the scope of application of the crimes of direct attacks on civilians and/or civilians objects.

What needs to be clarified, however, is whether there should be a direct intent to target the civilians or civilian objects as such, as finalistic purpose of the suspect (under *dolus directus* in the first degree), or whether it would be sufficient that the perpetrator has knowledge that his action will bring about protected persons and objects being struck jointly with the lawful targets, even in absence of a direct, purposeful intent.[61]

4.2.4. The Contradictory Elements of the Crime of (Clearly) Disproportionate Attacks

Before answering questions related to direct attacks on civilians sustained by a lower *mens rea* than direct intent (or *dolus directus* in the first degree), as it is more often than not the case in indiscriminate attacks, it is essential to understand the legal boundaries of the crime of disproportionate attacks, and how such attacks differ from indiscriminate attacks, legally and factually. One of the concerns of the jurisprudence analysed, as it has been shown, was to discern between indiscriminate attacks which may constitute crimes of direct attacks on civilians from other unlawful attacks, characterised by different elements, and violating a different targeting rule: proportionality.

The elements of the crime of clearly disproportionate attacks, considering the compromise formulas resulting in the Rome Statute definition and in the Elements of the Crimes, can easily confuse interpreters without a robust understanding of the law of targeting.

The relevant provision in this regard is Article 8(2)(b)(iv) of the Rome Statute, which punishes:

> Intentionally launching an attack in the knowledge that such attack will cause incidental loss of life or injury to civilians or damage to civilian objects or widespread, long-term

[60] *Prosecutor v Ntaganda*, Judgment, ICC-01/04-02/06, 8 July 2019, para 921 (emphasis added).
[61] Considering its complexity, navigating this issue requires a specific analysis, articulated in ch 5.

> and severe damage to the natural environment which would be *clearly* excessive in relation to the concrete and direct *overall* military advantage anticipated.

This offence translates into ICL the provision of Article 85(3)(b) AP I, combining the prohibition of indiscriminate and disproportionate attacks, and classifying as a grave breach to launching 'any attack which may be expected to cause incidental loss of civilian life, injury to civilians, damage to civilian objects, or a combination thereof, which would be excessive in relation to the concrete and direct military advantage anticipated'.[62] The offence is however placed among the other serious violations of the law of international armed conflicts in Article8(2)(b), rather than in letter 'a', punishing the grave breaches. Such collocation does not exclude that the relevant crime needs to be interpreted coherently with the relevant IHL regime, for the reasons of systematic coherence already explained.

Unlike in the grave breach provision, in addition, the Rome Statute offence adds the cumulative 'widespread, long-term *and* severe damage to the natural environment' to the proportionality assessment relevant for the crime.[63]

Even for this crime, in the Preparatory Commission there were doubts surrounding the necessity of a result requirement. Requiring the verification of the civilian damage in this case would have set a consequence threshold even higher than that established by AP I for grave breaches – that is causation of 'death or serious injury to body or health' – vis-à-vis the materialisation of the 'excessive loss of life or injury to civilians or damage to civilian objects or … to the environment' of the Rome Statute. For this reason, even for the commission of clearly disproportionate attacks the result element was held to be unnecessary.

The first element of the crime, therefore, requires that 'The perpetrator *launched* an attack'. If the attack had the characteristics specified in the subsequent elements, the crime does not require the material verification of the prohibited result. The crime is thus perfected when the perpetrator sets in motion the causal processes (launching the attack) which would have led, in the ordinary course of events, to the clearly excessive incidental impact of the attack on civilians, civilian structures, or the environment.

The second element of the crime qualifies the attack prohibited, object of the offence, stating:

> The attack was *such that it would cause* incidental death or injury to civilians or damage to civilian objects or widespread, long-term and severe damage to the natural environment and that such death, injury or damage *would be* of such an extent as to be *clearly* excessive in relation to the concrete and direct *overall* military advantage anticipated.[64]

[62] See Art 85(3)(b), with its explicit reference to Art 57(2)(a)(iii) AP I.

[63] For this profile of the offence (not discussed in the present treatise focusing on harm to civilians and civilian objects) see inter alia JC Lawrence and KJ Heller, 'The Limits of Article 8(2)(b)(iv) of the Rome Statute, the First Ecocentric Environmental War Crime' (2007) 20 *Georgetown International Environmental Law Review* 61.

[64] Emphasis added.

The concept of 'excessive' civilian harm arising from IHL worried some delegations, who could foresee the risk of radical compression of the prerogatives and margins of appreciation of their military commanders. Those delegations proposed to a adopt a more flexible criterion: damage 'not justified by military necessity'. This formulation, however, would have imposed a binary evaluation of the judges (justified v. not justified by military necessity), obstructing any assessment of an incidental civilian harm not entirely unjustified per se, but rather for its extent (which is much more coherent with the IHL prohibition). The complex discussion led to the compromise resulting in the final wording of the article, which adds to the IHL formulation the terms 'clearly', referring to the civilian and environmental harm, and 'overall', referring to concrete and direct military advantage.[65] The result of this formulation, setting the bar higher than the IHL proportionality rule, is to grant an additional lawyer of protection to the margin of appreciation of military commanders. This profile, however, cannot be read as condoning an excessive incidental civilian or environmental harm not evaluated by the perpetrators themselves as 'clearly' excessive. In addition, this element perplexingly expands the military advantage to be balanced in the proportionality assessment, producing the oxymoronic formulation of a military advantage which is at the same time a 'concrete and direct', and an 'overall' one.

The ICRC noted at the Rome Conference that the addition of the word 'overall' could not modify the concept of military advantage as consolidated in customary IHL. The Committee noted that:

> The word 'overall' could give the impression that an extra unspecified element has been added to a formulation that was carefully negotiated during the 1974–1977 Diplomatic Conference that led to Additional Protocol I to the 1949 Geneva Conventions and this formulation is generally recognised as reflecting customary law. The intention of this additional word appears to be to indicate that a particular target can have an important military advantage that can be felt over a lengthy period of time and affect military action in areas other than the vicinity of the target itself. As this meaning is included in the existing wording of Additional Protocol I, the inclusion of the word 'overall' is redundant.[66]

Validating this view, which is shared by the present author, requires a brief zoom-in on the issue. It has been noted, in this regard, that the adjunction of the term 'overall' was meant to cover attacks where the military advantage is legitimately planned to materialise at a later time and in a different place, therefore beyond

[65] See R Arnold 'Art. 8(2)(b)(iv)' in O Triffterer and K Ambos (eds), *The Rome Statute of the International Criminal Court. A Commentary* (Hart-Nomos, 2015) 341 ff; K Dörmann, *Elements of War Crimes Under the Rome Statute of the International Criminal Court: Sources and Commentary* (Cambridge University Press, 2003) 160.

[66] Official Records of the United Nations Diplomatic Conference of Plenipotentiaries on the Establishment of an International Criminal Court, Rome, 15 June–17 July 1998, Volume III (A/CONF.183/INF/10 of 13 July 1998) 225.

the capture or destruction of the specific objective of the attack. This debate was ongoing since the entry into force of the first Additional Protocol. At the time of the ratification of the Protocol itself, in fact, some states attached to the ratification an interpretative declaration affirming that:

> In applying the rule of proportionality in Article 51 and Article 57, 'military advantage' is understood to refer to the advantage anticipated from the attack as a whole and not only from isolated or particular parts of the attack.[67]

While the concept of 'attack as a whole' is unclear, a common example is that of the feigned attacks on the German military during World War II to allow the allied forces to land in Normandy. Those supporting a broad conceptualisation of the notion of concrete and direct military advantage often refer to Solf, who contended in an early commentary to Article 52 AP I:

> Whether a definite military advantage would result from an attack must be judged in the context of the military advantage anticipated from the specific military operation of which the attack is a part considered as a whole, and not only from isolated or particular parts of that operation. It is not necessary that the contribution made by the object to the Party attacked be related to the advantage anticipated by the attacker from the destruction, capture or neutralisation of the object. Thus, prior to the 1944 cross channel operation, the Allies attacked a large number of bridges, fuel dumps, airfields and other targets in the Pas de Calais. These targets made an effective contribution to German military action in that area. The primary military advantage of these attacks anticipated by the Allies, however, was not to reduce German military strength in that area, but to deceive the Germans into believing that the Allied amphibious assault would occur in the Pas de Calais instead of the beaches of Normandy. Therefore, the military advantage expected from these air raids was not related to their value to the adverse Party.[68]

Solf's reasoning referred, however, to the notion of 'definite military advantage', which is part of the tests to be fulfilled under Article 52 AP I to determine the legal status (military or civilian) of an object. Such determination, despite the terminological similitude, in IHL is antecedent and preliminary to the proportionality assessments requiring to weight, on one of the two proportionality 'scale pans', the 'concrete and direct military advantage' anticipated.[69]

In other words, an object might well be a military objective under IHL, provided it makes an effective contribution to the military action of the enemy, because it offers to attackers a military advantage of a *tactical* nature elsewhere on the battlefield, rather than an immediate one, such as inducing enemy forces to move troops in the attempt to defend the attacked object. Whether this definite

[67] See See BR-Drs 64/90 of 2 February 1990, 132, cited in J Gardam, *Necessity, Proportionaliy and the Use of Force by States* (Cambridge University Press, 2009) 102.

[68] WA Solf, 'Article 52' in M Bothe, KJ Partsch and WA Solf (eds), *New Rules for Victims of Armed Conflicts: Commentary on the Two 1977 Protocols Additional to the Geneva Conventions* (Martinus Nijhoff, 1982) 324.

[69] See E Raunch, 'Conduct of Combat and Risks Run by the Civilian Population' (1982) 21 *Military Law and Law of War Review* 292.

military advantage, tactically materialising elsewhere on a battlefield (and in a different time), can modify the 'concrete and direct military advantage' of an individual attack, under proportionality, is a different, and rather debatable, matter. An attack on a less important military outpost to induce enemy forces to defend it by concentrating around it, in other words, if expected to cause incidental civilian harm, may kill and/or injure civilians per se.

Subsequently, attacks in the areas of major importance with reduced enemy presence (as a consequence of the successful tactic) may well be expected to cause additional civilian harm, and thus to kill and/or injure more civilians in themselves. Balancing the incidental civilian harm of the former, feigned attack with the higher military advantage of the subsequent one in the area of main military importance, in other words, would deceive proportionality, since it would: 1) discount from the proportionality assessment of the first attack the incidental civilian harm to be expected in the second; and 2) double the weight of the military advantage anticipated from the first attack. It is therefore crucial to apply the same scale to both the military advantage, and the incidental civilian harm.[70] In other words, when attackers intend to construe the concrete and direct military advantage as deriving from an operation as a whole, they need to construe *symmetrically* the incidental civilian harm side of the proportionality assessment, evaluating the harm to civilians that can be expected from the operation as a whole.

In sum, considering that the Court must apply the 'established principles of the international law of armed conflict', included proportionality, the concept of military advantage in Article 8(2)(b)(iv) AP I needs to be interpreted in accordance with its IHL lineaments. The element therefore designates an advantage that:

(1) Must have a specifically military character, and cannot be merely psychological, eg aimed at breaking the enemies' determination to fight;
(2) Even if it can be anticipated from a military operation considered as a whole, and not solely from isolated or particular segments of the operation, it cannot be interpreted as broadly as to transform in a political advantage, or worse to morph into the overall aims of the war (which would conflate *ius in bello* with *ius ad bellum* proportionality);
(3) Remains a substantial and relatively close advantage, and not a hypothetical or speculative.[71]

The delicate compromise between instances of legal precision and military realism giving rise to the controversial formulation of Article 8(2)(b)(iv) AP I is reflected in a clarificatory footnote attached to third element of the crime, stating:

> The expression 'concrete and direct overall military advantage' refers to a military advantage that is foreseeable by the perpetrator at the relevant time. Such advantage

[70] Dörmann (n 66) 173.
[71] See ch 2, section 2.1.2.

> *may or may not* be temporally or geographically related to the object of the attack. The fact that this crime admits the possibility of lawful incidental injury and collateral damage does not in any way justify any violation of the law applicable in armed conflict. It does not address justifications for war or other rules related to jus ad bellum. It reflects the proportionality requirement inherent in determining the legality of any military activity undertaken in the context of an armed conflict.[72]

The robust anchorage of this footnote to the applicable IHL rules, therefore, specifying that the article cannot be interpreted as allowing violations thereof, supports the reasoning just articulated.

An additional lawyer of legal problems surrounding this offence, however one may interpret the concept of 'concreted and direct overall military advantage', is the determination of the scope of the proportionality assessment. In particular, the crucial problem remains understanding whose proportionality assessment must count in relevant investigations and trials.

As has been previously discussed, the main issue with the rule of proportionality in IHL is the necessity to balance between two sets of values of a radically different nature: the need to avoid civilian loss of life, injury and damage to civilian objects, on the one hand, and the pursuit of concrete and direct military advantages, on the other, insofar as they are lawful ones. During the drafting of the Rome Statute, the formulation of proportionality in Article 8(2)(b)(iv) triggered intense debate. Under IHL, as has been extensively discussed, the rule outlaws civilian damage that 'would be excessive in relation to the concrete and direct military advantage anticipated'. The emphasis of the IHL prescriptions is thus on the incidental civilian harm foreseeable before launching the attack. In Rome, many delegations were afraid that such a formulation would have enabled the Court to impose an excessively strict application, based on the judges' evaluation of the circumstances of the attack informed by their ex post knowledge, and thus in an unfair advantage if compared to the position and knowledge of the suspects in their *ex ante* assessments.[73] Overall, however, behind these concerns on the functioning of proportionality assessments under this offence the overarching preoccupation of many delegations was to minimise the constraints that the provisions would have imposed to their militaries.

The option to confer centrality to the position and stance of the alleged perpetrator at the moment of launching the attack resulted thus in the third, controversial element of the crime:

> The perpetrator *knew* that the attack would cause incidental death or injury to civilians or damage to civilian objects or widespread, long-term and severe damage to the natural environment and that such death, injury or damage would be of such an extent as to be clearly excessive in relation to the concrete and direct overall military advantage anticipated.[74]

[72] ICC (n 41) 19.
[73] See section 4.3.3 below.
[74] Emphasis added.

This element requires thus that the perpetrator had knowledge of the excessiveness of the incidental civilian or environmental harm. However, such assertion remains ambiguous. Delegations discussed what kind of evaluation was required from the perpetrator. Some delegations argued in favour of a more objective approach, according to which the Court would have had to review the evaluation of the suspects, based on the requisite information available to them. According to this orientation, to be punishable, the perpetrator was only required to be aware of the foreseeable *extent* of the incidental civilian harm that the attack would have caused. The excessiveness of this harm in comparison to the military advantage, instead, should have been determined by the Court through a prognostic evaluation, inherited from the ICTY jurisprudence, based on the 'reasonable commander' standard.[75] Other delegates, in contrast, argued in favour of a more subjective approach, emphasising the need of a psychological stance of the perpetrator worthy of legal blame and punishment. According to this perspective, the perpetrators had to be themselves aware of the excessiveness of the civilian harm foreseeable, and launch the attack nonetheless.[76]

The debate resulted in the wording of the second footnote included in the elements, which indicates what is meant by 'knowledge' in the definition of this war crime. In opposition to the general rule set forth in the general introduction of the Elements of Crimes document, indicating that expressions contained in the Statute such as 'inhumane' and 'severe' do not generally require the perpetrator to personally complete a particular value judgement, the footnote states that in relation to disproportionate attacks:

> [T]his knowledge element requires that the perpetrator makes the value judgement as described therein. An evaluation of that value judgement must be based on the requisite information available to the perpetrator at the time.[77]

Such specification remains highly problematic. A perpetrator can be considered to have knowledge of the excessiveness of the foreseeable incidental harm in an objective sense, meaning simply being aware of the actual extent of the incidental harm that the attack will cause, which in turn will be appreciated by judges as excessive, or not excessive.

[75] Trying to limit, and in order to review, the subjective margins of appreciation of military commanders in proportionality assessments, international criminal jurisprudence – as it has been recalled in ch 2 – developed a standard, based on a general and abstract point of reference, in order to judicially evaluate the proportionality assessments of those in charge of attacking decisions. The ICTY referred to this standard as that of a 'reasonably well-informed person in the circumstances of the actual perpetrator'. This standard was then developed by considering the ideal position not of any reasonably well-informed person, but that of a reasonably well-informed war professional, strong of training and expertise, ie the military commander. Actual, and potentially wrong/unlawful, proportionality assessments by commanders could in this way be re-evaluated by judges on the basis of the parameters of what a reasonably well-informed commander would have determined in comparison to the one under actual scrutiny.

[76] Dörmann (n 66) 165.

[77] ICC (n 41) 19.

Alternatively, a perpetrator could be considered to have knowledge of the excessiveness of the harm in a subjective sense, meaning that the perpetrators would need themselves to evaluate the foreseeable incidental civilian harm as excessive.

While the footnote perplexingly leans toward the second interpretation, such an approach would substantially neutralise the meaningfulness and applicability of this crime. Should perpetrators themselves need to formulate the relevant value judgement on the excessiveness, in order to be liable for this crime, then they would become the unreviewable sovereign of proportionality assessments, to the point of marginalising or even rendering irrelevant the Court's own prosecutorial and judicial review. The excessiveness of the incidental civilian harm, in fact, could be excluded by a grossly wrong, and manifestly unlawful value judgement of the perpetrator under IHL, erroneously considering, for example, extensive, or even immense incidental civilian harm 'proportionate' to the military advantage pursued. Suspect perpetrators, as noted by Bothe, would thus become nothing less than 'judges in their own cause' since, for example, an unreasonable moral indifference toward incidental mass killing of civilians would 'exclude the necessary intent'.[78] Such a reading would be tantamount to reducing the provision to an empty simulacre, transforming the subjective perception of a perpetrator devaluing or ignoring the right to life of discriminated civilians, or worse, an hypothetically genocidal military commander, in ultimate and *legibus solutus* monarch of proportionality assessments, with the ICC itself subdued by his own *mens rea*.

It is therefore crucial to reject the latter view and preserve an interpretation of the knowledge element specified in the footnote as knowledge of the objective entity of the incidental civilian harm, as part of the prognostic proportionality assessment of the suspect. It will then be the role of judges to evaluate whether the relevant suspect should have refrained from launching the attack in light of the excessiveness of the harm foreseen.

4.2.5. Old Challenges and New Possibilities: Toward the First ICC Adjudication of Disproportionate Attacks

The defects of the Article 8(2)(b)(iv) AP I offence, and the oxymoronic elements of the crime analysed so far have decisively contributed to an out-and-out stalling of the adjudication of disproportionate attacks, which it has suffered since the beginning of the ICC activities.

As has been recalled, the absence of any charges for the relevant crime until 2024 has not allowed the development of judicial reasoning that disentangles the interpretative knots connatural to the defects and contradictions of

[78] Bothe (n 18) 400.

the 1998 codification. It would appear that state powers allegedly concerned with the risk of an excessively strict application of proportionality by the Court have not only secured an extremely limited possibility for judges to review the proportionality assessments of their militaries, but have also succeeded in neutralising the applicability of the crime entirely. Heller and Laurence, referring to the nearly impossible threshold of environmental harm to be met, warned in 2007: 'If the Court does import Protocol I's definitions into Article 8(2)(b)(iv) the Article would have become "a virtual nullity".'[79] The reality was somehow even worse than the prediction: the article remained for the subsequent 15 years a virtual nullity, not only in cases of excessive harm inflicted on the natural environment, but in countless cases of clearly disproportionate and hardly incidental mass killing of civilians.

Comparatively, even in the absence of an explicit criminalisation in Article 8 of the Statute, ICC jurisprudence has supported the conclusion that indiscriminate attacks, when incorporating an intent to also target the civilian population, individual civilians, or civilian objects, even if jointly with lawful targets, fall under the scope of application of the crimes of direct attacks on civilians and/or civilians objects. On the contrary, despite a dedicated provision, clearly disproportionate attacks have only been alluded to in more than 20 years of judicial decision.

The world now faces the first chance to invert this trend. As has been mentioned, in March 2024 PTC II judges issued arrest warrants for Russian Federation top military commanders, Sergei Kobylash, Lieutenant General and the Commander of the Long-Range Aviation of the Aerospace Force, and Viktor Sokolov, an Admiral and the Commander of the Black Sea Fleet, for the crime of clearly disproportionate attacks. The same charge is also contained in the subsequent warrants against Sergei Kuzhugetovich Shoigu and Valery Vasilyevich Gerasimov, respectively Minister of Defence and Chief of the General Staff of the Armed Forces. The attacks which are the object of the charges were directed against electrical power stations, by declared military policy of the Russian forces. Even if the power stations qualified as lawful military objectives at the relevant time, the prosecutor and the judges have found reasonable grounds to believe that the expected incidental civilian harm and damage of these attacks would have been clearly excessive to the anticipated military advantage. PTC II also considered that the alleged campaign of strikes could qualify as a course of conduct involving the multiple commission of acts against a civilian population, pursuant to a state policy, in the meaning of Article 7 of the Statute. As such, pre-trial judges were satisfied that there are reasonable grounds to believe that the suspects bear responsibility for the crime against humanity of 'other inhumane acts … intentionally causing great suffering, or serious injury to body or to mental or physical health', under Article 7(1)(k) of the Rome Statute.[80]

[79] Lawrence and Heller (n 64) 66.

[80] See I. Marchuk, 'Justice for Victims of Missile Attacks in Ukraine: New ICC Arrest Warrants for Russian Top Military Commanders', *Opinio Juris*, 15 March 2024, opiniojuris.org/2024/03/15/justice-for-victims-of-missile-attacks-in-ukraine-new-icc-arrest-warrants-for-russian-top-military-commanders.

At stake in the cases stemming from these warrants, in other words, there is not only the first adjudication of the war crime of disproportionate attacks but even, relatedly, a trial strategy basing on a campaign of disproportionate attacks a charge of crimes against humanity.

Intuitively, the cases which should follow these warrants could be a crucial test bench for the Court, finally addressing the many limits of the offence, and the tensions inscribed in its elements. Leaving aside the blatant unlawfulness of the Russian campaign under *ius ad bellum*, following other wars of aggression in the precedent decades, different *ius in bello* interpretations could bring to opposed results. The interpretation of the notion of 'concrete and direct overall military advantage', the requirement for the incidental civilian harm to be 'clearly excessive', the uncertainties surrounding the *mens rea* standards for the punishment, in other words, will all make a decisive difference in the relevant cases, and could start to dissipate a number of issues which, in the last decades, have obstructed the international criminal adjudication of unlawful attacks in combat situations.

As much as the *Gotovina* case marked the development of international criminal law with a setback still exerting effects unfolding against civilian populations in current conflicts, these future adjudications will determine the future of *ius in bello* and, with it, the ways in which war are fought, potentially for decades to come.

The specific challenges posed, and possibilities offered by the cases underway at the ICC, are analysed in the following sections.

4.3. An 'Unduly Expanded Legal Shield' for the Military?

With the Rome Statute just approved, the debate around the treaty, its features, its limits, and how it compares with the earlier developments of international criminal law began to attract the reflections of the most revered international law scholars. Among them, and of particular relevance to this analysis, Cassese stands out for his foresight.

In 1999, Cassese wrote an initial critical appraisal of the Statute, focusing on both substantive and procedural profiles. In the reflection, he acknowledged the merits of the Statute, included codifying for the first time the general principles of criminal law, and achieving a new level of specificity in the definition of the offences. In contrast, he found that 'in many areas of substantive criminal law the Statute marks a retrogression with respect to existing international law', and that such regression was particularly evident in the area of war crimes, as notable in

> (i) the [initial] exclusion of the use of modern weapons that are inherently indiscriminate or cause unnecessary suffering from this category of crimes;
>
> …

(iii) the exclusion of liability for *reckless* commission of international crimes …;
(iv) the fact that Article 124 allows states to declare, upon becoming parties to the Statute, that the Court's jurisdiction over war crimes committed by their nationals or on their territory shall not become operative for a period of seven years. One is therefore left with the impression that the framers have been eager to shield their servicemen as much as possible from being brought to trial for, and possibly convicted of, war crimes.[81]

As will be shown, these 'retrogressions' identified by Cassese contributed to the setbacks under scrutiny of this analysis. The exclusion of recklessness as sufficient *mens rea* for the commission of unlawful attacks intersects precisely the limits and contradictions of the war crimes law framework observed so far. Cassese noted that

> international law must be taken to allow for recklessness: for example, it is admissible to convict a person who, when shelling a town, takes a high and unjustifiable risk that civilians will be killed – without, however, intending, that they be killed – with the result that the civilians are, in fact, thereby killed.[82]

As has been extensively discussed, such admission of recklessness for the war crimes consisting of attacks violating the IHL targeting rules was the key allowing the ICTY to punish indiscriminate and disproportionate attacks,[83] with the limits already analysed. Cassese underlined that

> on this score the Rome Statute marks a step backwards with respect to *lex lata*, and possibly creates a loophole: persons responsible for war crimes, when they acted recklessly, may be brought to trial and convicted before national courts, while they would be acquitted by the ICC," concluding [it] would seem that the draughtsmen have unduly expanded the shield they intended to provide to the military.[84]

Cassese's conclusion foresaw the egregious effects that the contradictory compromise formulas of the Statute (and the Elements), resulting from the efforts of states to protect their militaries from war crimes accountability, produced on the adjudication of unlawful attacks for two decades to come. Indiscriminate and disproportionate attacks have indeed accumulated in a climax, until arriving at instances of systematic commission and transformation into military policy, and routine attacks, in current conflicts. Some factual examples can elucidate this trend.

[81] Cassese (n 30) 170–71.
[82] ibid, 154.
[83] Recklessness was reaffirmed by the ICTY as admissible *mens rea* threshold in several cases, see eg *Prosecutor v Kordić and Čerkez*, Judgment, Appeals Chamber, IT-95-14/2-A, 17 December 2004, para 36; *Prosecutor v Prlić et al*, Judgment, Volume I, Trial Chamber, IT-04-74-T,29 May 2013, para 112; *Prosecutor v Delalić et al*, Judgment, Appeals Chamber, IT-96-21-A 20 February 2001, para 422; *Prosecutor v Blaškić*, Judgment, Trial Chamber, IT-95-14-T, 3 March 2000, para 217; *Prosecutor v Perišć*, Judgment, Trial Chamber, IT-04-81-T 6, September 2011, para 102; *Prosecutor v Naletilić and Martinović*, Judgment, Trial Chamber, IT-98-34-T, 31 March 2003, para 248; *Prosecutor v Stakić*, Judgment, Trial Chamber, IT-97-24-T, 31 July 2003; *Prosecutor v Strugar*, Judgment, Trial Chamber, IT-01-42-T 31 January 2005, para 235.
[84] Cassese (n 30) 154.

4.3.1. The 2015 Attack against the Kunduz MSF Hospital: The Problem of Recklessness

Among many attacks against civilians and civilian objects, including protected medical facilities, in numerous armed conflicts, intense discussions followed the US aerial attack on the Médecins Sans Frontières (MSF) hospital in Kunduz, Afghanistan, on 3 October 2015, killing 42 patients and medical personnel.[85]

In response to the incident, the US Government issued a 120-page report after investigating the attack,[86] accompanied by a summary.[87] The Government concluded that the targeting of the hospital had been a tragic mistake, 'caused by a combination of human errors, compounded by process and equipment failures. Fatigue and high operational tempo also contributed to the incident.'[88] The report itself acknowledged that, despite inconsistent information, the US forces failed to verify the contrasting accounts they had, with no accurate target grid location, advancing the attacking procedure against 'a vaguely described compound'.[89] An aircrew operator 'raised doubt'[90] about intelligence not matching a ground force commander's description of the scene. Instead of attempting to get more information, the US forces continued with the attack. Despite lack of indication of a 'time-sensitive' target, 211 rounds were fired at nine people. The investigation also concluded, concerningly, that 'The GFC and the Aircraft Commander *failed to exercise* the principle of proportionality in relation to the direct military advantage'.[91]

The report appeared to characterise the attack, as an unlawful failure to take all feasible precautions, both those required to avoid or minimise civilian harm, and even more crucially, those required to verify that the target was a lawful one, and not a protected civilian, as imposed by IHL.

The investigation identified 16 US service members whose conduct warranted consideration for appropriate administrative or disciplinary action, including a

[85] Among the numerous reports, *ex multiis*, see M Ryan and T Craig, 'Top U.S. general in Afghanistan: Hospital was "mistakenly struck"' *Washington Post*, 6 October 2015, at www.washingtonpost.com/world/national-security/top-us-general-in-afghanistan-hospital-was-mistakenly-struck/2015/10/06/0da262e8-6c34-11e5-9bfe-e59f5e244f92_story.html.

[86] United States Central Command, Investigation Report of the Airstrike on the Medecins Sans Frontieres I Doctors Without Borders Trauma Center in Kunduz, Afghanistan on 3 October 2015, 29 April 2016, at www.justsecurity.org/wp-content/uploads/2022/02/Investigation-Report-of-the-Airstrike-on-the-Medecins-Sans-Frontieres-I-Doctors-Without-Borders-Trauma-Center-in-Kunduz-Afghanistan-on-3-October-2015-2016-report.pdf.

[87] 'United States Central Command, CENTCOM releases investigation into airstrike on Doctors Without Borders trauma center', Press Release 29 April 2016, at www.centcom.mil/MEDIA/PRESS-RELEASES/Press-Release-View/Article/904574/april-29-centcom-releases-investigation-into-airstrike-on-doctors-without-borde.

[88] ibid.

[89] United States Central Command (n 87) 94.

[90] ibid.

[91] ibid, 76 (emphasis added).

general officer. Nonetheless, the investigation did not conclude that relevant failures constituted a war crime;

> The label 'war crimes' is typically reserved for *intentional* acts – *intentionally* targeting civilians or *intentionally* targeting protected objects. The investigation found that the tragic incident resulted from a combination of unintentional human errors and equipment failures, and that none of the personnel knew that they were striking a medical facility.[92]

The investigation did not dwell on the meaning of 'intentional', nor with IHL and the existing ICTY jurisprudence, already analysed, indicating that purposeful, direct targeting of civilians as such was only *one* of the possible subjective elements of criminal violations of the international law of targeting. As argued by authors at the time,[93] customary international law already supported punishability of war crimes for reckless attacks directed at or disproportionately impacting civilians.

Intuitively, the issue revolves around the understanding of the notion of 'intent' in penal theory cultures and traditions, and how these interact with the Rome Statute of the ICC. Continental criminal law doctrine typically frames *dolus eventualis* among the forms of intent. *Dolus eventualis* can be synthesised as the perpetrators' awareness of the likely, prohibited result of an action, with acceptance of its verification. Penal theory suggests in these cases the author either remains 'indifferent' to, or 'reconciles himself' with the prohibited outcome.[94] In contrast, Common Law criminal systems do not recognise this concept, nor its distinctive elements (which in Civil Law systems differentiate it from the category of 'conscious culpability', which can be defined as awareness of the likely harmful outcome of an action, with confidence that its verification will be avoided).[95] Rather, Anglo-American penal traditions bring these states of mind under the notion of recklessness.[96]

Scholars took different approaches around this issue, which led to a debate in relation to the Kunduz attack. Ohlin applied to the incident a previous reflection on the different manners in which distinct penal traditions understand the concept of intent, and the relevant intersections with war crimes law.[97] According to this reflection, the ICTY jurisprudence had contributed to a 'disappearance

[92] United States Central Command (n 88).

[93] S Knuckley, A Parrin and K Nimmala, 'US Government Concludes no "War Crimes" in Kunduz Strike, But Fails to Explain Why' *Just Security*, 29 April 2016, at www.justsecurity.org/30831/government-concludes-war-crimes-kunduz-strike-fails-explain.

[94] See GP Fletcher, *Rethinking Criminal Law* (Oxford University Press, 2000) 445–46.

[95] This distinction between *dolus eventualis* and conscious negligence is a *vexata quaestio* in the continental penal theory, since it is extremely difficult to identify firm parameters to identify the two figures in the concrete reality of the cases, the first being based on the author's acceptance of the realisation of the wrongful harm as a possible consequence of his actions, the second, instead, being based on the author's confidence in avoiding this wrongful harm.

[96] See ch 3, section 3.3.

[97] JD Ohlin, 'Targeting and the Concept of Intent' (2013) 35 *Michigan Journal of International Law* 79.

of proportionality' in war crimes adjudication, because judges embraced the tendency to prosecute disproportionate attacks as direct attacks on civilians.[98] Such tendency was supported, according to the author, by a typically continental understanding of recklessness as a form of intent, analogous to *dolus eventualis*, in opposition to how recklessness is understood in Anglo-American, Common Law penal traditions.[99]

The core argument by this author in relation to the Kunduz attack was that admitting recklessness as sufficient *mens rea* for Rome Statute war crimes would have conflated the offences of direct attacks on civilians and that of disproportionate attacks. In attacks knowingly causing (lawful) collateral damage, Ohlin contended, the attacker kills the civilians with knowledge that the civilians will die. Hence, according to the author, 'If intent = recklessness, then all cases of legitimate collateral damage would count as violations of the principle of distinction.'[100] The concern of the author, in sum, was that admitting recklessness as mental element sufficient to commit the war crimes under the ICC Rome Statute would have transformed every attack launched expecting incidental harm to civilians, even if not excessive in comparison to the military advantage sought, thus lawful under IHL, in an attack punishable as direct attack on civilians. The author therefore proposed to consider the different option of codifying a new war crime of reckless attacks on civilians, so to 'create a duty on the part of attacking forces and then penalize them for failing to live up to it' and 'signal the moral difference between intentionally killing civilians and recklessly killing them'.[101]

Some reflection is necessary in relation to this critique, and proposal. The analysis of the present research corroborates that the ICTY jurisprudence assessed in

[98] Referring to distinction and proportionality in the law of targeting, Ohlin argued, 'One might describe this as a two-track system, where what separates the two tracks is the concept of intent. Under the first track, an attack violates IHL if it is intentionally directed at civilians. Under the second track, an attack violates IHL, even in the absence of intent, if it produces disproportionate civilian casualties. More ink has been spilled analyzing the second track's concept of proportionality than perhaps any other issue in the law of targeting. It is fraught with vagueness and much is at stake. … Given the intensity of these legal disputes, it might seem surprising that there are almost no examples of track-two prosecutions before international tribunals that might provide guiding precedent on the nature of proportionality. This Part concludes that there is a simple reason why the second track, and its principle of proportionality, has so rarely been applied by international tribunals. Instead of dealing with the fraught legal complications, of proportionality, both prosecutors and international judges squeeze almost all of the targeting cases into the first track, thus accusing the commander in question of directly targeting civilians or indiscriminately bombarding civilian areas. When the analysis is shifted to the first track, proportionality is sidestepped as legally irrelevant.' (ibid, 86–87).

[99] In relation to intent, comparatively and internationally, see eg ME Badar, *The Concept of Mens Rea in International Criminal Law: The Case for a Unified Approach* (Hart Publishing, 2013); J van der Vyver, 'The International Criminal Court and the Concept of Mens Rea in International Criminal Law' (2004) 12 *University of Miami International and Comparative Law Review* 57, 62–63; and GP Fletcher, *The Grammar of Criminal Law. Volume Two: International Criminal Law* (Oxford University Press, 2019) 175–84.

[100] JD Ohlin, 'Was the Kunduz Hospital Attack a War Crime?' *Opinio Juris*, 1 May 2016, at opiniojuris.org/2016/05/01/was-the-kunduz-hospital-attack-a-war-crime.

[101] ibid.

many cases disproportionate harm to civilians as indicator of a potential *mens rea* of reckless attacks on civilians.

What Ohlin did not appear to consider, however, is that in such ICTY cases neither intention, nor the potential recklessness of attackers, was related to the lawful collateral damage element of the attacks, ie the incidental and not-excessive harm to civilians. Rather, the recklessness of the relevant perpetrators covered the unlawful excessiveness of this incidental harm, fully anticipated as such by relevant commanders, and yet not barring the decision to launch the attacks in the manner they were launched. This knot renders Ohlin's analysis highly debatable.

Heller, appreciating this profile, contended *contra* Ohlin that the war crimes of direct attacks on civilians and on civilian objects are completed when:

> (1) a defendant 'means to engage' in an attack against a specific group of people; (2) that specific group of people objectively qualifies as a civilian population; and (3) the defendant 'is aware' that the specific group of people qualifies as a civilian population. Thus understood, the war crime requires not one but two mental elements: (1) intent for the prohibited conduct (understood as purpose, direct intent, or *dolus directus*); (2) knowledge for the necessary circumstance (understood as oblique intent or *dolus indirectus*).[102]

Based on this understanding, Heller proposed that in attacks calculating a proportionate collateral damage for civilians the attackers know that the attack will injure or kill civilians but have no intent of doing so. In these cases, according to the author, commanders mean 'to attack *only* the military objective' and not the group of civilians.[103]

At a closer analysis, this dispute hinges on the understanding of the relationship between the rules of distinction and proportionality, and the criminal violations thereof. As it has been proposed in this research, a correct understanding of the IHL notion of 'incidentality' of the civilian harm, interpreted as premise for proportionality assessments, can help disentangle the relevant knots.

Reiterating what has been submitted, this notion indicates that only harm expected during attacks directed *solely* at lawful targets can be qualified as incidental, provided the harm to civilians is expected to be a side consequence of a main result pursued, which, in contrast, is anticipated to be of military character. This understanding, whether a legal framework admits recklessness, oblique intent, or both, can provide guidance to prosecutors and avoid conflating collateral killing and direct attacks on civilians. In opposition to the concerns prospected by Ohlin, such an understanding can provide guidance even to avoid conflations between the charge of disproportionate attacks and the charge of direct attacks on civilians. Only attacks which were 1) directly aiming at civilians

[102] KJ Heller, 'Thoughts on Jens's Post about the Kunduz Attack' *Opinio Juris*, 3 May 2016, at opiniojuris.org/2016/05/03/thoughts-on-jens-post-about-the-kunduz-attack.
[103] ibid (emphasis added).

and civilian objects (particularly if in large groups), even if they were 2) *jointly* with lawful targets, will be subject to charges of direct attacks on civilians. On the other hand, the offence of disproportionate attacks will be charged in the different scenario where attacks were: 1) directed at lawful targets; 2) expected to impact only incidentally civilians and civilian objects; and 3) launched despite foreseeing that this incidental harm would have been clearly excessive in comparison to the military advantage sought.

In the case of the Kunduz attack, however, the ICC jurisprudence explicitly excluded that recklessness or *dolus eventualis* are sufficient to perfect the relevant crimes under the material jurisdiction of the Court.[104] At the same time, the Kunduz MSF attack appeared characterised by a massive failure to take mandatory precautions to verify that the targets to be attacked were lawful targets, that is (in this instance) combatants. The ICC Trial Chamber VI, in the *Ntaganda* case judgment, referred to such situations as potentially falling under the scope of application of the crime of direct attacks on civilians, affirming they

> may encompass attacks that are carried out in an indiscriminate manner, that is by targeting an area, as opposed to specific objects, or not targeting specific military objects or persons taking a direct part in hostilities, so long as the perpetrator was aware of the presence of civilians in the relevant area. It may also include attacks that are launched *without taking necessary precautions* to spare the civilian population or individual civilians.[105]

It remains to be seen in future ICC case law developments how the duty to take mandatory precautions, imposed by customary law, will be weighed by the Court in cases concerning unlawful attacks not supported by a direct intent to strike exclusively civilians.

Such possibility, however, remains bound to the will of the Court to expand its investigations on conduct of hostilities crimes across the situations under its scrutiny. As a minimum, according to this author, failures to take mandatory precautions to verify the status of the objects or persons to be attacked should exclude the applicability of defences based on mistakes of fact (eg mistakes on the civilian status of a target, wrongly considered a combatant).[106] A mistake of fact is only relevant for the Rome Statute when it excludes the requisite mental element for the relevant crime.[107] In cases of failures to take precautions, it would be the violation of a customary law prescription to be the basis of mistakes on the status of the attacked persons or objects. In these cases, the reasonably well-informed

[104] See section 4.2.
[105] *Prosecutor v Bosco Ntaganda*, Judgment, ICC-01/04-02/06, 8 July 2019, para 921 (emphasis added).
[106] For an analysis of the problems arising from mistakes of fact, see A Eser, 'Mental Elements – Mistake of Fact and Mistake of Law' in A Cassese, P Gaeta and JRWD Jones (eds), The Rome Statute of the International Criminal Court: A Commentary (Oxford University Press, 2002); E van Sliedregt, Individual Criminal Responsibility in International Law (Oxford University Press, 2012) 269–86. On the distinct but related issue of mistake of law, see A Coco, *The Defence of Mistake of Law in International Criminal Law: A Study on Ignorance and Blame* (Oxford University Press, 2022).
[107] Art 32(1) Rome Statute.

commander standard (elaborated to adjudicate proportionality assessments in international criminal trials) could serve the purpose of distinguishing merely negligent failures to take precautions, from failures so serious as to indicate that it was impossible for the suspect not to know that the lack of precautions would have resulted, in the ordinary course of the events, and considering the circumstances, in attacks against targets of unverified status.[108]

4.3.2. Western Loopholes for Russian War Crimes? Indiscriminate and Disproportionate Attacks in the War against Ukraine

Since the full-scale Russian Federation invasion of Ukraine in February 2022, international institutions have denounced numerous attacks against civilians and civilian objects. The UN Independent International Commission of Inquiry reported, in line with the Office of the High Commissioner for Human Rights, that in slightly more than a month (from 24 February to 31 March 2022), in the provinces under the Commission's investigation, 1,237 civilians, including 112 children, were killed.[109] The Commission denounced patterns of indiscriminate attacks and attacks against civilian infrastructures.[110] Similarly, the OSCE Report on Violations of IHL and IHRL, War Crimes and Crimes Against Humanity Committed in Ukraine, while warning that '[a] detailed assessment of most allegations of International Humanitarian Law (IHL) violations and the identification of war crimes concerning particular incidents has not been possible', found nonetheless

> clear patterns of IHL violations by the Russian forces in their conduct of hostilities. If they had respected their IHL obligations in terms of distinction, proportionality and precautions in attack and concerning specially protected objects such as hospitals – the Report added – the number of civilians killed or injured would have remained much lower. Similarly, considerably fewer houses, hospitals, cultural properties, schools, multi-story residential buildings, water stations and electricity systems would have been damaged or destroyed.[111]

[108] For a comprehensive discussion of the issues related to mistakes of fact and unlawful attacks, see M. Milanović, 'Mistakes of Fact When Using Lethal Force in International Law' (Part I, Part II, and Part III), *EJILTalk!*, 14 January 2020, at www.ejiltalk.org/mistakes-of-fact-when-using-lethal-force-in-international-law-part-i.

[109] Report of the Independent International Commission of Inquiry on Ukraine, A/77/553, 18 October 2022, para 33, in which the Commission also warned that final figures were 'likely to be much higher'.

[110] ibid, paras 34–59.

[111] Report on Violations of International Humanitarian Law and International Human Rights Law, War Crimes and Crimes Against Humanity Committed in Ukraine since 24 February 2022, OSCE, ODIHR.GAL/26/22/Rev.1, 13 April 2022, i, 29–31.

Furthermore, in March 2023, the UN Independent International Commission of Inquiry on Ukraine released a final report that found Russian forces in Ukraine conducted 'indiscriminate and disproportionate attacks' against civilians,[112] affirming inter alia that

> in some of the situations examined, the Commission could not identify a military objective. When objects of military value that might have been the intended targets of the attacks were present in the vicinity of some of the impact sites, the Commission has generally found that Russian armed forces used weapons that struck both military and civilian objects without distinction.[113]

In sum, grave patterns of indiscriminate and disproportionate attacks were found concordantly by several competent bodies, concurring to bring about the charges by the Office of the Prosecutor of the ICC.

ICC judges are likely to dwell precisely on the issues discussed in this research, since trials should ensue for the war crime of directly attacking civilian objects (under Article 8(2)(b)(ii) Rome Statute), and the crime of disproportionate attacks (under Article 8(2)(b)(iv) Rome Statute), both charged in the arrest warrants issued against Kobylash and Sokolov, and in those issued against Shoigu and Gerasimov.

In both the warrants, the ICC informed that:

> Pre-Trial Chamber II considered that there are reasonable grounds to believe that the two suspects bear responsibility for missile strikes carried out by the forces under their command against the Ukrainian electric infrastructure from at least 10 October 2022 until at least 9 March 2023. During this time-frame, there was an alleged campaign of strikes against numerous electric power plants and sub-stations, which were carried out by the Russian armed forces in multiple locations in Ukraine.
>
> Pre-Trial Chamber II found that there are reasonable grounds to believe that the alleged strikes were directed against civilian objects, and for those installations that may have qualified as military objectives at the relevant time, the expected incidental civilian harm and damage would have been clearly excessive to the anticipated military advantage.[114]

In the face of these charges, many of the interpretations of the law of targeting discussed assume central relevance. Trials for direct attacks against civilian objects will probably revolve around the status determination of the relevant objects, with dangers arising from expansive interpretations of Article 52(2) AP I and the correspondent customary rule. As it has been discussed, part of laws of war scholarship has often accredited the idea that partial military uses of a civilian tower, eventually military uses of a single unit thereof, transform the entire object in a military objective. Some authors even contend that in such cases 'a military commander is

[112] Report of the Independent International Commission of Inquiry on Ukraine, A/HRC/52/62, 15 March 2003, summary.

[113] ibid, para 30.

[114] ICC (n 12) 5 March 2024; and ICC (n 12) 25 June 2024.

not obligated to consider the civilian use of a military objective in the context of a proportionality assessment'.[115] Similar views have been advanced for some time,[116] even if due to their arguments

> a fairly minor military use has turned a civilian object into a military objective (assuming that it fulfils the definition of Article 52 AP I), the damage caused to the remaining civilian part – however important it is – would have no bearing on the decision to launch an attack.[117]

An example might elucidate the implications of such views, and how they could affect assessment of attacks in Ukraine. Among various instances of violations of the law of targeting, and probable war crimes, one of the deadliest Russian attacks in the ongoing war took place on 2 March 2022, against a residential building in the Kharkiv Oblast city of Izium, killing 44 civilians.[118] Attacks against civilian object have been reported not only in Izium but also in Chernihiv, Dnipro, Kharkiv, Kramatorsk, Kremenchuk, Marinka, Mariupol, Mykolaiv and numerous other cities.[119] In an extensive analysis of the Izium attack by Human Rights Watch, it was reported that in some sections of the attacked civilian building a dozen casings fired from small arms projectiles (manufactured in both Russian and Ukrainian factories) has been found, concluding it was impossible to determine who used this ammunition, when it was used, or how it ended up in the building.[120] This finding did not impede the organsation to conclude – correctly in the opinion of this analysis – that the attack, using ammunition with a delayed-action fuze designed to detonate after piercing different segments of the building, was in any event a serious violation of IHL, indicating criminal intent of those in charge of the attacking decision, since they did not distinguish between a military objective and civilian objects, or at least launched the attack in the knowledge of the clearly excessive civilian harm that it would have caused.[121] The organisation concluded also that 'Anyone who commits serious violations of the laws of war, such as indiscriminate or disproportionate attacks, with criminal intent – that is, deliberately or recklessly – is responsible for war crimes',[122] somehow eluding the

[115] O Pomson, 'Proportionality and Civilian Use of a Military Objective' *Opinio Juris*, 24 June 2021.

[116] WH, Parks 'Asymmetries and the Identification of Legitimate Military Objectives' in WH von Heinegg and V Epping (eds), *International Humanitarian Law Facing New Challenges* (Springer, 2007) 106–07.

[117] L Gisel, *The Principle of Proportionality in the Rules Governing the Conduct of Hostilities under IHL*, International Expert Meeting 22–23 June 2016 (ICRC, 2018) 37.

[118] See Human Rights Watch, 'A Thousand Explosions in My Ears. Russian Attack Killed Dozens of Civilians in Izium Residential Building', 22 March 2023, at www.hrw.org/video-photos/interactive/2023/03/22/attack-in-izium.

[119] The list of attacks on Ukrainian civilian objects is tragically too long to be accounted for in this reflection. An updated record of the attacks denounced as unlawful and criminal by the Ukrainian Government can be found at under 'Attacking Civilians or Civilian Objects' at war.ukraine.ua/russia-war-crimes/attacking-civilians-or-civilian-objects.

[120] Human Rights Watch (n 119).

[121] ibid.

[122] Human Rights Watch, 'Ukraine: Izium Apartment Victims Need Justice Digital Reconstruction Highlights Russian Forces' Deadly Attack', 22 March 2023, at hrw.org/news/2023/03/22/ukraine-izium-apartment-victims-need-justice.

issue of the exclusion of recklessness as relevant *mens rea* for war crimes under the ICC jurisprudence. However, this does not invalidate the conclusion in relation to the attack under scrutiny.

In this as in many other possible examples, the equal applicability of IHL targeting obligations makes expansive readings of the notion of military objectives, collateral damage, as well as those capsizing the notion of incidentality of the civilian harm,[123] entirely transposable to all hostilities in residential areas in all armed conflicts. On the basis of the same visions of the laws of war criticised so far, the mere presence (hypothetical and for the sake of argument) of military items of Ukrainian defending forces in some of the residential buildings struck by Russian attacks would have rendered the attacked buildings lawful targets in their entirety.[124] Among the views supporting this interpretation of the notion of military objective, some would imply that damage to the civilian parts of those residential buildings ostensibly turned into 'military objectives', and obviously harm to civilians therein, should have been factored into precaution and proportionality assessments (thus not excluding the commission of a war crime),[125] whereas some others discussed in this research would even go as far as excluding the applicability of proportionality assessments altogether,[126] with civilian segments of the buildings and the civilians in them paradoxically (and lethally) 'subsumed' as component parts of the military objective (excluding any possible war crimes convictions).[127] It is therefore to be hoped that ICC judges will reject such interpretations.

Similar complexities are likely to affect potential trials for the war crime of disproportionate attacks against power grids. Power infrastructures that serve military purposes, such as military installations, equipment or activities, qualify under IHL as military objectives. This status is not excluded by dual-use purposes, such as the simultaneous uses for civilian functions, such as providing power to

[123] Deconstructed in ch 2, sections 2.4 and 2.5.

[124] '[T]he majority of the SG took the position that if a given floor of a building can be attacked, this does not mean that only that floor is a military objective and that the remaining parts of the building remain civilian objects. When looking at one individual object partly used for military purposes, for example a multi-story building when only the roof or one apartment is used for military purposes, today's prevailing understanding of the notion of military objective is that once an object is used in such a way as to fulfil the definition of military objective, the entire object becomes a lawful target.' (ILA Study Group on the Conduct of Hostilities in the 21st Century, 'The Conduct of Hostilities and International Humanitarian Law: Challenges of 21st Century Warfare' (2017) 93 *International Law Studies* 322, 334).

[125] 'Whether an object qualifies in whole or in part as a military objective has clear implications for the prohibition of indiscriminate attacks' (ibid, 335).

[126] See Pomson (n 115).

[127] 'This military use, even if it is secondary to the primary civilian use, satisfies the conditions of article 52(2) of AP-I, and qualifies the otherwise civilian object as a military objective. The question is whether the civilian elements of the target – either the object itself or the civilians within it – *are now all considered part of a legitimate military target*, or whether they remain in the civilian category, such that proportionality analysis should be applied.' (A Cohen and D Zlotogorski, *Proportionality in International Humanitarian Law: Consequences, Precautions, and Procedures* (Cambridge University Press, 2012) 157 (emphasis added)).

housing units. According to some authors, this remains the case even 'when the extent of civilian use far outweighs military reliance on it.[128]

Provided that the power infrastructures attacked served military purposes and qualified as military objectives, the problem becomes determining the disproportion, ie the clear excessiveness, of the incidental civilian harm foreseeable in relation to the relevant attacks. The UN Independent International Commission of Enquiry on Ukraine, in this regard, concluded that attacks after October 2022

> targeted systematically powerplants and other infrastructure critical for the transmission of electricity and the generation of heat across Ukraine. Based on these factors, the Commission has found that the attacks on energy infrastructure since 10 October 2022 were widespread and systematic and that the objective was to disrupt the energy system of the entire country, with the predictable effects on the heating system.
>
> The disruption of electric substations, power plants, and other installations which produce the energy and the heating indispensable to the survival of the population, has inflicted significant harm to civilians. Entire regions and millions of people have for periods been left without electricity or heating, particularly during winter, and consequently, with an impaired access to, notably, water, sanitation, food, healthcare, and education. …
>
> The Commission has concluded that these attacks by the Russian armed forces were disproportionate and that they constituted the war crime of excessive incidental death, injury, or damage.[129]

As the Office of Prosecutor did, the Commission also hypothesised a campaign of disproportionate attacks constituting a course of conduct involving the multiple commission of acts against a civilian population, pursuant to a state policy, and thus amounting to crimes against humanity.[130] The evaluation of the disproportionate harm to civilians therefore becomes crucial for the configurability not only of war crimes, but also of crimes against humanity.

As has been shown, however, the wording of Article 8(2)(b)(iv) Rome Statute does not facilitate such evaluation. It will need to be proved that Russian commanders launched the attacks in the knowledge of their disproportion. This will determine the necessity to assess the 'overall' concrete and direct military advantage anticipated, arguably including accumulative military advantages, not just the advantage anticipated from the single strikes, and not limited to the location and time of the relevant attacks. Relatedly, the prosecution will need to convince judges that the civilian harm foreseeable was 'clearly' excessive in comparison to the mentioned military advantage. Third, these elements will need to converge in the evaluation of the *mens rea*

[128] MN Schmitt, 'Attacking Power Infrastructure under IHL' *Articles of War* (Lieber Institute, West Point), 20 October 2022, at https://lieber.westpoint.edu/attacking-power-infrastructure-under-international-humanitarian-law.

[129] Report of the Independent International Commission of Inquiry on Ukraine, A/HRC/52/62, 15 March 2003, paras 41–43.

[130] ibid, para 43.

of the attackers. In this regard, the problematic footnote of the elements of crimes analysed in chapter two[131] will no doubt be invoked by the defence, which is likely to interpret it as requiring that the commanders formulated the value judgement on the disproportion of the attacks, subjectively, ie that they themselves considered the incidental harm foreseen for civilians as clearly excessive. The combined effect of these requirements would jeopardise accountability even if pursued by the most experienced and able prosecutor imaginable. Even in this regard, it is to be hoped that ICC judges will reject the interpretations centralising the subjective determination of the suspects, and rather valorise the knowledge element of the crime as knowledge of the objective extent of the civilian harm, which will be for judges to assess as clearly excessive, or not, in line with *lex lata* criteria, and existing jurisprudential parameters, such as that of the reasonably well-informed commander.

The loopholes and unreasonable prosecutorial burdens Western states and big military powers planted in the compromise formulas of the Rome Statute war crimes provisions, in other words, might now be working in favour of their rival powers' impunity, other than to the detriment of Ukrainian victims' right to justice. This represents a paradigmatic example of how weakening accountability for some powers is not only unethical but ultimately unfeasible, as it quickly results in diminished accountability for all powers, including those that the proponents of these barriers to accountability would want to cast out.

From the legal point of view, these loopholes and barriers to accountability will need to be tackled by the judges. In turn, however, this challenge represents a unique opportunity to provide interpretative solutions to structural defects of the Statute, which have for three decades contributed to obstruct the pursuit of accountability for conduct of hostilities war crimes and egregious violations of the law of targeting causing mass civilian victimization.

4.3.3. Gaza 2023–24: A Genocide by Means of Indiscriminate and Disproportionate Attacks?

Genocides, premised on the denial of the right of a people to exist as such, and the subsequent attempt or success in destroying the relevant group, entail various modes of elimination. As recently indicated by this and other authors,[132] when the Polish-Jewish jurist Raphael Lemkin coined the concept of genocide, after the Holocaust, he specifically observed that genocide is 'a composite of different acts of persecution or destruction',[133] ranging from physical elimination to the

[131] See section 2.4. The footnote states 'this knowledge element requires that the perpetrator makes the value judgement as described therein. An evaluation of that value judgement must be based on the requisite information available to the perpetrator at the time' (see ICC (n 41)).

[132] See Albanese, Daniele and Perugini (n 14).

[133] R Lemking, *Axis Rule in Occupied Europe. Laws of Occupation, Analysis of Government, Proposals of Redress* (Carnegie Endowment for International Peace, 1944) 92.

forced 'disintegration of the political and social institutions, culture, language, national feelings, religion, and the economic existence of national groups'.[134] As practices of elimination of protected groups, genocides in history have always been complex processes, not events, nor single actions.[135] Within these processes, exterminations are only one among many stages of development of the relevant processes, functionally converging toward the eliminationist purpose (*dolus specialis*) constituting the defining feature of the international crime of genocide in contemporary international law.[136] Eliminationist techniques culminating in genocide can include mass removals of populations from their lands (forcible transfer, ethnic cleansing), movement restrictions (segregation, mass incarceration), assimilation (cultural erasure), births prevention or control, and mass killing (direct or indirect, through eg murder, disease or starvation). In a climax of rights denials,[137] victim groups are dehumanised as total enemies, hold collectively 'guilty' of their undesirable, 'dangerous' existence, without any 'innocent' members, until international crimes against the group become accepted policies.

The definition of genocide in international law is narrower than genocide processes, usually composed by different international crimes,[138] and includes only the conduct codified in Article II of the 1948 Genocide Convention, and Article 6 of the Rome Statute; that is 'killing members of the group; causing serious bodily or mental harm to members of the group; deliberately inflicting on the group conditions of life calculated to bring about its physical destruction in whole or in part; imposing measures intended to prevent births within the group; forcibly transferring children of the group to another group',[139] if committed with the 'intent to destroy, in whole or in part'; a 'national, ethnic, racial, or religious' group.[140]

It is undisputed that both the Genocide Convention prohibitions and the crime of genocide codified in the ICC Rome Statute apply both in peacetime, and even more crucially in times of armed conflict. As a general and abstract legal issue, therefore, it is entirely legitimate to ask whether indiscriminate and disproportionate attacks can become means of execution of genocides.

[134] ibid, 79.

[135] See GH Stanton, 'The Ten Stages of Genocide' *Genocide Watch*, 2023 update, at www.genocidewatch.com/tenstages; R Segal, *Genocide in the Carpathians: War, Social Breakdown, and Mass Violence, 1914–1945* (Stanford University Press, 2016); M Shaw, *What is Genocide?*, 2nd edn (Wiley, 2015); M Shaw, *War and Genocide. Organised Killing in Modern Society* (Polity Press, 2003).

[136] On the legal definition and boundaries of the crime of genocide, see W Schabas, *Genocide in International Law. The Crime of Crimes*, 2nd edn (Cambridge University Press, 2009).

[137] M O'Brien, *From Discrimination to Death. Genocide Process Through Human Rights Lens* (Routledge, 2023).

[138] See eg G Mattraux, 'Genocide and Crimes Against Humanity' in G Mattraux, *International Crimes and the Ad Hoc Tribunals* (Oxford University Press, 2006) 329–40.

[139] Art II, Convention on the Prevention and Punishment of the Crime of Genocide, UNTS, vol 78, 277, approved 9 December 1948, entered into force 12 January 1951; and Art 6 ICC Rome Statute.

[140] ibid.

The question, more precisely, is whether it is possible, legally, to commit a genocide by means of indiscriminate and disproportionate attacks. Such unlawful attacks per se (as argued so far) amount to war crimes, but one could ask: how many of such war crimes against a civilian population does it take to make a genocide? And how many of such war crimes consistently committed in regular patterns allow (or even impose) us to infer genocidal intent by perpetrators (even in absence of an explicit, stated genocidal intent)?

What if the relevant war crimes are committed in the hundreds, or in the thousands, while their commission is sanctioned by state policies? What if relevant state policies exclude the premise that such crimes can be committed against the civilian populations of the territories they occupy or annex militarily? It would be paradoxical to consider the crime of genocide as relevant only when patterns of war crimes, eventually committed systematically for years against the same civilian population, have successfully extinguished the collective life of the protected group. This would obviously neutralise the preventive obligations imposed by the 1948 Convention. It is therefore crucial to scrutinise military policies of parties to conflicts with an open mind about the possibility that precisely in these policies (when they blur and cross the most fundamental red lines imposed by the law of war) judges could identify building blocks of genocidal intent.

An imaginary example could be that of a state claiming that, under the law of war, it is perfectly proportionate and lawful to (knowingly) kill 1,000 civilians 'collaterally' in attacks aimed at eliminating a senior commanders of the enemy armed forces. Should the relevant enemy force have hundreds of senior commanders, then the state would be prepared and determined to kill hundreds of thousands of civilians, constituting part of a relatively small national group. Would the relevant state thus have the requisite intent to physically destroy a substantial part of the group, even if this destruction is not the sole and ultimate purpose the perpetrators? Would this legal determination change if the state position contended that not a thousand, but hundreds of civilians and children can be killed proportionately and lawfully in each attack, for years?

Such a scenario is not too far from the reality of Gaza. Mass civilian victimisation in Gaza unfolded at unprecedented levels and at a unique rate in 2023–24. At least 12,000 Palestinian children and 6,500 adults were killed in less than 12 months of conflict, to which all the civilians among the remaining 14,000 adult men must be added.[141] According to Oxfam, Israel's military campaign has killed Palestinians at an average rate which exceeds the daily death toll of any other conflict of the twenty-first century.[142] According to Save the Children, the number of children killed in just the

[141] See OCHA, 'Reported impact snapshot | Gaza Strip', 18 September 2024, at www.ochaopt.org/content/reported-impact-snapshot-gaza-strip-18-september-2024.

[142] 'Daily death rate in Gaza higher than any other major 21st Century conflict', Oxfam, 11 January 2024, at www.oxfam.org/en/press-releases/daily-death-rate-gaza-higher-any-other-major-21st-century-conflict-oxfam.

first three weeks of Israeli bombardments in Gaza surpassed the number of those killed in armed conflict globally – across more than 20 countries – over the course of the last three years.[143] The same organisation has denounced the killing of 100 children every day for the first 100 days of the war,[144] and 10 per day have lost one of or both their legs.[145] In addition, thousands among the 41,000 victims remained unidentified or unidentifiable, 10,000 more have been reported missing under the rubble of entire cities, more than 95,000 have been maimed and injured, and almost the entirety of the population has been forcibly displaced.[146]

While this mass civilian victimisation unfolded, the misuse of IHL to justify this mass killing and injuring of civilians, as well as destruction of cities and forced displacement, has been stretched to unparalleled extents. However, it is not in itself a new phenomenon.

Regularly in the last 20 years, the victimisation of Palestinian civilians has been accompanied by the production of justificatory legal discourses eroding their civilian protections. These discourses systematically presented the killing of Palestinian civilians as negligible, collateral and 'proportionate', accurately limited, carefully authorised by a highly professional army, extremely well trained on its legal responsibilities, and allegedly restraining itself to spare civilians above and beyond the limits imposed by the law.

In 2015, leading authors dedicating specific analyses to Israeli targeting practices, and overall praised their compliance with IHL, indicating that in 2014 the Israel Defense Forces (IDF) estimated 'that around half of those killed were fighters who would not be factored into the collateral damage assessments performed for individual attacks', and that 'with respect to identifying a target, Israeli ISR [intelligence, surveillance, reconnaissance] capabilities are impressive, and undeniably enhance the accuracy of likely military advantage and collateral damage estimations'.[147] However, according to the United Nations Office for the Coordination of Humanitarian Affairs (OCHA) – cautious in comparison to the

[143] 'Gaza: 3,195 children killed in three weeks surpasses annual number of children killed in conflict zones since 2019', Save the Children, Press Release, 29 October 2023, at www.savethechildren.net/news/gaza-3195-children-killed-three-weeks-surpasses-annual-number-children-killed-conflict-zones.

[144] 'Gaza: 10,000 children killed in nearly 100 days of war', Save the Children, 11 January 2024, at www.savethechildren.net/news/gaza-10000-children-killed-nearly-100-days-war.

[145] 'Gaza: more than 10 children a day lose a limb in three months of brutal conflict', Save the Children, 7 January 2024, at www.savethechildren.net/news/gaza-more-10-children-day-lose-limb-three-months-brutal-conflict.

[146] Israel-Gaza war in maps and charts: Live tracker', *Al Jazeera*, at www.aljazeera.com/news/longform/2023/10/9/israel-hamas-war-in-maps-and-charts-live-tracker (these latter data have been object of contestations but see BQ Huynh, ET Chin and PB Spiegel, 'No evidence of inflated mortality reporting from the Gaza Ministry of Health' (2024) 403 *The Lancet* 23, at www.thelancet.com/journals/lancet/article/PIIS0140-6736(23)02713-7/fulltext.

[147] MN Schmitt and J Merriam, 'The Tyranny of Context: Israeli Targeting Practices in Legal Perspective' (2015) 37 *University of Pennsylvania Journal of International Law* 53, 126.

estimates of non-governmental organisations[148] – at least 1,462 victims turned out to be civilians, including 550 children and minors, and 330 women, while 11,231 Palestinians were injured (including 3,540 women and 3,436 children, with more than 1,000 of the latter suffering permanent disabilities as a result).[149] In other words, the overwhelming majority of the Palestinian victims of operation Protective Edge (65 per cent) were civilians.[150] The 'accuracy-enhancing' role of the IDF capabilities on proportionality assessments, therefore, revealed an either far from undeniable, or conversely, and somehow more concerningly, index of highly problematic conceptions of the entity of civilian killing and injuring that can be considered 'collateral' under IHL.

The ICRC itself singled out the tendency to compress IHL protections and expand beyond the law what it permits in its 2024 Report on the challenges to IHL. In it, the Committee affirmed:

> Over several decades now, expedient interpretations of IHL – often proposed at the height of armed conflict in order to preserve states' leeway to kill and detain – have compounded to undermine its protective force. In one conflict after another, some states have sought an increasingly expansive vision of what is permissible, and a contracted notion of what is considered prohibited. When faced with pressure to better protect civilians and detainees, these states have tended to argue that IHL allowed them greater latitude than what was being demanded of them. When responding to appreciation for their more protective policies, these states have tended to suggest that their actions were simply voluntary good practices – implying that meeting IHL's standards required much less of them.[151]

In the latest rounds of the ongoing conflict, however, this tendency exceeded the limits of reasonability, and narratives on the law of war developed far more concerning tendencies. Concepts borrowed from this legal framework have been appropriated, distorted and definitively re-functionalised to justify an indiscriminate conduct of hostilities, reaching apexes whereby IHL-mimicking categories morphed into code words for annihilatory means and methods of warfare.

[148] Estimates from NGOs are cited, inter alia, in Institute for Middle East Understanding (IMEU), '50 Days of Death & Destruction: Israel's "Operation Protective Edge"', at imeu.org/article/50-days-of-death-destruction-israels-operation-protective-edge.

[149] UN Office for the Coordination of Humanitarian Affairs (OCHA), 'Key figures on the 2014 hostilities', 23 June 2015, at www.ochaopt.org/content/key-figures-2014-hostilities#_ftnref1, as featured in UN Human Rights Council (HRC), *Report of the Independent Commission of Inquiry on the 2014 Gaza Conflict* (A/HRC/29/52), at www.ohchr.org/en/hrbodies/hrc/coigazaconflict/pages/reportcoigaza.aspx.

[150] See, for the international legal implications, S Weill and V Azarova, 'The 2014 Gaza War: Reflections on Jus Ad Bellum, Jus in Bello, and Accountability' in A Bellal (ed), *The War Report: Armed Conflict in 2014* (Oxford University Press, 2015) 360 ff; and L Trigeaud, 'L'operation Bordure Protectrice Menée par Israël Dans la Bande de Gaza (8 Juillet – 26 Août 2014)' (2014) *Annuaire Français de Droit International* 171 ff.

[151] ICRC, *International Humanitarian Law and the Challenges of Contemporary Armed Conflicts. Building a culture of compliance for IHL to protect humanity in today's and future conflicts*, Report, September 2024, 6 and 73, at rcrcconference.org/app/uploads/2024/09/34IC_10.6-IHL-Challenges-Report-EN.pdf.

4.3.3.1. Pre-Justifying Indiscriminate and Disproportionate Attacks: Entire Populations of 'Human Shields'

This is the case, among others, of the *ius in bello* prohibition against the use of the 'presence or movements of the civilian population or individual civilians … to render certain points or areas immune from military operations, in particular in attempts to shield *military objectives* from attacks or to shield, favour or impede military operations',[152] that is the prohibition against the use of human shields. 'Utilizing the presence of a civilian or other protected person to render certain points, areas or military forces immune from military operations'[153] is also punished as a war crime by the Rome Statute of the ICC. The commission of the relevant crime and the violation of the relevant prohibitions occur when the conduct is the result of a deliberate tactical choice of the relevant forces, or perpetrator, and not merely arising from the contextual constraints of the battlefield, such as hostilities in (besieged) urban areas.[154] This is confirmed by the elements of the relevant crime, requiring that 'The perpetrator moved or otherwise took advantage of the location of one or more civilians or other persons protected', and that 'The perpetrator intended to shield a military objective from attack or shield, favour or impede military operations'.[155] Concluding that violations of the prohibition of shielding have occurred, therefore, requires circumstantial, attack-specific assessments, since the relevant provisions explicitly refers to using civilian presence or movement to 'render *certain* points or areas' immune from attacks.[156] The same applies to the reference about shielding 'military objectives, which presupposes as a minimum that the relevant objects 'shielded' need to be lawful targets under IHL. Legal evaluations, therefore, should be cognisant of the circumstances imposed by context (for example, of hostilities in extremely densely populated areas, particularly when under total siege), as opposed to deliberate tactical choices (which are more likely, yet not to be assumed, in urban warfare).

[152] See 'Rule 97', ICRC Customary IHL Database, at ihl-databases.icrc.org/en/customary-ihl/v1/rule97; Art 23(1) Convention (III) relative to the Treatment of Prisoners of War, Geneva, adopted 12 August 1949, entered into force 21 October 1950, 75 UNTS 135; Art 28 Convention (IV) relative to the Protection of Civilian Persons in Time of War, adopted 12 August 1949, entered into force 21 October 1950, 75 UNTS 135; Arts 12 and 51(7), Protocol Additional to the Geneva Conventions of 12 August 1949 and relating to the Protection of Victims of International Armed Conflicts (Protocol I), adopted 8 June 1977, entered into force 7 December 1978, 1125 UNTS 3.

[153] Art 8(2)(b)(xxiii) Rome Statute.

[154] See SB De belle, 'Chained to Cannons or Wearing Targets on Their T-shirts: Human Shields in International Humanitarian Law' (2008) 90 *International Review of the Red Cross* 883; and R Geiß and JG Devaney, 'Zealots, Victims and Captives: Maintaining Adequate Protection of Human Shields in Contemporary International Humanitarian Law' (2017) 47 *Israel Yearbook on Human Rights* 11.

[155] ICC (n 41) Art 8(2)(b)(xxiii).

[156] 'The presence or movements of the civilian population or individual civilians shall not be used to render certain points or areas immune from military operations, in particular in attempts to shield military objectives from attacks or to shield, favour or impede military operations. The Parties to the conflict shall not direct the movement of the civilian population or individual civilians in order to attempt to shield military objectives from attacks or to shield military operations.'

The implications and dangers of human shields narratives to justify indiscriminate and disproportionate attacks have recently become more evident after the narrative has been redundantly wielded by Russian Federation officials to blame Ukrainian armed forces for the death of civilians killed by Russian unlawful attacks.[157] Systematically around deadly attacks with tragic civilian victims' tolls, Russian officials claimed that 'Ukrainian troops continue to station in public premises, including schools, just as they use civilians as human shields',[158] and repeated during the whole invasion that the Ukrainian army 'continues to use terrorist methods' and 'civilians as human shields'.[159] These claims around the use of human shields have revealed to interpreters how, in many conflicts, the prohibition against the use of human shields can be easily distorted into a blame-shifting narrative for breaches of IHL, displacing the prohibition of indiscriminate and disproportionate attacks. As convincingly suggested by Schmitt, the redundant mobilisation of human shields claims by Russian officials, particularly in response to evidences of indiscriminate and disproportionate conduct of hostilities,[160] has shown an 'aggressive disinformation (lawfare) campaign designed to shift blame for civilian casualties to Ukraine, a campaign to which human shielding might nefariously contribute'.[161]

This nefarious contribution to blame-shifting narratives for serious violations, however, has hardly raised similar concerns for civilian casualties in Gaza. Despite acknowledging the unique civilian population density of the latter theatre (rendering it 'an almost entirely urban battlefield'), in fact, the same author argued that in 'every round of hostilities' since the Israeli disengagement, 'Hamas has fought almost exclusively from among the civilian population', employing 'both voluntary and involuntary … human shields'.[162] The problem with these generalising assertions, particularly in one of the most densely populated areas

[157] See, inter alia, 'Russian Army Says Ukraine Civilians Being Used As "Human Shields" Can "Freely Leave" Kyiv', AFP News Agency, 28 February 2022, at www.barrons.com/news: 'Kiev regime continues to use terrorist methods. … They use civilians as human shields, not hesitating to shoot refugees.'

[158] Russian Embassy UK, 4 May 2022, at twitter.com/RussianEmbassy/status/1521914358896467968.

[159] Russian Embassy UK, 29 April 2023, at twitter.com/RussianEmbassy/status/1652407466171289609.

[160] OSCE, *Report on Violations of International Humanitarian and Human Rights Law, War Crimes and Crimes Against Humanity Committed in Ukraine Since 24 February 2022*, ODIHR.GAL/26/22/Rev.1, 13 April 2022, 46–48.

[161] See MN Schmitt, 'Weaponizing Civilians: Human Shields in Ukraine' *Articles of* (Lieber Institute, West Point), 11 April 2022, at lieber.westpoint.edu/weaponizing-civilians-human-shields-ukraine.

[162] See Schmitt and Merriam (n 148) 69. While indiscriminate attacks by armed groups in Gaza are self-evident, and episodes of uses of human shields under the meaning of the relevant international legal prohibition are documented, the generalising assertion cited seems not to consider at least three issues: 1) decades of unsubstantiated, regular human shields claims becoming the refrain of the IDF narratives over the civilian loss of life and damage to civilian objects produced by its military operations in the Strip (see eg O Ezra, 'Israel's Human Shields Defense: Shielding Israeli War Crimes' (2015) 30 *Tikkun* 32; 2) the Israeli army's domestic litigation to mitigate the prohibition against the use of human shields, and violations thereof (see eg B'Tselem, 'Human Shields: Use of Palestinian Civilians as Human Shields in Violation of High Court Justice Order', November 2002, at www.btselem.org); and, most of all, 3) the military ethics doctrines openly exhorting the IDF to dismiss proportionality obligations under IHL when factoring in the killing of involuntary shields, including those qualified as such for mere proximity (see section 4.3.3.1).

in the world, and under land and sea blockade, is that the prohibition against the use of human shields under IHL is circumstantial, requires evaluations of collocation,[163] specific tactical options, and should not serve the purpose of delineating identikit armed groups in general, and in premise, but rather be interpreted as placing on those who claim the prohibition has been breached the burden to provide circumstantial evidence and persuasive analyses indicating when and how the prohibition has been breached, in context. This exact standard, posing the burdens of 'persuasion and proof'[164] on those levelling the charges, has been at the core of the vehement criticisms[165] against much less radical claims on failures to take passive precautions by Amnesty International, linked to allegations of conduct by Ukrainian military forces endangering civilians.[166]

In this context, unlike in Gaza, it has been observed that, under *ius in bello*, 'there is no absolute prohibition on being in the vicinity of civilians and civilian objects or any absolute duty to remove them', and that 'To suggest otherwise would be operationally insensible', as 'It would effectively make defending the areas concerned impossible, either because military forces sometimes need to be in the area to operate or because removing nearby civilians sometimes would be impractical or even practically impossible'.[167] Similarly, it has been underlined how worrisome was the 'assertion that Ukrainian forces have launched strikes from populated civilian areas', considering in particular the enemy's 'operational advantages such as air superiority and the range of fires', leading to the conclusion that 'If Ukrainian forces had launched those strikes from non-urban areas, it would sometimes have enhanced Russia's ability to locate and destroy them.'[168] In sum, the same analysis emphasised the need of specific, circumstantiated evaluations of feasibility before alleging civilians have been endangered by Ukrainian armed forces, contesting that the criticised report did not 'indicate *why* the soldiers were there or what alternative locations might have been available to them'. In this estimation, 'Amnesty International … acted irresponsibly by making the claim without providing supporting evidence.'[169]

[163] As duly noted, 'Whether a particular situation amounts to permitted or prohibited collocation is important not only with regard to the prior determination of whether a particular military objective may legally be placed in a certain location, but is also critical in determining the legal liability of the party conducting the attack' (see Geiß and Devaney (n 155).

[164] See MN Schmitt, 'Amnesty International's Allegations of Ukrainian IHL Violations', *Articles of War* (Lieber Institute, West Point), 8 August 2022, at lieber.westpoint.edu/amnesty-allegations-ukrainian-ihl-violations.

[165] See Amnesty International, 'Report of the legal review panel on the Amnesty International press release concerning Ukrainian fighting tactics of 4 August 2022', 8 April 2023, at www.amnesty.org/en/documents/org60/6731/2023/en.

[166] Amnesty International, 'Ukraine: Ukrainian fighting tactics endanger civilians', Press Release, 4 August 2022, at www.amnesty.org/en/latest/news/2022/08/ukraine-ukrainian-fighting-tactics-endanger-civilians.

[167] Schmitt (n 165).

[168] ibid.

[169] ibid.

The same need for supporting evidence, however, seems to have been considered to large extents superfluous when human shields narratives were mobilised in Gaza, where attacking forces' general assertions on the use of the population as human shields have often been assumed as premise of legal analyses. From the point of view of this chapter, on the contrary, scholarly legal scrutiny should be at least as strict, if not more so, when evaluating the assertions of the armed forces actually bombarding (and thus potentially motivated to devise blame-shifting narratives for civilian killing), in comparison to those by NGOs and human rights groups, for the simple reason that the latter actors do not actually kill anyone even when their legal assessments are wrong.

On the contrary, military analysts often demand stricter legal rigour and more scrupulous scrutiny from rights groups than from armies themselves. The authors of a dated but elucidative NATO report, for example, contended that proportionate and collateral civilian harm in Palestine is unduly criticised by international institutions ('any collateral damage caused by the IDF usually yields harsh criticism from the UN and its institutes'), and affirmed that, after the Goldstone report,[170] the former UN Secretary General's calls for accountability of *all parties*' violations of international law, including war crimes, demonstrated 'Hamas' triumph in controlling the [UN and international community] narrative'.[171] The authors suggested that allied military powers refine their human shields narratives, with a subtext revealing degrees of bitterness about the tendency of public opinion 'to be influenced more by images depicting the suffering of innocent civilians than by well-thought-out legal arguments'.[172] Well-thought-out legal arguments, the sentence omits, about the killing of unarmed civilians by an army reported to consider so-called 'voluntary shields' (which would include civilians not leaving their houses after advance warnings)[173] as direct participants in the hostilities,[174] whose killing would thus need not be factored into proportionality or precautions-in-attack assessments.

[170] See *Human Rights in Palestine and Other Occupied Arab Territories: Report of the United Nations Fact-Finding Mission on the Gaza Conflict*, A/HRC/12/48, 25 September 2009.

[171] See J Pamment et al, 'Hybrid Threats: Hamas' use of human shields in Gaza' in S Aday et al, *Hybrid Threats. A Strategic Communications Perspective*, NATO Strategic Communications Centre of Excellence, Riga, 2019, at stratcomcoe.org/publications/hybrid-threats-a-strategic-communications-perspective/79, 60–61.

[172] 'Even if a targeted strike may be justifiable from a legal perspective, first impressions frame the narrative. Public opinion tends to be influenced more by images depicting the suffering of innocent civilians than by well-thought-out legal arguments. National governments should be able to publicly justify their position and reveal their adversary's use of civilians in combat. This can only be accomplished by thoroughly documenting incidents, *preparing supportive messages*, and working across multiple channels to *convey those narratives*' (ibid; see 'Hybrid Threats: Hamas' use of human shields in Gaza – Executive Summary', NATO Strategic Communications Centre of Excellence, 6 June 2019, annex, at stratcomcoe.org/publications/hybrid-threats-hamas-use-of-human-shields-in-gaza/87 (emphasis added)).

[173] See *Report of the Detailed Findings of the Commission of Inquiry on the 2014 Gaza Conflict*, A/HRC/29/CRP.4, 24 June 2015, para 400.

[174] See HCJ 769/02 The Public Committee Against Torture in Israel v. The Government of Israel 2006 (2) Isr L Rep 459 [December 14, 2006], para 36 ff.

The Israeli Supreme Court itself supported this view. It affirmed:

> What is the law regarding civilians serving as a 'human shield' for terrorists taking a direct part in the hostilities? Certainly, if they are doing so because they were forced to do so by terrorists, those innocent civilians are not to be seen as taking a direct part in the hostilities. They themselves are victims of terrorism. However, if they do so of their own free will, out of support for the terrorist organization, they should be seen as persons taking a direct part in the hostilities.[175]

It is difficult to see how before a bombardment an air force could precisely determine whether a family or group of families is not leaving a building or an area out of 'support' for an armed group, and how it could discern those cases from those in which the relevant civilians simply do not want to or cannot leave their locations (for example due to injured or sick family members unable to move from their houses).

Affirming that 'voluntary human shields' are direct participants in hostilities, in other words, is an assertion capable of legalising the killing of countless unarmed civilians, transformed into targets on the mere basis of their location. While practices by both parties to this conflict infringing the prohibition against the use human shields have been documented,[176] the violation of the prohibition, by any parties to any conflict, does not release aerial attackers from their targeting obligations, since even civilians effectively used as human shields (in the legal sense) do not cease to be civilians or become legitimate targets, and should they even voluntarily refuse to leave their homes after advance warnings, such an act does not amount to direct participation in hostilities.[177]

After the attack and the international crimes of 7 October 2023 against Israeli civilians, human shields claims became a mantra[178] of Israeli and Western politics, repeated around each of the deadliest attacks for Palestinian civilians. In November 2023, Israel's Ministry of Foreign Affairs published a position paper referring indistinctly to '*the* civilian population' and '*the* residents of Gaza Strip' as 'human shields',[179] leaving little doubt that the Israeli military policy assumed as a generalised premise what must be, instead, verified circumstantially in each attacking procedure, before levelling the accusation of human shielding. The Ministry, within this framing, also affirmed that 'civilians taking a direct

[175] *The Public Committee against Torture in Israel et al v The Government of Israel et al*, Supreme Court of Israel, 14 December 2006, para 36, with reference to MN Schmitt, 'Direct Participation in Hostilities and 21st Century Armed Conflict' in H Fischer (ed), *Crisis Management and Humanitarian Protection: Festshrift Fur Dieter Fleck* (BWV, 2004) 521.

[176] See eg *Report of the Detailed Findings of the Commission of Inquiry on the 2014 Gaza Conflict*, A/HRC/29/CRP.4, 24 June 2015, paras 320–323 and 483.

[177] See extensively on these points De belle (n 155).

[178] See N Gordon and N Perugini, *Human Shields. A History of People in the Line of Fire* (University of California Press, 2020) and N Gordon and N Perugini, 'The Politics of Human Shielding: On the Resignification of Space and the Constitution of Civilians as Shields in Liberal Wars' (2016) 34 *Environment and Planning D:Society and Space* 170.

[179] Ministry of Foreign Affairs, 'Hamas-Israel Conflict 2023: Key Legal Aspects' (Israeli Government, 2023), 7, 9 ff, at www.gov.il/en/pages/hamas-israel-conflict2023-key-legal-aspects.

part in the hostilities' are 'legitimate targets'.[180] While this is true in abstract legal terms, in context this assertion must be weighed by considering that the Israeli Supreme Court frames so-called 'voluntary' human shields as direct participants in the hostilities. As a consequence of using the frail construct of 'voluntary' shielding, and thereby implicating the whole of the Gaza population as actual or potential human shields, the Government position suggests that all civilians in the vicinity of lawful targets can be easily designated as direct participants in the hostilities, and thus transformed into legitimate targets of proximity, in irreconcilable contrast with the prohibition of indiscriminate attacks. In fact, the Government position insists that the embedding of Hamas in civilian areas is of such an extent that it 'cannot be concluded from the mere fact that *seeming* "civilians" or "civilian objects" have been targeted, that an attack was unlawful.'[181] Substantially, the protections of civilians, as well as the legal presumption of civilian status in cases of doubt, are de facto revoked on a large scale, proposing that unarmed protected persons can be either hostiles in disguise, or putting their lives in the line of fire out of 'support' for 'terrorists' and thus becoming voluntarily 'lawful' targets. In sum, the notion of human shields has been stretched to the point of characterising the entirety of the Gaza population, arguably functioning as preventive justification for every possible indiscriminate or disproportionate attacks, or even for the exclusion of their configurability altogether, in premise.

4.3.3.2. Indiscriminate and Disproportionate Attacks Nipped in the Bud: 'Every School, Every Mosque, Every Second House' as a 'Military Objective'

The mentioned Government views were also accompanied by public narratives, in Israel and abroad, going as far as contending that every civilian object and infrastructure in Gaza was a military objective. For example, in an interview with LBC the Israeli Ambassador to the United Kingdom declared that in Gaza 'every school, every mosque, every second house has access to a tunnel'. When LBC's Iain Dale contested that this was an argument functional to destroying 'every single building' in Gaza, the Ambassador responded: 'Do you have another solution?'[182]

This uncommonly honest exchange illuminates how for the Israeli political and military leadership every protected civilian object in Gaza is seen as a potential target. This view was reflected in official legal positions of the Israeli

[180] ibid.

[181] ibid (emphasis added).

[182] '"Do you have another solution?" Israeli Ambassador defends destruction of Gaza', LBC, 4 January 2024, at www.youtube.com/watch?v=cQtqvSYjMIc; and S Brown, 'LBC: Israeli ambassador to UK says every Gaza building is a target', *The National*, 4 January 2024, at www.thenational.scot/news/24026946.lbc-israeli-ambassador-uk-says-every-gaza-building-target.

Government and military. In a document entitled 'Hamas-Israel Conflict 2023: Key Legal Aspects', the Israeli MFA affirmed that 'Hamas systematically and unlawfully embeds its military assets within heavily populated areas, and carries out its military activities *amongst, behind, and under* its own civilians.'[183] Gaza and its civilian population are presented as pervasive obstructions living and existing amongst, in front of and above Israeli targets. Through this prism, the protection accorded by IHL to civilian objects, and the presumption of their protection in case of doubts, is capsized in a presumption of 'militarisation', representing the whole living space of the protected Palestinian group as a *continuum* of military objectives. As Israel's MFA further articulated, 'many ostensibly civilian objects may become legitimate targets'.[184] This potential to become a target, construed in premise and in general, disregarding any circumstantial determination or evidence, can be activated to systematically deny, ex post, that civilian objects were shelled. Given such premises, the prohibition of indiscriminate and disproportionate attacks, in the mind of attackers, becomes impossible to breach, because 'military objective' is everything.

As has been shown, the determination of what is a military objective under IHL is not categorical but rather circumstantial, based on the specific circumstances ruling in the place and time of each specific attack. Customary law clarifies that attacks should be '*strictly* limited' to objects which 'by their nature, location, purpose or use make an effective contribution to military action', and whose 'total or partial destruction, capture or neutralization', in the circumstances ruling at the time, offer 'a definite military advantage'.[185] Attackers' suspicions about speculative military uses, however, do not meet the tests for this status determination. IHL unequivocally dictates that 'in case of doubt whether an object which is normally dedicated to civilian purposes, such as a place of worship, a house or other dwelling or a school, is being used to make an effective contribution to military action, it shall be presumed not to be so used'.[186] In the war on Gaza, the Israeli executive completely overturned this presumption, generating a mechanism of *à la carte* militarisation of civilian objects. Discourses on this conflict went as far as proposing that any object that had allegedly been (in the past, retrospectively) or might have been (speculatively, in future) used militarily, was lawfully destroyable.[187]

[183] State of Israel Ministry of Foreign Affairs, 'Hamas-Israel Conflict 2023: Key Legal Aspects', 2 November 2023, 9, at www.gov.il/en/pages/hamas-israel-conflict2023-key-legal-aspects (emphases added).

[184] Henckaerts and Doswald-Beck (n 46) *Vol I*, 29–36.

[185] ibid.

[186] Art 52(3) Protocol Additional to the Geneva Conventions of 12 August 1949 and relating to the Protection of Victims of International Armed Conflicts (Protocol I), adopted 8 June 1977, entered into force 7 December 1978, 1125 UNTS 3.

[187] This is evidenced by the numerous official statements reclaiming the success of demolishing 'terrorist residences'; see Israel Defence Forces, *Central Command – Press Release Regarding Israel-Hamas War*, 6 April 2024; 'Demolition of Terrorists' Residencies' at www.idf.il/en/mini-sites/idf-press-releases-regarding-the-hamas-israel-war/april-24-press-releases/war-against-hamas-6-months-operational-update/the-central-command; and by the idea itself of total destruction of every building in the so-called 'buffer zone'; see '"Buffer zone" possible war crime: UN human rights chief', UN News, 8 February 2024, at news.un.org/en/story/2024/02/1146352.

By this logic, obviously no civilian object in any armed conflict fought in besieged urban areas can ever resist its transformation into an ostensibly legitimate target. Ultimately, this appears precisely the outcome of the mass characterisation of every object, in its entirety, from churches,[188] mosques,[189] schools and[190] UN facilities[191] to universities,[192] ambulances and hospitals[193] as military objectives, nurturing the perception of a relationship of military continuity and pervasive complicity,[194] removing the intransgressible red lines drawn by IHL around protected persons and objects, and displacing the applicability of war crimes law. This rationale resulted in the policy of destruction of Gaza's inhabited areas, whereby innumerable controlled demolitions and extensive destruction of civilian objects were carried out,[195] even after the control of the structures was acquired by the Israeli army, removing any plausible justification based on military necessity or advantages. As a consequence, houses, schools, university buildings, courts, municipal offices, parliamentary assembly buildings and entire civilian neighbourhoods were razed to the ground.[196] This followed aerial bombardments of entire multi-storey buildings,[197] with patterns of attacks levelling them while still full of civilians, and without advance warnings, knowingly killing hundreds of them in single strikes.[198] In just the first three weeks of the offensive in 2023, entire residential areas in cities across the Northern parts of the besieged enclave have been erased (as shown internationally by satellite imagery of Beith Hanoun, Beit Lahiya,

[188] See eg 'Israel bombs Greek Orthodox Gaza church sheltering displaced people', Al Jazeera, 20 October 2023, at www.aljazeera.com/news/2023/10/20/war-crime-israel-bombs-gaza-church-sheltering-displaced-people.

[189] Inter alia, Israel Defense Forces, 'Holy places, such as mosques, should not be used as fronts for terrorism' (X, 2023) at x.com/IDF/status/1727059761466650632.

[190] See eg Israel Defense Forces, 'RPGs, mortar shells, and other weapons were found by IDF troops a kindergarten and an elementary school in northern Gaza', X, 2023, x.com/IDF/status/1725683576522334603.

[191] In the media, see eg P Falk, 'Israel says these photos show how Hamas places weapons in and near U.N. facilities in Gaza, including schools', CBS News, 2023, at www.cbsnews.com/news/israel-photos-hamas-gaza-weapons-un-facilities-including-schools.

[192] P Jack, 'Academia in Gaza "has been destroyed" by Israeli "educide"', *Times Higher Education*, 2024 www.timeshighereducation.com/news/academia-gaza-has-been-destroyed-israeli-educide.

[193] Israel Defense Forces 'Terrorists operating within hospitals can be a hard pill to swallow …', X, 2023, x.com/IDF/status/1725455901824323697?s=20.

[194] See Albanese, Daniele and Perugini (n 14).

[195] N Waters, '"We've Become Addicted to Explosions" The IDF Unit Responsible for Demolishing Homes Across Gaza', *Bellingcat*, 29 April 2024, at www.bellingcat.com/news/2024/04/29/weve-become-addicted-to-explosions-the-idf-unit-responsible-for-demolishing-homes-across-gaza.

[196] L Abraham et al, 'Israel Controlled Demolitions Are Razing Neighborhoods in Gaza, *New York Times*, 1 February 2024, at www.nytimes.com/interactive/2024/02/01/world/middleeast/Israel-gaza-war-demolish.html.

[197] G Alkurd et al, 'Why Did Israel Bomb This Residential Building in Gaza City?', *Spiegel International*, 1 July 2024, at www.spiegel.de/international/world/gaza-city-possible-war-crime-why-did-israel-bomb-this-residential-building-a-a7e9e4f9-9879-404a-bb87-4a17cef81f8c.

[198] See N Erakat et al, *Report of the Independent Task Force on the Application of National Security Memorandum-20 to Israel*, 18 April 2024 31–41, at www.justsecurity.org/wp-content/uploads/2024/04/NSM20-TF-Report-_-Final.pdf.

Al-Athatra and Al Karameh),[199] with simultaneous, severe bombardments of civilian neighbourhoods also taking place in the South (where civilian residents of the North were forcibly displaced *en masse*).[200] The flattening of cities continued unabated in the following months, sparing substantially no built-up civilian area of the Strip.[201] By the end of November, the devastation of cities in Northern Gaza already far exceeded that of Dresden at the end of WWII.[202] By mid-December, Israel had dropped 29,000 bombs, munitions and shells, destroying 70 per cent of Gaza's 439,000 homes and damaging many more.[203] By early 2024, Gaza did not exist anymore.

4.3.3.3. Rewriting IHL Proportionality to Accommodate the Destruction of Victim Groups as 'Collateral': Of 'Incidental' and 'Proportionate' Genocides

When individual strikes in Gaza began to regularly kill and injure hundreds of civilians, most of whom were children,[204] the distortive 'humanitarian camouflage'[205] misusing IHL to claim unlimited leeway to kill and destroy turned to one of the most debated customary IHL rules: the rule of proportionality in attacks.

Proportionality, as already discussed, is legally inoperative unless the distinction between civilians and combatants is fully respected, and prohibits even attacks against lawful targets if the incidental harm to civilians (including killing, injuring or damaging civilian objects) is expected to be '*excessive* in relation to the concrete and direct military advantage anticipated'.[206] Determining how much foreseeable incidental harm to civilians is 'excessive' in comparison to the

[199] 'Gaza before and after: satellite images show destruction following Israeli airstrikes' *The Guardian*, 27 October 2023, at www.theguardian.com/world/2023/oct/27/gaza-before-and-after-satellite-images-show-destruction-after-israeli-airstrikes.

[200] 'Israel orders Gazans to flee, bombs where it sends them' Reuters, 4 December 2023, at www.reuters.com/video/watch/idRW320104122023RP1.

[201] N de Hoog et al, 'How war destroyed Gaza's neighbourhoods – visual investigation' *The Guardian*, 30 January 2024, at www.theguardian.com/world/ng-interactive/2024/jan/30/how-war-destroyed-gazas-neighbourhoods-visual-investigation.

[202] JP Rathbone, 'Military Briefing. The Israeli Bombs Raining on Gaza' *Financial Times*, 5 December 2023, at www.ft.com/content/7b407c2e-8149-4d83-be01-72dcae8aee7b.

[203] J Malsin and S Shah, 'The Ruined Landscape of Gaza After Nearly Three Months of Bombing' *Wall Street Journal*, 30 December 2023, at www.wsj.com/world/middle-east/gaza-destruction-bombing-israel-aa528542.

[204] 'Earlier, the surgical director of the Indonesian hospital, Mohamed el-Ron, told the BBC it received 400 casualties, including 120 dead, and the majority were women and children': E Graham-Harrison et al, 'Cratered ground and destroyed lives: piecing together the Jabalia camp airstrike' *The Guardian*, 1 November 2023, at www.theguardian.com/world/2023/nov/01/jabalia-camp-airstrike-gaza.

[205] F Albanese, *Anatomy of a Genocide. Report of the Special Rapporteur on the situation of human rights in the Palestinian territory occupied since 1967 to Human Rights* Council, A/HRC/55/73, 24 March 2024, at documents.un.org/doc/undoc/gen/g24/046/11/pdf/g2404611.pdf.

[206] See ch 2, sections 2.1 and 2.4.

military advantage anticipated is, obviously, an issue that has kept laws of war experts debating for decades, while costing the lives of innumerable civilians in many armed conflicts.[207] The relative indeterminacy and subjectivity of this test, however, cannot be used for removing any reasonable limit to the entity of civilian harm that can be considered incidental and not excessive, depicting entire crowds of civilians and children knowingly killed in attacks as 'collateral damage'.

In Israel's version of the laws of war,[208] this is precisely what has happened. Proportionality has been altered to increasingly diminish the value of Palestinian civilians' right to life. During multiple rounds of the hostilities between armed Israeli and Palestinian groups over the past two decades, Palestinian civilians have been framed as mere proximities to military targets, whose killing, even when indiscriminate, was portrayed as an unfortunate but proportionate cost of Israel's legitimate pursuit of its military advantages.[209] Not long before the current assault on Gaza, during Israel's 2021 attacks which resulted in the killing of 66 Palestinian children and injuring 600 more, IDF personnel publicly proposed that, when 'considering the military advantage gained by eliminating senior terrorists, it is irrelevant to ask how many children were *incidentally* killed'.[210] In this rationale, IHL proportionality is reinterpreted to render the conscious killing of children, regardless of how many, as irrelevant when targeting senior 'terrorists'. According to this subculture of disproportion, no amount of foreseeable mass killing of

[207] E Cannizzaro, 'Contextualizing Proportionality: *Jus ad Bellum* and *Jus in Bello* in the Lebanese War' (2006) 88 *International Review of the Red Cross* 779; W Fenrick, 'The Rule of Proportionality and Protocol I in Conventional Warfare' (1982) 98 *Military Law Review* 541; J Gardam, 'Proportionality as a Restraint on the Use of Force' (1999) 20 *Australian Yearbook of International Law* 161; J Hollande, 'Military Objective and Collateral Damage: Their Relationship and Dynamics' (2004) 7 *Yearbook of International Humanitarian Law* 35; T Parker, 'The Proportionality Principle in the War on Terror' (2002) 15 *Hague Yearbook of International Law* 3; K Watkin, 'Assessing Proportionality: Moral Complexity and Legal Rules' (2005) 8 *Yearbook of International Humanitarian Law* 3; WH von Heinegg, 'Considerations of Necessity under Article 57(2)(a)(ii), (c), and (3) and Proportionality under Article 51(5)(b) and Article 57(2)(b) of Additional Protocol I: Is There Room for an Integrated Approach?' in C Kreß and R Lawless (eds), *Necessity and Proportionality in International Peace and Security Law* (Oxford University Press, 2020) 437; A Haque, 'A Theory of *Jus in Bello* Proportionality' in JD Ohlin, L May and C Finkelstein (eds), *Weighing Lives in War* (Oxford University Press, 2017) 188–216.

[208] See L Daniele, 'Incidentality of the Civilian Harm in International Humanitarian Law and its Contra Legem Antonyms in Recent Discourses on the Laws of War' (2024) 29 *Journal of Conflict and Security Law* 21.

[209] See L Daniele, 'A lethal misconception, in Gaza and beyond: disguising indiscriminate attacks as potentially proportionate in discourses on the laws of war' *EJILTalk!*, 2023, at www.ejiltalk.org/a-lethal-misconception-in-gaza-and-beyond-disguising-indiscriminate-attacks-as-potentially-proportionate-in-discourses-on-the-laws-of-war.

[210] M Hirsch, 'Considering the military advantage gained by eliminating these senior terrorists …' (X, 2023) at x.com/MauriceHirsch4/status/1655840611704897536. The words were chosen by the senior officer, bafflingly, to repropose his own reflection on proportionality under IHL concluding that 'as much as … haters may opt to distort its meaning, proportionality in IHL is very clear and its meaning does not change into what they would like you to believe it means'; see M Hirsch, 'What is Proportionality in International Law When it Comes to Israel?' *Jerusalem Post* (10 August 2022), at www.jpost.com/opinion/article-714398.

Palestinian children in attacks can be deemed anything other than incidental, proportionate and inherently lawful.[211]

This exterminatory logic has become the norm in the ongoing offensive in Gaza.[212] Areas with a population density of 35,000 people per km^2 have been systematically attacked with destructive, wide-area impact weapons, often without any prior warning. The examples are innumerable. On the afternoon of 25 October 2023, the Al-Yarmouk neighbourhood in Gaza City was bombarded. A densely populated area of nearly 6 km^2 was largely flattened, including a high-rise residential tower. According to the UN OHCHR, 91 Palestinians were killed, including 28 women and 39 children. On 31 October 2023, Israeli strikes on the Al-Tarnis area of the Jabalia refugee camp killed at least 126 civilians, including 69 children. A further 280 civilians were injured, as reported by the director of the Indonesian Hospital. On the same day, an Israeli airstrike on a six-story apartment building near the Nuseirat refugee camp killed at least 106 civilians, including 54 children.[213] In each of these attacks, the mass killing of civilians, according to the war crimes *mens rea* categories discussed so far, was intentional. Flattening dense civilian neighbourhoods through aerial bombardment without advance warnings signals purposeful acceptance that the civilians on the ground will inevitably be killed *en masse*. By distorting the IHL notions of incidental civilian harm and proportionality, Israel has portrayed its relentless, daily extermination of civilians as a sum of unintended, collateral, proportionate, and thus 'lawful' costs of legitimate attacks. Through the semantic fraud of the 'collateral' killing, and dismantling the legal boundaries of the notion, entire Palestinian families, spanning three to five generations, have been wiped out[214] under this pretence of proportionality.

More than ever before, the distortion of IHL proportionality has been further elaborated and formalised in the official legal positions of the Israeli Government. While *ius in bello* proportionality indisputably refers to each individual attack, Israel's MFA propose that 'military advantage … may refer to the advantage anticipated from an operation as a whole',[215] alluding to the overall aims of the war. In sum, while IHL proportionality seeks to strike fair balance, in the hands of a reasonable commander, weighing up the tactical military advantage sought and the harm to civilians expected in individual attacks, the Israeli Government proposes that

[211] L Daniele, 'Incidentality of the civilian harm in international humanitarian law and its Contra Legem antonyms in recent discourses on the laws of war' (2024) 29 *Journal of Conflict and Security Law* 21.

[212] See OHCHR, *Thematic Report – Indiscriminate and disproportionate attacks during the conflict in Gaza (October–December 2023)*, 19 June 2024, 6–9, at www.ohchr.org/sites/default/files/documents/countries/opt/20240619-ohchr-thematic-report-indiscrim-disprop-attacks-gaza-oct-dec2023.pdf.

[213] See Erakat et al (n 214) 31–41.

[214] Sarah El Deeb, 'The war in Gaza has wiped out entire Palestinian families. AP documents 60 who lost dozens or more' Associated Press, 16 June 2024, apnews.com/article/gaza-palestinians-families-israel-war-deaths-a9f8bcfe402c17f1f78903eae67b7a7d.

[215] State of Israel Ministry of Foreign Affairs, 'Hamas-Israel Conflict 2023: Key Legal Aspects', 2 November 2023, at www.gov.il/en/pages/hamas-israel-conflict2023-key-legal-aspects.

the harm to civilians in each attack, including their anticipated killing, can and possibly must be balanced, as clearly indicated by Rubenstein, against the overall military advantage of the war.[216] A war, in addition, that is deemed to be existential by the Israeli executive, hence potentially factoring into each proportionally assessment the total elimination of Hamas and the survival of the state and its population. In this operation, the military advantage side of IHL proportionality becomes indeterminate, enormous, all-encompassing.

This operation completely disrupts the normative balance that IHL tries to strike between military necessity and humanity. Once this 'rule of disproportionality' is operationalised, in fact, there is virtually no entity of foreseeable killing of civilians in each attack, whether in the dozens or in the hundreds, that will ever be deemed excessive in comparison to the overall aims of the war. At the same time, according to this engine of distortions of the laws of war, no attack will ever be indiscriminate because every measure of anticipated killing of protected persons and destruction of protected objects will be per definition, in the mind of the attackers, incidental and never excessive.[217]

Nimer Sultany noted how the Israeli army, guided by the combined effect of the various distortions analysed in this section, appears to perceive the indiscriminate killing of civilians in areas subject to evacuation orders as lawful. The author noted that senior military officers commented to Israeli press agencies that once a population has been ordered to evacuate from cities, the army should have no concerns about collateral damage, because any civilians remaining, if killed *en masse* by Israeli forces, would be the responsibility of Palestinian armed groups 'holding them as hostages'.[218] As Jess White argued, these distortions represent 'the extreme form of an argumentative strategy that views the destruction of peoples and whole worlds as "incidental" to military necessities'.[219] This is, in other words, the expression of what could be labelled an 'incidental and proportionate genocide' theory, where the cumulative physical destruction of a substantial part of the victim group is represented as a sum of lawful collateral damages, and thus as an aggregate collateral damage in its entirety. In this way, collateral damage and proportionate civilian harm become code words not only for routinely exterminating civilians in attacks but, more profoundly, for cumulatively eliminating, one indiscriminate and one disproportionate attack after another, a substantial part of a group protected under the Genocide Convention.[220]

[216] L. Rubenstein, 'Israel's Rewriting of the Law of War' *Just Security*, 21 December 2023, at www.justsecurity.org/90789/israels-rewriting-of-the-law-of-war.

[217] On how the IHL notion of incidentality of the civilian harm is completely capsized in this reasoning, see Daniele (n 212) 32 ff.

[218] N Sultany, 'A Threshold Crossed: On Genocidal Intent and the Duty to Prevent Genocide in Palestine' (2024) 1 *Journal of Genocide Research* 10.

[219] J Whyte, 'A "Tragic Humanitarian Crisis": Israel's Weaponization of Starvation and the Question of Intent' (2024) 1 *Journal of Genocide Research* 14.

[220] See Albanese, Daniele and Perugini (n 14).

These legal distortions, in addition, were accompanied by discourses from the Israeli executive, military and political leaders, which repeatedly depicted the Gaza civilian population as collectively 'not innocent', 'not uninvolved', or even as a 'terrorist' population,[221] converging in an ideology of collective removal of the civilian protections descending from IHL, in turn reinforcing the perception of perpetrators about the irrelevance of the Genocide Convention framework in a total war against an enemy comprising both fighters and 'their' people.[222]

It is important to underline that the requisite special intent of the crime of genocide is not excluded by the simultaneous existence of parallel or ulterior motives, such as fighting a self-defensive war, eliminating a non-state armed group, preserving the future security of a nation, or protecting a group by threats perceived as existential, insofar as the destruction of a substantial part of the victim group is considered by perpetrators as a 'legitimate' means to achieve such aims. Genocidal intent, in fact, does not require that perpetrators intend the destruction of a substantial part of the group as the sole and ultimate purpose of their actions. Historically, perpetrators of genocide have hardly presented the destruction of their victim groups as an end in itself, nor as their sole and ultimate purpose, perceiving it, rather, as a necessary means; one they were forced to adopt as course of action to achieve further, compelling objectives.[223]

In sum, the Gaza war offers a paradigmatic and tragic example of how the lack of accountability for indiscriminate and disproportionate attacks can incentivise not only the adoption of war crimes as military policies but even their elevation to techniques of de-population of territories, within broader unlawful designs of aggressive military powers to occupy and annex foreign territories, up to the elimination of other nation-states and peoples.

4.4. Cassese's Prognosis Confirmed, and the Normalisation of Indiscriminate and Disproportionate Attacks

In conclusion, the expansion of discourses legitimising indiscriminate and disproportionate attacks accompanied a symmetrical, exponential growth in their actual

[221] See the numerous statement listed in the *Letter dated 29 May 2024 from the Permanent Representative of South Africa to the United Nations addressed to the President of the Security Council*, 29 May 2024, S/2024/419, at documents.un.org/doc/undoc/gen/n24/151/97/pdf/n2415197.pdf.

[222] A theorisation of this 'indistinction' between civilians and armed enemies in Gaza can be found in the vision articulated by the Defense Minister Advisor G Eiland, 'Let's not be intimidated by the world', *Yedioth Ahronoth*, 19 November 2023, tr T Shapira, at mondoweiss.net/2023/11/influential-israeli-national-security-leader-makes-the-case-for-genocide-in-gaza.

[223] See – without any undue analogy with the case under scrutiny, but rather to understand the issues of genocidal intent – B Ferencz, 'Mass Murderers Seek to Justify Genocide' *Ben Ferencz.Org* Stories 1946–1949, at benferencz.org/stories/1946-1949/mass-murderers-seek-to-justify-genocide.

commission, worldwide, as it can be observed through the examples analysed here. This curve of desensitisation toward accountability for unlawful attacks under *ius in bello* appears to have reached its climax in Gaza, where the commission of indiscriminate and disproportionate attacks has attracted political, media and legal discourses substantially declaring their commission a necessity and a 'civilizational' moral duty.[224]

A reckoning with the recent past might elucidate how this curve of normalisations has grown. Two decades ago, the killing of 15 civilians, including eight children, in Gaza in an operation to kill a senior member of Palestinian armed groups, was enough to prompt the then US President, George W Bush, to condemn the attack as 'heavy-handed' and 'not contributing to peace'.[225] Recently, while this work was in its final stages, the Israeli attack in Lebanon killing Hezbollah's Hassan Nasrallah was reported to have killed at least 300 civilians,[226] by likely use of 2,000 pound, GBU-31 bunker buster bombs on several residential buildings in the Beirut suburb of Dahiyeh.[227] Despite the civilian casualties tool, US President Biden affirmed the strike was a 'measure of justice' for the leader's 'many victims',[228] without a single reference to the civilian victims of the attack itself. This appears particularly significant after the likely indiscriminate attacks of the preceding days in Lebanon in crowded street markets, shops, cars in transit, killing and injuring thousands of civilians.[229]

This opposition between past and present symbolises how political, military and legal discourses culminated in Western political elites actively normalising the killing of civilians by allied powers in armed conflicts, in turn offering aggressive rival powers grounds to delegitimise the international institutions pursuing their accountability as biased, political, one-sided tools of hybrid warfare. This appears a principal ground, therefore, of the risks of breakdown of the international legal order, assaulted by opposed but symmetrical delegitimisations.

[224] See E Semerdjian, 'A World Without Civilians' (2024) *Journal of Genocide Research – Forum: Israel-Palestine: Atrocity Crimes and the Crisis of Holocaust and Genocide* at doi.org/10.1080/14623528.2024.2306714.

[225] See D Stout, 'White House Rebukes Israel for Attack, Calls It "Heavy-Handd"', *New York Times*, 23 July 2002, at www.nytimes.com/2002/07/23/international/white-house-rebukes-israel-for-attack-calls-it-heavyhanded; and M Oliver, 'Bush joins in condemnation of Israeli attack' *The Guardian*, 23 July 2002, at www.theguardian.com/world/2002/jul/23/israel2.

[226] A Harel et al, 'Israel Targets Hezbollah Chief Nasrallah in Massive Beirut Strike; Israeli Officials Estimate 300 Killed' *Haaretz*, 27 September 2024, at www.haaretz.com/israel-news/2024-09-27/ty-article/.premium/israel-targets-hezbollah-chief-nasrallah-in-massive-beirut-strike.

[227] H Ammar, 'AP images offer a close-up look at the smoldering site of Nasrallah's assassination', Associated Press, 29 September 2024, at apnews.com/article/lebanon-hezbollah-beirut-nasrallah-israel-airstrike-dahiyeh-.

[228] 'Statement from President Joe Biden on the Death of Hassan Nasrallah', White House, 28 September 2024, www.whitehouse.gov/briefing-room/statements-releases/2024/09/28/statement-from-president-joe-biden-on-the-death-of-hassan-nasrallah.

[229] See M Milanović, 'Were the Israeli Pager and Walkie-Talkie Attacks on Hezbollah Indiscriminate? *EJILTalk!*, 20 September 2024, at www.ejiltalk.org/were-the-israeli-pager-and-walkie-talkie-attacks-on-hezbollah-indiscriminate.

Such political normalisation of unlawful attacks increasingly surrounding the killing of civilians by allied powers, threatening the hold and endurance of the international legal architecture, would have not been possible without a decisive stall of international criminal justice, since the late 1990s, in charging, prosecuting and convicting indiscriminate and disproportionate attacks.

From this point of view, the prognosis offered by Cassese about the drafting of the Rome Statute ultimately shielding the militaries of powerful states from war crimes accountability[230] appears entirely confirmed and indeed exceeded, with nearly three decades of unpunished indiscriminate and disproportionate attacks, and many sectors of the law of war scholarship consistently mobilising to increasingly expand the conception of what is permissible, and progressively contract the consensus on what is prohibited in attacks. The combined effects of the Rome Statute war crimes provisions codified, as result of compromise, as blunt legal tools, war lawyers' mobilisations to constantly expand the boundaries of legality around the killing of civilians 'collaterally', and the political normalisation of indiscriminate and disproportionate attacks by allied powers, have ultimately culminated in a global threat to civilians.

In fact, once indiscriminate and disproportionate attacks are de facto accepted, if not promoted, when committed by allies, the principles of equal application and equality of belligerents under *ius in bello* immediately project the same acceptance and promotion in the hands of rival powers, in analogous circumstances. The unprecedent pace of mass civilian victimisation in the most recent armed conflicts, therefore, poses a most alarming threat, not only to civilians worldwide, but to the international legal order and global security, since no security of any state or human group can be allowed to be pursued through international crimes. Wars fought by means of indiscriminate and disproportionate attacks that evade any international law enforcement measures are actually moving the world into conflicts of total annihilation.

A vigilant ICC, therefore – one better equipped by its Statute for enforcing war crimes law without fear of favour – could decisively counter such threat, as the most egregious indiscriminate and disproportionate attacks would be singled out, scrutinised and punished, 'outcasting'[231] the unlawful attacks that lack of enforcement and accountability have, to date, integrated and incentivised.

For this reason, the conclusions of this research attempt to delineate avenues for addressing the failures in ensuring accountability for indiscriminate and disproportionate attacks, assessing both the *lex lata* and *lex ferenda* alternatives to be evaluated by international, state and non-governmental actors interested in effectively addressing this critical challenge, the urgency of which has never been more tragically evident than in the present historical moment.

[230] Cassese (n 30).

[231] See O Hathaway and S Shapiro, 'Outcasting: Enforcement in Domestic and International Law' (2011) 121 *Yale Law Journal* 252.

5

Bridging the Accountability Gap: Delivering Justice for Indiscriminate and Disproportionate Attacks

5.1. Jurisprudential Avenues for Ensuring Accountability, *Lex Lata*

The analysis so far has demonstrated that, despite some judicial determination opening windows for meaningful enforcement, international criminal law (ICL) has, for 20 years, de facto stopped the prosecuting and punishing of the most recurring forms of indiscriminate and disproportionate attacks, contributing to their normalisation when committed by allied powers. This normalisation, in turn, has led to a climax of increasingly exterminatory uses of these unlawful attacks, ultimately revealing their genocidal potential in armed conflicts fought by the annexing powers of contemporaneity.[1] Around the challenge to ensure accountability for indiscriminate and disproportionate attacks, therefore, it appears that the very survival of the international legal architecture of the post-World War II order is at risk.[2]

After exploring the persistent, concerning gaps obstructing the pursuit of international criminal accountability for indiscriminate and disproportionate attacks, the conclusions of this research bear the onus of indicating potential solutions, offering a reasoned *pars construens*.

In this respect, two directions for addressing the urgent challenges identified need to be evaluated. On the one hand, it is necessary to enquire whether it is possible to address the relevant challenges on the bases of the existing, codified Rome Statute war crimes. This avenue for restoring accountability requires an interpretative effort to reframe our understanding of the relevant war crimes, against the hegemonic distortions, misconceptions, and reversals of the protective purposes of the laws of war criticised so far, ultimately converging in weakening

[1] See eg Legal Consequences arising from the Policies and Practices of Israel in the Occupied Palestinian Territory, including East Jerusalem, 2024 ICJ Rep, 162–73.

[2] See I Brunk and M Hakimi, 'The Prohibition of Annexations and the Foundations of Modern International Law' (2024) 118 *American Journal of International Law* 417; A Kotova and N Tzouvala, 'In Defense of Comparisons: Russia and the Transmutations of Imperialism in International Law' (2022) 116 *American Journal of International Law* 710.

the war crimes regime of the Statute, and drastically reducing its enforceability and impact.

On the other hand, after articulating this *lex lata* analysis by suggesting the interpretations to be followed to punish and prevent these unlawful attacks, it becomes essential to acknowledge the limits of interpretative solutions, entrusted to the variable orientations of judges, operating within institutions inevitably captured by a reality of power relations between states and states blocks. This reality has revealed its capacity to hinder these institutions from fulfilling their mandates applying the law without fear or favour, by withstanding the pressures descending from power relations, including pressures on how to interpret the law. It is in this light that providing these institutions with reformed legal tools appears essential for correcting the defects of the Rome Statute and removing the 'unduly expanded legal shield' it has offered so far to aggressive military powers, with the catastrophic consequences we have witnessed in the last 20 years and, paradigmatically, in 2023–24.

The following sections therefore explore the possible *de iure condito*, interpretative solutions to the legal issues identified, whereas the remaining sections of the chapter indicate the alternatives *de jure condendo*, outlining avenues of legal reform, and assessing their potential advantages in comparison to solutions relying exclusively on interpretative correctives.

5.1.1. Indiscriminate Attacks as Direct Attacks on Civilians: The Missing Piece of the Puzzle

As the previous chapter showed, the ICC jurisprudence has in several cases indicated the international criminal relevance of indiscriminate attacks under the Rome Statute war crimes framework. This section recaps the findings of the analysis so far and indicates what jurisprudential developments, coherent with both Rome Statute mental element discipline and case law, appear inescapable to address the gaps in accountability identified.

In the *Katanga* case, judges determined that indiscriminate attacks fall under the scope of application of the crime of direct attacks on civilians. Discussing the elements of Article 8(2)(b)(i), they found that the crime of direct attacks on civilians is committed when the suspects, in their conduct of hostilities, have both the aim of attacking lawful targets, and, 'simultaneously', the aim of targeting the civilian population or individual civilians in the vicinity of the lawful targets.[3] The situation considered by the judges appeared to resemble that of attacks qualified by international humanitarian law (IHL) as area bombardments; that is, launching indiscriminate attacks on areas with high concentrations of civilians, ignoring the

[3] *Prosecutor v Katanga*, Decision on the confirmation of charges, ICC-01/04-01/07, 30 September 2008, para 273.

clear separation between distinct military objectives located therein. However, area bombardments are only an example of indiscriminate attacks under IHL, and do not exhaust the relevant category of unlawful attacks. Such normative indication, therefore, appears important to underline that attacking a village, residential area or neighbourhood as a whole simply because it is controlled by enemy forces, and of strategic relevance, can integrate the war crime of direct attacks on protected persons. As has been noted, this is coherent with consolidated case law indicating that the presence of some combatants amidst group of civilians does not alter the civilian status of the group, and thus its protection from direct attacks, both as a group and for the individual components thereof.[4]

It has also been clarified that this does not mean – despite military lawyers often suggesting otherwise – that armed forces are unable to target combatants if they are in the vicinity of civilians. The *Katanga* case judges, in fact, underlined the difference between, on the one hand, these indiscriminate attacks targeting simultaneously protected persons and lawful targets and, on the other, attacks launched with the aim of targeting *only* a military objective, albeit with awareness that incidental loss of life or injury to civilians would result from the attack.[5] This indication is crucial to correctly construe the dividing line between indiscriminate attacks and attacks causing either lawful collateral damage or, in contrast, disproportionate attacks.[6] Armed forces are not absolutely prohibited from causing incidental harm to civilians and civilian objects in their attacks (unless this is feasible in the circumstances), insofar as their objectives are only the lawful targets. In these cases, the decisive factor is whether attackers aimed *exclusively* at combatants, taking the relevant, mandatory precautions, or whether they substantially renounced distinguishing between them and the protected persons or objects in their vicinity. Only in the first situation does the issue becomes one of proportionality of the collateral damage, whereas in the second case it is the preliminary obligation of distinction, with its precautions corollaries, to be breached, in turn triggering the applicability of Article 8(2)(b)(i)–(ii) of the Statute. In sum, the *Katanga* case confirms that proportionality is operative exclusively when lawful targets are the *sole* objectives of direct attacks. On the contrary, the simultaneous targeting of civilians and civilian objects (even if jointly with lawful targets) can never be balanced by military advantages, as it is absolutely prohibited, and extraneous to proportionality assessments.

[4] *Prosecuto v Tadić*, Judgment, IT-94-1-T, 7 May 1997, para 638, ('it is clear that the targeted population must be of a predominantly civilian nature. The presence of certain non-civilians in their midst does not change the character of the population'); *Prosecutor v Jelisić*, Judgment, IT-95-10-T, 14 December 1999, para 54; *Prosecutor v Kordić and Čerkez*, Judgment, T-95-14/2-T, 26 February 2001, para 180; *Prosecutor v Naletilić and Martinović*, Judgment, IT-98-34-T, 31 March 2003, para 235; *Prosecutor v Blaskić*, Appeals Judgment, IT-95-14-A, 29 July 2004, para 115; *Prosecutor v Galić*, Appeal Judgment, IT-98-29-A, 30 November 2006, para 137.

[5] *Prosecutor v Katanga*, Decision on the confirmation of charges, ICC-01/04-01/07, 30 September 2008, para 274 (emphasis added).

[6] See ch 2, section 2.5, outlining the premises, in the opinion of this author, of a correct interpretation of the mentioned dividing line.

In addition, ICC judges dealt with the simultaneous targeting of combatants and civilians in the *Mbarushimana* case. In the confirmation of charges, it was clarified that the war crime of attacking civilians pursuant to Article 8(2)(e)(i) of the Statute does not presuppose that the civilian population is the *sole and exclusive* target of the attack. This case reiterated the reasoning of the *Katanga* case, affirming that the targeting of civilians and combatants jointly integrates the war crime of direct attacks on civilians.[7] The same approach was followed in the *Mudacumura* case.[8]

The relevant ICC judgments added some pieces to the puzzle, while generating some confusion. In the *Katanga* judgment, while reaffirming that indiscriminate attacks may constitute direct attacks on civilians, the Chamber clarified that to this purpose it is necessary to establish that the *primary object* of the attack was the civilian population or individual civilians. It also stated that the Court can reach such a conclusion where the damage caused to civilians is so great that it appears that the perpetrator meant to target civilians.[9]

Consequently, the Chamber seemed to require no less than direct intent to target the civilians as such, as the primary object of the attack, thus implying that the simultaneous targeting of combatants must appear to be a secondary objective. Simplifying this, the Chamber implied that for the configuration of the war crime of direct attacks on civilians the targeting of combatants must be a side (one could say 'collateral') element of what the attackers were anticipating as result of the attack, thus concealing an intent to strike *mainly* civilians. Consequently, the judgment also affirmed that the intention of targeting civilians can be inferred from the scale of the damage to civilians themselves,[10] which (when expected and understood by the suspects) can be so extensive as to indicate that the civilians were the real object of the attack. This reasoning appears similar to that of the ICTY when it discussed certain *apparently* disproportionate attacks which, due to the hugely disproportionate harm to civilians, concealed an intent to target the latter as such. Given this reasoning, the expression 'primary object' cannot be interpreted as 'primary purpose', because attackers can rely on the pursuit of high military advantages to affirm that such extensive harm to civilians was, for them, just incidental and not excessive, that is to say lawful collateral damage, and in any case not the desired result of their action.

Would such a subjective stance suffice to exclude the direct intent to strike civilians (determining eventually the relevance of the attack, alternatively, under Article8(2)(b)(iv))? In the opinion of this author, the answer is negative. Judges

[7] *Prosecutor v Mbarushimana* (Decision on the confirmation of charges), ICC-01/04-01/10, 16 December 2011, para 142 (first emphasis added).

[8] *Prosecutor v Mudacumura*, Decision on the Prosecutor's Application under Article 58, ICC-01/04-01/12, 13 July 2012, para 38.

[9] *Prosecutor v Katanga*, Judgment, ICC-01/04-01/07, 7 March 2014, para 802 (emphasis added).

[10] ibid.

meant to indicate the primary *object* of the attack, a concept to be appreciated objectively, as a main component of the group of persons and objects which it suspects to be engaged in direct attacks, even if the attacks include a small subset of lawful targets. 'Directly attacking', in such cases, must be understood in opposition to attacking with knowledge of causing incidental civilian ham, which requires that the lawful targets were the sole objects of the attack.

The *Katanga* Trial Chamber problematically added that indiscriminate attacks do not automatically amount to a war crime under Article 8(2)(e)(i). What the judges need to find for the war crime is, in good substance, the *mens rea*: the intent to target civilians as such.[11] This finding, importantly, is not confined to attacks directed solely at civilians, and can be inferred, as indicated by the judges, from the expected killing and injuring of civilians so extensive as to indicate that the civilians were indeed the primary object of the attack. Notwithstanding this possible inference, the framing remains unconvincing. Under IHL, the essence of indiscriminate attacks lies precisely in the conscious shelling of civilians alongside lawful targets. As a consequence, the suggestion that there might be indiscriminate attacks not implying any degree of intent to target civilians is incoherent with IHL, and potentially confusing. The key element for the relevance of indiscriminate attacks under ICL is the knowledge that the attack will directly kill civilians, indiscriminately. Absent this knowledge, there can still be intent to injure or kill civilians indirectly, but disproportionately, under Article8(2)(b)(iv). It should follow that without any degree of intent to strike civilians, crucially including knowledge that this prohibited consequence will occur, there is no indiscriminate attack (in the IHL sense). From this point of view, it appears that the Trial Chamber erred in referring to indiscriminate attacks which might not be supported by the intent to target civilians, and thus not amount to the relevant war crime of directly attacking civilians.

In the *Ntaganda* judgment, it was affirmed that crimes of direct attacks on civilians and civilian objects may encompass indiscriminate attacks; that is, targeting an area, as opposed to specific objects, or not targeting specific military objectives or persons taking a direct part in hostilities, on condition that the perpetrator was aware of the presence of civilians in the relevant area.[12] Importantly, the judges indicated that indiscriminate attacks amounting to direct attacks on civilians may also include attacks that are launched without taking necessary precautions to spare the civilian population or individual civilians.[13] ICC case law, except in this instance, has never dealt with how the duty to take mandatory precautions, imposed by customary law,[14] must be weighed by the Court in cases concerning unlawful attacks, and how unlawful failures to take mandatory precautions might

[11] ibid.
[12] *Prosecutor v Ntaganda*, Judgment, ICC-01/04-02/06, 8 July 2019, para 921 (emphasis added).
[13] ibid.
[14] See JM Henckaerts and L Doswald-Beck, *Customary International Humanitarian Law*, vol I (ICRC – Cambridge University Press, 2005) rules 15–21, 51–68.

impact the assessment of the intent to target civilians. Haque, analysing the defects of the Statute war crimes legal framework, concluded that

> under the Rome Statute, it does not matter why or how a combatant comes to mistake civilians for combatants. It does not matter if this mistaken belief was made despite 'doing everything feasible to verify that the objectives to be attacked are n[ot] civilians ... but are military objectives' or was made because the combatant did not even attempt to distinguish civilians from military targets. It does not matter if combatants fulfill their duties under humanitarian law or flout those duties. Any such mistake regarding civilian status, however unreasonable, means that the mistaken combatant did not intend to attack or knowingly kill civilians.[15]

This view, understandably concerned for the outcome of a literal interpretation, construes war crimes law as indifferent to IHL, excluding any chance of systematic interpretation and interpretative coherence between the two legal frameworks, pitting them against each other, irreconcilably. In the opinion of this author, judges should rather develop interpretative efforts in the opposite direction, harmonising as much as possible the discipline descending from the Rome Statute with the content of customary IHL obligations. From the perspective of this analysis, as a minimum, unreasonable failures to take mandatory precautions to verify the status of the objects or persons to be attacked should exclude the applicability of defences based on mistakes of fact (eg mistakes on the civilian status of a target, wrongly considered a combatant).[16] As already noted, a mistake of fact is only relevant for the Rome Statute when it excludes the requisite mental element for the relevant crime.[17] Would then unreasonable failures to take precautions, determining a mistake on the status of the attacked persons or objects, per se deny the relevant intent to target civilians? In these cases, it would be the violation of a customary law prescription to be the basis of mistakes on the status of the attacked persons or objects. The issue becomes then evaluating whether the mistake arose from negligence, or whether the failure to take precautions denoted, in the circumstances of the attack and the case, the moral indifference of the suspects toward the status of the persons or objects to be attacked. The reasonably well-informed commander standard (elaborated to adjudicate proportionality assessments in international criminal trials) could in such instances serve the purpose of distinguishing merely negligent failures to take precautions (for example, due to forces' fatigue, high-intensity and high-velocity battle, imminent risks of lethal counter-attacks, etc) from failures so unreasonable in the given circumstances and so serious as to indicate that it was

[15] A Haque, 'Protecting and Respecting Civilians: Correcting the Substantive and Structural Defects of the Rome Statute' (2011) 14 *New Criminal Law Review* 519, 529.

[16] See A Eser, 'Mental Elements–Mistake of Fact and Mistake of Law' in A Cassese, P Gaeta and JRWD Jones (eds), *The Rome Statute of the International Criminal Court: A Commentary* (Oxford University Press, 2002); E van Sliedregt, *Individual Criminal Responsibility in International Law* (Oxford University Press, 2012) 269–86.

[17] Art 32(1) Rome Statute.

impossible for the suspect not to know that the lack of precautions would have resulted, in the ordinary course of the events, in attacks against persons and objects of unverified status.[18]

In these latter cases, criminal liability should not be obstructed. Deciding to launch a strike against persons or object of unverified status in circumstances where it was entirely feasible to take the prescribed precautions, in fact, violates not only the customary rule of precautions but breaches also the IHL-imposed presumptions of protection in cases of doubts, clearly stated in Additional Protocol I (AP I) in relation to both persons and objects.[19] In these instances, unreasonable failures to take entirely feasible precautions would produce a mistake somehow preordained by the suspect. Such a circumstance presents similarities with the 'wilful blindness' doctrine emerged from common law criminal systems, as well as with the *actio libera in causa* developed by continental penal doctrine. In a narrow interpretation of wilful blindness, it was proposed that the perpetrator 'suspected the fact; he realized its probability; but he refrained from obtaining the final confirmation because he wanted in the event to be able to deny knowledge. This, and this alone, is wilful blindness.'[20]

The notion of *actio libera in causa*, used for cases of voluntary intoxication before committing an offence, similarly postulates that even if the persons were not liable during the course of action while performing an offence (in this case for a mistake of fact allegedly denying the mental element), they can still be held responsible for it if they voluntarily created a condition ('cause') for the offending action (eg unreasonably omitting to take any feasible precautions).[21] It is paradoxical that such notions are commonly applied domestically to punish perpetrators of ordinary offences across the world and remain unexplored in the punishment of the most egregious crimes of concern to the international community as a whole. This is only one of the many profiles in need of jurisprudential clarifications by the ICC judges, who are not bound to interpret the Statute in contrast with IHL.

[18] For a comprehensive discussion of the issues related to mistakes of fact and unlawful attacks, see M Milanović, 'Mistakes of Fact When Using Lethal Force in International Law' (Part I, Part II, and Part III), *EJILTalk!* (first post 14 January 2020), at www.ejiltalk.org/mistakes-of-fact-when-using-lethal-force-in-international-law-part-i.

[19] Art 50(1) AP I states: 'In case of doubt whether a person is a civilian, that person shall be considered to be a civilian'; Art 52(3) AP I affirms: 'In case of doubt whether an object which is normally dedicated to civilian purposes, such as a place of worship, a house or other dwelling or a school, is being used to make an effective contribution to military action, it shall be presumed not to be so used.' On presumptions of civilian status in cases of doubt, the US Department of Defense has recently codified the rule, with important implications for its customary status (on the top of nearly universal ratification of AP I); see CD Krass, 'Department of Defense Issues Update to DoD Law of War Manual on Presumption of Civilian Status and Feasible Precautions to Verify Military Objectives' *Just Security* (31 January 2023), at www.justsecurity.org/87430/department-of-defense-issues-update-to-dod-law-of-war-manual-on-presumption-of-civilian-status-and-feasible-precautions-to-verify-military-objectives.

[20] G Williams, *Criminal Law: The General Part*, 2nd edn (Stevens & Sons, 1961) 159.

[21] See eg S Dimock, 'Actio Libera in Causa' (2013) 7 *Criminal Law and Philosophy* 549.

In conclusion, in relation to indiscriminate attacks, neither the *Ntaganda* judgment nor the *Katanga* judgment provided specific indications about what degree of intent by suspects launching an indiscriminate attack is necessary to commit the war crime of direct attacks on civilians or civilian objects. The problem thus remains unresolved. It will be submitted in the next section that the issue remains unsolvable by exclusive reference to direct intent, centred on purposeful volition, triggering the inescapable necessity to valorise instead the cognitive element of the *mens rea.*

5.1.2. A Long-Overdue Step Forward: Applicability of the *Dolus Directus* in the Second Degree/Indirect Intent *Mens Rea* Standard

It remains impossible to solve the riddles of indiscriminate and disproportionate attacks under war crimes law without an enquiry into the *mens rea* thresholds relevant under the Rome Statute. The first two decades of ICC jurisprudence on the matter have seen oscillations between different interpretations, and internal dialectic between different chambers and judges.

In the early years of the Court, a Pre-Trial Chamber, in the *Lubanga* case (the Confirmation of Charges decision), appeared to embrace an interpretation of Article 30 of the Statute as including *dolus eventualis.* The Chamber stated that the default mental element of the Statute, 'intent and knowledge'

> also encompasses other forms of the concept of dolus which have already been resorted to by the jurisprudence of the ad hoc tribunals, that is:
>
> i. situations in which the suspect, without having the concrete intent to bring about the objective elements of the crime, is aware that such elements will be the necessary outcome of his or her actions or omissions (also known as dolus directus of the second degree); and
> ii. situations in which the suspect (a) is aware of the risk that the objective elements of the crime may result from his or her actions or omissions, and (b) accepts such an outcome by reconciling himself or herself with it or consenting to it (also known as dolus eventualis).
>
> [...] the latter type of situation, two kinds of scenarios are distinguishable.
>
> - Firstly, if the risk of bringing about the objective elements of the crime is substantial (that is, there is a likelihood that it 'will occur in the ordinary course of events'), the fact that the suspect accepts the idea of bringing about the objective elements of the crime can be inferred from:
>
> i. the awareness by the suspect of the substantial likelihood that his or her actions or omissions would result in the realisation of the objective elements of the crime; and
> ii. the decision by the suspect to carry out his or her actions or omissions despite such awareness.

- Secondly, if the risk of bringing about the objective elements of the crime is low, the suspect must have clearly or expressly accepted the idea that such objective elements may result from his or her actions or omissions.[22]

Much below the standard of virtual certainty for establishing 'intent', therefore, the judges in this decision explicitly admitted *dolus eventualis* even in cases characterised by low risks that the conduct would have brought about the objective elements of the crimes, if accompanied by a clear acceptance of the prohibited (eventual) results by the suspect. On a sort of sliding scale between cognition and volition, in this conception knowledge of a low risk of realisation of the prohibited consequence is punishable if the author has firmly accepted its verification, whereas a substantial likelihood of realisation of the prohibited consequence determines liability if the author has acted despite the awareness of its likely verification (much like recklessness).

In the *Katanga* case (Confirmation of Charges decision), pre-trial judges decided instead not to rely on *dolus eventualis*, considering it irrelevant.[23] At the same time, they clarified the admissibility and relevance of *dolus directus* in the second degree, broadly corresponding to indirect/oblique intent in Common Law penal systems, affirming:

> The cumulative reference to 'intent' and 'knowledge' requires the existence of a volitional element on the part of the suspect. This volitional element encompasses, first and foremost, those situations in which the suspect: (i) knows that his or her actions or omissions will bring about the objective elements of the crime; and (ii) undertakes such actions or omissions with the express intent to bring about the objective elements of the crime (also known as *dolus directus* of the first degree).
>
> The above-mentioned volitional element also encompasses another form of the concept of dolus which has been explained by the jurisprudence of this Chamber, relied on by the jurisprudence of the ad hoc tribunals and commonly accepted in the legal literature. This form of dolus concerns those situations in which although the suspect does not have the intent to bring about the objective elements of the crime, he is nonetheless 'aware that it (the consequence) will occur in the ordinary course of events' (also known as dolus directus of the second degree), as expressed in article 30(2)(b), second part of the Statute.[24]

In this interpretation, which has been influential for subsequent Trial and Appeal Chambers judgments, intent and knowledge under the Statute cannot be limited to cases where the suspect has a desire, a purposeful will to bring about the prohibited consequence per se. In fact, judges clarify that intent includes conduct in which the authors know that the development of the causal forces put in motion by their actions will result, ordinarily, in the realisation of the objective elements

[22] *Prosecutor v Lubanga Dyilo*, PTC I, Decision on the Confirmation of Charges, ICC-01/04-01/06, 29 January 2007, paras 252–254.

[23] ibid, para 531.

[24] *Prosecutor v Germain Katanga and Mathieu Ngudjolo Chui*, PTC I, Decision on the Confirmation of Charges, ICC-01/04-01/07, 30 September 2008, paras 529–30.

of the relevant crime. This *mens rea* is fundamental to capture an entire spectrum of subjective approaches in which, even without desire/purposeful will, the perpetrators decide otherwise that the objective elements of the crime which will knowingly result from their actions are acceptable.

The question triggered by this decision was therefore what level of awareness that a consequence will occur is necessary for this subjective element of the crime to be met.

A response was contained in the 2009 Confirmation of Charges decision in the *Bemba* case. The judges articulated a more comprehensive reasoning on the forms of *dolus* captured by the Statute, affirming:

> The Chamber stresses that the terms 'intent' and 'knowledge' as referred to in article 30(2) and (3) of the Statute reflect the concept of dolus, which requires the existence of a volitional as well as a cognitive element. Generally, dolus can take one of three forms depending on the strength of the volitional element vis-à-vis the cognitive element – namely, (1) dolus directus in the first degree or direct intent, (2) dolus directus in the second degree – also known as oblique intention, and (3) dolus eventualis – commonly referred to as subjective or advertent recklessness.
>
> In the view of the Chamber, article 30(2) and (3) of the Statute embraces two degrees of dolus. Dolus directus in the first degree (direct intent) requires that the suspect knows that his or her acts or omissions will bring about the material elements of the crime and carries out these acts or omissions with the purposeful will (intent) or desire to bring about those material elements of the crime. According to the dolus directus in the first degree, the volitional element is prevalent as the suspect purposefully wills or desires to attain the prohibited result.
>
> Dolus directus in the second degree *does not* require that the suspect has the actual intent or will to bring about the material elements of the crime, but that he or she *is aware that those elements will be the almost inevitable outcome of his acts or omissions*, i.e., the suspect 'is aware that … [the consequence] will occur in the ordinary course of events' (article 30(2)(b) of the Statute). In this context, *the volitional element decreases substantially and is overridden by the cognitive element*, i.e. the awareness that his or her acts or omissions 'will' cause the undesired proscribed consequence.
>
> With respect to dolus eventualis as the third form of dolus, recklessness or any lower form of culpability, the Chamber is of the view that such concepts are not captured by article 30 of the Statute. This conclusion is supported by the express language of the phrase 'will occur in the ordinary course of events', which does not accommodate a lower standard than the one required by dolus directus in the second degree (oblique intention)[25]

The Chamber further argued that, under a literal interpretation of Article 30, the wording about awareness that a prohibited result 'will occur' indicated an event that is entirely expected to happen as an almost inevitable consequence

[25] *Prosecutor v Jean-Pierre Bemba Gombo*, PTC II, Decision Pursuant to Art 61(7)(a) and (b) of the Rome Statute on the Charges of the Prosecutor against Bemba, ICC-01/05-01/08-424, 15 June 2009, paras 357–360 (emphases added).

of their actions by perpetrators. The judges contended that, had the drafters of the ICC Statute intended to convey the idea that author could be found to have intent in case of awareness of a possibility, based on likelihood, they could have employed the formula 'may' or 'might occur', in opposition to 'will occur'. In the same paragraphs, they contended that the phrasing 'in the ordinary course of events' in Article 30(2)(b) expressed that the degree of likelihood of occurrence, which can objectively never be absolutely certainty, must be nonetheless one that borders with certainty, establishing a standard of 'virtual certainty'. As the judges specified:

> [T]he Chamber considers that, by way of a literal (textual) interpretation, the words '[a consequence] will occur' serve as an expression for an event that is 'inevitably' expected. Nonetheless, the words 'will occur', read together with the phrase 'in the ordinary course of events', clearly indicate that *the required standard of occurrence is close to certainty*. In this regard, the Chamber defines this standard as 'virtual certainty' or 'practical certainty', namely that *the consequence will follow*, barring an unforeseen or unexpected intervention that prevent its occurrence.[26]

From this moment on in the ICC case law, *dolus eventualis* and recklessness were then confirmed to be excluded from the Rome Statute framework. First in the Lubanga Trial Judgment,[27] then in the *Katanga* Trial Judgment,[28] judges adhered to the *Bemba* Confirmation of Charges interpretation of the mental element. As the *Katanga* judgment stated, intent under the Rome Statute

> presupposes that the person knows that his or her actions will necessarily bring about the consequence in question, barring an unforeseen or unexpected intervention or event to prevent its occurrence. In other words, it is nigh on impossible for him or her to envisage that the consequence will not occur.[29]

This orientation was then confirmed at Appeals Chambers level, settling the debate on *dolus eventualis*. In the *Lubanga* Appeals Judgment, the Chamber stated:

> The Appeals Chamber notes that these provisions do not refer to the notion of 'risk' but employ the term of occurrence of a consequence 'in the ordinary course of events'. The Appeals Chamber considers that the words '[a consequence] will occur' refer to future events. The verb 'occur' is used with the modal verb 'will', and not with 'may' or 'could'. Therefore, this phrase conveys, as does the French version, certainty about the future occurrence. However, absolute certainty about a future occurrence can never exist; therefore, the Appeals Chamber considers that the standard for the foreseeability of events is virtual certainty.[30]

While most of the debate, included on the intent for war crimes of unlawful attacks, focused on the exclusion of *dolus eventualis*/recklessness from this framework, the

[26] ibid, para.362 (emphases added).
[27] *Prosecutor v Lubanga Dyilo*, TC I, Judgment, ICC-01/04-01/06, 14 March 2012, para 1012.
[28] *Prosecutor v Germain Katanga*, TC II, Judgment, ICC-01/04-01/07, 7 March 2014, para 777.
[29] ibid.
[30] *Prosecutor v Lubanga Dyilo*, AC, Judgment, ICC-01/04-01/06 A 5, 1 December 2014, para 447.

scholarly debate neglected that following the *Bemba* Confirmation of Charges decision also meant following the indication that indirect/oblique intent, unlike recklessness, is fully compatible with the Statute. When relevant judges affirmed that the volitional element can decrease substantially and be overridden by the cognitive element, ie, the awareness that acts or omissions 'will' cause the undesired proscribed consequence in the ordinary course of events, they provided a crucial indication for solving the legal issues under scrutiny.

Fully appreciated, and considering all of the above, this applicability of *dolus directus* in the second degree, or indirect/oblique intent, counters the concerns advanced by scholars like Ohlin who focus on the risk of transforming every case of lawful collateral damage in a case of direct attacks on civilians.[31] The opposite risk was indeed radically underestimated: the risk of transforming every case of indiscriminate harm to civilians in a case of presumedly lawful collateral damage. As has been shown, this risk was actually revealed to be the most concerning, since systematically, in the wars analysed, aggressive military powers killing civilians indiscriminately, so much as to induce the OTP to charge extermination as a crime against humanity, have characterised their attacks as causing only lawful collateral damage.

Ultimately, the applicability of indirect intent, ie, the valorisation of the cognitive element of intent in cases of virtual certainty, allows the full punishment of indiscriminate attacks as direct attacks on civilians or on civilian objects. Any indiscriminate attack, in fact, even if launched with purposeful will – the desire to kill just combatants – is prohibited under IHL because it is indeed launched despite the cognitive acceptance that it 'will' kill and destroy, alongside the desired targets, entire groups of protected persons as such, and/or of protected objects, particularly in populated urban centres.

Outside of the Rome Statute framework, this cognitive acceptance, in cases of virtual certainty, has thus no legal basis. Indiscriminately killing groups civilians, and indiscriminately destroying groups of civilian objects, directly shelling them alongside lawful targets (for example, via wide-area-impact explosive weapons in densely populated areas), should therefore be punished as a direct attack on civilians or on civilian objects.

In these cases, in fact, when the perpetrator is virtually certain that the proscribed consequence of killing and destroying groups of protected persons and objects will occur in the ordinary course of events, the Rome Statute *mens rea* threshold is met. The certainty of causing this prohibited and criminal consequence, does not change even if the perpetrator assumes a stance of moral indifference toward its verification, or eventually of regretful certainty. The Statute does not require desire, enthusiasm or satisfaction for the prohibited consequence; it requires virtual certainty.

[31] JD Ohlin, 'Was the Kunduz Hospital Attack a War Crime?' *Opinio Juris* (1 May 2016), at opiniojuris.org/2016/05/01/was-the-kunduz-hospital-attack-a-war-crime.

The scholarship concerned mainly with protecting from liability attacks anticipating lawful incidental killing of civilians/collateral damage, in other words, has produced the effect of obscuring the centrality of indirect intent from war crimes law enforcement. Behind the lines of these scholarly concerns, in fact, the misconception according to which liability for the war crime of attacking civilians has to be limited exclusively to unlawful attacks supported by direct intent, reserved for perpetrators with a primary purpose or desire to kill civilians or destroy civilian objects, has concerningly gained traction in public debates.

By so doing, this scholarship has facilitated an exceptionally narrow construction of the war crime of direct attacks on civilians, with a number of actors and observers de facto construing 'intent' for this war crimes as a *dolus specialis*, a specific intent to bring about the killing of the civilians. This is not what the Rome Statute and the Elements of Crimes indicate. Such misconceptions have thus further restricted the scope of application of war crimes already requiring mental element thresholds much higher than those of any penal system in the world, for ordinary offences. It is unreasonable to do so for crimes of concern of the international community as a whole.

Opposing this *dolus specialis* misconception for the war crimes of attacking civilians and/or civilian objects, it appears therefore that virtual certainty must be decisively valorised by judges scrutinising cases of indiscriminate attacks, amounting, precisely via indirect intent, to the war crimes of direct attacks on civilians and/or civilian objects. Once this indirect intent, or *dolus directus* in the second degree, where the cognitive element becomes the main formant of intent, is valorised, it becomes important to refine the interpretative guidelines to distinguish these war crimes of direct attacks on civilians, including indiscriminate attacks, from the war crime of disproportionate attacks, so that indirect intent does not translate into criminalisation of all cases of virtual certainty of collateral damage, reproducing the same concerns of the mentioned scholarship in relation to *dolus eventualis*.

5.1.3. The War Crime of Disproportionate Attacks: Achieving Harmonisation with IHL Proportionality Through Indirect Intent

5.1.3.1. Distinguishing Disproportionate Attacks from Indiscriminate Attacks under War Crimes Law

Before analysing how the valorisation of indirect intent can help the interpretation and application of the war crime of (clearly) disproportionate attacks under Article8(2)(b)(iv) of the Rome Statute, it is essential to recap the results of this research about the difference between indiscriminate and disproportionate attacks, as a premise for a correct interpretation and application of the relevant war crimes.[32]

A crucial challenge for the case law and the scholarship discussed so far has been, and continues to be, discerning between indiscriminate and disproportionate attacks. It is submitted that indiscriminate attacks, supported by indirect intent, in cases of virtual certainty of their amount to war crimes of direct attacks on civilians or civilian objects. These attacks must be differentiated from other unlawful attacks, characterised by the intentional violation of the rule of proportionality.

This first requires correctly differentiating between these types of unlawful attacks under IHL. In this regard, it has been argued in this research that the notion of *incidental* civilian harm is the decisive element to differentiate between lack of discrimination and disproportion.

The possibility to qualify the civilian harm expected from an attack as incidental, it has been submitted, is a pre-condition to weight this harm in IHL proportionality assessments. Proportionality and precautions in fact require a prognostic evaluation of what the attack *may be expected* to cause. Then, within the range of expectable consequences of the attacks, attackers need to discern between incidental and non-incidental consequences in their objective measure. In doing so, they must make sure that the expected civilian harm falls in the former camp, that of the *side* consequences of the attack. Only after this step it is possible to weight the civilian harm expectable and the military advantage anticipated against each other, in the balancing operation required under proportionality. Without this precondition, civilian harm that was not expected as an incidental consequence of the attack, or worse civilian harm expected to be the chief consequence of the attack, falls either under the prohibition of direct attacks or under that of indiscriminate attacks.

The question becomes then how to delimit the boundaries of disproportionate attacks, in which a civilian harm that can be considered incidental was nonetheless expected to be excessive, thus stopping the attack. In the relevant IHL prohibitions, disproportion (ie excessive incidental civilian harm) crosses the legal red lines separating civilians from combatants only: 1) *indirectly*, because civilians and civilian objects in these cases are not a *direct* target, nor do attackers juxtapose them to lawful targets in their lines of fire; plus 2) *collaterally*, because attackers in these cases aim solely at lawful targets, singularly identified, but accept at the same time that the incidental harm to civilians will be an excessive and foreseeable *side* consequence of the attack.

Obviously, in cases of clear excessiveness of the incidental civilian harm, the harm to civilians expected might be so great as to border on a lack of discrimination, blurring the boundaries between the two types of unlawful attacks, which remains elusive.

[32] This interpretative proposal completes what was mentioned but not fully developed in H van der Wilt, 'Towards a Better Understanding of the Concept of 'Indiscriminate Attack' – How International Criminal Law Can Be of Assistance' (2019) 22 *Yearbook of International Humanitarian Law* 29.

However, the Rome Statute mental element regime can decisively help in identifying when an expected civilian harm can be considered incidental, in order for prosecutors, judges and practitioners to determine whether the relevant conduct has relevance, *lex lata*, under the war crime of direct attacks on civilians, or whether it is exclusively relevant for the war crime of disproportionate attacks. It has been already established, in fact, that virtual certainty amounts to intent. As a consequence, the expected civilian harm of an attack, in order to lawfully enable access of attackers to proportionality assessments (as it has been submitted already under IHL and is equally valid under ICL),[33] must be anticipated as *incidental* in a threefold sense:

(a) the civilian harm must be incidental in relation to, and in contrast to, the main result of the attack *pursued*, from the volitional point of view (ie the attacker must have singularly identified the targets to be attacked purposefully and done everything feasible to attack them only);
(b) the civilian harm must be incidental in relation, and in contrast to the main result of the attack *foreseeable*, from the cognitive/prognostic point of view (ie the attacker must foresee what the attack will cause, in the ordinary course of events, and must not be accepting the virtual certainty of killing mainly civilians, particularly in large groups);
(c) the civilian harm must be incidental in relation, and in contrast to the main result – of military nature – of the attack *objectively*, from the material point of view, which needs as a minimum to be logically distinguishable and preponderant in comparison to the, secondary and indirect, impact on civilians and civilian objects (ie. the attack must not be confusing the conscious killing of entire crowds of civilians with a side-consequence of killing one or a few combatants, unreasonably inverting the camps of the main and lateral anticipated consequences of an action).

When this threefold demarcation line can reasonably be said to have been respected, the suspect might not be charged with direct attacks on civilians (including indiscriminate attacks), and might only be scrutinised under the war crime of disproportionate attacks, because in such cases it will be the entity (clearly excessive) of the incidental civilian harm foreseen in comparison to the military advantage sought to eventually justify a war crime charge.

This might be particularly relevant in cases of intense co-location of comparable numbers of lawful targets and protected persons, in the same populated areas. In such cases, absent any chance of attacking in less harmful ways (eg via ground forces), even harm to civilians expected to be high might be reasonably be identified as incidental, should the attack be aiming, for example, at killing an entire platoon of armed enemy forces, constituting the majority of those which will be hit by the attack. When, instead, some combatants are interspersed among

[33] See ch 2, 2.4 and 2.5.

entire crowds of civilians, killing, and/or gravely injuring the entire crowd of protected persons should not be considered an incidental consequence of the attack.

If, in fact, the civilian harm is expected to be, from an objective point of view, the largely prevalent result of the attack in comparison, quantitatively, to a secondary impact on legitimate (included high value) military targets, plus the foreseeability of the main result of impact on civilians is so high as to be equivalent to virtual certainty, then it can be said that this prevalent result of the attack on civilians is substantially intended, under the Rome Statute, for the simple reason that it is no more a 'collateral' one, and – in addition – it is expected with virtual certainty by the attacking forces.

In these cases, it is the war crime of direct attacks on civilians (or the war crime of direct attacks on civilian objects, or eventually both) that must be scrutinised, because the conditions to qualify the harm expected by attackers as incidental are absent. These evaluations could be particularly relevant particularly for the Office of the Prosecutor, suggesting alternative charges and alternative trial strategies based on the facts of cases, and based on indicators with a firm legal basis in IHL.

On the contrary, when the prosecution is convinced that this threefold dividing line between non-incidental and incidental civilian harm is respected, the potential crime of relevance becomes that of disproportionate attacks; that is, of clearly excessive *incidental* civilian harm.

5.1.3.2. Indirect Intent against the 'Monarchy' of the Military Commander

The elements of the crime of clearly disproportionate attacks, already discussed, present several issues.[34]

These elements require that:

1. The perpetrator launched an attack.
2. The attack was such that it would cause incidental death or injury to civilians or damage to civilian objects … and that such death, injury or damage would be of such an extent as to be clearly excessive in relation to the concrete and direct overall military advantage anticipated.
3. The perpetrator knew that the attack would cause incidental death or injury to civilians or damage to civilian objects … and that such death, injury or damage would be of such an extent as to be clearly excessive in relation to the concrete and direct overall military advantage anticipated.

To recap what was highlighted in chapter four, this crime does not have a result requirement. The test on the first element is whether the suspect launched an

[34] The treatise has not discussed and does not discuss issues related to the qualification of the armed conflict and the damage to the environment, since the focus of this analysis is on civilian harm in international armed conflicts.

attack, setting in motion the causal process which would have brought about the prohibited consequences. If the attack integrates the other elements, the crime is thus perfected when the perpetrator launches an attack which would have led, in the ordinary course of events, to the clearly excessive incidental civilian harm.

The second element of the crime qualifies the attack prohibited, from the objective point of view. The attack must possess the features indicated in the second element; that is, the clear disproportion between incidental civilian harm foreseeable and military advantage sought. The element characterises the incidental civilian harm and the military advantage object of the proportionality assessment with a different wording to the relevant IHL prohibition. While under IHL proportionality evaluations concern the balancing of the concrete and direct military advantage anticipated, on the one hand, and the incidental civilian harm which may be expected, on the other, Article 8(2)(b)(iv) refers to a concrete and direct 'overall' military advantage, and to a 'clearly' excessive incidental civilian harm (with the word 'clearly' nowhere to be found in the relevant IHL norms).

Concerning the military advantage, this research considers that the better view is that offered by the ICRC during the Rome Conference,[35] noting that the word 'overall' cannot alter an IHL concept consolidated into customary prohibitions. As has been discussed, the 'overall' wording was added following the literature suggesting that military objectives, provided they makes an effective contribution to the military action of the enemy, might be identified as lawful targets not only for the immediate advantage their capture, neutralisation or destruction offers in the single, specific and geographically circumscribed battle, but also for the less immediate, tactical advantage the attack could trigger elsewhere on the wider battlefield (eg feigned attacks to attract the focus of the enemy in order to weaken other positions hold by enemy forces).[36] However, the advantage needed to design an object as a military objective, identified as 'definite military advantage' under IHL, is different and less circumscribed than the advantage object of proportionality assessments, identified as 'concrete and direct'. Admitting that this latter advantage may consider tactical benefits manifesting in unspecified different times and places than those of the attack is thus extremely risky. Balancing the incidental civilian harm of a feigned attack with the advantage emerging elsewhere and at a different time in the war can radically alter proportionality: such operation would: 1) discount from the proportionality assessment of the first attack the incidental civilian harm to be expected in the second; and 2) double the weight of the military advantage anticipated from the first attack with that anticipated from the second. It is therefore crucial to apply the same scale to both the military advantage, and the incidental civilian

[35] Official Records of the United Nations Diplomatic Conference of Plenipotentiaries on the Establishment of an International Criminal Court, Rome, 15 June–17 July 1998, Volume III (A/CONF.183/INF/10 of 13 July 1998) 225.

[36] See WA Solf, 'Art 52' in M Bothe, KJ Partsch and WA Solf (eds), *New Rules for Victims of Armed Conflicts: Commentary on the Two 1977 Protocols Additional to the Geneva Conventions* (Martinus Nijhoff, 1982) 324.

harm.[37] In other words, a symmetry is required. When attackers intend to construe the concrete and direct military advantage as deriving from an operation as a whole, they must *symmetrically* construe the incidental civilian harm side of the proportionality assessment, evaluating the harm to civilians that can be expected from the operation as a whole.

This interpretation is backed by the footnote that accompanies the second element of the war crime, which affirms that the military advantage '*may or may not* be temporally or geographically related to the object of the attack', but also specifying that 'the possibility of lawful incidental injury and collateral damage does not in any way justify any violation of the law applicable in armed conflict'.[38] This footnote substantially states that the element cannot be interpreted as allowing violations of or derogations to IHL.

Concerning the incidental civilian harm, the offence affirms that liability is bound to knowledge of a 'clearly excessive' incidental civilian harm. It is doubtful how interpreters must read this qualifier, absent in the IHL prohibition. As noted critically by Haque 'The adjective 'clearly' might refer to the objective magnitude of the excessiveness that is prohibited: the Rome Statute might prohibit incidental civilian killing that is very or grossly excessive but allow incidental civilian killing that is only somewhat excessive.'[39] In contrast, Dormann has indicated that 'the addition of the words "clearly" and "overall" in the definition of collateral damage is not reflected in any existing legal source. Therefore, the addition must be understood as not changing existing law.'[40]

The alternative is about whether the word 'clearly' generates an inescapable gap with IHL, or whether footnote 36 of the Elements of Crimes (previously mentioned)[41] can be invoked to address this gap in the sense of compliance with the IHL rule. The same footnote states that the crime of disproportionate attacks 'reflects the proportionality requirement inherent in determining the legality of any military activity undertaken in the context of an armed conflict'.[42] It is difficult, considering such specifications, and the assertion that the formulation of the crime 'does not *in any way* justify *any* violation' of IHL,[43] to see how a correct application of the offence might depart, in significant ways, from IHL proportionality. It is unlikely, however, due to the formulation of the offence, plus the gravity of cases as requirement for their admissibility under Article 17(1)(d) of the Statute, that any prosecutor would charge the crime of disproportionate attacks in cases of excessiveness of the incidental civilian harm which is not manifest, at least at the preliminary examinations and investigations stage, under the reasonable commander standard.

[37] K Dörmann, *Elements of War Crimes under the Rome Statute of the International Criminal Court: Sources and Commentary* (Cambridge University Press, 2003) 173.
[38] ICC, Elements of Crimes, at 13, fn 36.
[39] Haque (n 15) 519–75.
[40] Dörmann (n 37) 169.
[41] ibid 19.
[42] ibid.
[43] ibid.

The element of the crime in relation to which the 'clear excessiveness' wording might generate the most serious issues is the mental element, requiring that the perpetrator

> *knew* that the attack would cause incidental death or injury to civilians or damage to civilian objects … and that such death, injury or damage would be of such an extent as to be clearly excessive in relation to the concrete and direct overall military advantage anticipated.[44]

It has been submitted that this element requires that the perpetrator had knowledge of the objective *extent* of the incidental civilian harm that the attack would have caused. The clear excessiveness of this harm in comparison to the military advantage, instead, should be determined by the Court, guided by the 'reasonable military commander' standard inherited by the ICTY case law.[45] Footnote 37 of the Elements of Crimes affirms that the knowledge element 'requires that the perpetrator makes the value judgement as described therein'.[46] This led eminent authors to conclude that the perpetrator has to be personally convinced of the clear excessiveness of the civilian harm.[47] Similarly, Heller and Lawrence suggested that 'the drafters specifically rejected the idea that the excessiveness of an attack should be determined by the Court from the perspective of the reasonable commander'.[48] In affirming this, they refer to Dormann, who in reality, in the opinion of the present author, has rather indicated that there was division on the point among the delegations and the relevant footnote was ultimately adopted without clarifying the issue.[49]

Concerningly, the need of a psychological stance of the perpetrator worthy of legal blame and criminal punishment should never mean that a perpetrator, at the time of the relevant conduct, was subjectively convinced of his own criminality in taking the course of action he opted for. This would produce the paradox of perpetrators becoming the ultimate 'judges in their own cause'.[50] Such a reading would

[44] ibid, Art 8(2)(b)(iv), 3 (emphasis added).

[45] Trying to limit, and to review, the subjective margins of appreciation of military commanders in proportionality assessments, international criminal jurisprudence, as it has been recalled in ch 2, developed a standard, based on a general and abstract point of reference, in order to judicially evaluate the proportionality assessments of those in charge of attacking decisions. The ICTY referred to this standard as that of a 'reasonably well-informed person in the circumstances of the actual perpetrator'. This standard was then developed by considering the ideal position not of any reasonably well-informed person, but that of a reasonable well-informed war professional, strong of training and expertise, that is the military commander. Actual, and potentially wrong/unlawful proportionality assessments by commanders could in this way be re-evaluated by judges based on the parameter of what a reasonably well-informed commander would have determined in comparison to the one under actual scrutiny. See eg I Henderson and K Reece, 'Proportionality under International Humanitarian Law: The 'Reasonable Military Commander' Standard and Reverberating Effects' (2021) 51 *Vanderbilt Law Review* 835.

[46] Dörmann (n 37) 19.

[47] Haque (n 15) 521.

[48] L Lawrence and KJ Heller, 'The Limits of Article 8(2)(b)(iv) of the Rome Statute: The First Ecocentric Environmental War Crime' (2007) 20 *Georgetown International Environmental Law Review* 61.

[49] Dörmann (n 37) 164–65.

[50] M Bothe, 'War Crimes' in A Cassese, P Gaeta and JRWD Jones (eds), *The Rome Statute of the International Criminal Court: A Commentary*, vol 1 (Oxford University Press, 2002) 400.

transform the subjective perception of all potential perpetrators of the crime, eventually devaluing the life of civilians (eg civilians considered accomplices of enemies in populated areas considered hostile), in *legibus soluti* 'monarchs' of proportionality assessments. Their discretion to decide how much incidental killing of civilians is acceptable would thus become absolute, and unreviewable, transforming the codification of the crime in an inapplicable, symbolic gesture. Think about the hypothetical example of a military commander conditioned by a genocidal ideology to consider the civilian population of a given national group as a mass of terrorism supporters, or of terrorists themselves, not deserving their own life.[51]

Such an ideological conditioning would obviously lead the commander to consider the incidental mass killing of discriminated, dehumanised civilians, whenever there is a lawful target in their vicinity, as never excessive and always proportionate. The commander might even be convinced that he is entitled to do so by the law of armed conflict. Such a commander might have led an entire campaign of disproportionate attacks, each launched with the certainty that hundreds of civilians would have certainly been killed in each attack, ultimately killing thousands in the campaign. The ICC itself, should the overly subjective reading of the crime be followed, would be subdued by the commander's own *mens rea*, and forced to accept that even genocidal ideologies distorting the commander's proportionality assessments must prevail over the Court's own assessment!

Against this reading, neutralising meaningfulness, and applicability of the war crime of disproportionate attack, valorising indirect intent can lead to a different interpretation. A correct interpretation of the crime needs to be conscious that, for a start, in contrast to the uncertainties during the drafting

[51] On the nexus between counter-guerrilla warfare and genocidal war ideologies, see JP Sartre, 'Genocide' (1968) 48 *New Left Review* 14, 17: 'It is not by mere chance that the "popular" war, with its principles, its strategy, its tactics and its theoreticians, begins at the same time as the industrial powers brought total war to its ultimate stage with the harnessing of nuclear fission. Nor is it by chance that it resulted in the ruin of colonialism. The contradiction that gave victory to the FLN in Algeria was typical of the time; in fact, popular war eradicates classical war (as does the hydrogen bomb). Against partisans backed by the entire population, colonial armies are helpless. They have only one way of escaping from the harassment which demoralises them and tends towards a Dien Bien Phu. This is to eliminate the civilian population. As it is the unity of a whole people that is containing the conventional army, the only anti-guerrilla strategy which will be effective is the destruction of that people, in other words, the civilians, women and children. Torture and genocide were the colonialists' answers to the uprising of the natives. And that answer, as we know, is useless if it is not definitive and total. A determined population, unified by its fierce and politicised partisan army, will not let itself be intimidated, as it was in the heyday of colonialism, by a massacre "as a lesson". On the contrary, this will only increase its hatred. It is no longer a matter of arousing fear but of physically liquidating a people. And as this is not possible without at the same time eliminating the colonial economy and the colonial system; the settlers panic, the colonial powers grow tired of sinking manpower and money into a conflict with no solution, the masses at home end up opposing the continuation of barbaric wars and the colonies become independent states. There do exist, however, cases where the genocidal solution to popular wars is not held back by innate contradictions. Total genocide then reveals itself as the foundation of anti-guerrilla strategy. And, under certain circumstances, it would even present itself as the ultimate objective, either immediately or gradually.'

(of both Statute and Elements of Crimes) ICC judges have now excluded *dolus eventualis*/recklessness from the Rome Statute framework. As a consequence, the footnotes added to the elements of this crime to preserve the professional margins of appreciation of (reasonable) military commanders have lost much of their weight. The judicial exclusion of *dolus eventualis*/recklessness, in fact, already protects commanders taking risks, including unjustifiable risks, of causing clearly excessive civilian harm. In such cases, in fact, the likelihood, including high likelihood of causing excessive civilian harm, would not meet the virtual certainty test for intent.

This jurisprudential development, the virtual certainty test, already sets the threshold for protection of the margin of appreciation of military commanders at a particularly high level. There is therefore no legally appreciable reason to disregard the virtually certain consequences of the attack, those which would have necessarily manifested in the ordinary course of the events. Such virtually certain consequences must be appreciated on the basis of the circumstances faced by and knowledge of the commander at the moment of launching the attack. The prognostic evaluation characterising the proportionality assessment as an *ex ante* balancing operation, preceding the attack, would thus be fully respected. What is crucial is moving away from the paradoxical interpretations requiring the excessiveness of the incidental killing of civilians to be 'clear' in the inner temple of the perpetrator's own conscience. In order to do so, prosecutors and judges must focus on the cognitive component of intent, applying the virtual certainty test, as clarified by ICC case law, to the war crime under Article 8(2)(b)(iv) Rome Statute.

By so doing, a military commander that launches an attack despite the virtual certainty of incidentally killing whole crowds of civilians, while acting with the direct intent of eliminating a number of lawful targets interspersed among the protected persons, will not escape accountability, because indirect/oblique intent will cover the virtually certain civilian harm foreseen and appreciated by the commander. It will then be for the trial and for judges to determine, beyond reasonable doubt, whether or not this extensive incidental civilian harm, expected with virtual certainty and appreciated in its objective extent by the commander, was clearly excessive in comparison to the military advantage sought, within IHL parameters. These IHL parameters should include the assessment of the combination of incidental killing and injuring of civilians, and incidental damage to civilian objects, in accordance with customary *ius in bello* proportionality.

Considering all of the above, the second element of the crime of disproportionate attacks should be interpreted with a focus on the wording 'of such an extent', referring to the incidental civilian harm. This would allow the objective entity of the incidental civilian harm predicted by the perpetrator to be valorised. The third element of the crime, in turn, should be interpreted focusing on the subjective stance of the perpetrator. It is in relation to this element that virtual certainty can play a decisive role. Virtual certainty would also mean near impossibility (for any reasonable commander) to expect a different, lesser extent of incidental civilian harm from attack. This virtually certain harm must be of the 'extent' indicated in the second element. Once it can be established that the suspect was virtually certain that the incidental civilian harm would have been of the objective extent required by the second element, than trial and judges can decide whether it was clearly excessive.

This interpretation would give back meaning to the formulation of the offence in the Rome Statute; that is, 'intentionally launching an attack … in the knowledge' that it would cause clearly disproportionate incidental civilian harm. This formulation is entirely compatible with an interpretation of the offence understanding direct intent as connected to the launching of the attack, with the purpose of directly targeting exclusively lawful targets. At the same time, the knowledge (ie *dolus indirectus*/oblique intent) element must be connected to the virtually certain incidental harm to civilians of a disproportionate, ie clearly excessive extent in comparison to the military advantage sought.

It is submitted, in conclusion, that the elements of the crime should be interpreted as requiring that:

(1) The perpetrator launched an attack.
(2) The attack, based on the circumstances at the time of its launch, was such that it would have caused incidental loss of civilian lives, injury to civilians, damage to civilian objects, or a combination thereof, of such an objective extent as to be clearly excessive in relation to the concrete and direct military advantage anticipated.
(3) The perpetrator, based on the circumstances ruling at the time of launching the attack, was virtually certain that the attack would have caused, in the ordinary course of events, the above-mentioned extent of incidental loss of civilian lives, injury to civilians, damage to civilian objects, or a combination thereof.

5.2. The Limits of Interpretative Solutions: Racialised Hierarchies of Civilian Protection and Racialised Hierarchies of War Crimes Law Enforcement

The interpretative proposals advanced in the previous sections have the virtue of being systematically coherent with the Rome Statute mental element framework, IHL customary obligations, and ready to be employed for ensuring accountability for the most egregious indiscriminate and disproportionate attacks under the Court's scrutiny. This includes first and foremost the two ICC situations in Ukraine and Palestine, which present epochal challenges that threaten the dawn of a new age of normalised, unpunished mass atrocities in the armed conflicts of the future. *Legibus sic stantibus* they appear the only reasonable way forward in countering distorted visions of what is legally permissible in war. These distorted visions have reached the paradoxical extent, in 2024, of denying that any violation of *ius in bello* was detectable[52] in war theatres where the conduct of hostilities was so indiscriminate and disproportionate as to be considered genocidal by numerous states,[53] UN institutions[54] and scholars.[55]

As affirmed by the ICRC, a most 'corrosive tendency at work diminishing IHL's ability to save lives' has produced tragic effects in disempowering the protection of civilians in contemporary armed conflicts, because

> over several decades now, expedient interpretations of IHL – often proposed at the height of armed conflict in order to preserve states' leeway to kill and detain – have compounded to undermine its protective force. In one conflict after another, some states have sought an increasingly expansive vision of what is permissible, and a contracted notion of what is considered prohibited.[56]

What the ICRC did not underline, due to its structure and mandate, is that these corrosive tendencies have not simply manifested horizontally, across war theatres, as a unitary tendency and without relations with the lines of privilege and alliance established by Western big powers. This corrosion, and then disruption, of civilian protections of victim groups construed as 'terrorist populations' have, on the contrary, manifested themselves along lines of radical racialisation, actualising the most regressive and discriminatory hierarchies entangled in the development of modern international law.[57]

[52] See inter alia J Spencer, 'Opinion: I'm an expert in urban warfare. Israel is upholding the laws of war' CNN, 7 November 2024, at edition.cnn.com/2023/11/07/opinions/israel-hamas-gaza-not-war-crimes-spencer/index.html.

[53] Starting from the states intervening in the *South Africa v Israel* ICJ proceedings for violations of the Genocide Convention (ie Nicaragua, Colombia, Libya, Mexico, Palestine, Spain, Türkiye, Chile, Maldives and Bolivia), see ICJ, *Application of the Convention on the Prevention and Punishment of the Crime of Genocide in the Gaza Strip* (South Africa v Israel), 'Latest Developments', at www.icj-cij.org/case/192.

[54] See eg *Report of the Special Committee to Investigate Israeli Practices Affecting the Human Rights of the Palestinian People and Other Arabs of the Occupied Territories*, A/79/363, at www.ohchr.org/en/documents/thematic-reports/a79363-report-special-committee-investigate-israeli-practices-affecting, and 'UN Special Committee finds Israel's warfare methods in Gaza consistent with genocide, including use of starvation as weapon of war', UN News, 14 November 2024, at www.ohchr.org/en/press-releases/2024/11/un-special-committee-finds-israels-warfare-methods-gaza-consistent-genocide.

[55] See inter alia R Segal, 'A Textbook Case of Genocide' *Jewish Currents* 13 October 2023), at jewishcurrents.org/a-textbook-case-of-genocide; E Traversl, *Gaza Faces History* (tr by W Wood) (Other Press, 2024); A Mahdawi, 'We are witnessing the final stage of genocide in Gaza. Omer Bartov is an Israeli American professor of Holocaust and genocide studies. He has issued a grim warning on Gaza' *The Guardian* (6 November 2024), at www.theguardian.com/commentisfree/2024/nov/06/we-are-witnessing-the-final-stage-of-genocide-in-gaza; A Goldberg, 'Yes, it is Genocide' *Swiss Policy Research* (9 May 2024), at swprs.org/professor-amos-goldberg-yes-it-is-genocide.

[56] ICRC, 'International Humanitarian Law and the Challenges of Contemporary Armed Conflicts. Building a culture of compliance for IHL to protect humanity in today's and future conflicts', Report, September 2024, 6, at rcrcconference.org/app/uploads/2024/09/34IC_10.6-IHL-Challenges-Report-EN.pdf.

[57] See inter alia W Schabs, *The International Legal Order's Colour Line: Racism, Racial Discrimination, and the Making of International Law* (Oxford University Press, 2023); AAVV, *Race, Racism, and International Law* (2023) 177 *AJIL Unbound*, particularly N Erakat, D Li and J Reynolds, 'Race,

A new *ethos* of inequality and global discrimination has installed its rule in Western powers at an unprecedented intensity in recent years, building racial hierarchies of colonial heritage, demanding the removal of any legal restraint and the dismissal of accountability for the conduct of allies in war. The geopolitical collocation of suspects of brutal international crimes in the enemy/ally camps has become the sole criterion of evaluation of military actions, irrespective of their manifest criminality, dismantling any semblance of the formal equality before the law that liberal democracies had tried to maintain in the post-World War II international order.

This new *ethos* of global inequality has regularly narrated the killing of white civilians in indiscriminate or disproportionate attack by US rival powers as nefarious atrocities, admitting no possible justifications and screaming for accountability. Almost simultaneously, the same *ethos* has systematically represented the mass killing of Brown civilians and children in the daily indiscriminate or disproportionate attacks by the closest US ally as an unfortunate but entirely justified self-defensive necessity, to be understood by the public as, at best, a mistake by benevolent and law-abiding actors. The same situationist, alternative moral parameters have invested violations of every international legal red line built to protect civilians individually and national groups collectively from annihilatory armed violence, including forcible annexations of foreign territory and denationalisation of unlawfully occupied territories. The very same violations of the very same fundamental norms – norms constituting pillars of the international legal architecture – have been presented, at the same time, as supreme offences when committed by rival powers, and as incoercible rights when committed by allied powers.

This tendency has produced new depths of racialisation, with the paradox of victim groups threatened by annihilation having to wish to be victimised by the correct annexing power in order to be considered worthy of the activation of the full spectrum of international law enforcement measures, from sanctions against responsible states to arrest warrants against states' leaders overseeing campaigns of probable international crimes.

It is therefore not only an *ethos* of inequality that has invested the international arena, with the G7 states lining up in its service, but more profoundly an *ethos* of active destruction of equality, and morality, where it is irrelevant whether an action amounts to an international crime, and whether or not fundamental norms have been violated. What is relevant is solely whose conduct is under scrutiny, with the law being increasingly construed as a tool for enemies only, rather than as a way to restrain and constrain the conduct of allies.

Palestine, and International Law' 77–81 in that issue; E Tendayi Achiume, 'The In- or Ex-clusiveness of International Law' (2023) 34 *European Journal of International Law* 225; M Koskenniemi, 'Race, Hierarchy and International Law: Lorimer's Legal Science' (2016) 27 *European Journal of International Law* 415.

This Manichaeism of the ally–enemy dichotomy, in sum, has over-run legality as the parameter to be assumed by liberal democracies in determining their foreign policies, transforming it rather into a variable of the same dichotomy. The action of the ally is lawful by mere virtue of the alliance, even if it transforms international crimes in state policies. The action of the enemy is unlawful by mere virtue of the enmity, so that total war until total defeat is the only available option. In other words, the ally–enemy dichotomy invests, subsumes and substitutes the lawful–unlawful dichotomy.

When the doublespeak of states' hypocrisy evolves in such a mindset, it becomes a paradigm, and produces an internationalised nationalism, a form of global tribalism by blocks of allied states refusing to be subject to the same norms they want to see enforced against their rivals. In this process, legality is inevitably diminished as a criterion to rule over the alliances themselves and becomes rather an articulation of enmity, only relevant to outcast rivals and enemies. Building upon the formants of race and profits,[58] therefore, this global tribalism is reproduced by the most powerful centres of interest and policy-making of our societies, of both presumedly progressive and conservative political orientations, almost indistinguishably. In this massive mobilisation of power and pressure groups, the first casualty is obviously international law enforcement, ultimately (and somehow coherently with the described ethos) construed as an affront *in re ipsa* if and when directed at allies.

In this scenario, for the same reasons analysed in the introduction to this research, it is extremely unlikely that legal and jurisdictional institutions can maintain their impartiality and performativity independently from pressures from states, particularly pressures from the richest states whose financial contribution determine the survival of the said institutions. In other words, the hegemony of double standards, the militarisation of legal debate as a continuation of war by other means, and the dominance of this new ethos of destruction of equality are inevitably destined to produce their effects on legal and jurisdictional institutions themselves.

To offer a comparison, the situations in Ukraine and Palestine at the ICC offer a paradigmatic example of this new ethos. Several US senators, among other Western policy makers, have publicly threatened the ICC and its prosecutor with legal action (alluding also to military action) if arrest warrants are issued against Israeli suspects of international crimes,[59] reproducing in the camp of liberal democracies orders of the discourse indistinguishable from those employed by Russian Federation officials after the arrest warrants against Russian suspects of international crimes.[60] Beyond these extreme instances,

[58] See N Tzouvala, *Capitalism as Civilization* (Cambridge University Press, 2020).

[59] See J Eskauriatza, '"Wait a Minute, Mr. Postman": Legal Implications of Threats Issued by U.S. Republican Senators', *Opinio Juris* (30 May 2024), at opiniojuris.org/2024/05/30/wait-a-minute-mr-postman-legal-implications-of-threats-issued-by-u-s-republican-senators.

[60] See J Jochecova, 'Russia blasts back at ICC over Putin arrest warrant', *Politico*, 20 March 2023, at www.politico.eu/article/putin-russia-icc-criminal-case-moscow-ukraine-war.

even ICC Member States championing other initiatives in the Assembly of State Parties, and supporting fully the action of the ICC in the situation in Ukraine, have firmly opposed the action of the Court in the situation in Palestine,[61] and denied, despite the full jurisdictional analogy with Russian conduct in occupied Ukrainian territory, that the Court had jurisdiction over Israeli conduct in the occupied Palestinian territory.[62]

The consequence of these alternative stances is that even the protection of civilians, including the protection descending from accountability for war crimes, and thus from war crimes law enforcement, is antithetically construed for civilian victims of enemies and allies, with the consequence of exponentially aggravating the racial hierarchies of deservedness of protection.

With this multiform and polycentric mobilisation to exacerbate racial hierarchies involving dominant interests, even war crimes law enforcement is infested by the same mobilisations, translating racial hierarchies of civilian protection in racial hierarchies of accountability and war crimes law enforcement. Within such a background, confidence in judicial hermeneutics and purely interpretative solutions to tackle the persistent impunity gaps analysed in this research appears insufficient. International judicial institutions are not an empyrean of pure legal reasoning, impermeable to power politics, ideological mobilisations and financial threats. They are, on the contrary, actors inserted in the very same field of political conflicts, facing the profound risk that the composition of these conflicts might impacts judgments and judicial interpretations, particularly interpretations of war crimes offences.

As has been shown, in the history of war crimes law enforcement, from Nuremberg to the ICTY to the ICC, the effectiveness of the conduct of hostilities war crimes applicable to big military powers' warfare has always been antagonised by the same powers' pressures on the processes of codification. The Ohlendorf trial judgment's passages on the atomic bombing of Japan, the ICTY Gotovina case 'scandal', the Report of the Committee Established to Review the NATO Bombing Campaign Against the Federal Republic of Yugoslavia, and the more recent decisions of the ICC Office of the Prosecutor not to request the opening of an investigation into the potential crimes committed by UK forces in Iraq, as well as the 'de-prioritization' of the profiles of the investigation in Afghanistan concerning probable crimes committed by US officials, are all part of the same trajectory of systematic retractions of international criminal justice from the challenge of adjudicating the war crimes of the most powerful.

[61] K Ambos, 'Complementarity and the German Amicus Curiae Submission in the ICC Palestine Arrest Warrant Proceedings', *EJILTalk!* (19 August 2024), at www.ejiltalk.org/complementarity-and-the-german-amicus-curiae-submission-in-the-icc-palestine-arrest-warrant-proceedings.

[62] N Landau, 'Siding With Israel, Germany Says ICC Has No Jurisdiction in Palestinian Territories', *Haaretz*, 15 February 2020, at www.haaretz.com; and S Talmon, 'Germany publicly objects to the International Criminal Court's ruling on jurisdiction in Palestine,' *GPIL* (11 February 2021), at gpil.jura.uni-bonn.de/2021/02/germany-publicly-objects-to-the-international-criminal-courts-ruling-on-jurisdiction-in-palestine.

Whenever large margins of indeterminacy persisted in war crimes offences, they were systematically exploited by hegemonic powers to safeguard their militaries, and their conduct in war, incrementally reducing the chances for accountability. The actors of the international legal community declaring their allegiance to the fight against impunity, therefore, from practitioners, to scholars, civil society groups, NGOs, as well as policy makers, would have the duty of considering not only *lex lata* avenues to address the accountability gaps demonstrated in this work, but also more definitive *lege ferenda* solutions, capable of radically reducing these margins of indeterminacy.

5.3. An Agenda for the Assembly of the State Parties to the Rome Statute: *Lex Ferenda* Avenues for Restoring Accountability

The interpretative efforts proposed in the previous sections can address the impunity gaps demonstrated, but only at the price of new antagonisms between the ICC and big powers. Ideally, therefore, while these proposed interpretations are the only avenue for delivering justice to the many victims of indiscriminate and disproportionate attacks committed by aggressive military powers, preventing their normalisation as routine conduct of hostilities requires more than reliance on judicial hermeneutics. The 'contagion' of this normalisation has already reached a breadth and depth requiring a codification effort.

Therefore, in the opinion of this work, thinking about a perspective of war crimes legal reform, for all the reasons articulated, is an intellectual duty for practitioners and scholars taking accountability and equal enforcement seriously. The indeterminacy persisting in some of the war crimes offences codified in the Rome Statute, and the absence of offences translating into war crimes law customary IHL prohibitions, demand an effort of improved legal certainty, capable of triggering a new culture of compliance, in countertendency to the subcultures of mass killing that distorted visions of the law of war have encouraged.

As Radbruch wrote, 'Legal certainty (which is characteristic of every positive-law statute simply in virtue of the statute's having been enacted) takes a curious middle place between' two other values of the law; that is

> purposiveness and justice, because it is required not only for the public benefit but also for justice. That the law be certain and sure, that it not be interpreted and applied one way here and now, another way elsewhere and tomorrow, is also a requirement of justice.[63]

[63] G Radbruch, 'Gesetzliches Unrecht und Übergesetzliches Recht', first published in *Süddeutsche Juristen-Zeitung* 1, (1946) 105–08, BL Paulson and SL Paulson (tr), 'Statutory Lawlessness and Supra-statutory Law (2006) 26 *Oxford Journal of Legal Studies* 6.

From this point of view, legal uncertainty and injustice descending from the lack of equal enforcement of war crimes law have nurtured each other. Reforming the Rome Statute, therefore, with the limited interventions proposed in the next sections, would present the decisive advantage of establishing stringent and well-defined types of offence for unlawful attacks in armed conflicts, which are not subject to the variable pressures of hegemonic powers on judicial institutions, and empowering future prosecutors and judges to simply apply the law without fear or favour, with lesser uncertainties descending from the defects of the offences themselves.

By so doing, legal reform could provide the structural changes needed for restoring accountability for the most egregious and recurring forms of indiscriminate and disproportionate attacks, and decisively enhance their preventions. Increasing legal certainty, in service of justice and toward equal enforcement, appears an urgent step against a new age of mass atrocities in warfare which appears to be increasingly promised by the current successes in presenting war crimes as a moral necessity for occupying and annexing powers, as means justified by the aim of ensuring 'permanent security'[64] to their citizens, thus opening the doors to the most extreme inhumanities.

The Assembly of the State Parties of the ICC should, in conclusion, be induced to discuss proposals of enhancement of the war crimes regime of the Statute, of which those below are only some possible versions.

5.3.1. Toward a New War Crime Offence of Indiscriminate Attacks

It has been submitted that, by reliance on the cognitive component of intent in cases of virtual certainty of indiscriminate civilian harm, and in accordance with the most recent ICC jurisprudence, the war crimes of direct attacks on civilians, under Article 8(2)(b)(i), and of direct attacks on civilian objects, under Article(2)(b)(ii), should be interpreted as applicable to the attacks that IHL categorises as indiscriminate attacks. Indiscriminate attacks, under IHL, are indeed a form of direct attacks on civilians and/or civilian objects, with the feature of being simultaneously directed at them and, jointly, at some lawful target or targets interspersed among them, or in their vicinity. This is particularly the case in urban warfare and hostilities in densely populated areas.

The boundary of this interpretation is represented by cases of intense co-location of combatants and civilians in the same areas and in comparable numbers, when (due to the features of the attack) it cannot be affirmed that IHL prohibited it as indiscriminate. This can only be the case when the harm to civilians, even if

[64] See AD Moses, *The Problems of Genocide. Permanent Security and the Language of Transgression* (Cambridge University Press, 2021) 241–92.

high, is anticipated to be just an incidental, collateral consequence of the attacks themselves. It is a boundary which can be interpretatively determined, through the hermeneutical steps proposed in this research, and recapped in the previous section, indicating criteria to discern, under war crimes law, cases of indiscriminate attacks and cases of attacks to be assessed solely under proportionality. This boundary is illuminated by understanding the incidentality of the civilian harm as *conditio sine qua non* for proportionality assessments.

When the proposed requirements of incidentality of the civilian harm foreseen are not met, and when this principal harm to civilians (including killing, injuring, destruction of or damage to civilian objects) is expected from an attack with virtual certainty, then the attack will be qualifiable as an indiscriminate attack and punishable under the crimes of direct attacks on civilians and civilian objects.

Since this interpretation is coherent with both the Rome Statute framework on the *mens rea* and customary IHL, there appears to be no legal reason barring the introduction of a new war crime in the Rome Statute that explicitly criminalises indiscriminate attacks as war crimes.

A potential Article 8(2)(b)(ii bis), codifying a war crime of indiscriminate attacks modelled on the IHL prohibition, should therefore read as follows:

> Launching an indiscriminate attack in the knowledge that
>
> (a) it was not directed at a specific military objective;
> (b) it employed a method or means of combat which could not be directed at a specific military objective; or
> (c) it employed a method or means of combat the effects of which could not be limited as required by the law of armed conflict.

The elements of this crime would require that:

(1) The perpetrator launched an attack
(2) The attack was such that it:
    (a) was not directed at a specific military objective;
    (b) employed a method or means of combat which could not be directed at a specific military objective; or
    (c) employed a method or means of combat the effects of which could not be limited as required by the law of armed conflict.
(3) The perpetrator was virtually certain that the attack, in the ordinary course of the events, would have struck military objectives and civilians or civilian objects without distinction.[65]

In just one amendment, the Rome Statute war crimes regime would be radically enhanced by anchoring it to a consolidated customary IHL prohibition and attaching a penal sanction to its most egregious violations.

[65] These proposed elements derive their wording from the indirect intent *mens rea* standard, combined with the defining feature of indiscriminate attacks under customary IHL.

The emphasis of the offence on the impossibility to discriminate in the cases under (a), (b), and (c) would ensure that the crime is not used to punish cases of attacks expected to cause lawful collateral damage. The *mens rea* (virtual certainty of the prohibited consequence) element already admitted by the Statute for all the other crimes under the default Article 30 mental element regime would ensure that the offence does not expose reasonable commanders to liability for mere negligence, or for merely taking the risk of a possibly indiscriminate impact of the attack. Such a subjective stance, eventually clouded by a dense fog of war on a challenging battlefield, would not fall under the scope of application of the crime. Thanks to the virtual certainty standard, only the cases in which a discriminate impact of the attack is nearly impossible would attract punishment, in full coherence with the gravity regime of the Statute. In addition, no arguments against such an offence could reasonably contend that it excessively constraints the professional margins of appreciation of military commanders.

5.3.2. Amending the War Crime of Disproportionate Attacks

So far, this work has proposed the interpretation of indiscriminate attacks as war crimes of direct attacks on civilians and/or civilian objects. At the same time, to bridge a persistent accountability gap between IHL and war crimes law, it has been submitted that a new war crime of indiscriminate attacks should be codified, punishing suspects whoorder such attacks despite virtual certainty of the lack of distinction/discrimination of their foreseen impact.

A contestation to the thesis could be that, in situations of intense co-location of combatants and civilians in the same areas and in comparable numbers, such an interpretation would impede and punish even lawful attacks, such as attacks calculated to cause only incidental and not excessive harm to civilians, substantially reproducing the same arguments advanced by Ohlin in relation to the strike on the Kunduz MSF trauma centre.

Against this contestation, it has been proposed that the decisive factor in deciding whether attacks can be assessed from the point of view of the proportionality of the incidental civilian harm is precisely that the civilian harm was anticipated by the suspect only as an incidental, side consequence of the attack itself.

This requires that the attack was such that it can be deemed by judges to be directed solely at lawful targets, and not at some lawful targets jointly with entire crowds of civilians and groups of civilian objects, far outnumbering the former. It is not possible, in cases of intense co-location, to rely on numerical formulas to solve the riddles about the legality of the relevant attacks. For this reason, the interpretative proposals advanced insisted on qualifying the incidentality of the civilian harm not as a subjective determination of the attackers but as a legal precondition of proportionality. More specifically, the proposal is to give legal depth to the IHL and ICL-required incidentality of the civilian harm in a threefold sense: 1) incidentality in the volition; 2) incidentality in the cognition; and 3) incidentality in the objective entity of civilian harm foreseen by the suspect.

Incidentality of the civilian harm in the volition means that the suspect does not directly intend (*dolus directus* in the first degree) to kill civilians and has the sole purpose of striking the lawful target/targets. However, this lack of desire to kill civilians, under the ICC virtual certainty test for indirect/oblique intent, is not enough to exclude indiscriminate attacks. Incidentality of the civilian harm in the cognition is thus necessary. Incidentality in the cognition means that the suspect, beyond not pursuing/desiring the killing of civilians, expects to harm them only incidentally, while predicting as a main consequence of the attack the one he/she actually pursues, that is the impact on lawful targets. Finally, incidentality in the objective entity of the civilian harm foreseen means that the attacker is reasonably discerning the main and collateral consequences of the attack, among those expected, and that the harm to civilians will fall objectively in the latter camp, that of the collateral, side, incidental consequences of the attack, in contrast to the main anticipated consequence (eg the destruction or neutralisation of lawful targets). This is because any reasonable agent, and an even more reasonable commander, needs to discern the objective entity of the several anticipated consequences of an attack, before being able to assign any comparative value to them, balancing these consequences in proportionality assessments.

Only if this threefold requirement of incidentality of the civilian harm is respected (that is, if the three tests are cumulatively met) is it possible to evaluate an attack exclusively under proportionality, excluding that it might have been an indiscriminate attack.

This understanding has guided the proposed interpretation of the crime of disproportionate attacks, construed under the guidance of IHL parameters. While the proposed interpretation appears the only one viable in order not to neutralise the applicability of the Rome Statute war crime of disproportionate attacks, the relevant offence remains one of the most problematic of the whole treaty, as demonstrated by the lack of any charge in the first 20 years of activity of the Court.

For all the reasons exposed in the present research, it is thus submitted that the crime under Article 8(2)(b)(iv) should be reformulated in the following manner:

> Launching an attack in the knowledge that such attack will cause incidental loss of civilian life, injury to civilians, damage to civilian objects, or a combination thereof, which would be clearly excessive in relation to the concrete and direct military advantage anticipated.[66]

[66] This formulation reproduces the wording of the customary IHL prohibition of disproportionate attacks. Attacks knowingly causing disproportionate harm to the environment should be decoupled from this amended crime, and reformulated under a new Art 8(2)(b)(iv bis). A specific war crime offence of attacks causing disproportionate harm to the environment should be mindful of the relevant customary IHL prohibitions, particularly rules 43 (at ihl-databases.icrc.org/en/customary-ihl/v1/

The proposed, amended formulation of the crime of disproportionate attacks would simply take due account of the exclusion of *dolus eventualis* from the framework of the Statute, which dissipates the concerns of delegations responsible of the most contradictory elements added to the current definition. The amendment would again realign the Rome Statute war crime discipline with the customary IHL prohibition of disproportionate attacks.

The debated phrase 'clearly excessive' could be maintained in order not to lose the compromise reached with the states most concerned with protecting the professional margins of appreciation of their military commanders. At the same time, the elements of the crime should be reformulated to finally dismiss the risks of an unreviewable 'monarchy' of military commanders on proportionality assessments, making clear in the elements that the Court will need to assess whether the incidental harm to civilians, anticipated in its objective entity (with virtual certainty) by the commander, was clearly disproportionate (from the point of view of the judges, after trials, and thus beyond reasonable doubt).

As has been proposed for a correct interpretation of the current elements, the new elements of the crime should thus require that:

(1) The perpetrator launched an attack.
(2) The attack, based on the circumstances ruling at the time of launching it, was such that it would have caused, in the ordinary course of the events, incidental loss of civilian lives, injury to civilians, damage to civilian objects, or a combination thereof, of such an objective extent as to be clearly excessive in relation to the concrete and direct military advantage anticipated.
(3) The perpetrator, based on the circumstances ruling at the time of launching the attack, was virtually certain that the attack would have caused, in the ordinary course of events, the above-mentioned extent of incidental loss of civilian lives, injury to civilians, damage to civilian objects, or a combination thereof.

5.3.3. Roxin and the Future Roles of Criminal Sciences

In one of his latest contributions, Claus Roxin reflected on the future roles of criminal sciences in a globalised world, focusing his attention on the universal achievements of contemporary penal theory, and how they could guide criminal sciences in tackling the incoming challenges that a new historical season would present for the dialectic between individual freedoms and punitive powers.[67]

rule43), 44 (https://ihl-databases.icrc.org/en/customary-ihl/v1/rule44),and 45 (at ihl-databases.icrc.org/en/customary-ihl/v1/rule45) of the Customary IHL ICRC Study, and transpose their emphasis on the duty to choose the least harmful means and methods of warfare for the environment in the relevant war crime offence.

[67] C Roxin, 'I compiti future della scienza penalistica' (2000) 43 *Rivista Italiana di Diritto e Procedura Penale* 3.

Synthetising the most important kernels of these universal achievements, owed to the juridical Enlightenment, he indicated three precepts which should guide the supranational development of criminal sciences: 1) criminal law must be based on social harm; 2) the use of criminal law must be a tool of last resort; and 3) social control should not sacrifice the protection of individual freedoms. In relation to the first point, Roxin reiterated that the task of criminal law must never be to promote morals, religion, or a given ideology or vision of the world, but exclusively the protection of individual security and social peace. Therefore, only socially harmful conduct (not morally reprehensible conduct) should be the object of penal sanctions. In relation to the second profile, the German scholar affirmed that criminal law is a double-edged sword and thus not just a tool of social control and stabilisation of society, but also a tool that can favour crime among the subaltern and the marginalised, and therefore produce social disintegration. As a consequence, its use must be reserved for the most socially harmful conduct which cannot be addressed by other means, such as social security and administrative controls. Third, he contended that the best model of criminal justice is not the one organsing a perfect system of repression, but rather one that balances the instances of indispensable social control with the maximum degree of individual freedoms safeguarded for the citizens. He therefore concluded that criminal sciences should hold vigil on the protection of fundamental freedoms against the expansion of state powers, their abuses and the overexpansion of surveillance and social control.

In the last two decades, we have witnessed criminal law disintegrating into the exact opposite of each of these tenets in most states. Criminal law has been increasingly used to impose the variable ideologies of ruling powers, presented as sole possible moralities, in turn punishing opinions, political opinions, even critique and denunciation of international crimes. Moreover, electoral uses of social fears and securitarian tactics to manufacture consent have produced a dramatic expansion of domestic uses of criminal law to add offences to domestic legislations, engulfing penal systems and producing dramatic conditions of detention in overcrowded jails. Finally, the instances of social control and surveillance have become one of the most lucrative businesses of late capitalism, decisively threatening individual freedoms and fundamental rights. Meanwhile, the punishment of the crime of concern to the international community as a whole has systematically failed to punish perpetrators using the relevant international crimes to increase the dominance of their power structures and states, included upon and against the jurisdictional determinations of international courts.

In relation to ICL, Roxin underlined that it is undoubtedly necessary to punish international crimes. He went as far as indicating the possibility that general prevention might be more profound and effective in international criminal justice than in domestic penal systems, if powerful perpetrators of international crimes are forced to stop relying on impunity. By so doing, in his opinion, international criminal justice could have even contributed to bringing humankind closer to the Kantian ideal of a perpetual peace. At the same time, he warned that the type of offences for these crimes were still largely imprecise, elastic and indeterminate. Due to these defects, Roxin foresaw that these offences could have enabled political instrumentalisation, in turn threating both failure in prevention and the triggering of new international conflicts.[68]

The new conflicts have arrived. They have done so with an annihilatory brutality that was unforeseen, one capable of dismantling the international legal architecture of modernity. The unprecedented civilian victimisation that is unfolding on a daily basis while this work is being concluded has reached levels of atrocity unseen in decades.

Against the failures that have enabled these atrocities, this work has tried to develop, in homage to the declared purposes of the legal frameworks object of the research, interpretative and legal reform proposals to restore accountability for crimes attacking the minimum moral dignity of every civilian and every national group, at least from the point of view of whoever takes universalism seriously.

The exceptional normalisation of indiscriminate and disproportionate attacks committed systematically by aggressive military powers requires exceptional attention by the international legal community. Seventy-five years after the codification of the Geneva Convention, the Universal Declaration of Human Rights and the Genocide Convention, executives, diplomats and too often scholars take refuge in a generic 'should' related to the world as it ought to be, and the law as it should be applied, omitting to call out and denounce the new savage powers that are de facto reconfiguring the world order, one violation after another, in an order of impunity and unrestrained military violence. These omissions, while exterminations of civilians unfold under our watch, and with the support of many of our own executives, is an exercise in wilful blindness which could cost this generation of international lawyers a judgement of history much more severe than the judgment that any court of law might deliberate.

The ethos of destruction of equality before the law, normalisation of massacres, racialisation and war tribalism that has infected societies must be answered by an unprecedented effort of mobilisation by all the actors of the international community taking seriously the interests and destiny of future generations, globally. Enforcing war crimes law equally, and reforming it, will not be sufficient as an answer to the epochal threat of a new age of mass atrocities. An international legal architecture that has failed to protect entire national groups, first stripped one by one of every right, then of the right to have rights, and finally of the right to bare life, individually and collectively, requires much more. However, restoring accountability for indiscriminate and disproportionate attacks would be a start, and a significant one. In a climate of readiness to new wars between great military powers, the principle of equality of belligerents under *ius in bello* reminds us that every millimetre of civilian protection we advocate to remove for the populations

[68] ibid.

targeted by our governments' allies, every inch of accountability we try to remove for the conduct of our own militaries and their allies in their wars, is a millimetre and inch of diminished protection and impunity that might soon fall back on us, in wars on our neighbourhoods, on the hospitals where our loved ones are treated for their injuries, in the schools in which our children are sheltering, and on the civilian infrastructures allowing the survival of our national groups. We should not wait for all of this to be perpetrated against us in order to gain the necessary determination to oppose the forces, the trends, and the legal and moral distortions that have allowed, and continue to allow, the relevant crimes to be perpetrated against others.

INDEX

Accountability (gap)
Cassese's prognosis confirmed, 209–11
Commission on the Responsibility of the Authors of the War and on Enforcement of Penalties 1919, 103
creation of the IMT, 106
developments in the pursuit of leadership accountability, 9–10
direct intent as *mens rea* threshold, 147
future of the ICC, 155
Gaza 2023–24, 200
Gotovina Scandal, 146
human rights violations, 152
impact of ICC jurisprudence, 98
jurisprudential avenues for ensuring accountability
applicability of *dolus directus* in *mens rea* standard, 219–24
indiscriminate attacks as direct attacks on civilians, 213–19
two directions for addressing the urgent challenges, 212–13
war crime of disproportionate attacks, 224–33
jurisprudential contribution of the tribunals, 123
lex ferenda avenues for restoring accountability
amending the war crime of disproportionate attacks, 241–3
need for new culture of compliance, 238–9
toward a new war crime offence of indiscriminate attacks, 239–41
'retrogressions' identified by Cassese, 181
Rome Statute, 192
Actio libera in causa, 218
Additional Protocol 1 *see* **Geneva Conventions, Additional Protocol 1**
Advantage *see* **Military advantage**
Aggression
Draft Rome Statute 1994, 157
post-1945 efforts to outlaw and punish the waging of aggressive war, 16–17
unequal institutional mobilisation to enforce the prohibition against aggression, 11–12
Atomic bombing
breach of the existing laws and customs of war, 111–12
conception of war as unlimited enmity between entire populations, 114–15
deaths and destruction, 110–11
Einsatzgruppen Case, 112–13
military necessity, 113–14
'total war' rationale, 113–14

Circular error probable (CEP)
ICTY jurisprudence, 140–1
importance, 73
Civilian harm
amending the war crime of disproportionate attacks, 241–2
conduct indicating the intent of direct attacks on civilians, 131–9
disproportionate attacks and indiscriminate attacks distinguished, 225–7
distinction, moderation, 'surgical precision' and minimisation of civilian harm as virtues, 15
elements of the crime of clearly disproportionate attacks, 228–30
Hiroshima and Nagasaki, 110–11
incidentality as conditio sine qua non for proportionality assessments, 93–5
intent, 82
legal boundaries of the crime of disproportionate attacks, 173–5
legality of non-incidental civilian harm, 97
toward a new war crime offence of indiscriminate attacks, 240
Civilian objects
basic cornerstones of IHL, 22
defined, 53
direct attacks on civilians and civilian objects
ICC jurisprudence, 167–71
Rome Statute, 163–7

Draft Rome Statute 1994, 159
ICTY jurisprudence on war crimes, 163–7
conduct indicating the intent of direct attacks on civilians, 131–9
recklessness, 128
jurisprudential avenues for ensuring accountability, 213–19
recklessness as sufficient *mens rea*, 186
Rome Statute
toward a new war crime offence of indiscriminate attacks, 240
Civilian resistance
cycles of insurgency and counterinsurgency, 30
different political options bearing upon the rules
definition of occupation, 24
levée en masse concept, 25–7
permitted methods of maintaining a military occupation, 24–5
question of legitimate combatancy, 25
emergence of large scale military resistance conducted by civilians, 23
friction surrounding the legal classification of legally unqualified fighters, 30
guerrilla warfare
contemporary *ius in bello*, 29
cycles of insurgency and counterinsurgency, 30
historical examples, 27–8
partisanship, 28–9
necessity for new categorisations of the subjects involved in armed conflict, 30
problems surrounding the principle of distinction between civilians and combatants, 23–5
Civilian status
defined, 49–50
direct participation in the hostilities (DPH), 51
distinction between civilians and combatants, 26
guerrilla warfare, 18
Civilian victimisation
distinction, moderation, 'surgical precision' and minimisation of civilian harm as virtues, 15
effect of war on terror, 17–18
European wars
post-1945 efforts to outlaw and punish the waging of aggressive war, 16–17
rationalisation and humanisation of war, 16
fundamental protective principles of contemporary law, 18–19
Gaza 2023–24, 194–5
impact of the rise and evolution of the nation-states, 15
Jus Publicum Europaeum (European Public Law)
failure to account for the problems of civilians in war, 22
'qualitative' accounts of traditional warfare, 20–2
successful juridical limitation of inter-state wars, 19–20
over the past three centuries, 31
'rationalisation' of war, 15–16
in recent armed conflicts
counterproductive strategy, 32–3
elemental strategic commitment, 32
fundamental analytical distinction between typologies of civilian victimisation, 33
staggering collision between common morals and common practice, 31–2
three main decisive factors determining the killing of non-combatants, 34–7
why non-combatants continue to be targeted, 33–4
targeting of non-combatants since the earliest times, 13–14
three main decisive factors determining the killing of non-combatants
crucial importance of analysis, 36–7
differences/collision in identity and culture, 35
organisational culture of the military, 34–5
regime-type factors, 35–6
universal functions behind military actions, 18
Collateral damage
civilian victimisation, 31, 34
crime of clearly disproportionate attacks, 227, 229
dividing line between the operative spheres of distinction and proportionality, 82–3
Gaza 2023–24, 205–9

irreconcilable principles, 18
proportionality, 57, 60–2
recklessness as sufficient *mens rea*, 185
toward a new war crime offence of indiscriminate attacks, 241

Colonialism
civilian victimisation
armed conflicts in history and theory, 13–16
identity-based theories on civilian victimisation, 35
ICC jurisdiction as an instrument of colonial domination, 9
Mao Tse-tung's framing of the partisan, 28
military supremacy and the subjugation of entire populations, 2
new ethos of inequality and global discrimination of Western powers, 235
option to use additional resources flexibly a, 23
significance of decolonisation and its contribution to the rise of contemporary international law, 7

Combatants
amending the war crime of disproportionate attacks, 241
atomic bombing of Hiroshima and Nagasaki, 114
cannot be punished for exercising their duty, 51
distinction between civilians and combatants, 26
guerrilla warfare, 18
mere presence does not change civilian objects, 133
no right to prisoner-of-war status, 51
right to directly participate in hostilities, 50–1

Crimes against humanity
Draft Rome Statute 1994, 157–8
Einsatzgruppen Case, 112–13
extermination as crime against humanity, 223
ICTY jurisprudence, 136
material jurisdiction of IMT, 106
pursuit of leadership accountability, 10
Russia/Ukraine war, 179, 179–80, 187, 191
victor's justice critique of the IMTs, 151

Crimes against peace, 106

Criminal sciences
destruction of equality before the law, 245–6
imposition of variable ideologies of ruling powers, 244
necessity to punish international crimes, 244–5
normalisation of indiscriminate and disproportionate attack, 245
reflections of Claus Roxin, 243–4
three precepts which should guide the supranational development of criminal sciences, 244

Customary international law
codification of pre-existing customary law by Additional Protocol 1, 71
crime of terror, 129
distinction, 48–9
grave breaches provisions of the four 1949 Geneva Conventions, 158
ICTY jurisdiction, 125
individual criminal responsibility, 127
origins of modern international criminal justice, 3
precautions, 66, 137
proportionality, 58, 137
punishability of war crimes, 183

Direct attacks on civilians, *see* **Civilian objects**

Direct participation in the hostilities (DPH)
differing consequences, 52–3
three cumulative criteria, 51–2
transformative effect on civilian status, 51

Disproportionate attacks *see* **Indiscriminate and disproportionate attacks**

Distinction
civilian objects defined, 53
civilian status defined, 49–50
combatant status defined
cannot be punished for exercising their duty, 51
no right to prisoner-of-war status, 51
right to directly participate in hostilities, 50–1
contemporary development of modern principle, 48
direct participation in the hostilities (DPH), 51–3
distinction, moderation, 'surgical precision' and minimisation of civilian harm as virtues, 15

dividing line between the operative spheres of distinction and proportionality
collateral killing of civilians and the collateral destruction of civilian objects, 82–3
importance, 81–2
importance and function of incidentality, 85–8
incidentality and precautions, 84–5
incidentality between distinction and proportionality, 83–4
simultaneous civilian and military uses of multi-component objects, 88–93
Geneva Conventions, Additional Protocol 1, 48
interplay of targeting principles, 80
interpretative auxilium of *mens rea* categories, 95–8
military objectives
according to their use by the enemy or potential use by the attacker, 53–4
necessity of a concrete and perceptible military advantage, 56
two-pronged test, 54–6
normative fabric of IHL, 45–6
recklessness as sufficient *mens rea*, 185–6
relation between distinction and proportionality, 58, 63–4
spectrum of legally required evaluation, 64
status of customary international law, 48–9
toward a new war crime offence of indiscriminate attacks, 240
traditional conception and development, 46–8
Dolus directus, 166, 171, 185, 219–24, 242
Dolus eventualis, 135, 183–4, 186, 219–24, 221–2, 232, 243
Dolus indirectus, 185, 233
Dolus specialis, 130, 193, 219
Double standards
ally/enemy dichotomies, 11, 236
discrimination against those who violate human rights on a citizenship basis, 9
Hiroshima, Nagasaki, and the *Einsatzgruppen* Case, 108–15
ICL enforcement, 9
new phase of principled pursuit of equal accountability, 155
reckless attacks on civilians and fragility of case-by-case inferences, 147–9
victors' justice, 36
Equality
of belligerents, 76–7, 211
breakthrough in modernity, 7–8
crucial relevance of war crimes, 10
current developments in the pursuit of leadership accountability, 9–10
destruction of equality before the law, 245–6
Gramsci's theory of hegemony, 6–7
inescapable tension between power relations, inequality, and the regulation of war, 2–3
new *ethos* of inequality and global discrimination, 235–6
nexus between victory and selective material jurisdiction as emblem of 'victors' justice', 3
power to establish the IMTs, 109
profound legal problems at Nuremberg, 115–21
risks of 'tale of two IHLs', 11–12
selective administration of international justice, 5
of sovereigns, 16
unequal enforcement of the laws of war, 4–5
unequal institutional mobilisation to enforce the prohibition against aggression, 11
European wars
Jus Publicum Europaeum (European Public Law)
failure to account for the problems of civilians in war, 22
'qualitative' accounts of traditional warfare, 20–2
successful juridical limitation of inter-state wars, 19–20
post-1945 efforts to outlaw and punish the waging of aggressive war, 16–17
rationalisation and humanisation of war, 16
Russia/Ukraine war
crime of clearly disproportionate attacks, 179
crimes against humanity, 191
developments in the pursuit of leadership accountability, 10
different future around indiscriminate and disproportionate attacks for ICC, 154–5

ICC warrants, 188
identification of war crimes, 187
military advantage, 191–2
military objectives, 188, 190–1
targeting, 188–90
unreasonable prosecutorial burdens, 192

Feasibility
bridging the accountability gap, 214, 217–18, 226
incidentality and precautions, 84–5
Kunduz MSF Hospital attack, 182
need of specific circumstantiated evaluations, 199
nexus between precautions and distinction, 81
normative fabric of IHL, 46
precautions, 64–70
proportionality, 60
proportionality assessments, 93
targeting decisions, 39
war crimes framework, 156

Gaza 2023–24
applicability of Genocide Convention and Rome Statute, 193
civilian victimisation, 194–5
definition of genocide in international law, 193
denial of the right of a people to exist, 192–3
developments in the pursuit of leadership accountability, 10
entire populations as human shields, 197–202
Israeli targeting, 195–6
military objectives, 202–5
proportionality, 205–9
relevant war crimes, 194
tendency to compress IHL protections and expand beyond the law what it permits, 196
Geneva Conventions, Additional Protocol 1
attacks designed to spread terror, 128
codification of pre-existing customary law, 71
culmination of the historical efforts to restrain the conduct of hostilities of belligerents, 10
'Grave Breaches', 124
ILC Report, 158
indiscriminate attacks
circular error probable (CEP), 73–4
continuing debate on what types of attacks are unequivocally prohibited, 74–6
defined, 71–2
means or methods of combat which cannot be directed against specific military objectives, 72–3
need for continuous vigilance and lasting effort to limit every aspect and effect of the attacks, 77–8
problems of implementation and effectiveness of proportionality, 78–9
'overall' military advantage, 173–4
precautions, 65–6
presumptions of protection, 218
principle of distinction, 48–9
proportionality, 58
realignment between the laws governing international and non-international armed conflicts, 123–4
weapons, projectiles and material and methods of warfare of a nature to cause superfluous injury or unnecessary suffering, 45
Genocide
Draft Rome Statute 1994, 157
Gaza 2023–24
applicability of Genocide Convention and Rome Statute, 193
civilian victimisation, 194–5
definition of genocide in international law, 193
denial of the right of a people to exist, 192–3
entire populations as human shields, 197–202
Israeli targeting, 195–6
military objectives, 202–5
proportionality, 205–9
relevant war crimes, 194
tendency to compress IHL protections and expand beyond the law what it permits, 196
legacy of legalisation of atomic bombing, 115
Rwandan genocide, 124
***Gotovina* 'Scandal',** 141–6, 180
Grave breaches
Geneva Conventions, Additional Protocol 1, 124, 172
ICTY Statute, 124–5

ILC Report, 158
intent, 135
particular category of violations, 99
prohibition of indiscriminate and disproportionate attacks, 172
Rome Statute, 160
special obligations of the states parties, 95
war crimes distinguished, 163–4

Guerrilla warfare
blurring of legal dichotomy between civilians and combatants, 18
against colonial powers, 14
contemporary *ius in bello*, 29
cycles of insurgency and counterinsurgency, 30
historical examples, 27–8
impact of technological developments of weaponry, 21
notions of legitimate guerrilla warfare, 24
partisanship
erosion of fundamental components of IHL, 29
significance for IHL, 28

Hague Regulations
acts of devastation without military justification or necessity, 107
precautions, 65
privileged belligerency, 23
prohibition against indiscriminate warfare, 71
war crimes, 158

Harm *see* **Civilian harm**

Hegemonic power
ability of ICC to prevent atrocity crimes, 153–4
consolidation and hegemony of humanitarian conceptions of the limits of warfare, 103
double standards, 236
equilibriums established by war, 4
erosion of protective purposes of the laws of war, 30
Gramsci's theory, 6–7
ICC jurisdiction as an instrument of colonial domination, 9
indeterminacy in war crimes offences, 238
jurisprudential avenues for ensuring accountability, 212
legality of non-incidental civilian harm, 97
light brought by human rights, 19
margin of judicial creativity used by the ICTY judges, 149
narratives deployed to impose their unilateralism into normative theories, 17–18
prescience of Schmitt's warning, 17
unequal enforcement of war crimes law, 239
western-centric approaches to legal history, 40

Hiroshima
breach of the existing laws and customs of war, 111–12
conception of war as unlimited enmity between entire populations, 114–15
deaths and destruction, 110–11
Einsatzgruppen Case, 112–13
failure of post-World War II international criminal tribunals, 4
military necessity, 113–14
'total war' rationale, 113–14

Human rights
axiomatic claims of universalism, 19
centrality of ICL, 122
double standards in ICL enforcement, 9
fundamental protective principles of contemporary law, 18–19
fundamental protective principles of contemporary law of armed conflicts, 18
Gaza 2023–24, 200
ICC aims, 151
ICTY teleological interpretation of IHL, 126
monitoring of civilian death tolls, 32
need for exceptional attention by the international legal community, 245
Preamble to the Rome Statute, 152
process leading to the codification of human rights law, 7
progressive action in international law, 7
punishment of specific categories of subjects, 110
Russia/Ukraine war, 187, 189

Human shields
Article 8(2)(b) Rome Statute, 163
Gaza 2023–24, 197–202
military objectives, 54

Humanity principle
civilian victimisation in recent armed conflicts, 32
European wars, 16

fundamental prescriptions governing targeting in IHL
distinction, 46–56
Lieber Code, 39–41
need for a realistic approach to the objective of governing warfare, 43–4
normative fabric of IHL, 45–6
precautions, 64–70
proportionality, 56–64
St Petersburg Declaration, 42–4
targeting decisions, 38–9
weapons, projectiles and material and methods of warfare of a nature to cause superfluous injury or unnecessary suffering, 44–5
legal attempts to outlaw aggressive wars, 17
legally balancing considerations military necessity and the principle of humanity
Additional Protocol I (1977), 10
normative fabric of contemporary IHL, 10–11
repercussions of these choices, 11
origins and early development of ICL, 103

Incidentality
see also **Collateral damage**
amending the war crime of disproportionate attacks, 241–2
between distinction and proportionality, 83–4
importance and function of incidentality, 85–8
interpretative auxilium of *mens rea* categories, 96
and precautions, 84–5
toward a new war crime offence of indiscriminate attacks, 240
Indiscriminate and disproportionate attacks
bridging the accountability gap
jurisprudential avenues for ensuring accountability, 212–33
lex ferenda avenues for restoring accountability, 238–46
crucial relevance of war crimes, 10
Gaza 2023–24
applicability of Genocide Convention and Rome Statute, 193
civilian victimisation, 194–5
definition of genocide in international law, 193
denial of the right of a people to exist, 192–3
entire populations as human shields, 197–202
Israeli targeting, 195–6
military objectives, 202–5
proportionality, 205–9
relevant war crimes, 194
tendency to compress IHL protections and expand beyond the law what it permits, 196
indiscriminate attacks under AP I
circular error probable (CEP), 73–4
continuing debate on what types of attacks are unequivocally prohibited, 74–6
defined, 71–2
means or methods of combat which cannot be directed against specific military objectives, 72–3
need for continuous vigilance and lasting effort to limit every aspect and effect of the attacks, 77–8
obligation to use precision ammunitions, 76–7
problems of implementation and effectiveness of proportionality, 78–9
international criminal law
critical knots in ICTY jurisprudence, 140–9
ICTY jurisprudence on war crimes, 121–39
institution and judgments of Nuremberg IMT, 105–8
origins and early development, 99–105
international humanitarian law
dividing line between the operative spheres of distinction and proportionality, 81–93
fundamental prescriptions governing targeting, 38–70
Geneva Conventions, Additional Protocol 1, 71–9
interplay of targeting principles, 79–80
interpretative auxilium of *mens rea* categories, 95–8
Médecins Sans Frontières (MSF) hospital attack in Kunduz
intent, 183–4
recklessness as sufficient *mens rea*, 184–6
US Government report, 182–3
normalisation, 209–11

Rome Statute (ICC)
Article 8 two-fold structure, 157–62
direct attacks on civilians and civilian objects under Rome Statute, 163–7
growing urgency of topic, 155–7
ICC jurisprudence on indiscriminate and direst attacks on civilians, 167–71
legal boundaries of the crime of disproportionate attacks, 171–8
out-and-out stalling of the adjudication of disproportionate attacks, 178–80
'retrogressions' identified by Cassese, 180–1
Russia/Ukraine war
crimes against humanity, 191
ICC warrants, 188
identification of war crimes, 187
military advantage, 191–2
military objectives, 188, 190–1
targeting, 188–90
unreasonable prosecutorial burdens, 192
Intent
civilian victimisation, 13, 20, 34
collateral damage, 60
conduct indicating the intent of direct attacks on civilians, 131–9
conduct indicating the intent of the crime of terror, 128–31
direct attacks on civilians and civilian objects under Rome Statute, 164
grave breaches, 135
incidentality of civilian harm, 82
indiscriminate attacks as direct attacks on civilians, 215–16, 219
joint criminal enterprise, 142
lack of distinction and lack of proportionality distinguished, 83
Médecins Sans Frontières (MSF) hospital attack in Kunduz, 183–4
recklessness as a form of intent, 184–5
targeting decisions, 55
war crime of disproportionate attacks
disproportionate attacks and indiscriminate attacks distinguished, 224–7
elements of the crime of clearly disproportionate attacks, 227–33
wrongful intent, 135
International Committee of the Red Cross
location of military objectives, 78
prohibition of superfluous injury, 45
Report on the challenges to IHL 2024, 196
International Court of Justice (ICJ)
distinction as customary international law, 48
prohibition of superfluous injury, 45
International Criminal Court (ICC)
see also **Rome Statute (ICC)**
bridging the accountability gap
applicability of *dolus directus* in *mens rea* standard, 219–24
jurisprudential avenues for ensuring accountability, 213–19
developments in the pursuit of leadership accountability, 10
different future around indiscriminate and disproportionate attacks, 154–5
importance as universalist achievement, 150–1
jurisprudence on indiscriminate and direst attacks on civilians, 167–71
out-and-out stalling of the adjudication of disproportionate attacks, 178–80
overload of goals, 150–3
Rome Statute (ICC) *see* **Rome Statute (ICC)**
unreasonable prosecutorial burdens, 192
warrants arising from Russia/Ukraine war, 188
International criminal law (ICL)
see also **International humanitarian law (IHL)**
critical knots in ICTY jurisprudence
circular error probable (CEP), 140–1
Gotovina 'Scandal', 141–6
reckless attacks on civilians and fragility of case-by-case inferences, 147–9
historically recurring problem in the analysis of armed conflict
omnipresent reference to the notorious sentence by Cicero, 1–2
war as an antithesis to law and equality, 2
ICTY jurisprudence on war crimes
conduct indicating the intent of direct attacks on civilians, 131–9
conduct indicating the intent of the crime of terror, 128–31
decisive contributions to development of ICL, 121–3
identification of two broader war crimes, 127–8
realignment between the laws governing international and non-international armed conflicts, 123–8
seminal Tadic judgment, 124–7

institution and judgments of Nuremberg IMT
contentious issue of prosecuting major war criminals, 106
development of ICL, 105–6
disregard of equality before the law and of equal enforcement of sanctions, 109–10
issue of the atomic bombing, 110–15
Judgement of the IMT, 107–8
material jurisdiction, 106
nexus between the victory in war and the law-making process, 108–9
profound legal problems, 110–15
war crimes indictments, 106–7
necessity to punish international crimes, 244–5
origins and early development, 99–105
origins of modern international criminal justice
Additional Protocol I (1977), 10–11
contemporary nexus between war, victory and law, 2–3
developments in the pursuit of leadership accountability, 9–10
Foucault's inversion of Clausewitz's proposition, 5–6
Gramsci's theory of hegemony, 6–7
legally balancing military necessity and the principle of humanity, 10
paradigm of the 'type of author', 3–4
persisting selectivity of IHL and ICL, 8–9
risks of 'tale of two IHLs', 11–12
theoretical and normative problem still affecting international law today, 4–5
victor's justice at Nuremberg and Tokyo, 3
profound legal problems at Nuremberg
ex-post facto nature of the law, 116–20
mark of victors' justice, 120–1
modes of liability, 116
International Criminal Tribunal for Rwanda (ICTR)
accusations of victors' justice, 151
jurisdiction of tribunal, 124
International Criminal Tribunal for the former Yugoslavia (ICTY)
accusations of victors' justice, 151
critical knots in ICTY jurisprudence
circular error probable (CEP), 140–1
Gotovina 'Scandal', 141–6
reckless attacks on civilians and fragility of case-by-case inferences, 147–9
jurisprudence on war crimes
conduct indicating the intent of direct attacks on civilians, 131–9
conduct indicating the intent of the crime of terror, 128–31
decisive contributions to development of ICL, 121–3
identification of two broader war crimes, 127–8
realignment between the laws governing international and non-international armed conflicts, 123–8
seminal Tadic judgment, 124–7
International human rights *see* **Human rights**
International humanitarian law (IHL)
see also **International criminal law (ICL)**
distinction, moderation, 'surgical precision' and minimisation of civilian harm as virtues, 15
dividing line between between radically conflicting interests, 22–3
dividing line between the operative spheres of distinction and proportionality
collateral killing of civilians and the collateral destruction of civilian objects, 82–3
importance, 81–2
importance and function of incidentality, 85–8
incidentality and precautions, 84–5
incidentality between distinction and proportionality, 83–4
simultaneous civilian and military uses of multi-component objects, 88–93
fundamental prescriptions governing targeting
distinction, 46–56
Lieber Code, 39–41
need for a realistic approach to the objective of governing warfare, 43–4
normative fabric of IHL, 45–6
precautions, 64–70
proportionality, 56–64
St Petersburg Declaration, 42–3
targeting decisions, 38–9
weapons, projectiles and material and methods of warfare of a nature to cause superfluous injury or unnecessary suffering, 44–5

fundamental protective principles of contemporary law, 18–19
Geneva Conventions, Additional Protocol 1
circular error probable (CEP), 73–4
codification of pre-existing customary law, 71
continuing debate on what types of attacks are unequivocally prohibited, 74–6
indiscriminate attacks, 71–2
means or methods of combat which cannot be directed against specific military objectives, 72–3
need for continuous vigilance and lasting effort to limit every aspect and effect of the attacks, 77–8
obligation to use precision ammunitions, 76–7
problems of implementation and effectiveness of proportionality, 78–9
treaty of reference, 71
historically recurring problem in the analysis of armed conflict
omnipresent reference to the notorious sentence by Cicero, 1–2
war as an antithesis to law and equality, 2
ICRC Report on the challenges to IHL 2024, 196
indiscriminate attacks as direct attacks on civilians, 213, 216–17
interplay of targeting principles, 79–80
interpretative auxilium of *mens rea* categories, 95–8
lex ferenda avenues for restoring accountability
amending the war crime of disproportionate attacks, 241–3
future role of criminal sciences, 243–6
toward a new war crime offence of indiscriminate attacks, 239–41
normative fabric of contemporary IHL, 10–11
only acceptable action in armed conflicts, 22
origins of modern international criminal justice
Additional Protocol I (1977), 10–11
contemporary nexus between war, victory and law, 2–3
developments in the pursuit of leadership accountability, 9–10
Foucault's inversion of Clausewitz's proposition, 5–6
Gramsci's theory of hegemony, 6–7
legally balancing military necessity and the principle of humanity, 10
paradigm of the 'type of author', 3–4
persisting selectivity of IHL and ICL, 8–9
risks of 'tale of two IHLs', 11–12
theoretical and normative problem still affecting international law today, 4–5
victor's justice at Nuremberg and Tokyo, 3
partisanship, 28–9
war crime of disproportionate attacks
disproportionate attacks and indiscriminate attacks distinguished, 224–7
elements of the crime of clearly disproportionate attacks, 227–33
Irregular warfare, *see* ***Guerrilla warfare***
Ius ad bellum/in bellum, 1, 175, 180
see also **International criminal law (ICL); International humanitarian law (IHL)**

Jus Publicum Europaeum **(European Public Law)**
failure to account for the problems of civilians in war, 22
'qualitative' accounts of traditional warfare, 20–2
successful juridical limitation of inter-state wars, 19–20

Kunduz *see* **Médecins Sans Frontières (MSF) hospital attack in Kunduz**

Levée en masse, 24–6, 50
Lex ferenda
avenues for restoring accountability, 238
Cassese's prognosis confirmed, 211
Lex lata
future of the ICC, 192
jurisprudential avenues for ensuring accountability, 213, 226
limits of interpretive solutions, 238
Rome Statute, 181
Lieber Code, 24, 39–41, 101–3

Médecins Sans Frontières (MSF) hospital attack in Kunduz
intent, 183–4
recklessness as sufficient *mens rea*, 184–6
US Government report, 182–3

Mens rea *see also* **Intent**
direct attacks on civilians and civilian objects under Rome Statute, 166
exclusion of recklessness under Rome Statute, 181
guilty intent and recklessness, 132
ICC jurisprudence, 170, 190
individual criminal liability, 10
interpretative auxilium of *mens rea* categories, 95–8
Rome Statute war crimes, 184
toward a new war crime offence of indiscriminate attacks, 240
Military advantage
Article 52(2) of AP I, 54
Article 57(2) AP I, 65
debated concept, 56
dividing line between the operative spheres of distinction and proportionality
collateral killing of civilians and the collateral destruction of civilian objects, 82
importance, 81–2
importance and function of incidentality, 85–8
incidentality between distinction and proportionality, 83
simultaneous civilian and military uses of their various components, 88, 91
elements of the crime of clearly disproportionate attacks, 227–9
humanity principle, 42
indiscriminate attacks, 79–80
interpretative auxilium of *mens rea* categories, 97
law of targeting, 39
legal boundaries of the crime of disproportionate attacks, 172–6
need for a realistic approach to the objective of governing warfare, 44
normative fabric of IHL, 46
'overall' military advantage, 173–4
proportionality, 57–63
Russia/Ukraine war, 191–2
targeting decisions, 68
Military necessity
atomic bombing of Hiroshima and Nagasaki, 113–14
customary prohibition of attacks on civilians, 133
fundamental prescriptions governing targeting in IHL
distinction, 46–56
Lieber Code, 39–41
need for a realistic approach to the objective of governing warfare, 43–4
normative fabric of IHL, 45–6
precautions, 64–70
proportionality, 56–64
St Petersburg Declaration, 42–3
targeting decisions, 38–9
weapons, projectiles and material and methods of warfare of a nature to cause superfluous injury or unnecessary suffering, 44–5
legally balancing military necessity and the principle of humanity
Additional Protocol I (1977), 10
normative fabric of contemporary IHL, 10–11
repercussions of these choices, 11
origins and early development of ICL, 102–3
underlying problem with proportionality, 63–4
Military objectives
according to their use by the enemy or potential use by the attacker, 53–4
atomic bombing of Hiroshima and Nagasaki, 114
basic cornerstones of IHL, 22
Gaza 2023–24, 202–5
Geneva Conventions, Additional Protocol 1
indiscriminate attacks, 71–2
means or methods of combat which cannot be directed against specific military objectives, 72–3
ICC jurisprudence on indiscriminate and direst attacks on civilians, 167
ICRC proposals, 78
indiscriminate attacks as direct attacks on civilians, 214
legal boundaries of the crime of disproportionate attacks, 174–5
necessity of a concrete and perceptible military advantage, 56
precautions, 69–70
Russia/Ukraine war, 188, 190–1

toward a new war crime offence of indiscriminate attacks, 240
two-pronged test, 54–6

Nagasaki
breach of the existing laws and customs of war, 111–12
conception of war as unlimited enmity between entire populations, 114–15
deaths and destruction, 110–11
Einsatzgruppen Case, 112–13
failure of post-World War II international criminal tribunals, 4
military necessity, 113–14
'total war' rationale, 113–14
Necessity *see* **Military necessity**
Non-combatants
civilian victimisation
as targets of organised violence since earliest times, 13–14
three main decisive factors determining the killing of non-combatants
crucial importance of analysis, 36–7
differences/collision in identity and culture, 35
organisational culture of the military, 34–5
regime-type factors, 35–6
why non-combatants continue to be targeted
fundamental analytical distinction between typologies of civilian victimisation, 33
they contribute to a nation's war-making capacity, 33–4
Nullum crimen sine proevia lege penali
centrality of Kelsen's reasoning, 118–19
contradiction in reasoning, 118
defence counsel motion at Nuremberg, 117
fundamentals tenet of modern penal theory, 116–17
judicial response to counsel's challenge, 117–18
Radrubch's theory, 119–20
Nuremberg IMT
contentious issue of prosecuting major war criminals, 106
development of ICL, 105–6
disregard of equality before the law and of equal enforcement of sanctions, 109–10
issue of the atomic bombing, 110–15
Judgement of the IMT, 107–8
material jurisdiction, 106
nexus between the victory in war and the law-making process, 108–9
nexus between victory and selective material jurisdiction, 3
profound legal problems
ex-post facto nature of the law, 116–12
mark of victors' justice, 120–1
modes of liability, 116
war crimes indictments, 106–7

Objectives *see* **Military objectives**
Occupation
categorisations of the law of armed conflicts, 36
defined, 24–5
distinction between civilians and combatants, 26
Gaza 2023–24, 209, 237
grave breaches, 160
irregular warfare, 27–8
material jurisdiction of IMT, 106
new *ethos* of global inequality, 235
nexus between war, victory and law, 2–3, 109
problems surrounding the principle of distinction, 22
Rome Statute (ICC), 163
Russia/Ukraine war, 237
war crimes as a moral necessity, 239
war crimes charges, 107–8

Paradigm of the 'type of author', 3–4
***Pars pro toto* determinations,** 88–93
Partisanship
erosion of fundamental components of IHL, 29
significance for IHL, 28
Passive precautions, 70, 199
Precautions
additional information gathering, 66–7
Article 57(2) AP I, 65–6
Article 57(2)(a)(iii), 58
choice between means and methods of attack, 68
concept of feasibility, 68–9
customary international law, 137
defences based on mistakes, 186–7
different stages of the attacks, 69–70
early treaty provisions, 64–5
Hague Regulations, 65

ICC jurisprudence on indiscriminate and direst attacks on civilians, 171
identification of target, 66
importance of accurate intelligence, 67
incidentality and precautions, 84–5
interplay of targeting principles, 80–1
Médecins Sans Frontières (MSF) hospital attack in Kunduz, 182
normative fabric of IHL, 45–6
obligations in relative and contextual terms, 67–8
passive precautions, 70, 199
symmetric and complementary precautions to be taken by the defending powers, 70
third spectrum of legally required evaluation, 64
underlying problem with proportionality, 63–4

Prisoners of war
civilian victimisation, 24
combatant status, 50–1
Judgement of the IMT, 108
Lieber Code, 39
origins and early development of ICL, 102, 104

Proportionality
amending the war crime of disproportionate attacks, 241
Article 51(5)(b) AP I, 58
collateral damage, 60–2
customary rule of IHL, 58
dividing line between the operative spheres of distinction and proportionality
collateral killing of civilians and the collateral destruction of civilian objects, 82–3
importance, 81–2
importance and function of incidentality, 85–8
incidentality and precautions, 84–5
incidentality between distinction and proportionality, 83–4
simultaneous civilian and military uses of multi-component objects, 88–93
foundation of the modern idea of proportionality, 56–7
Gaza 2023–24, 205–9
guide for decision-makers about whether or not to attack military objective, 58
harmful consequences on civilians, 60
ICTY jurisprudence on indiscriminate and disproportionate attacks, 134
indiscriminate attacks as direct attacks on civilians, 214
interplay of targeting principles, 80
interpretative auxilium of *mens rea* categories, 95–8
Médecins Sans Frontières (MSF) hospital attack in Kunduz, 184
military advantage, 174
need for concrete and direct military advantage, 59–60
normative fabric of IHL, 45–6
recklessness as sufficient *mens rea*, 185–6
relation between distinction and proportionality, 58
spectrum of legally required evaluation, 64
targeting practices, 59
war crime of disproportionate attacks
disproportionate attacks and indiscriminate attacks distinguished, 224–7
elements of the crime of clearly disproportionate attacks, 227–33
wide margin of appreciation, 61–3

Recklessness
dolus eventualis, 221–2, 232
exclusion of liability under Rome Statute, 181
as a form of intent, 184–5
ICC jurisprudence, 190
ICTY jurisprudence on war crimes
direct attacks on civilians, 128
intentionality of acts or omissions, 132
reckless attacks on civilians and fragility of case-by-case inferences, 147–9
terrorisation of civilians, 129
wrongful intent, 135
international law of targeting, 183
key in the ICTY jurisprudence, 147
Médecins Sans Frontières (MSF) hospital attack in Kunduz, 182–7
Russia/Ukraine war, 189

Reprisals
collective responsibility, 118
legality principle, 118
permitted methods of maintaining a military occupation, 24–5
Rome Statute (ICC), 158, 165

Requisitions
Commission on the Responsibility of the Authors of the War and on Enforcement of Penalties 1919, 24–5
permitted methods of maintaining a military occupation, 24–5
Resistance *see* **Civilian resistance**
Rome Statute (ICC)
Article 8 two-fold structure, 157–62
bridging the accountability gap
applicability of *dolus directus* in *mens rea* standard, 219–24
jurisprudential avenues for ensuring accountability, 213–19
lex ferenda avenues for restoring accountability, 238–46
war crime of disproportionate attacks, 224–33
defects of war crimes provisions, 153–4
direct attacks on civilians and civilian objects under Rome Statute, 163–7
ICC jurisprudence on indiscriminate and direst attacks on civilians, 167–71
lack of enforcement for the crimes committed by agents of hegemonic states, 9
legal boundaries of the crime of disproportionate attacks, 171–8
out-and-out stalling of the adjudication of disproportionate attacks, 178–80
overload of goals for ICC, 150–3
'retrogressions' identified by Cassese, 180–1
selective administration of international justice, 5
Russia/Ukraine war
crime of clearly disproportionate attacks, 179
crimes against humanity, 191
developments in the pursuit of leadership accountability, 10
different future around indiscriminate and disproportionate attacks for ICC, 154–5
ICC warrants, 188
identification of war crimes, 187
military advantage, 191–2
military objectives, 188, 190–1
targeting, 188–90
unreasonable prosecutorial burdens, 192
Rwanda, *see* **International Criminal Tribunal for Rwanda (ICTR)**

State practice *see* **Customary international law**
'Synecdoches' capsizing incident, 88–93

Targeting
defined, 38
fundamental prescriptions governing targeting in IHL
distinction, 46–56
identification of persons, places and objects, 38–9
Lieber Code, 39–41
need for a realistic approach to the objective of governing warfare, 43–4
normative fabric of IHL, 45–6
precautions, 64–70
proportionality, 56–64
St Petersburg Declaration, 42–3
weapons, projectiles and material and methods of warfare of a nature to cause superfluous injury or unnecessary suffering, 44–5
Gaza 2023–24, 195–6
Gotovina 'Scandal', 141–6
ICC jurisprudence on indiscriminate and direst attacks on civilians, 167
indiscriminate attacks as direct attacks on civilians, 214–17
international law of targeting, 183
interplay of targeting principles, 79–80
precautions, 66
proportionality, 59
Russia/Ukraine war, 188–90
when not justified by military necessity, 133
Terror
conduct indicating the intent of the crime of terror, 128–31
Judgement of the IMT, 107–8
prescience of Schmitt's warning, 17–18
Tokyo IMT
contentious issue of prosecuting major war criminals, 106
development of ICL, 105–6
nexus between victory and selective material jurisdiction, 3

Total wars
atomic bombing of Hiroshima and Nagasaki, 110, 113, 121
institution and the judgments of the Nuremberg and Tokyo IMTs, 105–8
irrelevance of the Genocide Convention framework, 209
only available option, 236
post-1945 efforts to outlaw and punish the waging of aggressive war, 17

Ukraine *see* **Russia/Ukraine war**
Unlawful combatants
interpretation of the notion of DPH, 53
necessity for new categorisations of the subjects involved in armed conflict, 30

Victimisation *see* **Civilian victimisation**
Victors' justice
double standards, 36
IMT war crimes law, 120–1, 151
nexus between victory and selective material jurisdiction, 3
reckless attacks on civilians, 147–9
Virtual certainty test, 220, 222–7, 232, 239–43

War crimes
crucial relevance, 10
defects of Rome Statute, 153–4
different future around indiscriminate and disproportionate attacks for ICC, 154–5
Draft Rome Statute 1994, 158–9
Einsatzgruppen Case, 112–13
Gaza 2023–24, 194
grave breaches distinguished, 163–4
ICTY jurisprudence on indiscriminate and disproportionate attacks
conduct indicating the intent of direct attacks on civilians, 131–9
conduct indicating the intent of the crime of terror, 128–31
decisive contributions to development of ICL, 121–3
identification of two broader war crimes, 127–8
realignment between the laws governing international and non-international armed conflicts, 123–8
seminal Tadic judgment, 124–7
IMT indictments, 106–7
indiscriminate and disproportionate attacks under Rome Statute
Article 8 two-fold structure, 157–62
direct attacks on civilians and civilian objects under Rome Statute, 163–7
growing urgency of topic, 155–7
ICC jurisprudence on indiscriminate and direst attacks on civilians, 167–71
legal boundaries of the crime of disproportionate attacks, 171–8
out-and-out stalling of the adjudication of disproportionate attacks, 178–80
'retrogressions' identified by Cassese, 180–1
indiscriminate attacks as direct attacks on civilians, 216, 219
Judgement of the IMT, 107–8
lex ferenda avenues for restoring accountability
amending the war crime of disproportionate attacks, 241–3
toward a new war crime offence of indiscriminate attacks, 239–41
material jurisdiction of IMT, 106
as a moral necessity, 239
proportionality through direst intent
disproportionate attacks and indiscriminate attacks distinguished, 224–7
elements of the crime of clearly disproportionate attacks, 227–33
Russia/Ukraine war, 187
violation of the established laws and customs of war, 110

www.ingramcontent.com/pod-product-compliance
Ingram Content Group UK Ltd.
Pitfield, Milton Keynes, MK11 3LW, UK
UKHW020909180926
475645UK00003B/40

9 781509 976072